LIVES

OF THE

MOST EMINENT

ENGLISH POETS,

WITH

CRITICAL OBSERVATIONS ON THEIR WORKS.

BY SAMUEL JOHNSON.

WITH NOTES CORRECTIVE AND EXPLANATORY

By PETER CUNNINGHAM, F.S.A.

IN THREE VOLUMES.—Vol. III.

LONDON:
JOHN MURRAY, ALBEMARLE STREET.
1854.

LONDON : PRINTED BY WILLIAM CLOWES AND SONS, STAMFORD STREET,
AND CHARING CROSS.

EDITOR'S POSTSCRIPT TO HIS PREFACE.

In the first volume of this work it was stated that some detailed reference to the strictly new information contributed to it, and first made public by its Editor, would be prefixed to the third and last volume. The following sentences, therefore, are now subjoined.

The discovery of Cowley's parentage, and a correction of all the received accounts of his birth, are here made ; and his Will —hardly less beautiful or characteristic than one of his Essays —is printed for the first time. Concerning Milton (—it is difficult to glean over a field so well eared by earlier gleaners), the slight but not uninteresting fact that Marvell intended to have written his Life, is communicated here ; and the dates of Sir John Denham's marriages have at length been made known. Here also the earliest public reference has been made to the will of Denham's father, and to the will of Waller's father, from both of which minutiæ of importance have been drawn for the illustration of their lives. The date of Waller's marriage, and the period when Butler ceased to be steward at Ludlow Castle, were first set forth by me ; and whoever will look into the Lives of Roscommon and Dryden will find much that is new. I have been careful in all cases to examine the wills, where such interesting documents exist, of the poets whose Lives have been written by Johnson ; and the result of this examination, besides the discovery of Cowley's, is shown in some important references, not before made, to the wills of eight of Johnson's heroes, viz. Waller, Roscommon, Garth, Blackmore, Somervile, West, Hammond, and Akenside.

The final disposition contemplated by Blackmore of his money
(it took a poetical turn) is new to our literary history ; and it
has not until now been known what John Philips received from
Tonson for his poem on Cider.   Four unpublished letters from
Prior to his patron and friend the witty Earl of Dorset, and
three unpublished letters from Swift to Arbuthnot, are to be
found in print for the first time in this edition of Johnson ;
and a highly interesting letter, hitherto unpublished, from Sir
William Temple, introducing and describing Swift, will be
found in the notes to Swift's Life.   Of the friendly liking
which the Whig Addison and the Tory Arbuthnot entertained
for one another, I have given a new and interesting proof ;
and, in Parnell's Life, several entries in Swift's Journal to Stella,
which his editors have wholly misunderstood, are here satisfactorily explained.   To the Life of Tickell I have been enabled
to add (through a descendant's kindness) some particulars that
cannot fail to interest the many admirers of a true poet ;
and Mr. Croker's friendship has enabled me to enrich, with
extracts from their unpublished correspondence, the Lives of
Pope and his two assistants, Fenton and Broome.   The letter
from Mrs. Montagu to Herbert Croft, to which such marked
allusion is made in the Life adopted by Dr. Johnson, was
also first printed by me ; and three long and hitherto unpublished letters from Akenside are included in the Appendix
to that poet's Life.   The kindness of a descendant has added
some new particulars to the Life of Dyer, and my researches
have brought to light some small matters of biographical importance in the life of Gray.   The date of Somervile's birth,
and the county and year of Ambrose Philips's birth, are first
correctly stated.   That Young had a pension from the Crown
rested solely on the authority of a couplet in Swift, till I had
the good fortune to discover the warrant fixing the pension, the

period when it was given, and the amount. To the enumeration of Thomson's works, a poem on the death of Congreve, not before known, is here added ; and for the first time attention has been directed to a printed poem by Parnell, which Pope properly suffered to expire, but which no biographer will, if he does his duty, omit hereafter to mention. With no desire to make any parade of these discoveries, of which the list might be yet more enlarged, have they thus been referred to, but simply with the hope of establishing a claim to the merit of careful and conscientious diligence, exercised always, I am sure, honestly and reverentially. It is impossible to add to the popularity of Johnson's great work—but one may add to its usefulness, and this I think is here done.

I cannot, however, quit a labour of love without a concluding paragraph. Few men now alive are so competent to understand the merits of Johnson's labours, or the difficulties any editor of his best work must seek to surmount, as the author of the 'Life and Times of Oliver Goldsmith :' to him therefore, having brought this labour of love to an end, I desire to dedicate it, and place together, in remembrance of two and twenty years of uninterrupted friendship and esteem, the names of MR. JOHN FORSTER and

PETER CUNNINGHAM.

Kensington, November 29, 1854.

CONTENTS OF VOL. III.

LIVES OF THE ENGLISH POETS.

ALEXANDER POPE.

POPE.

1688–1744.

Born in London — Both Parents Roman Catholics — Educated by Priests — Early distinguished as a Poet — Lives at Binfield in Berkshire — Sees Dryden — Becomes acquainted with Wycherley, Walsh, Sir W. Trumbull, &c. — Writes his 'Pastorals' — Publishes his 'Pastorals' in Tonson's Miscellany — Publishes 'An Essay on Criticism' — Dennis attacks the 'Essay' — Publishes 'The Rape of the Lock' in Lintot's Miscellany — His intimacy with Addison — Publishes 'Windsor Forest' — Commences a Translation of the 'Iliad' — History of the Subscription for the 'Iliad' — Lord Halifax and Pope — Collects his Poems — 'Eloisa to Abelard' — 'Verses on an Unfortunate Lady' — Commences a Translation of the 'Odyssey' — Fenton and Broome — Publication of his Letters to Cromwell — Curll — Edits Shakespeare — Theobald's Attack — The Bathos — History of 'The Dunciad' — Writes his 'Moral Epistles' and 'Epistle to Dr. Arbuthnot' — The 'Essay on Man' — Bolingbroke and Warburton — Quarrels with Lord Hervey and Lady Mary Montagu — His Imitations of Horace — Collects a Second Volume of his Poems — Publication of his Letters by Curll — Writes his two Dialogues, '1738' — Quarrels with Cibber — Writes a Fourth Book of 'The Dunciad' — Theobald dethroned — Death and Burial at Twickenham — Personal Character — Works and Character — Dryden and Pope compared — Criticism on his Epitaphs.

ALEXANDER POPE was born in London, May 22, 1688, of parents whose rank or station was never ascertained: we are informed that they were of " gentle blood;"[1] that his father was of a family of which the Earl of Downe was the head;[2] and that his mother was the daughter of William Turner, Esq., of York,[3] who had likewise three sons, one of whom had the

[1] Of gentle blood (part shed in honour's cause,
While yet in Britain honour had applause)
Each parent sprung.
        POPE: *Epistle to Arbuthnot.*

[2] Compare note in Warton's 'Essay on Pope,' ed. 1782, vol. ii. p. 262.

[3] " Pray what authority had you to say that Mr. Pope's mother was Cooper's daughter ? . . . In the parish of Worsbro, a village very near Lord Strafford, is the following entry:—'1643. Edith, the daughter of Mr. William Turner, bapt. 18 June.' Which Mr. Brooke, one of the Heralds, who is writing an account of Yorkshire families, says is the same person."—*Mason to Walpole, Dec.* 4, 1782. If

honour of being killed, and the other of dying, in the service
of Charles the First; the third [the eldest] was made a general
officer in Spain, from whom the sister inherited what sequestra-
tions and forfeitures had left in the family.[4]

This, and this only, is told by Pope, who is more willing, as I
have heard observed, to show what his father was not, than what
he was. It is allowed that he grew rich by trade, but whether
in a shop or on the Exchange was never discovered till Mr.
Tyers told, on the authority of Mrs. Rackett,[5] that he was a
linen-draper in the Strand.[6] Both parents were Papists.

Pope was from his birth of a constitution tender and delicate,
but is said to have shown remarkable gentleness and sweetness
of disposition. The weakness of his body continued through
his life;[7] but the mildness of his mind perhaps ended with his
childhood. His voice, when he was young, was so pleasing,
that he was called in fondness the "little Nightingale."

Being not sent early to school, he was taught to read by an
aunt; and when he was seven or eight years old, became a

this entry is correct, and the usual period only elapsed between birth and
baptism, Pope's mother was ninety, and not ninety-three, at her death on the
7th June, 1733.

[4] Pope's own note in his 'Epistle to Arbuthnot.'

[5] Magdalen Rackett—Pope's half-sister, it is said, by his mother's former
marriage. She survived Pope, and, with her three sons, is remembered by
him in his will. Pope's father in his will speaks of "My son-in-law Charles
Rackett, and my dear daughter Magdalen," by which it is clear that the woman
was nearer related to him than the man. A letter from Magdalen Rackett to
Mrs. Pope (the poet's mother) concludes, "Dear mother, your dutiful daughter, M. Rackett." She speaks, however, in the same letter of her "mother
Rackett," by which she may mean either her own or her husband's mother.
(MS. Iliad, vol. ii. 136ᵇ.) Pope in his will speaks of his "sister-in-law,"
Magdalen Rackett, meaning perhaps his half-sister. I incline to think that the
woman was the nearer related of the two to Pope, and that Magdalen Rackett
was the daughter of Mr. Pope by a previous marriage, and not (as hitherto
thought) of Mrs. Pope by a former husband. Compare Malone's note in his
edition of Spence, p. 68.

[6] No, in Lombard Street. Martha Blount described him as "a merchant
who dealt in hollands" (Spence by Singer, p. 357). The poet's father became
a convert to the Roman Catholic faith when still a youth, living with a merchant in Lisbon.

[7] This weakness was so great that he constantly wore stays, as I have been
assured by a waterman at Twickenham, who, in lifting him into his boat, had
often felt them. His method of taking the air on the water was to have a
sedan-chair in the boat, in which he sat with the glasses down.—SIR JOHN
HAWKINS. (Note in Johnson's 'Lives,' 4 vols. 8vo., 1791.)

lover of books. He first learned to write by imitating printed books; a species of penmanship in which he retained great excellence through his whole life, though his ordinary hand was not elegant.[8]

When he was about eight, he was placed in Hampshire under Taverner,[9] a Romish priest, who, by a method very rarely practised, taught him the Greek and Latin rudiments together. He was now first regularly initiated in poetry by the perusal of Ogilby's ' Homer,' and Sandys's ' Ovid.' Ogilby's assistance he never repaid with any praise; but of Sandys he declared in his notes to the ' Iliad,' that English poetry owed much of its beauty to his translations. Sandys very rarely attempted original composition.

From the care of Taverner, under whom his proficiency was considerable, he was removed to a school at Twyford, near Winchester, and again to another school about Hyde-Park Corner, from which he used sometimes to stroll to the play-house, and was so delighted with theatrical exhibitions, that he formed a kind of play from Ogilby's ' Iliad,' with some verses of his own intermixed, which he persuaded his school-fellows to act, with the addition of his master's gardener, who personated Ajax.

At the two last schools he used to represent himself as having lost part of what Taverner had taught him; and on his master at Twyford he had already exercised his poetry in a lampoon. Yet under those masters he translated more than a fourth part of the ' Metamorphoses.' If he kept the same proportion in his other exercises, it cannot be thought that his loss was great.

He tells of himself, in his poems,[10] that " he lisp'd in numbers;" and used to say that he could not remember the time when he began to make verses. In the style of fiction it might have been said of him as of Pindar, that when he lay in his cradle, " the bees swarmed about his mouth."

---

[8] This was not the case. His ordinary hand was far from inelegant, and his imitations of print made with the pen such as schoolmasters would admire. I possess his copy of some of Dryden's poems in quarto, with, on the fly-leaf, "Alexander Pope," in his best manner of printing with a pen.

[9] Johnson follows Ruffhead. By Spence (ed. Singer, pp. 192, 259, 283) he is called Banister.　　　[10] ' Epistle to Arbuthnot.'

About the time of the Revolution his father, who was undoubtedly disappointed by the sudden blast of Popish prosperity, quitted his trade, and retired to Binfield, in Windsor
Forest, with about twenty thousand pounds; for which, being
conscientiously determined not to entrust it to the Government,
he found no better use than that of locking it up in a chest,[11]
and taking from it what his expenses required; and his life
was long enough to consume a great part of it before his son
came to the inheritance.

To Binfield Pope was called by his father when he was
about twelve years old; and there he had for a few months
the assistance of one Deane, another priest, of whom he learned
only to construe a little of Tully's ' Offices.'   How Mr. Deane
could spend, with a boy who had translated so much of Ovid,
some months over a small part of Tully's ' Offices,' it is now
vain to inquire.[12]

Of a youth so successfully employed, and so conspicuously
improved, a minute account must be naturally desired; but
curiosity must be contented with confused, imperfect, and sometimes improbable intelligence.   Pope, finding little advantage
from external help, resolved thenceforward to direct himself,
and at twelve formed a plan of study which he completed with
little other incitement than the desire of excellence.

His primary and principal purpose was to be a poet, with
which his father accidentally concurred by proposing subjects,
and obliging him to correct his performances by many revisals;
after which the old gentleman, when he was satisfied, would say,
" These are good rhymes." [13]

In his perusal of the English poets he soon distinguished the

[11] This notion of the money-chest is a great absurdity. He soon found
opportunities of investing his capital in sound foreign securities.

[12] Thomas Deane, son of Edward Deane, of Malden in Kent. He was edu-
cated at University College, Oxford, of which he was made a Fellow 4th Dec.,
1684; but, becoming a convert in King James's reign, was declared Non-socius.
He stood in the pillory at Charing Cross (18th Dec., 1691), under the name of
Thomas Franks, for concealing the author of a libellous pamphlet against the
Government. He was fond of pamphleteering, and is described by Pope in
1727 as " all his life a dupe to some project or other." See Wood's ' Ath.
Ox.,' and ' The Athenæum' of 15th July, 1854.

[13] Warburton's note on ' Epistle to Arbuthnot;' and Spence, p. 8.

versification of Dryden, which he considered as the model to be studied, and was impressed with such veneration for his instructor, that he persuaded some friends to take him to the coffee-house which Dryden frequented, and pleased himself with having seen him.

Dryden died May 1, 1700, some days before Pope was twelve, so early must he therefore have felt the power of harmony and the zeal of genius.   Who does not wish that Dryden could have known the value of the homage that was paid him, and foreseen the greatness of his young admirer? [14]

The earliest of Pope's productions is his ' Ode on Solitude,' written before he was twelve, in which there is nothing more than other forward boys have attained, and which is not equal to Cowley's performances at the same age.

His time was now wholly spent in reading and writing.   As he read the Classics, he amused himself with translating them ; and at fourteen made a version of the first book of the ' Thebais,' which, with some revision, he afterwards published. He must have been at this time, if he had no help, [15] a considerable proficient in the Latin tongue.

By Dryden's ' Fables,' which had then been not long published, and were much in the hands of poetical readers, he was tempted to try his own skill in giving Chaucer a more fashionable appearance, and put ' January and May,' and the ' Prologue of the Wife of Bath,' into modern English.   He translated likewise the ' Epistle of Sappho to Phaon ' from Ovid, to complete the version which was before imperfect ; and wrote some other small pieces which he afterwards printed.

He sometimes imitated the English poets, and professed to have written at fourteen his poem upon ' Silence,' after Rochester's ' Nothing.' [16]   He had now formed his versification,

---

[14] I was informed by an intimate friend of Pope [Walter Harte] that when he was yet a mere boy Dryden gave him a shilling, by way of encouragement, for a translation he had made of the story of 'Pyramus and Thisbe,' from Ovid. —WARTON: *Essay on Pope*, i. 82, ed. 1782; and WARTON: *Life of Pope*, p. xiii.

[15] He appears to have had the assistance of Walsh.—*Spence by Singer*, p. 278.

[16] His earliest existing satire is an attack on Settle : ' To the Author of Successio,' written in imitation of the Earl of Dorset.

and the smoothness of his numbers surpassed his original : but this is a small part of his praise ; he discovers such acquaintance both with human and public affairs as is not easily conceived to have been attainable by a boy of fourteen in Windsor Forest.

Next year he was desirous of opening to himself new sources of knowledge by making himself acquainted with modern languages, and removed for a time to London, that he might study French and Italian, which, as he desired nothing more than to read them, were by diligent application soon despatched. Of Italian learning he does not appear to have ever made much use in his subsequent studies.

He then returned to Binfield, and delighted himself with his own poetry. He tried all styles and many subjects. He wrote a comedy, a tragedy, an epic poem, with panegyrics on all the princes of Europe ; and as he confesses, "thought himself the greatest genius that ever was." Self-confidence is the first requisite to great undertakings. He, indeed, who forms his opinion of himself in solitude, without knowing the powers of other men, is very liable to error ; but it was the felicity of Pope to rate himself at his real value.

Most of his puerile productions were, by his maturer judgment, afterwards destroyed : ' Alcander,' the epic poem, was burned by the persuasion of Atterbury. The tragedy was founded on the legend of St. Genevieve.[17] Of the comedy there is no account.

Concerning his studies it is related that he translated ' Tully on Old Age ;' and that, besides his books of poetry and criticism, he read Temple's ' Essays' and ' Locke on Human Understanding.' His reading, though his favourite authors are not known, appears to have been sufficiently extensive and multifarious ; for his early pieces show, with sufficient evidence, his knowledge of books.

He that is pleased with himself easily imagines that he shall please others. Sir William Trumbull, who had been ambassador at Constantinople, and Secretary of State when he retired from business, fixed his residence in the neighbourhood of

[17] Copied by Dodsley in his ' Cleone.'

Binfield. Pope, not yet sixteen, was introduced to the statesman of sixty, and so distinguished himself, that their interviews ended in friendship and correspondence. Pope was, through his whole life, ambitious of splendid acquaintance ; and he seems to have wanted neither diligence nor success in attracting the notice of the great ; for from his first entrance into the world (and his entrance was very early) he was admitted to familiarity with those whose rank or station made them most conspicuous.[18]

From the age of sixteen the life of Pope, as an author, may be properly computed. He now [1704] wrote his Pastorals, which were shown to the poets and critics of that time : as they well deserved, they were read with admiration, and many praises were bestowed upon them and upon the Preface, which is both elegant and learned in a high degree : they were, how-ever, not published till five years afterwards.

Cowley, Milton, and Pope are distinguished among the English poets by the early exertion of their powers ; but the works of Cowley alone were published in his childhood, and therefore of him only can it be certain that his puerile perform-ances received no improvement from his maturer studies.

At this time began his acquaintance with Wycherley, a man who seems to have had among his contemporaries his full share of reputation, to have been esteemed without virtue, and caressed without good humour. Pope was proud of his notice ; Wy-cherley wrote verses in his praise, which he was charged by Dennis with writing to himself ; and they agreed for a while to flatter one another. It is pleasant to remark how soon Pope learned the cant of an author, and began to treat critics with contempt, though he had yet suffered nothing from them.

But the fondness of Wycherley was too violent to last. His esteem of Pope was such that he submitted some poems to his revision, and when Pope, perhaps proud of such confidence, was sufficiently bold in his criticisms, and liberal in his altera-tions, the old scribbler was angry to see his pages defaced, and

---

[18] My comfort is, you begun to distinguish so confounded early that your acquaintance with distinguished men of all kinds was almost as ancient as mine. I mean, Wycherley, Rowe, Prior, Congreve, Addison, Parnell, &c.— Swift to Pope, Dec. 2, 1736.

felt more pain from the detection than content from the amendment of his faults. They parted, but Pope always considered him
with kindness, and visited him a little time before he died.[19]

Another of his early correspondents was Mr. Cromwell, of
whom I have learned nothing particular but that he used to
ride a-hunting in a tye-wig.[20]   He was fond, and perhaps vain,
of amusing himself with poetry and criticism; and sometimes
sent his performances to Pope, who did not forbear such remarks as were now and then unwelcome. Pope, in his turn, put
the juvenile version of 'Statius' into his hands for correction.

Their correspondence afforded the public its first knowledge
of Pope's epistolary powers; for his letters were given by
Cromwell to one Mrs. Thomas, and she many years afterwards sold them to Curll, who inserted them [1727] in a volume
of his Miscellanies.

Walsh, a name yet preserved among the minor poets, was
one of his first encouragers.[21]   His regard was gained by the
Pastorals, and from him Pope received the counsel from which
he seems to have regulated his studies. Walsh advised him to
correctness, which, as he told him, the English poets had
hitherto neglected, and which therefore was left to him as a
basis of fame; and being delighted with rural poems, recommended to him to write a pastoral comedy, like those which are
read so eagerly in Italy; a design which Pope probably did
not approve, as he did not follow it.

Pope had now declared himself a poet; and thinking himself
entitled to poetical conversation, began at seventeen to frequent Will's, a coffee-house on the north side of Russell-street, in
Covent-garden, where the wits of that time used to assemble, and
where Dryden had, when he lived, been accustomed to preside.

During this period of his life he was indefatigably diligent,

[19] My first friendship at sixteen was contracted with a man of seventy, and
I found him not grave enough or consistent enough for me, though we lived
well till his death. I speak of old Mr. Wycherley.—POPE to Swift, Nov. 28, 1729.

[20] Henry Cromwell, son of Henry Cromwell, of Ramsey, in Huntingdonshire, born 15th January, 1658–9, died 1728, and buried by his own desire in
the church of St. Clement's Danes. Several of his translations are in Dryden's
'Third Miscellany,' 1693.

[21] See vol. ii. p. 36.   Wycherley introduced him to Walsh.

and insatiably curious: wanting health for violent, and money for expensive pleasures, and having excited in himself very strong desires of intellectual eminence, he spent much of his time over his books; but he read only to store his mind with facts and images, seizing all that his authors presented with undistinguishing voracity, and with an appetite for knowledge too eager to be nice. In a mind like his, however, all the faculties were at once involuntarily improving. Judgment is forced upon us by experience. He that reads many books must compare one opinion or one style with another, and when he compares, must necessarily distinguish, reject, and prefer. But the account given by himself of his studies was, that from fourteen to twenty he read only for amusement, from twenty to twenty-seven for improvement and instruction; that in the first part of this time he desired only to know, and in the second he endeavoured to judge.

The 'Pastorals,' which had been for some time handed about among poets and critics, were at last printed (1709) in Tonson's [Sixth] 'Miscellany,' in a volume which began with the Pastorals of Philips, and ended with those of Pope.

The same year [1709] was written the 'Essay on Criticism;' a work which displays such extent of comprehension, such nicety of distinction, such acquaintance with mankind, and such knowledge both of ancient and modern learning, as are not often attained by the maturest age and longest experience. It was published about two years afterwards; and being praised by Addison in 'The Spectator,' [22] with sufficient liberality, met

---

[22] 'The Spectator,' No. 253, 20th Dec. 1711. They were not then known to one another. Pope, it is said by Warton ('Life of Pope,' p. xvii.), was displeased with a passage in which Addison censures some strokes of ill-nature. Warton's statement is in some measure confirmed by the letter which Pope wrote to Addison respecting the paper. As this letter is not included in any edition of Pope's Works, I shall give it entire:—

To Mr. Addison.

[January, 1711–12.]

Sir,—I have past part of this Xmas with some honest Country Gentlemen, who have Wit enough to be good-natured but no manner of Relish for Criticism or polite writing, as you may easily conclude when I tell you they never read the Spectator. This was the Reason I did not see that of ye 20th [Dec.

with so much favour as enraged Dennis, "who," he says,
" found himself attacked without any manner of provocation on
his side, and attacked in his person, instead of his writings, by
one who was wholly a stranger to him, at a time when all the
world knew he was persecuted by fortune ; and not only saw
that this was attempted in a clandestine manner, with the utmost
falsehood and calumny, but found that all this was done by a
little affected hypocrite, who had nothing in his mouth at the
same time but truth, candour, friendship, good nature, humanity,
and magnanimity."

How the attack was clandestine is not easily perceived, nor
how his person is depreciated ;[23] but he seems to have known

1711, No. 253] till yesterday at my Return home, wherein tho' it be ye highest satisfaction to find myself commended by a Person whom all ye world commends, yet I am not more obliged to you for that, than for your Candour and
Frankness in acquainting me with ye Errour I have been guilty of in speaking
too freely of my Brother-Moderns. Tis indeed ye common method of all coun-
terfeits in Wit, as well as in Physic, to begin with warning us of others' Cheats,
in order to make ye more Way for their own. But if ever this Essay be
thought worth a second edition, I shall be very glad to strike out all such
strokes which you shall be so kind as to point out to me: I shall really be proud
of being corrected; for I believe 'tis with ye Errors of ye Mind, as with y^e
Weeds of a Field, w^h if they are consumed upon ye Place, enrich and improve
it more, than if none had ever grown there. Some of ye Faults of that book,
I myself have found, and more (I am confident) others have, enough at least
to have made me very humble, had not you given this public approbation of
it, which I can look upon only as ye effect of that Benevolence you have ever
been so ready to show to any who but make it their endeavour to do well.
But as a little Rain revives a flower, which too much overcharges and de-
presses, so moderate praise encourages a young writer, but a great deal may
injure him; and you have been so lavish in this Point, that I almost hope,
(not to call in Question your Judgement in ye Piece,) that 'twas some particular partial Inclination to ye Author which carried you so far. This would
please me more than I can express, for I should in good earnest be fonder of
your Friendship than the World's applause. I might hope too to deserve it
better, since a man may more easily answer for his own sincerity, than his
own Wit. And if ye highest Esteem built on ye justest ground in ye World,
together with Gratitude for an obligation so unexpectedly conferred, can
oblige a Man to be ever yours, I beg you to believe no one is more so than

Sir, your most Faithful and ob^t
humble servant

—*Lucy Aikin's Life of Addison*, ii. 73.   A. POPE.

Pope returns to "the strokes of ill-nature in the Essay" in his last letter to
Addison, Oct. 10, 1714: ' Letters,' 4to. 1737, p. 118.

[23] The "threatening eye" and "stare tremendous" of Appius were Dennis's
peculiarities.

something of Pope's character, in whom may be discovered an appetite to talk too frequently of his own virtues.

The pamphlet is such as rage might be expected to dictate. He supposes himself to be asked two questions : whether the ' Essay ' will succeed, and who or what is the author.

Its success he admits to be secured by the false opinions then prevalent ; the author he concludes to be " young and raw."

" First ; because he discovers a sufficiency beyond his last ability, and hath rashly undertaken a task infinitely above his force.   Secondly ; while this little author struts and affects the dictatorian air, he plainly shows that at the same time he is under the rod ; and while he pretends to give law to others, is a pedantic slave to authority and opinion.   Thirdly ; he hath, like schoolboys, borrowed both from living and dead. Fourthly ; he knows not his own mind, and frequently contradicts himself. Fifthly ; he is almost perpetually in the wrong."

All these positions he attempts to prove by quotations and remarks ; but his desire to do mischief is greater than his power.   He has, however, justly criticised some passages in these lines :—

> " There are whom Heaven has bless'd with store of wit,
>   Yet want as much again to manage it ;
>   For wit and judgment ever are at strife—"

[First Edition, 4to., 1711, p. 7.]

It is apparent that wit has two meanings, and that what is wanted, though called wit, is truly judgment. So far Dennis is undoubtedly right ; but not content with argument, he will have a little mirth, and triumphs over the first couplet in terms too elegant to be forgotten.   " By the way, what rare numbers are here !   Would not one swear that this youngster had espoused some antiquated muse, who had sued out a divorce on account of impotence from some superannuated sinner ; and having been p—xed by her former spouse, has got the gout in her decrepit age, which makes her hobble so damnably." This was the man who would reform a nation sinking into barbarity.

In another place Pope himself allowed that Dennis had

detected one of those blunders which are called " bulls." [24]
The first edition had this line :

" What is this wit—
      Where wanted, scorned ; and envied where acquir'd ? "

" How," says the critic, " can wit be scorn'd where it is not ?
Is not this a figure frequently employed in Hibernian land ?
The person that wants this wit may indeed be scorned, but the
scorn shows the honour which the contemner has for wit." Of
this remark Pope made the proper use by correcting the
passage.

I have preserved, I think, all that is reasonable in Dennis's
criticism ; it remains that justice be done to his delicacy. " For
his acquaintance (says Dennis) he names Mr. Walsh, who had
by no means the qualification which this author reckons absolutely necessary to a critic, it being very certain that he was,
like this essayer, a very indifferent poet ; he loved to be well
dressed ; and I remember a little young gentleman whom Mr.
Walsh used to take into his company, as a double foil to his
person and capacity.   Inquire between Sunninghill and Oaking-
ham [25] for a young, short, squab gentleman, the very bow of
the God of Love, and tell me whether he be a proper author
to make personal reflections ?   He may extol the ancients, but
he has reason to thank the gods that he was born a modern ;
for had he been born of Grecian parents, and his father consequently had by law had the absolute disposal of him, his
life had been no longer than that of one of his poems, the life
of half a day.   Let the person of a gentleman of his parts be
never so contemptible, his inward man is ten times more ridiculous ; it being impossible that his outward form, though it be
that of downright monkey, should differ so much from human
shape as his unthinking, immaterial part does from human
understanding."   Thus began the hostility between Pope and
Dennis, which, though it was suspended for a short time, never
was appeased.   Pope seems, at first, to have attacked him

[24] I confess it is what the English call a bull in the expression, though the
sense be manifest enough.—POPE to Caryl, June 15, 1711.
[25] That is, inquire at Binfield.

wantonly ; but though he always professed to despise him, he discovers, by mentioning him very often, that he felt his force or his venom.[26]

Of this 'Essay' Pope declared that he did not expect the sale to be quick, because " not one gentleman in sixty, even of liberal education, could understand it." [27] The gentlemen and the education of that time seem to have been of a lower character than they are of this. He mentioned a thousand copies as a numerous impression.[28]

Dennis was not his only censurer : the zealous Papists thought the monks treated with too much contempt, and Erasmus too studiously praised ; but to these objections he had not much regard.

The 'Essay' has been translated into French by Hamilton, author of the 'Comte de Grammont,' whose version was never printed ; by Robotham, secretary to the King for Hanover, and by Resnel ; and commented by Dr. Warburton, who has discovered in it such order and connection as was not perceived by Addison, nor, as is said, intended by the author.

Almost every poem consisting of precepts is so far arbitrary and immethodical, that many of the paragraphs may change places with no apparent inconvenience ; for of two or more positions, depending upon some remote and general principle, there is seldom any cogent reason why one should precede the other. But for the order in which they stand, whatever

---

[26] Compare Addison's 'Life,' vol. ii. p. 138.

[27] Letter to Caryl, July 19, 1711. 'Letters,' 1737, 4to. p. 83.

Old Mr. Lewis, the bookseller in Russell Street, who printed the first edition of this Essay in quarto, without Pope's name, informed me that it lay many days in his shop unnoticed and unread ; and that, piqued with this neglect, the author came one day and packed up and directed twenty copies to several great men ; among whom he could recollect none but Lord Lansdown and the Duke of Buckingham ; and that in consequence of these presents, and his name being known, the book began to be called for.—WARTON : *Life of Pope,* p. xviii.

A second edition was advertised as ready in 'The Spectator' of 29th Nov. 1712. The first edition consisted of a thousand copies ('Letter to Caryl,' July 19, 1711 ; 'Letters,' 1737, 4to. p. 83).

[28] One of these gentlemen himself [Pope] can tell you that his admirable 'Essay on Criticism' lay upon the bookseller's hands for some time.— ARBUTHNOT : *Works,* i. 110.

it be, a little ingenuity may easily give a reason. " It is
possible," says Hooker, " that, by long circumduction from any
one truth, all truth may be inferred." Of all homogeneous
truths, at least of all truths respecting the same general end,
in whatever series they may be produced, a concatenation by
intermediate ideas may be formed, such as, when it is once
shown, shall appear natural; but if this order be reversed,
another mode of connection equally specious may be found or
made.   Aristotle is praised for naming Fortitude first of the
cardinal virtues, as that without which no other virtue can
steadily be practised ; but he might, with equal propriety, have
placed Prudence and Justice before it, since without Prudence
Fortitude is mad ; without Justice it is mischievous.

As the end of method is perspicuity, that series is sufficiently
regular that avoids obscurity ; and where there is no obscurity,
it will not be difficult to discover method.

In 'The Spectator'[29] was published the 'Messiah,' which he
first submitted to the perusal of Steele, and corrected in compliance with his criticisms.

It is reasonable to infer from his Letters that the verses on
the ' Unfortunate Lady' were written about the time when his
' Essay' was published. The lady's name and adventures I
have sought with fruitless inquiry.

I can therefore tell no more than I have learned from Mr.
Ruffhead, who writes with the confidence of one who could trust
his information.[30] She was a woman of eminent rank and
large fortune, the ward of an uncle, who, having given her a
proper education, expected like other guardians that she should
make at least an equal match ; and such he proposed to her,
but found it rejected in favour of a young gentleman of inferior
condition.

Having discovered the correspondence between the two lovers,
and finding the young lady determined to abide by her own
choice, he supposed that separation might do what can rarely

[29] Of May 14, 1712, No. 378.
[30] Ruffhead (p. 133) follows the account in Ayre's ' Life of Pope,' 2 vols.
12mo., 1745, vol. i. p. 75.

be done by arguments, and sent her into a foreign country, where she was obliged to converse only with those from whom her uncle had nothing to fear.

Her lover took care to repeat his vows, but his letters were intercepted and carried to her guardian, who directed her to be watched with still greater vigilance, till of this restraint she grew so impatient, that she bribed a woman servant to procure her a sword, which she directed to her heart.

From this account, given with evident intention to raise the lady's character, it does not appear that she had any claim to praise, nor much to compassion. She seems to have been impatient, violent, and ungovernable. Her uncle's power could not have lasted long; the hour of liberty and choice would have come in time. But her desires were too hot for delay, and she liked self-murder better than suspense.

Nor is it discovered that the uncle, whoever he was, is with much justice delivered to posterity as " a false Guardian ;" [31] he seems to have done only that for which a guardian is appointed ; he endeavoured to direct his niece till she should be able to direct herself. Poetry has not often been worse employed than in dignifying the amorous fury of a raving girl. [32]

[31] The epithet *false* is not in Ayre or in Ruffhead. Ayre calls him *severe*, Ruffhead calls him *rigid*.

[32] A posthumous note to the 'Verses,' when published by Warburton, has Pope's initial to it, and is as follows:—

"See the Duke of Buckingham's ' Verses to a Lady designing to retire into a Monastery,' compared with Mr. Pope's ' Letters to several Ladies,' p. 206, 4to. edition. She seems to be the same person whose unfortunate death is the subject of this poem."—P.

The Duke's verses were first printed in Tonson's 'Sixth Miscellany' (1709), in the same volume in which Pope's *Pastorals* were first published, and are there (p. 327) entitled, "To a Person who was designing to retire into a Monastery. Written by the E. of M—, now D. of B—." The verses, poor in themselves, are of no assistance in what Johnson calls his "fruitless inquiry;" and the page of the volume of ' Letters ' (4to. 1737) does not contain one word either about the lady or the poem. All that is known of the lady and her adventures with anything like accuracy is told by Joseph Warton :—

" After many and wide inquiries, I have been informed that her name was Wainsbury, and that (which is a singular circumstance) she was as ill-shaped and deformed as our author. Her death was not by a sword, but, what would less bear to be told poetically, she hanged herself."— *Warton's Pope*, 9 vols. 8vo., 1797, vol. i. p. 336.   Sir

Not long after he wrote 'The Rape of the Lock,' the most
airy, the most ingenious, and the most delightful of all his
compositions, occasioned by a frolic of gallantry rather too
familiar, in which Lord Petre [33] cut off a lock of Mrs. Arabella
Fermor's hair.[34]   This, whether stealth or violence, was so
much resented, that the commerce of the two families, before
very friendly, was interrupted.   Mr. Caryl, a gentleman who,
being secretary to King James's Queen, had followed his
mistress into France, and who, being the author of 'Sir Solomon
Single,' a comedy, and some translations,[35] was entitled to the
notice of a wit, solicited Pope to endeavour a reconciliation by
a ludicrous poem, which might bring both the parties to a

Sir John Hawkins, in a note in Johnson's 'Lives,' has given us a slightly
different name:—
    "I have in my possession a letter to Dr. Johnson, containing the name of
the lady; and a reference to a gentleman well known in the literary world for
her history.   Him I have seen; and from a memorandum of some particulars
to the purpose communicated to him by a lady of quality, he informs me
that the Unfortunate Lady's name was Withinbury, corruptly pronounced
Winbury; that she was in love with Pope, and would have married him; that
her guardian, though she was deformed in her person, looking upon such a
match as beneath her, sent her to a convent, and that a noose, and not a
sword, put an end to her life."—H.
    I suspect that Pope knew no more personally of Mrs. or Miss Wainsbury
than he knew of Mrs. Tempest, whom he has celebrated in his fourth Pastoral.
Mrs. Tempest was lamented to please Mr. Walsh, and the Unfortunate Lady
lamented to please the Duke of Buckingham.
    Since this was written an ingenious attempt has been made in 'The Athe-
næum' of 15th July, 1854, to identify the Unfortunate Lady with a Mrs.
Weston (born Elizabeth Gage), who married John Weston, of Sutton, near
Guildford, Esq., and died after a life of wedded misery at Guildford, in the
year 1724.   Mrs. Weston was well known to Pope, who took a warm interest
in her sorrows ; but I cannot call the supposition successful, for the *Verses* in
which she is said to be lamented as dead were actually published seven years
before her death.   She may, however, like Charles V., have taken a part in her
own funeral.
    [33] Robert, seventh Lord Petre, died 22nd March, 1712–13, in his 23rd year.
    [34] Mrs. or Miss Arabella Fermor was afterwards married to Francis Perkins,
Esq., of Ufton Court, in Berkshire. She died at Ufton in 1738.   (See 'Gent.'s
Mag.,' 1817, Part ii. p. 591.)   It is a singular fact, as Mr. Croker has observed
to me, that notwithstanding one of Pope's best letters was addressed to this
lady on her marriage, no one of his various editors or biographers had taken
the trouble to inquire, or at least to give us, the husband's name, or any particulars concerning Belinda beyond the loss of her Lock.   Mr. Carruthers was
the first to do so in his edition published in 1853.   There is a portrait of her
and another of Sir George Brown (Sir Plume) at Tusmore, in Oxfordshire.
    [35] He translated Briseis to Achilles, in Dryden's 'Ovid,' 1680.

better temper.[36] In compliance with Caryl's request, though his name was for a long time marked only by the first and last letter, C—l, a poem of two cantos was written (1711), as is said, in a fortnight, and sent to the offended lady, who liked it well enough to show it : and, with the usual process of literary transactions, the author, dreading a surreptitious edition, was forced to publish it.

The event is said to have been such as was desired ; the pacification and diversion of all to whom it related, except Sir George Brown, who complained with some bitterness that, in the character of Sir Plume, he was made to talk nonsense. Whether all this be true I have some doubt, for at Paris, a few years ago, a niece of Mrs. Fermor, who presided in an English convent, mentioned Pope's work with very little gratitude, rather as an insult than an honour ;[37] and she may be supposed to have inherited the opinion of her family.

At its first appearance[38] it was termed by Addison " merum sal." Pope, however, saw that it was capable of improvement ; and having luckily contrived to borrow his machinery from the Rosicrucians, imparted the scheme with which his head was teeming to Addison, who told him that his work, as it stood, was " a delicious little thing," [39] and gave him no encouragement to retouch it.

This has been too hastily considered as an instance of

---

[36] Here is an error. The Caryl who was " Secretary to King James's Queen " was John Lord Caryl, so created by King James in exile, who died 4th Sept. 1711, aged about 86. Pope could never have seen him. The Caryl of the 'Rape of the Lock' was either a son or nephew of the Secretary, and was buried at Harting, in Sussex, 17th April, 1736. At Pope's return from Greece, or—to drop Gay's poetical expression—at his completion of the 'Iliad,' among those who congratulated him on his successful labours, the Caryls, we are told, came by " dozens." Pope corresponded with at least three of this name; and to add to our difficulty in distinguishing the family, Pope's editors, misled by the initials, have, as Mr. Croker has pointed out to me, given some of the John Caryl letters to James Craggs. Three of the Caryls occur in 1715 as subscribers to Pope's 'Iliad,' viz. " The Honourable John Caryl, Esq.," " John Caryl, jun., Esq.," and " Richard Caryl, Esq."

[37] See Johnson's entry in his Diary : " She knew Pope, and thought him disagreeable."—*Boswell by Croker*, ed. 1848, p. 462.

[38] In Lintot's first ' Miscellany,' 8vo., 1712. The same ' Miscellany ' afterwards enlarged into two volumes, 12mo., and called ' Pope's Miscellany.'

[39] Warburton's note on ' Epistle to Arbuthnot,' v. 193.

Addison's jealousy; for as he could not guess the conduct of
the new design, or the possibilities of pleasure comprised in a
fiction of which there had been no examples, he might very
reasonably and kindly persuade the author to acquiesce in his
own prosperity, and forbear an attempt which he considered as
an unnecessary hazard.[40]

Addison's counsel was happily rejected. Pope foresaw the
future efflorescence of imagery then budding in his mind, and
resolved to spare no art or industry of cultivation. The soft
luxuriance of his fancy was already shooting, and all the gay
varieties of diction were ready at his hand to colour and
embellish it.

His attempt was justified by its success. 'The Rape of the
Lock'[41] stands forward, in the classes of literature, as the most
exquisite example of ludicrous poetry. Berkeley congratulated
him upon the display of powers more truly poetical than he had
shown before: with elegance of description and justness of precepts he had now exhibited boundless fertility of invention.

He always considered the intermixture of the machinery with
the action as his most successful exertion of poetical art. He
indeed could never afterwards produce anything of such unexampled excellence. Those performances which strike with
wonder, are combinations of skilful genius with happy casualty;
and it is not likely that any felicity, like the discovery of a new
race of preternatural agents, should happen twice to the same
man.

Of this poem the author was, I think, allowed to enjoy the
praise for a long time without disturbance. Many years afterwards [1728] Dennis published some remarks upon it, with very
little force and with no effect; for the opinion of the public was
already settled, and it was no longer at the mercy of criticism.

About this time he published 'The Temple of Fame,'[42] which,

[40] If this is true, Pope fairly balanced the bad counsel of Addison by ad-
vising him not to bring 'Cato' on the stage. (See Warburton's note on
verse 215 of 'Imitations of Horace,' B. ii. Ep. 1.)

[41] 'The Rape of the Lock,' thus amplified, was first published by Lintot
in 8vo., 1714.

[42] 'The Temple of Fame' did not appear till 1715.

as he tells Steele in their correspondence, he had written two
years before ; that is, when he was only twenty-two years old,[43]
an early time of life for so much learning and so much observation as that work exhibits.

On this poem Dennis afterwards published some remarks,[44]
of which the most reasonable is, that some of the lines represent
Motion as exhibited by Sculpture.[45]

Of the 'Epistle from Eloisa to Abelard' I do not know the
date.[46] His first inclination to attempt a composition of that
tender kind arose, as Mr. Savage told me, from his perusal of
Prior's 'Nut-brown Maid.' How much he has surpassed Prior's
work it is not necessary to mention, when perhaps it may be
said with justice that he has excelled every composition of the
same kind. The mixture of religious hope and resignation
gives an elevation and dignity to disappointed love, which
images merely natural cannot bestow. The gloom of a convent
strikes the imagination with far greater force than the solitude
of a grove.

This piece was, however, not much his favourite in his latter
years, though I never heard upon what principle he slighted it.

In the next year (1713) he published 'Windsor Forest ;'[47]
of which part was, as he relates, written at sixteen, about the
same time as his Pastorals ; and the latter part was added
afterwards : where the addition begins we are not told. The
lines relating to the Peace confess their own date. It is dedicated to Lord Lansdown, who was then high in reputation and

---

[43] Pope's note on Letter to Steele of 16th Nov. 1712.

[44] Remarks upon Mr. Pope's Translation of Homer; with two Letters concerning Windsor Forest and the Temple of Fame. By Mr. Dennis. London:
printed for E. Curll, in Fleet Street, 1717, 8vo. pp. 92.

[45] Dennis idly objected to these lines, because motion cannot be represented
in sculpture. But Virgil, in his shield, uses such; but in one instance perhaps
he carries it too far:

—— Mulcere alternos.

Motion may be represented, but not change of motion.—JOS. WARTON : *Pope*,
ed. 1797, ii. 67.

[46] 'Eloisa to Abelard' was first published in his collected 'Poems,' 4to. and
folio, 1717.

[47] 'Windsor Forest' was his first publication in folio.

influence among the Tories ; and it is said [48] that the conclusion
of the poem gave great pain to Addison, both as a poet and a
politician. Reports like this are often spread with boldness
very disproportionate to their evidence. Why should Addison
receive any particular disturbance from the last lines of 'Windsor Forest?' If contrariety of opinion could poison a politician,
he would not live a day; and, as a poet, he must have felt
Pope's force of genius much more from many other parts of his
works.

The pain that Addison might feel, it is not likely that he
would confess; and it is certain that he so well suppressed his
discontent that Pope now thought himself his favourite; for,
having been consulted in the revisal of 'Cato,' he introduced it
[14th April, 1713] by a Prologue; and, when Dennis published
his 'Remarks,' undertook not indeed to vindicate but to revenge
his friend, by *Dr. Norris's* 'Narrative of the Frenzy of Mr.
John Dennis.' [49]

There is reason to believe that Addison gave no encouragement to this disingenuous hostility; for, says Pope, in a letter to
him, "indeed your opinion, that 'tis entirely to be neglected,
would have been my own had it been my own case; but I felt
more warmth here than I did when I first saw his book against
myself (though indeed in two minutes it made me heartily
merry)." [50]   Addison was not a man on whom such cant of
sensibility could make much impression.   He left the pamphlet
to itself, having disowned it to Dennis, and perhaps did not
think Pope [51] to have deserved much by his officiousness.[52]

This year [1713] was printed in 'The Guardian'[53] the ironical
comparison between the pastorals of Philips and Pope; a com-

[48] By Joseph Warton, in his 'Essay on Pope,' vol. i. p. 30, ed. 1782.

[49] Dennis, in *two* distinct publications ('Remarks on Rape of the Lock,' 1728,
and 'Remarks on Dunciad,' 1729), distinctly accuses Pope of prevailing on
Lintot to engage Dennis " to write and publish" Remarks on 'Cato.'

[50] Letter to Addison, July 20, 1713.—*Letters,* 4to. 1737, p. 106.

[51] Through Steele, in a letter to Lintot, printed by Dennis in his 'Remarks
on the Dunciad' (1729).   Compare Johnson in Addison's 'Life,' ii. 357.

[52] In the same year (1713) in which 'Windsor Forest' appeared, he published his 'Ode on St. Cecilia's Day.'

[53] 'The Guardian,' No. 40, Monday, 27th April, 1713.

position of artifice, criticism, and literature, to which nothing equal will easily be found. The superiority of Pope is so ingeniously dissembled, and the feeble lines of Philips so skilfully preferred, that Steele, being deceived, was unwilling to print the paper lest Pope should be offended. Addison immediately saw the writer's design ; and, as it seems, had malice enough to conceal his discovery and to permit a publication which, by making his friend Philips ridiculous, made him for ever an enemy to Pope.

It appears that about this time Pope had a strong inclination to unite the art of Painting with that of Poetry, and put himself under the tuition of Jervas. He was near-sighted, and therefore not formed by nature for a painter : he tried, however, how far he could advance, and sometimes persuaded his friends to sit. A picture of Betterton, supposed to be drawn by him, was in the possession of Lord Mansfield : if this was taken from life, he must have begun to paint earlier ; for Betterton was now dead.[54] Pope's ambition of this new art produced some encomiastic verses to Jervas, which certainly show his power as a poet ; but I have been told that they betray his ignorance of painting.[55]

[54] It is a copy after Betterton, and still at Caen Wood, near Hampstead, the seat of Lord Mansfield. Betterton died 28th April, 1710.

[55] It has escaped Pope's editors that the first and, in point of penmanship, small and very rough sketch of his ' Epistle to Jervas' is to be found on the reverse page, 128ᵇ, of part of the 9th book of the ' Iliad':

> This small well-polish'd gem (yᵉ work of years)
> In Dryden's diction still more bright appears;
> Yet here how faint each image seems to shine,
> Match'd with thy soul's rich unexhausted mine—
> Whence endless streams of fair ideas flow,
> Rise on
> Strike on the sketch or on the canvass glow;
> Where Beauty, waking all her forms, supplies
> An Angel's sweetness or a Berkley's eyes!
>
> Nature to thee has all her graces shown,
> And gave thee words to make those graces known:
> *For this of Jervas Envy's self shall tell,*
> *None practis'd better, none explain'd so well.*
> Ev'n Fresnoy painted with unfruitful pains;
> The artist's lost, the critic yet remains.

If

He appears to have regarded Betterton with kindness and
esteem; and after his death published, under his name, a version into modern English of Chaucer's Prologues, and one of
his Tales, which, as was related by Mr. Harte, were believed to
have been the performance of Pope himself by Fenton, who
made him a gay offer of five pounds if he would show them in
the hand of Betterton.[56]

The next year (1713) produced a bolder attempt, by which
profit was sought as well as praise. The poems which he had
hitherto written, however they might have diffused his name,
had made very little addition to his fortune. The allowance
which his father made him, though, proportioned to what he
had, it might be liberal, could not be large; his religion hindered him from the occupation of any civil employment; and
he complained that he wanted even money to buy books.[57]

He therefore resolved [October 1713] to try how far the
favour of the public extended, by soliciting a subscription to a
version of the ' Iliad,' with large notes.

To print by subscription was, for some time, a practice peculiar
to the English. The first considerable work for which this
expedient was employed is said to have been Dryden's ' Virgil;'[58]
and it had been tried again with great success when the
' Tatlers ' were collected into volumes.

There was reason to believe that Pope's attempt would be

If Raphael writ, or if Leandro wrought,
Vasari
Thou only sawst what others could not know,
Or if they saw it, only thou canst show.

As sisters different, and as sisters like,
As twins they vary, and as twins are like.

The words in italics are scored out.

[56] Lintot's Account Book contains the entry of a payment to Mr. Betterton,
under the 7th of April, 1712, of 5*l*. 7*s*. 6*d*. for " The Miller's Tale, with some
characters from Chaucer." But Betterton was then dead. The payment may
have been made to Mrs. Betterton, for whose profit Pope interfered in the disposal of the husband's works. See J. C.'s letter, 23rd May, 1712.

[57] Spence.—JOHNSON.

[58] The first volume of verse published by subscription was the folio edition
(1688) of Milton's ' Paradise Lost.'

successful.   He was in the full bloom of reputation, and was
personally known to almost all whom dignity of employment or
splendour of reputation had made eminent; he conversed indif-
ferently with both parties, and never disturbed the public with
his political opinions; and it might be naturally expected, as
each faction then boasted its literary zeal, that the great men,
who on other occasions practised all the violence of opposition,
would emulate each other in their encouragement of a poet who
delighted all, and by whom none had been offended.

With those hopes he offered an English 'Iliad' to subscribers,
in six volumes in quarto, for six guineas; a sum, according to
the value of money at that time, by no means inconsiderable,
and greater than I believe to have been ever asked before.   His
proposal, however, was very favourably received; and the patrons
of literature were busy to recommend his undertaking and promote his interest.   Lord Oxford, indeed, lamented that such a
genius should be wasted upon a work not original; but proposed
no means by which he might live without it.   Addison recommended caution and moderation, and advised him not to be
content with the praise of half the nation, when he might be
universally favoured.[59]

The greatness of the design, the popularity of the author, and
the attention of the literary world, naturally raised such expectations of the future sale, that the booksellers made their offers
with great eagerness; but the highest bidder was Bernard
Lintot,[60] who became proprietor on condition of supplying, at
his own expense, all the copies which were to be delivered to
subscribers, or presented to friends, and paying two hundred
pounds for every volume.[61]

Of the quartos it was, I believe, stipulated that none should
be printed but for the author, that the subscription might not be

[59] Addison to Pope, 2nd Nov. 1713. 'Letters,' 4to. 1737, p. 108.
[60] Lintot's competitors were Jacob Tonson, Ben Tooke, &c.
[61] I had 1200l. for my translation of the 'Iliad,' and 600l. for the 'Odyssey,'
and all my books for subscribers and presents into the bargain.—POPE : *Spence
by Singer*, p. 295.
   As he only translated half the 'Odyssey,' the payment was the same as for
the 'Iliad.'

depreciated; but Lintot impressed the same pages upon a small folio, and paper perhaps a little thinner; and sold exactly at half the price, for half-a-guinea each volume, books so little inferior to the quartos, that by a fraud of trade those folios, being afterwards shortened by cutting away the top and bottom, were sold as copies printed for the subscribers.

Lintot printed two hundred and fifty on royal paper in folio, for two guineas a volume; of the small folio, having printed seventeen hundred and fifty copies of the first volume, he reduced the number in the other volumes to a thousand.

It is unpleasant to relate that the bookseller, after all his hopes and all his liberality, was, by a very unjust and illegal action, defrauded of his profit. An edition of the English 'Iliad' was printed in Holland in duodecimo, and imported clandestinely for the gratification of those who were impatient to read what they could not yet afford to buy. This fraud could only be counteracted by an edition equally cheap and more commodious; and Lintot was compelled to contract his folio at once into a duodecimo, and lose the advantage of an intermediate gradation. The notes, which in the Dutch copies were placed at the end of each book, as they had been in the large volumes, were now subjoined to the text in the same page,[62] and are therefore more easily consulted. Of this edition two thousand five hundred were first printed, and five thousand a few weeks afterwards; but indeed great numbers were necessary to produce considerable profit.

Pope, having now emitted his proposals, and engaged not only his own reputation, but in some degree that of his friends who patronised his subscription, began to be frightened at his own undertaking; and finding himself at first embarrassed with difficulties which retarded and oppressed him, he was for a time timorous and uneasy; had his nights disturbed by dreams of long journeys through unknown ways, and wished, as he said, "that somebody would hang him." [63]

---

[62] This is not quite correct. In the edition "London: printed by T. J. for B. L. and other Booksellers," 1718–21, 6 vols. 12mo., the notes are at the end of each volume.   [63] Spence.— JOHNSON. *Singer*, p. 218.

This misery, however, was not of long continuance; he grew by degrees more acquainted with Homer's images and expressions, and practice increased his facility of versification. In a short time he represents himself as despatching regularly fifty verses a day,[64] which would show him by an easy computation the termination of his labour.

His own diffidence was not his only vexation. He that asks a subscription soon finds that he has enemies. All who do not encourage him defame him. He that wants money will rather be thought angry than poor; and he that wishes to save his money conceals his avarice by his malice. Addison had hinted his suspicion that Pope was too much a Tory; and some of the Tories suspected his principles because he had contributed to 'The Guardian,' which was carried on by Steele.[65]

To those who censured his politics were added enemies yet more dangerous, who called in question his knowledge of Greek and his qualifications for a translator of Homer. To these he made no public opposition; but in one of his letters[66] escapes from them as well as he can. At an age like his (for he was not more than twenty-five), with an irregular education and a course of life of which much seems to have passed in conversation, it is not very likely that he overflowed with Greek. But when he felt himself deficient, he sought assistance; and what man of learning would refuse to help him? Minute inquiries into the force of words are less necessary in translating Homer than other poets, because his positions are general and his representations natural, with very little dependence on local or temporary customs, on those changeable scenes of artificial life which, by mingling original with accidental notions, and crowding the mind with images which time effaces, produces ambiguity in diction and obscurity in books. To this open display of unadulterated nature it must be ascribed that Homer has fewer passages of doubtful meaning than any other poet either in the

---

[64] Thirty or forty verses before I got up.—*Spence by Singer,* p. 218.   Often forty or fifty verses in a morning in bed.—*Ibid.* p. 142.

[65] See Pope's Letter to Addison [1713]. 'Letters,' 4to. 1737, p. 109.

[66] To Mr. Bridges, and first printed by Johnson. See p. 138.

learned or in modern languages. I have read of a man, who
being, by his ignorance of Greek, compelled to gratify his
curiosity with the Latin printed on the opposite page, declared
that from the rude simplicity of the lines literally rendered, he
formed nobler ideas of the Homeric majesty than from the
laboured elegance of polished versions.

Those literal translations were always at hand, and from them
he could easily obtain his author's sense with sufficient certainty;
and among the readers of Homer the number is very small of
those who find much in the Greek more than in the Latin,
except the music of the numbers.

If more help was wanting, he had the poetical translation of
Eobanus Hessus, an unwearied writer of Latin verses; he had
the French Homers of La Valterie and Dacier, and the English
of Chapman, Hobbes, and Ogilby. With Chapman, whose
work, though now totally neglected, seems to have been popular
almost to the end of the last century, he had very frequent con-
sultations, and perhaps never translated any passage till he had
read his version, which indeed he has been sometimes suspected
of using instead of the original.[67]

Notes were likewise to be provided; for the six volumes
would have been very little more than six pamphlets without
them. What the mere perusal of the text could suggest, Pope
wanted no assistance to collect or methodize; but more was
necessary; many pages were to be filled, and learning must
supply materials to wit and judgment. Something might be
gathered from Dacier; but no man loves to be indebted to his
contemporaries, and Dacier was accessible to common readers.
Eustathius was therefore necessarily consulted. To read Eustathius, of whose work there was then no Latin version, I suspect Pope, if he had been willing, not to have been able;[68]

----

[67] My copy [of Chapman's 'Homer'] once belonged to Pope; in which he
has noted many of Chapman's absolute interpolations, extending sometimes to
the length of a paragraph of twelve lines. A diligent observer will easily discern that Pope was no careless reader of his rude predecessor.—THOS. WARTON:
Hist. of English Poetry, iii. 358, ed. 1840.

[68] All the crime that I have committed is saying that he is no master of
Greek; and I am so confident of this, that if he can translate ten lines of

some other was therefore to be found who had leisure as well as abilities; and he was doubtless most readily employed who would do much work for little money.

The history of the notes has never been traced.   Broome, in his preface to his Poems, declares himself the commentator " in part upon the Iliad ;" and it appears from Fenton's letter, pre-served in the Museum,[69] that Broome was at first engaged in consulting Eustathius ; but that after a time, whatever was the reason, he desisted ; another man of Cambridge was then employed, who soon grew weary of the work ; and a third, that was recommended by Thirlby, is now discovered to have been Jortin, a man since well known to the learned world, who com-plained that Pope, having accepted and approved his perform-ance, never testified any curiosity to see him, and who professed to have forgotten the terms on which he worked.   The terms which Fenton uses are very mercantile : " I think at first sight that his performance is commendable enough, and have sent word for him to finish the 17th book, and to send it with his demands for his trouble. . . . I have here enclosed the speci-men ; if the rest come before you return, I will keep them till I receive your orders."[70]

Broome then offered his service a second time, which was probably accepted, as they had afterwards a closer correspond-ence.   Parnell contributed the Life of Homer, which Pope found so harsh that he took great pains in correcting it ;[71] and by his own diligence, with such help as kindness or money could procure him, in somewhat more than five years he completed his version of the 'Iliad,' with the notes.   He began it in 1712, his twenty-fifth year ; and concluded it in 1718, his thirtieth year.[72]

Eustathius, I'll own myself unjust and unworthy.—BROOME to Fenton, 15th June, 1727. (Unpublished letter in Mr. Croker's possession.)

[69] Pope having written part of his translation of Homer upon the back of it.

[70] MS. Iliad, vol. ii. 107[b], part of 21st book.

[71] It is still stiff, and was written much stiffer.—POPE : *Spence by Singer*, p. 138.

[72] This is not quite correct. " He began the 'Iliad' in 1713, and finished it in 1719." So Pope's own note in his own edition of 'The Dunciad,' 12mo. 1736, p. 224.

When we find him translating fifty lines a day,[73] it is natural to suppose that he would have brought his work to a more speedy conclusion. The 'Iliad,' containing less than sixteen thousand verses, might have been despatched in less than three hundred and twenty days by fifty verses in a day. The notes, compiled with the assistance of his mercenaries, could not be supposed to require more time than the text. According to this calculation the progress of Pope may seem to have been slow; but the distance is commonly very great between actual performances and speculative possibility. It is natural to suppose that as much as has been done to-day may be done to-morrow; but on the morrow some difficulty emerges, or some external impediment obstructs. Indolence, interruption, business, and pleasure, all take their turns of retardation; and every long work is lengthened by a thousand causes that can, and ten thousand that cannot, be recounted. Perhaps no extensive and multifarious performance was ever effected within the term originally fixed in the undertaker's mind. He that runs against Time has an antagonist not subject to casualties.

The encouragement given to this translation, though report seems to have over-rated it, was such as the world has not often seen. The subscribers were five hundred and seventy-five. The copies for which subscriptions were given were six hundred and fifty-four; and only six hundred and sixty were printed. For those copies Pope had nothing to pay; he therefore received, including the two hundred pounds a volume, five thousand three hundred and twenty pounds four shillings without deduction, as the books were supplied by Lintot.

By the success of his subscription Pope was relieved from those pecuniary distresses with which, notwithstanding his popularity, he had hitherto struggled. Lord Oxford had often lamented his disqualification for public employment, but never proposed a pension. While the translation of Homer was in its progress, Mr. Craggs, then Secretary of State, offered to

---

[73] Which he never said he did translate. See 'Spence by Singer,' p. 142, and p. 218. He would do as many as fifty at a heat, but not regularly every day; and these fifty were in the rough.

procure him a pension,[74] which, at least during his ministry, might be enjoyed with secrecy.   This was not accepted by Pope, who told him, however, that if he should be pressed with want of money he would send to him for occasional supplies.[75]   Craggs was not long in power, and was never solicited for money by Pope, who disdained to beg what he did not want.

With the product of this subscription, which he had too much discretion to squander, he secured his future life from want by considerable annuities.[76]   The estate of the Duke of Buckingham was found to have been charged with five hundred pounds a-year,[77] payable to Pope, which doubtless his translation enabled him to purchase.

It cannot be unwelcome to literary curiosity that I deduce thus minutely the history of the English 'Iliad.'   It is certainly the noblest version of poetry which the world has ever seen ; and its publication must therefore be considered as one of the great events in the annals of learning.

To those who have skill to estimate the excellence and difficulty of this great work, it must be very desirable to know how it was performed and by what gradations it advanced to correctness.   Of such an intellectual process the knowledge has very rarely been attainable ; but happily there remains the original copy of the 'Iliad,' which, being obtained by Bolingbroke as a curiosity, descended from him to Mallet, and is now by the solicitation of the late Dr. Maty reposited in the Museum.

Between this manuscript, which is written upon accidental fragments of paper, and the printed edition, there must have

[74] Pope, in 'Spence by Singer,' p. 307.
[75] Ibid.

[76] But (thanks to Homer) since I live and thrive
      Indebted to no prince or peer alive.
                    POPE: *2nd Epist. of 2nd Book of Horace.*

      Appealing to the nation's taste,
      Above the reach of want is placed:
      By Homer dead was taught to thrive,
      Which Homer never could alive.
                    SWIFT: *A Libel on Dr. Delany.*

[77] Rather 200*l.* a-year. The deed by which it was granted was once in the custody of Sir John Hawkins.'

been an intermediate copy, that was perhaps destroyed as it
returned from the press.[78]

From the first copy I have procured a few transcripts,[79] and
shall exhibit first the printed lines; then, in a small print, those
of the manuscripts, with all their variations. Those words in
the small print which are given in Italics are cancelled in the
copy and the words placed under them adopted in their stead.

The beginning of the *first book* stands thus :—

> The wrath of Peleus' son, the direful spring
> Of all the Grecian woes, O Goddess, sing !
> That wrath which hurl'd to Pluto's gloomy reign
> The souls of mighty chiefs untimely slain.

> The stern Pelides' *rage*, O Goddess, sing,
>   wrath
> Of all the woes *of Greece* the fatal spring,
>   Grecian
> That strew'd with *warriors* dead the Phrygian plain,
>   heroes
> And *peopled the dark hell with heroes* slain;
>   fill'd the shady hell with chiefs untimely

> Whose limbs unburied on the naked shore,
> Devouring dogs and hungry vultures tore,
> Since great Achilles and Atrides strove ;
> Such was the sovereign doom, and such the will of Jove.

> Whose limbs, unburied on the hostile shore,
> Devouring dogs and greedy vultures tore,
> Since first *Atrides* and *Achilles* strove;
> Such was the sovereign doom, and such the will of Jove.

> Declare, O Muse, in what ill-fated hour
> Sprung the fierce strife, from what offended Power ?
> Latona's son a dire contagion spread,
> And heap'd the camp with mountains of the dead ;
> The King of men his reverend priest defied,
> And for the King's offence, the people died.

> Declare, O Goddess, what offended Power
> Enflam'd their *rage*, in that *ill omen'd* hour;
>   anger   fatal, hapless

---

[78] This was the case. The copy sent to the press was made by a Mr. Doncastle, one of Pope's neighbours at Binfield. (Pope's Letters to Doncastle,
in 'Gentleman's Magazine' for October, 1831, and Doncastle's Letter to Pope,
MS. 'Iliad,' vol. ii. 160ᵇ.)

[79] Made by Mrs. Thrale, in her very beautiful handwriting.

Phœbus himself the *dire* debate procur'd,
        fierce
T' avenge the wrongs his injur'd priest endur'd;
For this the God a dire infection spread,
And heap'd the camp with millions of the dead:
The King of Men the Sacred Sire defied,
And for the King's offence the people died.

For Chryses sought with costly gifts to gain
His captive daughter from the victor's chain ;
Suppliant the venerable Father stands,
Apollo's awful ensigns grace his hands ;
By these he begs, and, lowly bending down,
Extends the sceptre and the laurel crown.

  For Chryses sought by *presents to regain*
                costly gifts to gain
  His captive daughter from the victor's chain;
  Suppliant the venerable Father stands,
  Apollo's awful ensigns grac'd his hands.
  By these he begs, and lowly bending down
  The golden sceptre and the laurel crown,
   Presents the sceptre
  For these as ensigns of his God he bare,
  The God that sends his golden shafts afar ;
  Then low on earth, the venerable man,
  Suppliant before the brother kings began.

He sued to all, but chief implor'd for grace,
The brother-kings of Atreus' royal race ;
Ye kings and warriors, may your vows be crown'd,
And Troy's proud walls lie level with the ground ;
May Jove restore you, when your toils are o'er,
Safe to the pleasures of your native shore.

  To all he sued, but chief implor'd for grace
  The brother kings of Atreus' royal race.
  Ye *sons of Atreus*, may your vows be crown'd,
   Kings and warriors
  Your labours, by the Gods be all your labours crown'd ;
  So may the Gods your arms with conquest bless,
  And Troy's proud walls lie level with the ground;
  Till   *laid*
  And crown your labours with desir'd success ;
  May Jove restore you, when your toils are o'er,
  Safe to the pleasures of your native shore.

But, oh ! relieve a wretched parent's pain,
And give Chryseis to these arms again ;
If mercy fail, yet let my presents move,
And dread avenging Phœbus, son of Jove.

> But, oh! relieve a hapless parent's pain,
> And give my daughter to these arms again;
> *Receive my gifts;* if mercy fails, yet let my present move,
> And fear *the God that deals his darts around,*
> > avenging Phœbus, son of Jove.

> The Greeks, in shouts, their joint assent declare
> The priest to reverence, and release the fair.
> Not so Atrides ; he, with kingly pride,
> Repuls'd the sacred Sire, and thus replied.

> He said, the Greeks their joint assent declare,
> *The father said, the gen'rous Greeks relent,*
> T' accept the ransom, and release the fair:
> *Revere the priest, and speak their joint assent :*
> Not so *the tyrant;* he, with kingly pride,
> > Atrides
> Repuls'd the sacred Sire, and thus replied.
> > [Not so the tyrant. Dryden.]

Of these lines, and of the whole first book, I am told that there was yet a former copy, more varied, and more deformed with interlineations.

The beginning of the *second book* varies very little from the printed page, and is therefore set down without any parallel; the few differences do not require to be elaborately displayed.

> Now pleasing sleep had seal'd each mortal eye ;
> Stretch'd in their tents the Grecian leaders lie ;
> Th' Immortals slumber'd on their thrones above,
> All but the ever-watchful eye of Jove.
> To honour Thetis' son he bends his care,
> And plunge the Greeks in all the woes of war.
> Then bids an empty phantom rise to sight,
> And thus *commands* the vision of the night :
> > directs
> Fly hence, delusive dream, and, light as air,
> To Agamemnon's royal tent repair ;
> Bid him in arms draw forth th' embattled train,
> March all his legions to the dusty plain.
> *Now tell the King* 'tis given him to destroy
> Declare ev'n now
> The lofty *walls* of wide-extended Troy ;
> > tow'rs
> For now no more the Gods with Fate contend ;
> At Juno's suit the heavenly factions end.
> Destruction *hovers* o'er yon devoted wall,
> > hangs
> And nodding Ilion waits th' impending fall.

Invocation to the Catalogue of Ships.—Book II.

Say, Virgins, seated round the throne divine,
All-knowing Goddesses! immortal Nine!
Since earth's wide regions, heaven's unmeasur'd height,
And hell's abyss, hide nothing from your sight,
(We, wretched mortals! lost in doubts below,
But guess by rumour, and but boast we know)
Oh say what heroes, fir'd by thirst of fame,
Or urg'd by wrongs, to Troy's destruction came!
To count them all, demands a thousand tongues,
A throat of brass and adamantine lungs.

> Now, Virgin Goddesses, immortal Nine!
> That round Olympus' heavenly summit shine,
> Who see through heaven and earth, and hell profound,
> And all things know, and all things can resound;
> Relate what armies sought the Trojan land,
> What nations follow'd, and what chiefs command;
> (For doubtful Fame distracts mankind below,
> And nothing can we tell, and nothing know)
> Without your aid, to count th' unnumber'd train,
> A thousand mouths, a thousand tongues were vain.

Book V. v. 1.

But Pallas now Tydides' soul inspires,
Fills with her force, and warms with all her fires :
Above the Greeks his deathless fame to raise,
And crown her hero with distinguish'd praise,
High on his helm celestial lightnings play,
His beamy shield emits a living ray ;
Th' unwearied blaze incessant streams supplies,
Like the red star that fires th' autumnal skies.

> But Pallas now Tydides' soul inspires,
> Fills with her *rage,* and warms with all her fires;
>   force
> O'er all the Greeks decrees his fame to raise,
> Above the Greeks *her warrior's* fame to raise,
>   his deathless
> And crown her hero with *immortal* praise:
>   distinguish'd
> *Bright from* his beamy *crest* the lightnings play,
> High on   helm
> From his broad buckler flash'd the living ray,
> High on his helm celestial lightnings play,
> His beamy shield emits a living ray.
> The Goddess with her breath the flame supplies,
> Bright as the star whose fires in Autumn rise;

                                                    D 2

Her breath divine thick streaming flames supplies,
Bright as the star that fires th' autumnal skies;
Th' unwearied blaze incessant streams supplies,
Like the red star that fires th' autumnal skies:

When fresh he rears his radiant orb to sight,
And bath'd in ocean shoots a keener light,
Such glories Pallas on the chief bestow'd,
Such from his arms the fierce effulgence flow'd ;
Onward she drives him, furious to engage,
Where the fight burns, and where the thickest rage.

> When fresh he rears his radiant orb to sight,
> And gilds old Ocean with a blaze of light,
> Bright as the star that fires th' autumnal skies,
> Fresh from the deep, and gilds the seas and skies.
> Such glories Pallas on her chief bestow'd,
> Such sparkling rays from his bright armour flow'd,
> Such from his arms the fierce effulgence flow'd;
> Onward she drives him *headlong* to engage,
>   furious
> Where the *war bleeds*, and where the *fiercest* rage.
>   fight burns   thickest

The sons of Dares first the combat sought,
A wealthy priest, but rich without a fault ;
In Vulcan's fane the father's days were led,
The sons to toils of glorious battle bred ;

> There liv'd a Trojan—Dares was his name,
> The priest of Vulcan, rich, yet void of blame;
> The sons of Dares first the combat sought,
> A wealthy priest, but rich without a fault.

Conclusion of Book VIII., v. 687.

As when the moon, refulgent lamp of night,
O'er heaven's clear azure spreads her sacred light ;
When not a breath disturbs the deep serene,
And not a cloud o'ercasts the solemn scene ;
Around her throne the vivid planets roll,
And stars unnumber'd gild the glowing pole :
O'er the dark trees a yellower verdure shed,
And tip with silver every mountain's head :
Then shine the vales—the rocks in prospect rise,
A flood of glory bursts from all the skies ;
The conscious swains, rejoicing in the sight,
Eye the blue vault, and bless the useful light.
So many flames before proud Ilion blaze,
And lighten glimmering Xanthus with their rays ;
The long reflections of the distant fires
Gleam on the walls, and tremble on the spires :

A thousand piles the dusky horrors gild,
And shoot a shady lustre o'er the field ;
Full fifty guards each flaming pile attend,
Whose umber'd arms by fits thick flashes send ;
Loud neigh the coursers o'er their heaps of corn,
And ardent warriors wait the rising morn.

As when in stillness of the silent night,
As when the moon in all her lustre bright,
As when the moon, refulgent lamp of night,
O'er heaven's *clear* azure *sheds* her *silver* light;
    pure spreads sacred
As still in air the trembling lustre stood,
And o'er its golden border shoots a flood;
When *no loose gale* disturbs the deep serene,
   not a breath
And *no dim* cloud o'ercasts the solemn scene;
  not a
Around her silver throne the planets glow,
And stars unnumber'd trembling beams bestow;
Around her throne the vivid planets roll,
And stars unnumber'd gild the glowing pole:
Clear gleams of light o'er the dark trees are seen,
      o'er the dark trees a yellow sheds,
O'er the dark trees a yellower *green* they shed,
      gleam
      verdure
And tip with silver all the *mountain* heads
      forest
And tip with silver every mountain's head.
The valleys open, and the forests rise,
The vales appear, the rocks in prospect rise,
Then shine the vales, the rocks in prospect rise,
All nature stands reveal'd before our eyes;
A flood of glory bursts from all the skies.
The conscious shepherd, joyful at the sight,
Eyes the blue vault, and numbers every light.
The conscious *swains rejoicing at the* sight
     shepherds gazing with delight
Eye the blue vault, and bless the *vivid* light,
      glorious
      useful
So many flames before *the navy* blaze,
    proud Ilion
And lighten glimmering Xanthus with their rays,
Wide o'er the fields to Troy extend the gleams,
And tip the distant spires with fainter beams;
The long reflexions of the distant fires
Gild the high walls, and tremble on the spires;
Gleam on the walls, and tremble on the spires;
A thousand fires at distant stations bright,
Gild the dark prospect, and dispel the night.

Of these specimens every man who has cultivated poetry, or who delights to trace the mind from the rudeness of its first conceptions to the elegance of its last, will naturally desire a greater number; but most other readers are already tired, and I am not writing only to poets and philosophers.

The 'Iliad' was published volume by volume, as the translation proceeded; the four first books appeared in [June] 1715. The expectation of this work was undoubtedly high, and every man who had connected his name with criticism or poetry was desirous of such intelligence as might enable him to talk upon the popular topic. Halifax, who, by having been first a poet and then a patron of poetry, had acquired the right of being a judge, was willing to hear some books while they were yet unpublished. Of this rehearsal Pope afterwards gave the following account.

"The famous Lord Halifax was rather a pretender to taste than really possessed of it.—When I had finished the two or three first books of my translation of the 'Iliad,' that Lord desired to have the pleasure of hearing them read at his house. Addison, Congreve, and Garth were there at the reading. In four or five places Lord Halifax stopt me very civilly, and with a speech each time much of the same kind, 'I beg your pardon, Mr. Pope, but there is something in that passage that does not quite please me. Be so good as to mark the place, and consider it a little at your leisure. I am sure you can give it a better turn.' I returned from Lord Halifax's with Dr. Garth, in his chariot; and, as we were going along, was saying to the Doctor, that my Lord had laid me under a good deal of difficulty by such loose and general observations; that I had been thinking over the passages almost ever since, and could not guess at what it was that offended his Lordship in either of them. Garth laughed heartily at my embarrassment; said I had not been long enough acquainted with Lord Halifax to know his way yet; that I need not puzzle myself about looking those places over and over when I got home. 'All you need do (said he) is to leave them just as they are; call on Lord Halifax two or three months hence, thank him for his kind observations on those passages, and then read them to him as altered. I have known him much longer than you have, and will be answerable for the event.' I followed his advice ; waited on Lord Halifax some time after ; said, I hoped he would find his objections to those passages removed ; read them to him exactly as they were at first : and his Lordship was extremely pleased with them, and cried out, 'Ay, now, Mr. Pope, they are perfectly right ; nothing can be better.' " [80]

It is seldom that the great or the wise suspect that they are despised or cheated. Halifax, thinking this a lucky opportunity of securing immortality, made some advances of favour and some overtures of advantage to Pope, which he seems to have received with sullen coldness. All our knowledge of this transaction is derived from a single letter (Dec. 1, 1714), in which Pope says, "I am obliged to you, both for the favours you have done me, and for those you intend me. I distrust neither your will nor your memory when it is to do good ; and if I ever become troublesome or solicitous, it must not be out of expectation, but out of gratitude. Your Lordship may either cause me to live agreeably in the town, or contentedly in the country, which is really all the difference I set between an easy fortune and a small one. It is, indeed, a high strain of generosity in you to think of making me easy all my life, only because I have been so happy as to divert you some few hours : but, if I may have leave to add it is because you think me no enemy to my native Country, there will appear a better reason ; for I must of consequence be very much (as I sincerely am) yours, &c." [81]

[80] Spence.—Johnson. Ed. Singer, p. 134.
[81] 'Letters of Mr. Alexander Pope and several of his Friends.' 4to. 1737, p. 120.
The letter printed by Pope differs from the original as sent to Lord Halifax, now in the British Museum :—

[Addit. MSS. British Museum, No. 7121.]

Decemb^r 3^d, 1714.

My Lord,—While you are doing justice to all the world, I beg you will not forget Homer, if you can spare an hour to attend his cause. I leave him with you in that hope, and return home full of acknowledgments for the Favours

These voluntary offers, and this faint acceptance, ended without effect. The patron was not accustomed to such frigid gratitude, and the poet fed his own pride with the dignity of independence. They probably were suspicious of each other. Pope would not dedicate till he saw at what rate his praise was valued; he would be "troublesome out of gratitude, not expectation." Halifax thought himself entitled to confidence; and would give nothing, unless he knew what he should receive. Their commerce had its beginning in hope of praise on one side, and of money on the other, and ended because Pope was less eager of money than Halifax of praise. It is not likely that Halifax had any personal benevolence to Pope; it is evident that Pope looked on Halifax with scorn and hatred.[82]

The reputation of this great work failed of gaining him a patron; but it deprived him of a friend. Addison and he were now [1715] at the head of poetry and criticism; and both in such a state of elevation, that, like the two rivals in the Roman state, one could no longer bear an equal, nor the other a superior. Of the gradual abatement of kindness between friends the beginning is often scarcely discernible by themselves, and the process is continued by petty provocations, and incivilities sometimes peevishly returned, and sometimes contemptuously neglected, which would escape all attention but that of pride,

your L^dship has done me and for those you are pleas'd to intend me. I distrust neither your will, nor your memory, when it is to do good, and if ever I become troublesome or sollicitous it must not be out of expectation but out of gratitude. Your Lordship may either cause me to live agreeably in the Towne or contentedly in the Country; which is really all the difference I sett between an easy Fortune and a small one. It is indeed a high strain of generosity in you, to think of making me easie all my Life, only because I have been so happy as to divert you an hour or two; But if I may have leave to add, because you think me no enemy to my country, there will appear a better Reason, for I must be of consequence as I sincerely am

My Lord
Your most obliged, most obedient and faithful humble servant,

A. POPE.

[82] This is over-charged. That he disliked Halifax I believe; but compare Pope's posthumous praise of him in the Preface to the 'Iliad.' The character of Bufo (in the 'Epistle to Arbuthnot'), supposed to represent Halifax, is only true in parts to Halifax's character.

and drop from any memory but that of resentment. That the quarrel of these two wits should be minutely deduced is not to be expected from a writer to whom, as Homer says, " nothing but rumour has reached, and who has no personal knowledge."

Pope doubtless approached Addison, when the reputation of their wit first brought them together, with the respect due to a man whose abilities were acknowledged, and who having attained that eminence to which he was himself aspiring, had in his hands the distribution of literary fame. He paid court [1713] with sufficient diligence by his Prologue to 'Cato,' by his abuse of Dennis [1713], and with praise yet more direct by his poem on the 'Dialogues on Medals,' of which the immediate publication was then intended.[83] In all this there was no hypocrisy ; for he confessed that he found in Addison something more pleasing than in any other man.[84]

It may be supposed that as Pope saw himself favoured by the world, and more frequently compared his own powers with those of others, his confidence increased and his submission lessened ; and that Addison felt no delight from the advances of a young wit, who might soon contend with him for the highest place. Every great man, of whatever kind be his greatness, has among his friends those who officiously or insidiously quicken his attention to offences, heighten his disgust, and stimulate his resentment. Of such adherents Addison doubtless had many ; and Pope was now too high to be without them.

From the emission and reception of the proposals for the ' Iliad,' the kindness of Addison seems to have abated. Jervas the painter once pleased himself (Aug. 20, 1714) [85] with imagining that he had re-established their friendship ; and wrote to Pope that Addison once suspected him of too close a confederacy with Swift, but was now satisfied with his conduct. To this Pope answered, a week after, that his engagements to Swift

---

[83] Pope's poem on the Dialogues was first published (after Addison's death) in Tickell's edition of 'Addison's Works,' 4 vols. 4to., 1721.

[84] See vol. ii. p. 152. ' Spence by Singer,' p. 50.

[85] 'Pope's Letters,' 4to. 1737, p. 115.

were such as his services in regard to the subscription demanded, and that the Tories never put him under the necessity of asking leave to be grateful. " But," says he,[86] " as Mr. Addison must be the judge in what regards himself, and has seemed to be no very just one to me, so I must own to you I expect nothing but civility from him." In the same letter he mentions Philips as having been busy to kindle animosity between them; but in a letter to Addison he expresses some consciousness of behaviour inattentively deficient in respect.

Of Swift's industry in promoting the subscription there remains the testimony of Kennet, no friend to either him or Pope.

" Nov. 2, 1713, Dr. Swift came into the coffee-house and had a bow from everybody but me, who, I confess, could not but despise him. When I came to the ante-chamber to wait, before prayers, Dr. Swift was the principal man of talk and business, and acted as master of requests. Then he instructed a young nobleman that the *best Poet in England* was Mr. Pope (a Papist), who had begun a translation of Homer into English verse, for which *he must have them all subscribe;* for, says he, the author *shall not* begin to print till *I have* a thousand guineas for him."

About this time it is likely [87] that Steele, who was, with all his political fury, good-natured and officious, procured an interview between these angry rivals, which ended in aggravated malevolence. On this occasion, if the reports be true, Pope made his complaint with frankness and spirit, as a man undeservedly neglected or opposed; and Addison affected a contemptuous unconcern, and, in a calm, even voice, reproached Pope with his vanity, and telling him of the improvements which his early works had received from his own remarks and those of Steele, said that he, being now engaged in public business, had no longer any care for his poetical reputation; nor had any other desire with regard to Pope than that he should not, by too much arrogance, alienate the public.

---

[86] 'Pope's Letters,' 4to. 1737, p. 116.

[87] " It is likely " is surely a strange kind of fact for a Life.

To this Pope is said to have replied with great keenness and
severity, upbraiding Addison with perpetual dependence, and
with the abuse of those qualifications which he had obtained at
the public cost, and charging him with mean endeavours to
obstruct the progress of rising merit. The contest rose so high,
that they parted at last without any interchange of civility.

The first volume of ' Homer ' was (1715) in time published ;
and a rival version of the first ' Iliad,' for rivals the time of their
appearance inevitably made them, was immediately printed,
with the name of Tickell.[88]   It was soon perceived that, among
the followers of Addison, Tickell had the preference, and the
critics and poets divided into factions. " I, like the Tories," says
Pope, " have the town in general, that is, the mob, on my side ;
but 'tis usual with the smaller party to make up in industry what
they want in numbers. . . . . I appeal to the people as my rightful judges, and while they are not inclined to condemn me, I
fear no arbitrary, high-flying proceedings from the small court
faction at Button's."[89] This opposition he immediately imputed
to Addison, and complained of it in terms sufficiently resentful
to Craggs,[90] their common friend.

When Addison's opinion was asked, he declared the versions
to be both good, but Tickell's the best that had ever been
written ; and sometimes said that they were both good, but that
Tickell had more of ' Homer.'[91]

Pope was now sufficiently irritated ; his reputation and his
interest were at hazard. He once intended to print together
the four versions of Dryden, Maynwaring, Pope, and Tickell,
that they might be readily compared and fairly estimated. This
design seems to have been defeated by the refusal of Tonson,[92]
who was the proprietor of the other three versions.

Pope intended at another time a rigorous criticism of Tickell's
translation, and had marked a copy, which I have seen, in all

[88] Both made their appearance in June, 1715.
[89] ' Letters,' 4to. 1737, p. 128.
[90] Letter, July 5, 1715. ' Letters,' 4to. 1737, p. 127.
[91] Gay to Pope, July 8, 1715. Roscoe's ' Pope,' ed. 1847, viii. 40.
[92] Lintot to Pope, June 22, 1715. Pope's MS. Iliad, vol. i. 108[b].

places that appeared defective.[93]   But while he was thus meditating defence or revenge, his adversary sunk before him without a blow ; the voice of the public was not long divided, and the preference was universally given to Pope's performance.[94]

He was convinced, by adding one circumstance to another,[95] that the other translation was the work of Addison himself ; but if he knew it in Addison's lifetime, it does not appear that he told it.   He left his illustrious antagonist to be punished by what has been considered as the most painful of all reflections, the remembrance of a crime perpetrated in vain.

The other circumstances of their quarrel were thus related by Pope :[96]

"Philips seemed to have been encouraged to abuse me in coffee-houses and conversations : Gildon wrote a thing about Wycherley, in which he had abused both me and my relations very grossly.[97]   Lord Warwick himself told me one day, that it was in vain for me to endeavour to be well with Mr. Addison ; that his jealous temper would never admit of a settled friendship between us : and, to convince me of what he had said, assured me that Addison had encouraged Gildon to publish those scandals, and had given him ten guineas after they were published.   The next day, while I was heated with what I had heard, I wrote a letter to Mr. Addison, to let him know that I was not unacquainted with this behaviour of his ; that if I was

[93] Mr. Pope, in his first resentment of this usage, was resolved to expose this new version in a severe critique upon it.   I have now by me the copy he had marked for this purpose, in which he has classed the several faults in translation, language, and numbers, under their proper heads.—WARBURTON: *Pope's Works,* 8vo. 1752, iv. 26.

[94] Tickell, whose skiff (in partnership they say)
    Set forth for Greece, but founder'd in the way.

        GAY : *Mr. Pope's Welcome from Greece.*

[95] Compare Life of Tickell, in ii. 321.
[96] Spence.—JOHNSON.   Ed. Singer, p. 148.   Spence's statement is confirmed by Warburton's Notes on Pope (Works, 8vo. 1752, iv. 27).
[97] He [Gildon] abused Mr. P. very scandalously in an anonymous pamphlet of the Life of Mr. Wycherley, printed by Curll.—POPE: *The Dunciad,* 4to. 1729, p. 21.

This pamphlet I have failed in finding.

to speak severely of him in return for it, it should be not in such a dirty way ; that I should rather tell him, himself, fairly of his faults, and allow his good qualities ; and that it should be something in the following manner :—I then subjoined the first sketch of what has been since called my Satire on Addison. He used me very civilly ever after, and never did me any injustice that I know of, from that time to his death, which was about three years after." [98]

The verses on Addison, when they were sent to Atterbury, were considered by him as the most excellent of Pope's performances ; and the writer was advised, since he knew where his strength lay, not to suffer it to remain unemployed. [99]

This year (1715) being, by the subscription, enabled to live more by choice, having persuaded his father to sell their estate at Binfield, he purchased, I think only for his life, that house at Twickenham to which his residence afterwards procured so much celebration, and removed thither with his father and mother. [100]

Here he planted the vines and the quincunx which his verses

---

[98] Spence adds: "Dr. Trapp, who was by at the time of this conversation, said that he wondered how so many people came to imagine that Mr. Pope did not write this copy of verses till after Addison's death; since so many people, and he himself for one, had seen it in Addison's lifetime."—*Spence by Singer*, p. 149.

The character of Addison was first printed as a 'Fragment of a Satire' ('Miscellanies, the last volume,' 1728, 8vo.) ; the volume with the Preface signed by Swift and Pope, in which Preface this passage occurs: "In regard to two persons only, we wish our raillery, though ever so tender, or resentment, though ever so just, had not been indulged. We speak of Sir John Vanbrugh, who was a man of wit and of honour; and of Mr. Addison, whose name deserves all respect from every lover of learning."

[99] Atterbury to Pope, Feb. 26, 1721–2. 'Letters,' 4to. 1737, p, 239.

[100] He did not remove from Chiswick to Twickenham till after his father's death. His father died in October, 1717, at Chiswick, and is buried at Chiswick.

"At last the Gods and Fate have fixed me on the borders of the Thames, in the districts of Richmond and Twickenham: it is here I have passed an entire year of my life, without any fixed abode in London, or more than casting a transitory glance (for a day or two at most in a month) on the pomps of the town."—POPE to Jervas, Dec. 12, 1718 ('Letters,' 4to. 1737, p. 205).

This, however, is a wrong date; for Garth, who is mentioned as dead in the same letter, did not die till 18th January, 1718–19. Pope, I suspect, has thrown two letters into one.

mention; and being under the necessity of making a subter-
raneous passage to a garden on the other side of the road, he
adorned it with fossil bodies, and dignified it with the title of a
grotto; a place of silence and retreat, from which he endeavoured
to persuade his friends and himself that cares and passions could
be excluded.

A grotto is not often the wish or pleasure of an Englishman,
who has more frequent need to solicit than exclude the sun;
but Pope's excavation was requisite as an entrance to his
garden, and, as some men try to be proud of their defects, he
extracted an ornament from an inconvenience, and vanity produced a grotto where necessity enforced a passage. It may be
frequently remarked of the studious and speculative, that they are
proud of trifles, and that their amusements seem frivolous and
childish; whether it be that men conscious of great reputation
think themselves above the reach of censure, and safe in the
admission of negligent indulgences, or that mankind expect
from elevated genius an uniformity of greatness, and watch its
degradation with malicious wonder; like him who, having
followed with his eye an eagle into the clouds, should lament
that she ever descended to a perch.

While the volumes of his ' Homer' were annually published,
he collected his former works (1717) into one quarto volume,
to which he prefixed a Preface, written with great sprightliness
and elegance, which was afterwards reprinted, with some passages subjoined that he at first omitted;[101] other marginal
additions of the same kind he made in the later editions of his
poems. Waller remarks, that poets lose half their praise,
because the reader knows not what they have blotted. Pope's
voracity of fame taught him the art of obtaining the accumulated
honour both of what he had published, and of what he had
suppressed.[102]

In this year [1717] his father died suddenly, in his seventy-
fifth year, having passed twenty-nine years in privacy. He is
not known but by the character which his son has given him.

---

[101] The omitted passages were not printed by Pope.
[102] ' Eloisa to Abelard ' appeared for the first time in the quarto of 1717.

If the money with which he retired was all gotten by himself, he had traded very successfully in times when sudden riches were rarely attainable.

The publication of the 'Iliad' was at last completed in 1720. The splendour and success of this work raised Pope many enemies, that endeavoured to depreciate his abilities. Burnet, who was afterwards a judge of no mean reputation, censured him in a piece called 'Homerides' before it was published. Ducket likewise endeavoured to make him ridiculous.[103] Dennis was the perpetual persecutor of all his studies. But, whoever his critics were, their writings are lost; and the names which are preserved, are preserved in 'The Dunciad.'

In this disastrous year (1720) of national infatuation, when more riches than Peru can boast were expected from the South Sea, when the contagion of avarice tainted every mind, and even poets panted after wealth, Pope was seized with the universal passion, and ventured some of his money. The stock rose in its price; and for a while he thought himself the lord of thousands. But this dream of happiness did not last long; and he seems to have waked soon enough to get clear with the loss of what he once thought himself to have won, and perhaps not wholly of that.[104]

Next year [105] he published some select poems of his friend Dr. Parnell, with a very elegant Dedication to the Earl of Oxford; who, after all his struggles and dangers, then lived in retirement, still under the frown of a victorious faction, who could take no pleasure in hearing his praise.

He gave the same year (1721 [106]) an edition of 'Shakespeare.' His name was now of so much authority, that Tonson thought

[103] He assisted Burnet in the tract called 'Homerides,' of which two editions in different types appeared in one year (1715).

[104] He [Pope] has engaged to translate the 'Odyssey' in three years; I believe rather out of a prospect of gain than inclination; for I am persuaded he bore his part in the loss of the South Sea.—GAY to Swift, Jan. 24, 1722.

[105] That is, 1721; but the edition did not appear until 1722. The verses to Lord Oxford are dated September 25, 1721, and are written in honest emulation of Tickell's excellent Elegy on Addison, addressed to the young Lord Warwick, and then newly the subject of great admiration.

[106] Another confusion of dates. The edition, six volumes 4to. (Tonson), did not appear till 1725.

himself entitled, by annexing it, to demand a subscription of six guineas for Shakespeare's plays in six quarto volumes; nor did his expectation much deceive him; for of seven hundred and fifty which he printed, he dispersed a great number at the price proposed. The reputation of that edition indeed sunk afterwards so low, that one hundred and forty copies were sold at sixteen shillings each.

On this undertaking, to which Pope was induced by a reward of two hundred and seventeen pounds twelve shillings, he seems never to have reflected afterwards without vexation; for Theobald, a man of heavy diligence, with very slender powers, first [1726] in a book called 'Shakespeare Restored,' and then [1733] in a formal edition, detected his deficiencies with all the insolence of victory; and as he was now high enough to be feared and hated, Theobald had from others all the help that could be supplied by the desire of humbling a haughty character.

From this time Pope became an enemy to editors, collators, commentators, and verbal critics; and hoped to persuade the world that he miscarried in this undertaking only by having a mind too great for such minute employment.

Pope in his edition undoubtedly did many things wrong, and left many things undone; but let him not be defrauded of his due praise. He was the first that knew, at least the first that told, by what helps the text might be improved. If he inspected the early editions negligently, he taught others to be more accurate. In his Preface he expanded with great skill and elegance the character which had been given of Shakespeare by Dryden; and he drew the public attention upon his works, which, though often mentioned, had been little read.[107]

[107] The edition of Shakespeare (which he undertook merely because he thought nobody else would) took up near two years more in the drudgery of comparing impressions, rectifying the scenery, &c.—POPE: *Note in Dunciad*, 12mo. 1736, p. 224.

'I have retained all his [Pope's] notes, that no fragment of so great a writer may be lost; his Preface, valuable alike for elegance of composition and justness of remark, and containing a general criticism on his author, so extensive that little can be added, and so exact that little can be disputed, every editor has an interest to suppress, but that every reader would demand its insertion. —JOHNSON: *Preface to Shakespeare*.

Soon after the appearance of the 'Iliad,' resolving not to let the general kindness cool, he published proposals[108] for a translation of the 'Odyssey,' in five volumes, for five guineas.   He was willing, however, now to have associates in his labour, being either weary with toiling upon another's thoughts, or having heard, as Ruffhead relates,[109] that Fenton and Broome had already begun the work, and liking better to have them confederates than rivals.

In the patent, instead of saying that he had "translated" the 'Odyssey,' as he had said of the 'Iliad,' he says that he had "undertaken" a translation; and in the proposals, the subscription is said to be not solely for his own use, but for that of "two of his friends who have assisted him in this work."

In 1723, while he was engaged in this new version, he appeared before the Lords at the memorable trial of Bishop Atterbury, with whom he had lived in great familiarity, and frequent correspondence.   Atterbury had honestly recommended to him the study of the Popish controversy, in hope of his conversion ; to which Pope answered in a manner that cannot much recommend his principles or his judgment.   In questions and projects of learning they agreed better.   He was called at the trial to give an account of Atterbury's domestic life, and private employment, that it might appear how little time he had left for plots.   Pope had but few words to utter, and in those few he made several blunders.

His Letters to Atterbury express the utmost esteem, tenderness, and gratitude : " perhaps," says he, " it is not only in this world that I may have cause to remember the Bishop of Rochester."   At their last interview in the Tower, Atterbury presented him with a Bible.[110]

Of the 'Odyssey' Pope translated only twelve books ; the

---

[108] Dated 10th January, 1724-5.

[109] Ruffhead's statement is confirmed by a passage in Spence, ed. Singer, p. 326.   Parts of Books vii. and xiii. he had already printed in Steele's 'Miscellany,' 12mo. 1714.

[110] This Bible was afterwards used in the chapel at Prior Park.   Pope was remembered by Atterbury in his will: " I give to Mr. Pope any book he shall think fit to choose out of my small collection, to be preserved by him in memory of me."—(See Nichols's 'Atterbury,' iii. 518, and iv. 492.)

rest were the work of Broome and Fenton : the notes were
written wholly by Broome, who was not over-liberally rewarded.
The public was carefully kept ignorant of the several shares ;
and an account was subjoined at the conclusion, which is now
known not to be true.[111]

The first copy of Pope's books, with those of Fenton, are to
be seen in the Museum. The parts of Pope are less interlined
than the 'Iliad ;' and the latter books of the 'Iliad' less than
the former. He grew dexterous by practice, and every sheet
enabled him to write the next with more facility. The books
of Fenton have very few alterations by the hand of Pope.[112]
Those of Broome have not been found ; but Pope complained,
as it is reported, that he had much trouble in correcting them.

His contract with Lintot was the same as for the 'Iliad,'
except that only one hundred pounds were to be paid him for
each volume. The number of subscribers were five hundred
and seventy-four, and of copies eight hundred and nineteen ; so
that his profit, when he had paid his assistants, was still very
considerable. The work was finished in 1725 ; and from that
time he resolved to make no more translations.

The sale did not answer Lintot's expectation ; and he then
pretended to discover something of fraud in Pope, and commenced or threatened a suit in Chancery.

On the English 'Odyssey' a criticism was published [1727]
by Spence, at that time [113] Prelector of Poetry at Oxford ; a man
whose learning was not very great, and whose mind was not
very powerful. His criticism, however, was commonly just ;
what he thought, he thought rightly ; and his remarks were
recommended by his coolness and candour. In him Pope had
the first experience of a critic without malevolence, who thought

[111] Compare passage in Broome's ' Life' by Johnson in this volume. He
claimed twelve books, with some parts of other books, in the Appendix (vii.)
to the 'Dunciad,' 4to. and 8vo., 1729.

[112] Only three of Fenton's four books are in the Museum, and one is free
from interlineations.

[113] No. Warton's father was Professor at this time. Spence succeeded Warton. (See Warton's ' Pope,' i. 35.) A second edition of Spence's ' Essay' was
published in 1737.

it as much his duty to display beauties as expose faults; who censured with respect, and praised with alacrity.

With this criticism Pope was so little offended that he sought the acquaintance of the writer,[114] who lived with him from that time in great familiarity, attended him in his last hours, and compiled memorials of his conversation. The regard of Pope recommended him to the great and powerful; and he obtained very valuable preferments in the church.

Not long after [Sept. 1726] Pope was returning home from a visit in a friend's coach,[115] which, in passing a bridge, was over-turned into the water; the windows were closed, and being unable to force them open, he was in danger of immediate death, when the postilion snatched him out by breaking the glass, of which the fragments cut two of his fingers in such a manner that he lost their use.

Voltaire, who was then in England, sent him a letter of con-solation. He had been entertained by Pope at his table, where he talked with so much grossness that Mrs. Pope was driven from the room. Pope discovered by a trick that he was a spy for the Court, and never considered him as a man worthy of confidence.

He soon afterwards (1727) joined with Swift, who was then in England, to publish three volumes of 'Miscellanies,' in which amongst other things he inserted the 'Memoirs of a Parish Clerk,' in ridicule of Burnet's importance in his own History, and a 'Debate upon Black and White Horses,' written in all the formalities of a legal process by the assistance, as is said, of Mr. Fortescue, afterwards Master of the Rolls. Before these 'Miscellanies' is a preface signed by Swift and Pope,[116]

[114] By the favour of Dr. Lowth, the late excellent Bishop of London, I have seen a copy of this Essay on the 'Odyssey,' with marginal observations, written in Pope's hand, and generally acknowledging the justice of Spence's observations; and in a few instances pleading, humorously enough, that some favourite lines might be spared.— *Warton's Pope*, i. 36.

[115] In a coach and six at Whitton, on his way home from Dawley. (Spence by Singer, p. 6 and p. 267; Arbuthnot to Swift, 20th Sept. 1726; Bolingbroke to Swift, 22nd Sept. 1726; and Pope to Swift, 8th March, 1726–7.) It was his right hand.

[116] Dated Twickenham, May 27, 1727; but the volume in which it appears is dated 1728, and is called "the last volume."

but apparently written by Pope; in which he makes a ridiculous
and romantic complaint of the robberies committed upon authors
by the clandestine seizure and sale of their papers.   He tells in
tragic strains how " the cabinets of the sick and the closets of
the dead have been broke open and ransacked ;" as if those
violences were often committed for papers of uncertain and
accidental value, which are rarely provoked by real treasures ;
as if epigrams and essays were in danger where gold and
diamonds are safe.   A cat hunted for his musk is, according
to Pope's account, but the emblem of a wit winded by booksellers.

His complaint, however, received some attestation ; for the
same year [117] the letters written by him to Mr. Cromwell, in his
youth, were sold by Mrs. Thomas to Curll, who printed them.

In these ' Miscellanies ' was first published the ' Art of Sinking
in Poetry,' [118] which, by such a train of consequences as usually
passes in literary quarrels, gave in a short time, according to
Pope's account, occasion to ' The Dunciad.'

In the following year (1728) he began to put Atterbury's
advice in practice, and showed his satirical powers by publishing ' The Dunciad,' [119] one of his greatest and most elaborate

[117] Rather two years before.   The 'Complaint' was published in 1728, and
Curll's ' Miscellanea,' in which they appeared, though dated 1727, was actually
published in 1726.   See Corinna's (Mrs. Thomas's) own letter before them,
dated 16th June, 1726; and Thomson's letter to Aaron Hill, of Oct. 20, 1726.

[118] In "the last volume," 1728, containing the Preface, signed by Swift and
Pope.

Mr. Pope has published a second volume of his ' Poetical Works ' [folio, 1735],
of which I suppose he has made you a present.   I am surprised to see he owns
so little in the four volumes [of Miscellanies], and speaks of these few things
as inconsiderable.   I am a stranger to what part of the copy-money he received; but you know better, are a competent judge whether he deserved it.   I
always thought the ' Art of Sinking ' was his, though he there disowns it.—BEN.
MOTTE (the publisher) to Swift, 31st July, 1735 (Scott, xviii. 356).

[119] Misled by a note of Pope's, no doubt meant to mislead, the date of
publication of the first edition of 'The Dunciad' has been a kind of puzzle to
the critics.   Pope's final account of its publication is as follows :—

"This Poem was written in the year 1726.   In the next year an imperfect
edition was published at Dublin, and reprinted at London, in twelves; another
at Dublin, and another at London, in octavo; and three others, in twelves, the
same year.   But there was no perfect edition before that of London, in quarto,
1729, which was attended with notes."   (Note on 'Dunciad,' B. i. p. 5, in the

performances, in which he endeavoured to sink into contempt all the writers by whom he had been attacked, and some others whom he thought unable to defend themselves.

At the head of the Dunces he placed poor Theobald, whom he accused of ingratitude, but whose real crime was supposed to be that of having revised 'Shakespeare' more happily than himself. This satire had the effect which he intended, by

'Works of Alexander Pope, Esq.,' vol. iii. part 1, containing 'The Dunciad.' Now first published according to the complete copy, found in the year 1741. London: printed for R. Dodsley, and sold by T. Cooper, 1743.)

Now it so happens that an edition of the year 1727 is unknown, though Pope positively states ('Dunciad,' 1736), that *five* imperfect editions were printed at Dublin and London, in octavo and duod., 1727. We have editions of 1728, and what is more to the point, no advertisement of its publication is to be found, or any reference to it be seen, in the newspapers of the time prior to May, 1728. The first known edition of 'The Dunciad' was first published on Saturday, the 18th of May, 1728, price 1s., with this imprint (transcribed from Malone's copy, now in my possession):—

THE

DUNCIAD

AN

Heroic Poem

IN

THREE BOOKS.

DUBLIN Printed   LONDON Reprinted for A. DODD 1728. [12mo.]

Now, what does Pope himself tell us? " 'The Dunciad,' imperfect as it was, had not been published two days, but the whole town gave it to Mr. Pope." (Note *f.* on 'Dunciad,' 1736, p. 7.) But Pope was not always correct in his dates. In the edition of 1736 he inserts an 'Advertisement to the first Edition, with Notes in quarto, 1728'—meaning 1729. (He has made the same error in the date of the quarto, at p. 70 of the same edition, but corrected his mistake in 1743.) What on the title-page is called "The second edition, with some additional notes," an octavo, of 1729, Pope calls, in a letter to Swift, "the eighth." (Letter, Nov. 28, 1729.)

I have seen in Mr. Croker's hands a letter from Pope to Lord Oxford, of the 20th May, 1728, in which he says, "I hope you have seen 'The Dunciad' in print, which is more than I have done." The second edition of 'The Dunciad; an Heroic Poem, in three books,' was advertised as this day published in 'The London Journal' of May 27, 1728, with the famous Spenser motto appended, which Spence tells us (p. 296) he remembers seeing "in the first MS. copy of 'The Dunciad.'"

A Dublin edition was printed in 1728, subsequent to the London edition. (See 'Notes and Queries,' x. 199.) If there was any Dublin edition of 'The Dunciad' prior to the London, it was doubtless paid for by Pope himself. (See Swift to Beach, 'Scott,' xviii. 300.)

blasting the characters which it touched. Ralph, who, unnecessarily interposing in the quarrel, got a place in a subsequent edition, complained that for a time he was in danger of starving, as the booksellers had no longer any confidence in his capacity.[120]

The prevalence of this poem was gradual and slow : the plan, if not wholly new, was little understood by common readers. Many of the allusions required illustration ; the names were often expressed only by the initial and final letters, and, if they had been printed at length, were such as few had known or recollected. The subject itself had nothing generally interesting, for whom did it concern to know that one or another scribbler was a dunce ? If therefore it had been possible for those who were attacked to conceal their pain and their resentment, ' The Dunciad ' might have made its way very slowly in the world.

This, however, was not to be expected : every man is of importance to himself, and, therefore, in his own opinion, to others ; and, supposing the world already acquainted with all his pleasures and his pains, is perhaps the first to publish injuries or misfortunes which had never been known unless related by himself, and at which those that hear them will only laugh, for no man sympathises with the sorrows of vanity.

---

[120] " He [Dryden] died nevertheless, in a good old age, possessed of the kingdom of Wit, and was succeeded by King Alexander, surnamed Pope. This prince enjoyed the crown many years, and is thought to have stretched the prerogative much farther than his predecessor. He is said to have been extremely jealous of the affections of his subjects, and to have employed various spies, by whom, if he was informed of the least suggestion against his title, he never failed of branding the accused person with the word *dunce* on his forehead in broad letters; after which the unhappy culprit was obliged to lay by his pen for ever, for no bookseller would venture to print a word that he wrote. He did indeed put a total restraint on the liberty of the press; for no person durst read anything which was writ without his licence and approbation; and this licence he granted only to four during his reign, namely, to the celebrated Dr. Swift, to the ingenious Dr. Young, to Dr. Arbuthnot, and to one Mr. Gay, four of his principal courtiers and favourites. But without diving any deeper into his character, we must allow that King Alexander had great merit as a writer, and his title to the kingdom of Wit was better founded, at least, than his enemies have pretended."—FIELDING : *Covent Garden Journal*, No. 23, Saturday, March 21, 1752.

The history of 'The Dunciad' is very minutely related by Pope himself, in a Dedication which he wrote to Lord Middlesex in the name of Savage.

"I will relate the war of the 'Dunces' (for so it has been commonly called), which began in the year 1727, and ended in 1730."

"When Dr. Swift and Mr. Pope thought it proper, for reasons specified in the preface to their 'Miscellanies,' to publish such little pieces of theirs as had casually got abroad, there was added to them the 'Treatise of the Bathos,' or the 'Art of Sinking in Poetry.' It happened that in one chapter of this piece the several species of bad poets were ranged in classes, to which were prefixed almost all the letters of the alphabet (the greatest part of them at random); but such was the number of poets eminent in that art, that some one or other took every letter to himself: all fell into so violent a fury, that, for half a year or more, the common newspapers (in most of which they had some property, as being hired writers) were filled with the most abusive falsehoods and scurrilities they could possibly devise; a liberty no way to be wondered at in those people, and in those papers, that for many years, during the uncontrolled licence of the press, had aspersed almost all the great characters of the age; and this with impunity, their own persons and names being utterly secret and obscure.

"This gave Mr. Pope the thought that he had now some opportunity of doing good, by detecting and dragging into light these common enemies of mankind; since, to invalidate this universal slander, it sufficed to show what contemptible men were the authors of it. He was not without hopes, that by manifesting the dulness of those who had only malice to recommend them, either the booksellers would not find their account in employing them, or the men themselves, when discovered, want courage to proceed in so unlawful an occupation. This it was that gave birth to 'The Dunciad;' and he thought it an happiness, that, by the late flood of slander on himself, he had acquired such a peculiar right over their names as was necessary to this design.

" On the 12th of March, 1728-9, at St. James's, that poem was presented to the King and Queen (who had before been pleased to read it) by the Right Honourable Sir Robert Walpole ; and some days after the whole impression was taken and dispersed by several noblemen and persons of the first distinction.

" It is certainly a true observation, that no people are so impatient of censure as those who are the greatest slanderers, which was wonderfully exemplified on this occasion. On the day the book was first vended, a crowd of authors besieged the shop ; entreaties, advices, threats of law and battery, nay cries of treason, were all employed to hinder the coming out of ' The Dunciad ;' on the other side the booksellers and hawkers made as great efforts to procure it. What could a few poor authors do against so great a majority as the public ? There was no stopping a torrent with a finger ; so out it came.

" Many ludicrous circumstances attended it. The ' Dunces ' (for by this name they were called) held weekly clubs to consult of hostilities against the author : one wrote a letter to a great minister, assuring him Mr. Pope was the greatest enemy the Government had ; and another bought his image in clay to execute him in effigy ; with which sad sort of satisfaction the gentlemen were a little comforted.

" Some false editions of the book having an owl in their frontispiece, the true one, to distinguish it, fixed in his stead an ass laden with authors. Then another surreptitious one being printed with the same ass, the new edition in octavo returned for distinction to the owl again.[121] Hence arose a great contest of booksellers against booksellers, and advertisements against advertisements ; some recommending the edition of the owl, and others the edition of the ass ; by which names they came to be distinguished, to the great honour also of the gentlemen of ' The Dunciad.' "

Pope appears by this narrative to have contemplated his victory over the ' Dunces ' with great exultation ; and such was his delight in the tumult which he had raised, that for a while

[121] The first *ass* edition is the quarto of 1729. Even the *owl* plates vary.

his natural sensibility was suspended, and he read reproaches and invectives without emotion, considering them only as the necessary effects of that pain which he rejoiced in having given.

It cannot, however, be concealed that, by his own confession, he was the aggressor ; for nobody believes that the letters in the ‘ Bathos’ were placed at random ; [122] and it may be discovered that, when he thinks himself concealed, he indulges the common vanity of common men, and triumphs in those distinctions which he had affected to despise.   He is proud that his book was presented to the King and Queen by the Right Honourable Sir Robert Walpole ; he is proud that they had read it before ; he is proud that the edition was taken off by the nobility and persons of the first distinction.

The edition of which he speaks was, I believe, that which, by telling in the text the names, and in the notes the characters of those whom he had satirised, was made intelligible and diverting.[123]   The critics had now declared their approbation of the plan, and the common reader began to like it without fear ; those who were strangers to petty literature, and therefore unable to decipher initials and blanks, had now names and persons brought within their view ; and delighted in the visible effect of those shafts of malice which they had hitherto contemplated as shot into the air.

Dennis, upon the fresh provocation now given him, renewed the enmity which had for a time been appeased by mutual civilities ; and published [1728] remarks, which he had till then suppressed, upon ‘ The Rape of the Lock.’   Many more

---

[122] Let us try and hit a few of these random letters :

A. H.	Aaron Hill.	C. C.	Colley Cibber.
C. G.	Charles Gildon.	J. D.	John Dennis.
L. T.	Lewis Theobald.	J. O.	John Oldmixon.
D. F.	De Foe.	E. W.	Edward Ward.
L. E.	Lawrence Eusden.	J. M., Esq.	James Moore, Esq.
W. B.	William Broome.	T. D., Gent.	Thomas Durfey, Gent.
L. W.	Leonard Welsted.	A. P.	Ambrose Philips.

[123] Yes, the 4to. of 1729 ; but a better edition is that of the octavo of 1729, “ the second edition, with some additional notes ;” printed for Lawton Gilliver, and recommended by Pope to Swift. (Letter, Oct. 9, 1729.) ‘ The Dunciad ’ was registered at Stationers’ Hall, by Lawton Gilliver, on 12 April, 1729. He was then the sole publisher, registering “ the whole.”

grumbled in secret, or vented their resentment in the newspapers by epigrams or invectives.

Ducket, indeed, being mentioned as loving Burnet with
" pious passion," pretended that his moral character was injured, and for some time declared his resolution to take vengeance with a cudgel.[124]   But Pope appeased him by changing
" pious passion " to " cordial friendship," [125] and by a note, in
which he vehemently disclaims the malignity of meaning imputed to the first expression.

Aaron Hill, who was represented as diving for the prize,[126]
expostulated with Pope in a manner so much superior to all
mean solicitation, that Pope was reduced to sneak and shuffle,
sometimes to deny, and sometimes to apologise; he first endeavours to wound, and is then afraid to own that he meant a
blow.

' The Dunciad,' in the complete edition, is addressed to Dr.
Swift: [127] of the notes, part were written by Dr. Arbuthnot, and
an apologetical letter was prefixed, signed by Cleland,[128] but
supposed to have been written by Pope.

After this general war upon Dulness, he seems to have in-

---

[124] Some one said to Lord Chesterfield, he wondered Pope was not beaten for
his personality in his satires.   Lord Chesterfield said, " What was everybody's
business, is no one's business."—HORACE WALPOLE: MS. *Note quoted in Mitford's Gray*, v. 182.

[125] This is not quite correct.   The couplet in which " pious passion " occurs
was retained with an explanatory note, and is to be found in the edition of
1736, 12mo.   " Cordial friendship " occurs in no edition that I have seen.

> [126] Then *   * try'd, but hardly snatch'd from sight,
> Instant buoys up, and rises into light.
>
>   Ed. 1729.
>
> Then * essay'd, scarce vanish'd out of sight,
> He buoys up instant, and returns to light.
>
>   Ed. 1736, *and all subsequent editions.*

Johnson has somewhat mistaken the exact point of the controversy.   The
first *blow* of which Hill complains in his manly letters to Pope is not in ' The
Dunciad,' but in ' The Art of Sinking.'   Hill accuses Pope of having attacked
him under the initials A. H. in ' The Art of Sinking.'   The diving scene, which
was a kind of palinode on Pope's part, is in ' The Dunciad.'

[127] The name of Swift appears for the first time before the 12mo. edition,
1736.

[128] Dated "St. James's, Dec. 22, 1728."

dulged himself awhile in tranquillity ; but his subsequent productions prove that he was not idle.   He published (1731) a
poem on ' Taste,' in which he very particularly and severely
criticises the house, the furniture, the gardens, and the entertainments of Timon, a man of great wealth and little taste.
By Timon he was universally supposed, and by the Earl of
Burlington, to whom the poem is addressed, was privately said,
to mean the Duke of Chandos ; a man perhaps too much
delighted with pomp and show, but of a temper kind and
beneficent, and who had consequently the voice of the public
in his favour.

A violent outcry was therefore raised against the ingratitude
and treachery of Pope, who was said to have been indebted to
the patronage of Chandos for a present of a thousand pounds,[129]
and who gained the opportunity of insulting him by the kindness of his invitation.

The receipt of a thousand pounds Pope publicly denied ;[130]
but from the reproach which the attack on a character so
amiable brought upon him, he tried all means of escaping.   The
name of Cleland was again employed in an apology,[131] by
which no man was satisfied ; and he was at last reduced to
shelter his temerity behind dissimulation, and endeavour to
make that disbelieved which he never had confidence openly to
deny.   He wrote an exculpatory letter to the Duke, which was
answered with great magnanimity, as by a man who accepted
his excuse without believing his professions.   He said, that to
have ridiculed his taste, or his buildings, had been an indifferent
action in another man ; but that in Pope, after the reciprocal
kindness that had been exchanged between them, it had been
less easily excused.[132]

Pope, in one of his letters, complaining of the treatment

[129] Only five hundred pounds.   (See ' Ingratitude.   To Mr. Pope, 1733,'
fol. p. 7.)

[130] In an undated letter to the Earl of Burlington, before the third edition
of the ' Epistle,' and included in his ' Letters,' 4to. 1737, p. 310.   He got into
a scrape with the critics by signing his letter " your faithful *affectionate*
servant."

[131] In the shape of a letter to Gay, dated Dec. 16, 1731.

[132] This does not agree with the account in Spence by Singer, p. 145.

which his poem had found, " owns that such critics can intimidate him, nay, almost persuade him to write no more, which
is a compliment this age deserves." [133]   The man who threatens
the world is always ridiculous ; for the world can easily go on
without him, and in a short time will cease to miss him.   I
have heard of an idiot who used to revenge his vexations by
lying all night upon the bridge.   " There is nothing," says
Juvenal, " that a man will not believe in his own favour."
Pope had been flattered till he thought himself one of the
moving powers in the system of life.   When he talked of laying
down his pen, those who sat round him intreated and implored ;
and self-love did not suffer him to suspect that they went away
and laughed.[134]

The following year [4th Dec., 1732] deprived him of Gay,
a man whom he had known early, and whom he seemed to love
with more tenderness than any other of his literary friends.
Pope was now forty-four years old ; an age at which the mind
begins less easily to admit new confidence, and the will to grow
less flexible, and when, therefore, the departure of an old friend
is very acutely felt.

In the next year [7th June, 1733] he lost his mother, not by
an unexpected death, for she had lasted to the age of ninety-
three ; but she did not die unlamented.   The filial piety of
Pope was in the highest degree amiable and exemplary ; his
parents had the happiness of living till he was at the summit
of poetical reputation, till he was at ease in his fortune, and
without a rival in his fame, and found no diminution of his
respect or tenderness.[135]   Whatever was his pride, to them he

[133] Letter to Lord Burlington, first prefixed to the *third* edition of ' The
Epistle on Taste.'

[134] There is a general outcry against that part of the poem which is thought
an abuse on the Duke of Chandos.   Other parts are quarrelled with as
obscure and unharmonious; and I am told there is an advertisement that promises a publication of Mr. Pope's Epistle versified. . . . I am surprised Mr.
Pope is not weary of making enemies.—DR. DELANY to Sir Thomas Hanmer,
23rd Dec. 1731 (Hanmer Corresp., p. 217).

The hundred footsteps scraping the marble hall indicated exactly, it was
said, the number for some years of the Duke's domestics at Canons.

[135] As to Pope's being born of honest parents, I verily believe it; and will

was obedient; and whatever was his irritability, to them he was gentle. Life has, among its soothing and quiet comforts, few things better to give than such a son.[136]

One of the passages of Pope's life which seems to deserve some inquiry was a publication of Letters between him and many of his friends, which falling into the hands of Curll, a rapacious bookseller of no good fame, were by him [May 1735] printed and sold. This volume containing some letters from noblemen,[137] Pope incited a prosecution against him in the House of Lords for breach of privilege, and attended himself to stimulate the resentment of his friends. Curll appeared at the bar, and, knowing himself in no great danger, spoke of Pope with very little reverence. " He has," said Curll, " a knack at versifying, but in prose I think myself a match for him." When the orders of the House were examined, none of them appeared to have been infringed; Curll went away triumphant; and Pope was left to seek some other remedy.

Curll's account was, that one evening a man in a clergyman's gown, but with a lawyer's band, brought and offered to sale a number of printed volumes, which he found to be Pope's epistolary correspondence; that he asked no name, and was told none, but gave the price demanded, and thought himself authorised to use his purchase to his own advantage.

That Curll gave a true account of the transaction, it is reasonable to believe, because no falsehood was ever detected; and

add one praise to his mother's character, that (though I only knew her very old) she always appeared to me to have much better sense than himself.— LADY M. W. MONTAGU to Dr. Arbuthnot, Jan. 3 [1734-5].

[136] The obelisk which Pope erected in his garden to his mother was bought by the present Earl Howe, and removed to his Lordship's seat, Gopsall, in Leicestershire. I remember it at Twickenham, and I have seen it at Gopsall.

[137] Johnson is here incorrect. The volume complained of does not contain a single letter from any nobleman, and Curll was acquitted, and the copies returned to him, on this ground alone, the Committee finding (15th May, 1735) that the publication was not contrary to the standing order of the House, of 31st January, 1721-2, though the advertisement in ' The Postboy ' expressly mentioned letters from Lords Halifax and Burlington. The standing order was founded on an advertisement by Curll of an intended publication, ' The Works and Life of Sheffield Duke of Buckingham,' for which Curll, on his knees, was reprimanded by the Lord Chancellor.

when some years afterwards I mentioned it to Lintot, the son
of Bernard, he declared his opinion to be, that Pope knew
better than any body else how Curll obtained the copies, because
another parcel was at the same time sent to himself, for which
no price had ever been demanded, as he made known his resolution not to pay a porter, and consequently not to deal with a
nameless agent.

Such care had been taken to make them public, that they
were sent at once to two booksellers : to Curll, who was likely
to seize them as a prey ; and to Lintot, who might be expected
to give Pope information of the seeming injury. Lintot, I
believe, did nothing, and Curll did what was expected. That
to make them public was the only purpose may be reasonably
supposed, because the numbers offered to sale by the private
messengers showed that hope of gain [138] could not have been
the motive of the impression.

It seems that Pope, being desirous of printing his letters,
and not knowing how to do, without imputation of vanity, what
has in this country been done very rarely, contrived an appearance of compulsion ; that when he could complain that his
letters were surreptitiously published, he might decently and
defensively publish them himself.[139]

Pope's private correspondence, thus promulgated, filled the
nation with praises of his candour, tenderness, and benevolence,
the purity of his purposes, and the fidelity of his friendship.
There were some letters which a very good or a very wise man
would wish suppressed, but, as they had been already exposed,
it was impracticable now to retract them.

From the perusal of those Letters, Mr. Allen first conceived
the desire of knowing him ; and with so much zeal did he cultivate the friendship which he had newly formed, that when Pope

[138] There cannot be a stronger proof of his [Pope's] being capable of any
action for the sake of gain than publishing his literary correspondence, which
lays open such a mixture of dulness and ingenuity that one would imagine it
visible even to his most passionate admirers.—LADY MARY W. MONTAGU to the
Countess of Bute, June 23, 1752.

[139] This account of the publication of Pope's letters is now the universally
received account.

told his purpose of vindicating his own property by a genuine edition, he offered to pay the cost.

This, however, Pope did not accept; but in time solicited a subscription for a quarto volume, which appeared (1737), I believe, with sufficient profit. In the Preface he tells that his Letters were reposited in a friend's library, said to be the Earl of Oxford's,[140] and that the copy thence stolen was sent to the press. The story was doubtless received with different degrees of credit. It may be suspected that the Preface to the ' Miscellanies ' [141] was written to prepare the public for such an incident ; and, to strengthen this opinion, James Worsdale, a painter, who was employed in clandestine negotiations, but whose veracity was very doubtful, declared that he was the messenger who carried, by Pope's direction, the books to Curll.[142]

When they were thus published and avowed, as they had relation to recent facts and persons either then living or not yet forgotten, they may be supposed to have found readers ; but, as the facts were minute, and the characters, being either private or literary, were little known or little regarded, they awaked no popular kindness or resentment ; the book never became much the subject of conversation ; some read it as a

[140] This was the case. Edward Earl of Oxford, son of Robert Harley Earl of Oxford to whom Pope addressed his touching and noble epistle prefixed to Parnell's Poems (1721). To this second Earl, Pope, in 1727, presented a silver cup, with this inscription upon it—" This is the least thing that Alex. Pope owed to Edward Earl of Oxford."

[141] The preface signed by Swift and Pope, and dated Twickenham, May 27, 1727.

[142] This is strengthened by a note made by Dr. Birch of a conversation held Aug. 17, 1749, with George Faulkner, the Dublin bookseller (see Warton's ' Pope,' ii. 330).

Worsdale was apprentice to Sir Godfrey Kneller, but marrying his wife's niece without their consent was dismissed by his master. On the reputation, however, of that education, by his singing, excellent mimicry, and facetious spirit, he gained many patrons and business.—HORACE WALPOLE: Anecd. of Painters. Ed. Dallaway, iv. 102.

He does not figure to advantage in a letter from Swift to Barber (Scott's ' Swift,' xix. 127, sec. ed.). Pope applied to Lord Oxford, as early as 1729, for permission to deposit his letters in his Lordship's library. Permission was at once granted. Early in the spring of 1735 he reborrowed his letters from the library—I will not say for what purpose.

contemporary history, and some perhaps as a model of epistolary
language; but those who read it did not talk of it.   Not much
therefore was added by it to fame or envy; nor do I remember
that it produced either public praise or public censure.

It had, however, in some degree the recommendation of
novelty.   Our language has few Letters, except those of statesmen.   Howel, indeed, about a century ago, published his
Letters, which are commended by Morhoff, and which alone of
his hundred volumes continue his memory.   Loveday's Letters
were printed only once; those of Herbert and Suckling are
hardly known.   Mrs. Phillips's [Orinda's] are equally neglected;
and those of Walsh seem written as exercises, and were never
sent to any living mistress or friend.   Pope's epistolary excellence had an open field; he had no English rival, living
or dead.

Pope is seen in this collection as connected with the other
contemporary wits, and certainly suffers no disgrace in the
comparison : but it must be remembered that he had the power
of favouring himself; [143] he might have originally had publication in his mind, and have written with care, or have afterwards
selected those which he had most happily conceived, or most
diligently laboured : and I know not whether there does not
appear something more studied and artificial in his productions
than the rest, except one long letter by Bolingbroke, composed
with all the skill and industry of a professed author.   It is
indeed not easy to distinguish affectation from habit; he that
has once studiously formed a style, rarely writes afterwards with
complete ease.   Pope may be said to write always with his
reputation in his head; Swift perhaps like a man who remembered that he was writing to Pope; but Arbuthnot like one
who lets thoughts drop from his pen as they rise into his mind.

Before these Letters appeared, he published the first part of
what he persuaded himself to think a system of ethics, under

[143] And did so. He not only made large omissions, but important alterations
and even additions, as Mr. Bowles has exhibited in ' The Athenæum' for
July 1854, and Mr. Croker's forthcoming edition of Pope will most amply
exhibit.

the title of an ' Essay on Man ;' which, if his Letter to Swift (of
Sept. 14, 1725) be rightly explained by the commentator,[144] had
been eight years under his consideration, and of which he seems
to have desired the success with great solicitude.   He had now
many open and doubtless many secret enemies.   The ' Dunces '
were yet smarting with the war ; and the superiority which he
publicly arrogated disposed the world to wish his humiliation.

All this he knew, and against all this he provided.   His own
name, and that of his friend to whom the work is inscribed
[Lord Bolingbroke], were in the first editions carefully suppressed ; and the poem, being of a new kind, was ascribed to
one or another, as favour determined or conjecture wandered :
it was given, says Warburton, to every man except him only
who could write it.[145]   Those who like only when they like the
author, and who are under the dominion of a name, condemned
it ; and those admired it who are willing to scatter praise at
random, which while it is unappropriated excites no envy.
Those friends of Pope that were trusted with the secret went
about lavishing honours on the new-born poet, and hinting that
Pope was never so much in danger from any former rival.

To those authors whom he had personally offended, and to
those whose opinion the world considered as decisive, and whom
he suspected of envy or malevolence, he sent his ' Essay ' as a
present before publication, that they might defeat their own
enmity by praises which they could not afterwards decently
retract.

With these precautions, in 1732 was published the first part
of the ' Essay on Man.'   There had been for some time a
report that Pope was busy upon a System of Morality ; but this
design was not discovered in the new poem, which had a form
and a title with which its readers were unacquainted.   Its

---

[144] By Warburton.   I agree with Warton that the allusion is so obscure that
Swift certainly could not guess at the subject.

[145] Warburton's note on verse 282 of ' *Epistle to Arbuthnot* ' (Prologue to the
' Satires ').   What threw off the scent from Twickenham was the name of
another publisher, J. Wilford, on the title-page—now becoming a common
practice with Pope—and the fact that he was issuing at the same time other
pieces of some length with the publisher he had been dealing with before.

reception was not uniform : some thought it a very imperfect
piece, though not without good lines.   While the author was
unknown, some, as will always happen, favoured him as an
adventurer, and some censured him as an intruder ; but all
thought him above neglect : the sale increased, and editions
were multiplied.[146]

The subsequent editions of the first Epistle exhibited two
memorable corrections.   At first, the poet and his friend

> " Expatiate freely o'er this scene of man,
> A mighty maze *of walks without a plan*."

For which he wrote afterwards,

> " A mighty maze, *but not without a plan :* "

for, if there was no plan, it was in vain to describe or to trace
the maze.

The other alteration was of these lines :

> " And spite of pride, *and in thy reason's spite*,
> One truth is clear, whatever is, is right :"

but having afterwards discovered, or been shown, that the
" truth " which subsisted " in spite of reason " could not be
very " clear," he substituted,

> " And spite of pride, *in erring reason's spite*."

To such oversights will the most vigorous mind be liable
when it is employed at once upon argument and poetry.

The second and third Epistles were published ; and Pope
was, I believe, more and more suspected of writing them : at
last, in 1734, he avowed the fourth, and claimed the honour
of a moral poet.[147]

[146] But truly I had not the least thought of stealing applause by suppressing
my name to that Essay.   I wanted only to hear truth, and was more afraid of
my partial friends than enemies. —POPE to Mr. Duncombe, 20th Oct. 1734.

[147] It was a sensible mortification that I could not find you and your son
yesterday. . . . I had a hundred things to talk to you of ; and among the rest
of the ' Essay on Man,' which I hear so much of.   Pray, what is your opinion
of it ?   I hear some cry it extremely up, others think it obscure in part, and
some (of whom I am sure you are not one) have said it is mine.   I think I

In the conclusion it is sufficiently acknowledged that the doctrine of the 'Essay on Man' was received from Bolingbroke, who is said to have ridiculed Pope, among those who enjoyed his confidence, as having adopted and advanced principles of which he did not perceive the consequence, and as blindly propagating opinions contrary to his own. That those communications had been consolidated into a scheme regularly drawn, and delivered to Pope, from whom it returned only transformed from prose to verse, has been reported, but hardly can be true. The 'Essay' plainly appears the fabric of a poet: what Bolingbroke supplied could be only the first principles; the order, illustration, and embellishments must all be Pope's.[148]

These principles it is not my business to clear from obscurity, dogmatism, or falsehood; but they were not immediately

could show you some faults in it, and believe you can show me more : upon the whole it is allowed to have merit, and I think so myself.—POPE to Richardson the painter. *Roscoe's Pope*, i. 305, ed. 1847.

Our author [Pope] told Mr. Harte, that in order to disguise his being the author of the second Epistle of the 'Essay on Man,' he made in the first edition the following bad rhyme :—

> "A cheat! a whore! who starts not at the *name*,
>   In all the inns of court or Drury *Lane* ? "

And Harte remembered to have often heard it urged, in inquiries about the author whilst he was unknown, that it was impossible it could be Pope's on account of this very passage.—WARTON's *Essay on Pope*, ii. 154. Ed. 1782.

[148] It was odd, as you observe, that Voltaire should translate the line from Pope as it is in the last edition. I persuaded the latter to alter *miracles* to prodigies, not only for the religion but the reason of the thing. . . . Yet this was one of the *speciosa dictata* of Bolingbroke, who was fond of the impiety, and yet did not see the blunder.—WARBURTON to Hurd (Letters, p. 110).

In the year 1763, being at London, I was carried by Dr. John Blair, prebendary of Westminster, to dine at old Lord Bathurst's, where we found the late Mr. Mallet, Sir James Porter, &c. The conversation turning on Mr. Pope, Lord Bathurst told us that the 'Essay on Man' was originally composed by Lord Bolingbroke in prose, and that Mr. Pope did no more than put it into verse; that he had read Lord Bolingbroke's manuscript in his own handwriting; and remembered well that he was at a loss whether most to admire the elegance of Lord Bolingbroke's prose or the beauty of Mr. Pope's verse. When Lord Bathurst told this, Mr. Mallet bade me attend, and remember this remarkable piece of information, as, by the course of nature, I might survive his Lordship, and be a witness of his having said so.—DR. HUGH BLAIR to Boswell, Sept. 21, 1779.

examined; philosophy and poetry have not often the same readers; and the 'Essay' abounded in splendid amplifications and sparkling sentences, which were read and admired with no great attention to their ultimate purpose ; its flowers caught the eye which did not see what the gay foliage concealed, and for a time flourished in the sunshine of universal approbation. So little was any evil tendency discovered, that, as innocence is unsuspicious, many read it for a manual of piety.

Its reputation soon invited a translator. It was first turned into French prose, and afterwards by Resnel into verse. Both translations fell into the hands of Crousaz, who first, when he had the version in prose, wrote a general censure, and afterwards reprinted Resnel's version, with particular remarks upon every paragraph.

Crousaz was a professor of Switzerland, eminent for his treatise of Logic, and his 'Examen de Pyrrhonisme,' and, however little known or regarded here, was no mean antagonist. His mind was one of those in which philosophy and piety are happily united. He was accustomed to argument and disquisition, and perhaps was grown too desirous of detecting faults ; but his intentions were always right, his opinions were solid, and his religion pure.

His incessant vigilance for the promotion of piety disposed him to look with distrust upon all metaphysical systems of theology, and all schemes of virtue and happiness purely rational; and therefore it was not long before he was persuaded that the positions of Pope, as they terminated for the most part in natural religion, were intended to draw mankind away from revelation, and to represent the whole course of things as a necessary concatenation of indissoluble fatality : and it is undeniable that, in many passages, a religious eye may easily discover expressions not very favourable to morals or to liberty.

About this time Warburton began to make his appearance in the first ranks of learning.[149] He was a man of vigorous

[149] The friendship of Pope and Warburton had its commencement in that bookseller's shop which is situate on the wayside of the gateway leading down the Inner Temple-lane. Warburton had some dealings with Jacob Robinson

faculties, a mind fervid and vehement, supplied by incessant and unlimited inquiry, with wonderful extent and variety of knowledge, which yet had not oppressed his imagination nor clouded his perspicacity. To every work he brought a memory full fraught, together with a fancy fertile of original combinations, and at once exerted the powers of the scholar, the reasoner, and the wit. But his knowledge was too multifarious to be always exact, and his pursuits too eager to be always cautious. His abilities gave him a haughty confidence, which he disdained to conceal or mollify ; and his impatience of opposition disposed him to treat his adversaries with such contemptuous superiority as made his readers commonly his enemies, and excited against the advocate the wishes of some who favoured the cause. He seems to have adopted the Roman emperor's determination, *oderint dum metuant;* he used no allurements of gentle language, but wished to compel rather than persuade.

His style is copious without selection, and forcible without neatness ; he took the words that presented themselves ; his diction is coarse and impure, and his sentences are unmeasured.

He had in the early part of his life pleased himself with the notice of inferior wits, and corresponded with the enemies of Pope. A letter was produced,[150] when he had perhaps himself

the publisher, to whom the shop belonged, and may be supposed to have been drawn there on business; Pope might have a call of the like kind: however that may be, there they met, and entering into a conversation which was not soon ended, conceived a mutual liking, and, as we may suppose, plighted their faith to each other. The fruit of this interview, and the subsequent communications of the parties, was the publication, in Nov. 1739, of a pamphlet with this title, 'A Vindication of Mr. Pope's Essay on Man. By the Author of The Divine Legation of Moses. Printed for J. Robinson.'—HAWKINS: *Life of Johnson,* p. 69.

Their very first interview was in Lord Radnor's garden, just by Mr. Pope's, at Twickenham. Dodsley was present, and was, he told me, astonished at the high compliments paid him by Pope as he approached him.—JOS. WARTON : *Pope's Works,* ix. 342.

[150] This remarkable letter was first printed in Malone's 'Supplement to Shakespeare,' i. 223, but was first referred to in print by Akenside in a note to his 'Ode to Thomas Edwards, Esq., on the late edition of Mr. Pope's Works, 1751.' See Dyce's ' Akenside,' p. lxxvi.

forgotten it, in which he tells Concanen, "Dryden, I observe, borrows for want of leisure, and Pope for want of genius; Milton out of pride, and Addison out of modesty." And when [1733] Theobald published 'Shakespeare,' in opposition to Pope, the best notes were supplied by Warburton.[151]

But the time was now come when Warburton was to change his opinion; and Pope was to find a defender in him who had contributed so much to the exaltation of his rival.

The arrogance of Warburton excited against him every artifice of offence, and therefore it may be supposed that his union with Pope was censured as hypocritical inconstancy; but surely to think differently at different times of poetical merit may be easily allowed. Such opinions are often admitted, and dismissed, without nice examination. Who is there that has not found reason for changing his mind about questions of greater importance?

Warburton, whatever was his motive, undertook, without solicitation, to rescue Pope from the talons of Crousaz, by freeing him from the imputation of favouring fatality, or rejecting revelation; and from month to month continued a vindication of the 'Essay on Man' in the literary journal of that time called 'The Republic of Letters.'

Pope, who probably began to doubt the tendency of his own work, was glad that the positions, of which he perceived himself not to know the full meaning, could by any mode of interpreta-

---

[151] Those villains who upbraid me with my acquaintance and correspondence with the gentlemen of 'The Dunciad' know I at the same time proclaimed it to the world in Theobald's edition of Shakespeare in Mr. Pope's lifetime. Till his Letters were published, I had as indifferent opinion of his morals as they pretended to have. Mr. Pope knew this, and had the justice to own to me that I fairly followed appearances, when I thought well of them and ill of him. He owned, indeed, that in reading that edition he was sorry to find a man of genius got amongst them; for he told me he was greatly struck with my notes. This conversation happened to pass in company. On one of them saying they wondered I would give anything to such a fellow as Theobald, Mr. Pope said immediately, there was no wonder at all: I took him for an honest man, as he had done, and on that footing had visited him—and then followed what I relate above. This was the only time the subject ever came upon the tapis, for he was too delicate to mention anything of it to me alone.—WAR-BURTON to Hurd, January 12, 1757.

tion be made to mean well.   How much he was pleased with his gratuitous defender the following letter evidently shows:

"April 11, 1739.

" Sir,—I have just received from Mr. R.[152] two more of your letters.   It is in the greatest hurry imaginable that I write this; but I cannot help thanking you in particular for your third letter, which is so extremely clear, short, and full, that I think Mr. Crousaz ought never to have another answerer, and deserved not so good an one.   I can only say, you do him too much honour, and me too much right, so odd as the expression seems ; for you have made my system as clear as I ought to have done, and could not.   It is indeed the same system as mine, but illustrated with a ray of your own, as they say our natural body is the same still when it is glorified. [153]   I am sure I like it better than I did before, and so will every man else.   I know I meant just what you explain ; but I did not explain my own meaning so well as you.   You understand me as well as I do myself; but you express me better than I could express myself. Pray accept the sincerest acknowledgments.   I cannot but wish these letters were put together in one book, and intend (with your leave) to procure a translation of part, at least, or of all of them into French ; but I shall not proceed a step without your consent and opinion, &c."

By this fond and eager acceptance of an exculpatory comment, Pope testified that, whatever might be the seeming or real import of the principles which he had received from Bolingbroke, he had not intentionally attacked religion ; and Bolingbroke, if he meant to make him, without his own consent, an instrument of mischief, found him now engaged, with his eyes open, on the side of truth.

It is known that Bolingbroke concealed from Pope his real opinions.   He once discovered them to Mr. Hooke, who related them again to Pope, and was told by him that he must have mistaken the meaning of what he heard ; and Bolingbroke, when Pope's uneasiness incited him to desire an explanation, declared that Hooke had misunderstood him.[154]

[152] Mr. Robinson the bookseller.

[153]   So will our God re-build man's perish'd frame,
            And raise him up much better, yet the same.

COWLEY to Sir W. Davenant.

[154]   Ruffhead's account of this matter (' Life of Pope,' 8vo. 1769, p. 219), which Warburton himself supplied, and of which the autograph is now in Mr. Croker's possession.   But compare ' Spence,' ed. Singer, p. 369.

Bolingbroke hated Warburton, who had drawn his pupil from him ; and a little before Pope's death they had a dispute, from which they parted with mutual aversion.[155]

From this time Pope lived in the closest intimacy with his commentator, and amply rewarded his kindness and his zeal ; for he introduced him to Mr. Murray, by whose interest he became preacher at Lincoln's Inn, and to Mr. Allen, who gave him his niece and his estate, and by consequence a bishopric.[156] When he died, he left him the property of his works, a legacy which may be reasonably estimated at four thousand pounds.

Pope's fondness for the 'Essay on Man' appeared by his desire of its propagation. Dobson, who had gained reputation by his version of Prior's 'Solomon,' was employed by him to translate it into Latin verse, and was for that purpose some time at Twickenham ; but he left his work, whatever was the reason, unfinished, and, by Benson's invitation, undertook the longer task of 'Paradise Lost.'[157] Pope then desired his friend to find a scholar who should turn his Essay into Latin prose, but no such performance has ever appeared.

Pope lived at this time *among the great*,[158] with that reception and respect to which his works entitled him, and which he had not impaired by any private misconduct or factitious partiality. Though Bolingbroke was his friend, Walpole was not his enemy,[159] but treated him with so much consideration

[155] It was this work [Letters concerning the use of reading History] which occasioned his [Bolingbroke's] aversion to me. There is a dissertation in it against the canon of Scripture, which I told Mr. Pope was full of absurdities and false reasoning, and would discredit the work; and at his desire, I drew up a paper of remarks upon it, which Lord Bolingbroke never forgave. He wrote an answer to it in great wrath and much acrimony, but, by the persuasion of a great man, suppressed it. It is possible it may now see the light. The paper it was an answer to was drawn up one summer's afternoon, as Mr. Pope sat by me, without taking my hand from the table till it was done; so that, as it contained several sheets, you will easily believe he had advantage enough of me.—WARBURTON to Hurd, Dec. 29, 1751.

[156] Compare 'Boswell by Croker,' p. 185 and p. 289.

[157] Two specimens of Dobson's translation may be seen in Singer's 'Spence,' p. 475.

[158] Envy must own I live among the great.—POPE.

[159] He has praised him in verse (Epilogue to the 'Satires'):—

as, at his request, to solicit and obtain [1728] from the French
Minister an abbey for Mr. Southcott, whom he considered himself as obliged to reward, by this exertion of his interest, for
the benefit which he had received from his attendance in a
long illness.[160]

It was said that, when the Court was at Richmond, Queen
Caroline had declared her intention to visit him. This may
have been only a careless effusion, thought on no more : the
report of such notice, however, was soon in many mouths ; and
if I do not forget or misapprehend Savage's account, Pope, pretending to decline what was not yet offered, left his house for
a time, not, I suppose, for any other reason than lest he should
be thought to stay at home in expectation of an honour which
would not be conferred. He was therefore angry at Swift,
who represents him as " refusing the visits of a Queen," because he knew that what had never been offered had never
been refused.[161]

Beside the general system of morality, supposed to be con-

> Seen him I have, but in his happier hour
> Of social pleasure, ill exchanged for power;
> Seen him uncumbered with the venal tribe,
> Smile without art, and win without a bribe.

Of his first wife he has said that she was "untainted by a court;" and her
son Horace has made the poet's encomium part of his mother's monument in
Westminster Abbey. He afterwards had a hit at Walpole : "besides, he was a
tyrant to his wife."

[160] Warburton's note on ver. 29 of Epilogue to the 'Satires,' Dial. i., and
Spence by Singer, p. 7.

> [161] Hail, happy Pope! whose generous mind,
> Detesting all the statesman kind,
> Contemning Courts, at Courts unseen,
> Refused the visits of a Queen.
>
> SWIFT: *A Libel on Dr. Delany*, 1729.
>
> The Court . . . .
> Where Pope will never show his face.
>
> SWIFT: *On Poetry, a Rhapsody.*

Why, pray, do you fancy I do not desire to cultivate Mr. Pope's acquaintance?
But, perhaps, if I seek it too much, I might meet with a rebuff, as you say her
Majesty did.—LADY BETTY GERMAINE to Swift, Feb. 10, 1735-6. (SCOTT'S
Swift, xviii. 450, 2nd ed.)

tained in the 'Essay on Man,' it was his intention to write distinct poems upon the different duties or conditions of life; one of which is the Epistle to Lord Bathurst (1732) on the 'Use of Riches,' a piece on which he declared great labour to have been bestowed.[162]

Into this poem some hints are historically thrown, and some known characters are introduced, with others of which it is difficult to say how far they are real or fictitious: but the praise of Kyrle, the Man of Ross, deserves particular examination, who, after a long and pompous enumeration of his public works and private charities, is said to have diffused all those blessings from *five hundred a year*. Wonders are willingly told, and willingly heard. The truth is, that Kyrle was a man of known integrity and active benevolence, by whose solicitation the wealthy were persuaded to pay contributions to his charitable schemes; this influence he obtained by an example of liberality exerted to the utmost extent of his power, and was thus enabled to give more than he had. This account Mr. Victor[163] received from the minister of the place, and I have preserved it, that the praise of a good man, being made more credible, may be more solid. Narrations of romantic and impracticable virtue will be read with wonder, but that which is unattainable is recommended in vain: that good may be endeavoured, it must be shown to be possible.[164]

[162] Spence.—JOHNSON. Ed. Singer, p. 304.

I remember Mr. Pope's repeating to my father and me, in his library at Twickenham, four verses designed for his 'Epistle on Riches,' which were an exquisite description of an old lady dying, and just raising herself up, and blowing out a little end of a candle that stood by her bedside with her last breath. These verses are not in the printed edition.—*Richardsoniana*, 8vo. 1776, p. 221.

This poem, 'Of the Use of Riches,' as Mr. Pope tells us himself, cost much attention and labour; and, from the easiness that appears in it, one would be apt to think as much.—GOLDSMITH: *Works by Cunningham*, iii. 437.

[163] Ben Victor, a dramatic writer and historian of the stage. Johnson (see vol. ii. p. 121) received the story of Addison's hard conduct to Steele from Ben Victor.

[164] The following highly interesting letter from Pope relative to the Man of Ross, and his poetical portrait of him, is not to be found in any edition of Pope's Works. Pope had written to Tonson, who lived at Ledbury, near Ross, for some particulars of Kyrle:—

This is the only piece in which the author has given a hint of his religion by ridiculing the ceremony of burning the Pope, and by mentioning with some indignation the inscription on the Monument.

When this poem was first published, the dialogue, having no

To Jacob Tonson, Senior.

Twickenham, June 7, 1732.

Dear Sir,—Before I received your last, I intended to write to you my thanks for the great diligence (or let me give it a higher title, zeal) you have shown in giving me so many particulars of the Man of Ross. They are more than sufficient for my honest purpose of setting up his fame, as an example to greater and wealthier men, how they ought to use their fortunes. You know, few of these particulars can be made to shine in verse, but I have selected the most affecting; and have added two or three which I learned from other hands. A small exaggeration you must allow me as a poet; yet I was determined the ground-work at least should be *truth*, which made me so scrupulous in my enquiries, and sure, considering that the world is bad enough to be always extenuating and lessening what virtue is among us, it is but reasonable to pay it sometimes a little over measure, to balance that injustice, especially when it is done for example and encouragement to others. If any man shall ever happen to endeavour to emulate the Man of Ross, it will be no manner of harm if I make him think he was something more charitable and more beneficent than really he was, for so much more good it would put the imitator upon doing. And farther, I am satisfied in my conscience (from the strokes in two or three accounts I have of his character) that it was in his will, and in his heart, to have done every good a poet can imagine.

My motive for singling out this man was two-fold: first, to distinguish real and solid worth from showish or plausible expense, and virtue from vanity; and, secondly, to humble the pride of greater men, by an opposition of one so obscure and so distant from the sphere of public glory, this proud town. To send you any of the particular verses will be much to the prejudice of the whole; which if it has any beauty, derives it from the manner in which it is *placed*, and the *contrast* (as the painters call it) in which it stands, with the pompous figures of famous, or rich, or high-born men.

I was not sorry he had no monument, and will put that circumstance into a note, perhaps into the body of the poem itself (unless you ontreat the contrary in youi own favour, by your zeal to erect one). I would however in this case, spare the censure upon his heir (so well as he deserves it), because I dare say, after seeing his picture, every body will turn that circumstance to his honour, and conclude the Man of Ross himself would not have any monument in memory of his own good deeds.

I have no thoughts of printing the poem (which is an epistle on the 'Use of Riches') this long time, perhaps not till it is accompanied with many others, and at a time when telling truths and drawing exemplary pictures of men and manners can be of no disservice to the author, and occasion no slanderer to mistake them, and apply them falsely, as I was lately served in the character of Timon. But I wish for nothing more than to see you here, on these quiet

letters of direction, was perplexed and obscure. Pope seems
to have written with no very distinct idea, for he calls that an
' Epistle to Bathurst,' in which Bathurst is introduced as
speaking.[165]

He afterwards (1733) inscribed to Lord Cobham his
' Characters of Men,' written with close attention to the operations of the mind and modifications of life. In this poem he
has endeavoured to establish and exemplify his favourite theory
of the *ruling passion*, by which he means an original direction
of desire to some particular object, an innate affection which
gives all action a determinate and invariable tendency, and
operates upon the whole system of life, either openly, or more
secretly by the intervention of some accidental or subordinate
propension.

Of any passion, thus innate and irresistible, the existence
may reasonably be doubted. Human characters are by no
means constant ; men change by change of place, of fortune, of
acquaintance ; he who is at one time a lover of pleasure, is at
another a lover of money. Those indeed who attain any excellence commonly spend life in one pursuit ; for excellence is
not often gained upon easier terms. But to the particular
species of excellence men are directed, not by an ascendant

banks of the Thames, where any of these things should be frankly shown to
you.

My portrait by Dahl, I have sent a week ago to your nephew. You oblige
me in the copy of my old friend Dr. Garth; and you will always oblige me in
continuing to write to me. As to Dr. Bentley and Milton, I think the one
above and the other below all criticism. Adieu, and health and peace and
fair weather attend you.

                                                          Yours,
—*Gent.'s Mag.* for January, 1836.   A. POPE.

See ' Spence by Singer,' p. 437, for a letter from Stephen Duck to Spence,
with particulars about the Man of Ross.

[165] " I never saw this very amiable old nobleman, whose wit, vivacity, sense,
and integrity are well known, but he repeatedly expressed his disgust, and
his surprise, at finding in later editions this Epistle awkwardly converted into
a Dialogue, in which he has but little to say. And I remember he once remarked that ' this line:—

          P. But you are tir'd.   I'll tell a tale.—B. Agreed.

was insupportably insipid and flat.' "—JOS. WARTON : *Life of Pope*, p. xliii.

planet or predominating humour, but by the first book which they read, some early conversation which they heard, or some accident which excited ardour and emulation.[166]

It must be at least allowed that this *ruling passion*, antecedent to reason and observation, must have an object independent on human contrivance, for there can be no natural desire of artificial good. No man therefore can be born, in the strict acceptation, a lover of money, for he may be born where money does not exist : nor can he be born, in a moral sense, a lover of his country ; for society, politically regulated, is a state contradistinguished from a state of nature, and any attention to that coalition of interests which makes the happiness of a country, is possible only to those whom inquiry and reflection have enabled to comprehend it.

This doctrine is in itself pernicious as well as false : its tendency is to produce the belief of a kind of moral predestination, or overruling principle which cannot be resisted ; he that admits it, is prepared to comply with every desire that caprice or opportunity shall excite, and to flatter himself that he submits only to the lawful dominion of Nature, in obeying the resistless authority of his *ruling passion*.

Pope has formed his theory with so little skill, that, in the examples by which he illustrates and confirms it, he has confounded passions, appetites, and habits.

To the ' Characters of Men ' he added soon after [1735], in an Epistle supposed to have been addressed to Martha Blount, but which the last edition [167] has taken from her, the ' Characters of Women.' This poem, which was laboured with great diligence, and in the author's opinion with great success, was neglected at its first publication, as the commentator supposes,

[166] The true genius is a mind of large general powers, accidentally determined to some particular direction. Sir Joshua Reynolds, the great painter of the present age, had the first fondness for his art excited by the perusal of Richardson's treatise.—JOHNSON : *Life of Cowley*, i. 4.

[167] Johnson alludes, I suppose, to Warburton's edition. But in no edition, even in Pope's lifetime, and when it was free from personal characters, did the Epistle appear otherwise than as it now appears, addressed simply ' To a Lady.'

because the public was informed, by an advertisement, that it contained *no character drawn from the life:* an assertion which Pope probably did not expect or wish to have been believed, and which he soon [168] gave his readers sufficient reason to distrust by telling them in a note that the work was imperfect, because part of his subject was *vice too high* to be yet exposed.[169]

The time, however, soon came in which it was safe to display the Duchess of Marlborough under the name of *Atossa;* and her character was inserted with no great honour to the writer's gratitude.[170]

He published from time to time (between 1733 and 1738) imitations of different poems of Horace, generally with his name, and once,[171] as was suspected, without it. What he was upon moral principles ashamed to own, he ought to have suppressed. Of these pieces it is useless to settle the dates, as they had seldom much relation to the times, and perhaps had been long in his hands.

This mode of imitation, in which the ancients are familiarised, by adapting their sentiments to modern topics, by making Horace say of Shakespeare what he originally said of Ennius,

[168] The same year when the Epistle was included with his other works in a duodecimo edition.

[169] He makes the same observation and quotation at the end of the first edition of the Fourth Book of 'The Dunciad.'

[170] The character of Atossa did not appear in any edition of 'The Characters of Women' published in Pope's lifetime. The Duchess outlived Pope. It was, however, inserted in an edition of the 'Four Epistles' that he had ready for publication at the time of his death. This edition was destroyed by his executors. Pope, I grieve to add, had received a "favour" from the Duchess for the suppression of the character. The favour, it is said, was 1000*l.* (See Bolingbroke to Marchmont (n. d.), in Marchmont Papers, vol. ii. p. 334.) Among his papers was left a finished character of the great Duke of Marlborough, still unpublished, and which I have seen in Mr. Croker's hands. It is in his best manner, and is part of the fourth epistle of the 'Essay on Man.'

[171] Johnson alludes to 'Sober Advice from Horace to the Young Gentlemen about Town. As delivered in his Second Sermon. Imitated in the manner of Mr. Pope. London: Printed for T. Boreman, at the Cock on Ludgate Hill,' folio, no date. When Pope collected his Imitations, 12mo., 1740, he inserted 'Sober Advice,' as an imitation of the Second Satire of the First Book. See Bolingbroke's interesting account of it in a letter to Swift of June 27, 1734.

and accommodating his satires on Pantolabus and Nomentanus to the flatterers and prodigals of our own time, was first practised in the reign of Charles the Second by Oldham and Rochester; at least I remember no instances more ancient. It is a kind of middle composition between translation and original design, which pleases when the thoughts are unexpectedly applicable, and the parallels lucky. It seems to have been Pope's favourite amusement, for he has carried it further than any former poet.

He published likewise a revival, in smoother numbers, of Dr. Donne's 'Satires,' which was recommended to him by the Duke of Shrewsbury and the Earl of Oxford. They made no great impression on the public. Pope seems to have known their imbecility, and therefore suppressed them while he was yet contending to rise in reputation, but ventured them when he thought their deficiencies more likely to be imputed to Donne than to himself.[172]

The Epistle to Dr. Arbuthnot, which seems to be derived in its first design from Boileau's Address *à son Esprit*, was published in January, 1734-5, about a month before the death of him to whom it is inscribed. It is to be regretted that either honour or pleasure should have been missed by Arbuthnot,—a man estimable for his learning, amiable for his life, and venerable for his piety.

Arbuthnot was a man of great comprehension, skilful in his profession, versed in the sciences, acquainted with ancient literature, and able to animate his mass of knowledge by a bright and active imagination; a scholar with great brilliance of wit; a wit who, in the crowd of life, retained and discovered a noble ardour of religious zeal.

In this poem Pope seems to reckon with the public. He vindicates himself from censures, and with dignity, rather than arrogance, enforces his own claims to kindness and respect.

Into this poem are interwoven several paragraphs which had been before printed as a fragment, and among them the

---

[172] They were never published separately, but introduced into the second volume of his works in folio and quarto.

satirical lines upon Addison, of which the last couplet has been
twice corrected.   It was at first,—

> " Who would not smile if such a man there be?
> Who would not laugh if Addison were he? "

Then,

> " Who would not grieve if such a man there be?
> Who would not laugh if Addison were he? "

At last it is,

> " Who but must laugh if such a man there be?
> Who would not weep if Atticus were he? " [173]

He was at this time at open war with Lord Hervey, who
had distinguished himself as a steady adherent to the Ministry,
and being offended with a contemptuous answer [174] to one of
his pamphlets, had summoned Pulteney to a duel.   Whether
he or Pope made the first attack perhaps cannot now be easily
known; [175] he had written an invective [176] against Pope, whom he

[173] Another reading is:—

> " What pity! Heaven! if such a man there be,
> Who would not weep if Addison were he?"

> (*Miscellanies. The last volume*, 1728, p. 129.)

[174] ' A proper Reply to a late Scurrilous Libel,' 1731.   The so-called libel
was 'Sedition and Defamation displayed,' 1731.

[175] It would be now idle to seek for a cause of quarrel which the parties
were, an hundred years ago, unable or unwilling to explain. . . . . But whatever may have been their private feuds, the first public offence was undoubtedly given by Pope.   In his ' Miscellanies ' (1727), Lord Hervey is sneered at
in several passages, both covertly and under his initials.   In the first edition
of ' The Dunciad ' (1728) we find—

> And high-born Howard, more majestic sire,
> Impatient waits till * * [*Hervey*] joins the quire.

These were, however, slight touches; and though no one could doubt who was
meant, they afforded Hervey no ground of complaint.   But towards the close
of 1732 appeared the *Imitation of the First Satire of the Second Book of Horace*,
in which Pope attacked Lady Mary, by the name of *Sappho*, in the most brutal
and indecent couplet ever printed, and Lord Hervey twice over by the contemptuous designation of *Lord Fanny*.—CROKER: *Lord Hervey's Memoirs*, i. xxxix.

[176] Verses addressed to the Imitator of the First Satire of the Second Book of
Horace.   By a Lady; in which he had the assistance of Lady Mary W. Mon-
tagu.   At Ickworth (the seat of the Herveys) is a copy without " By a
Lady."

calls, " Hard as thy heart, and as thy birth obscure," and
hints that his father was a *hatter*.[177] To this Pope wrote a
reply in verse and prose ; the verses are in this poem, and the
prose, though it was never sent, is printed among his Letters,[178]
but to a cool reader of the present time exhibits nothing but
tedious malignity.[179]

His last Satires, of the general kind, were two Dialogues,
named, from the year in which they were published, 'Seventeen Hundred and Thirty-eight.' In these poems many are
praised and many are reproached. Pope was then entangled
in the Opposition ; a follower of the Prince of Wales, who
dined at his house,[180] and the friend of many who obstructed
and censured the conduct of the Ministers. His political partiality was too plainly shown ; he forgot the prudence with
which he passed, in his earlier years, uninjured and unoffending,
through much more violent conflicts of faction.

In the first Dialogue, having an opportunity of praising
Allen of Bath, he asked his leave to mention him as a man not
illustrious by any merit of his ancestors, and called him in his
verses " low-born Allen." Men are seldom satisfied with praise
introduced or followed by any mention of defect. Allen seems
not to have taken any pleasure in his epithet, which was afterwards softened into " humble Allen."

In the second Dialogue he took some liberty with one of the
Foxes, among others ; which Fox, in a reply to Lyttelton, took
an opportunity of repaying, by reproaching him with the friend-

[177] The *hatter* accusation occurs in a different *invective,* and one wholly from
Lord Hervey's pen—' An Epistle [in Verse] from a Nobleman to a Doctor of
Divinity: in answer to a Latin Letter in Verse, Written from H[ampto]n
C[our]t. Aug. 28, 1733. London: Printed for J. Roberts, 1733,' folio.

[178] Warburton publishes his edition of Pope next week, with the famous
piece of prose on Lord Hervey, which he formerly suppressed at my uncle's
desire, who had got an abbey from Cardinal Fleury for one Southcott, a
friend of Pope's. My Lord Hervey pretended not to thank him.—HOR. WALPOLE
to Montagu, 13th June, 1751.

[179] This was said from Johnson's fondness for the Herveys; and he has said
elsewhere in the same Life that " the meanest passage " in the '*Prologue to the
Satires* ' is the Satire upon Sporus.

[180] The Prince visited him in 1735 (see Gent.'s Mag. for October, 1735,
p. 610).

ship of a lampooner, who scattered his ink without fear or
decency, and against whom he hoped the resentment of the
Legislature would quickly be discharged.[181]

About this time [1739] Paul Whitehead, a small poet, was summoned before the Lords for a poem called ' Manners,' together
with Dodsley, his publisher. Whitehead, who hung loose upon
society, sculked and escaped; but Dodsley's shop and family
made his appearance necessary. He was, however, soon dismissed ; and the whole process was probably intended rather to
intimidate Pope than to punish Whitehead.[182]

Pope never afterwards attempted to join the patriot with the
poet, nor drew his pen upon statesmen. That he desisted from
his attempts of reformation is imputed by his commentator[183]
to his despair of prevailing over the corruption of the time. He
was not likely to have been ever of opinion that the dread of
his satire would countervail the love of power or of money; he
pleased himself with being important and formidable, and gratified sometimes his pride, and sometimes his resentment ; till at
last he began to think he should be more safe if he were less
busy.

The ' Memoirs of Scriblerus,' published about this time,[184]
extend only to the first book of a work projected in concert
by Pope, Swift, and Arbuthnot, who used to meet in the time
of Queen Anne, and denominated themselves the " Scriblerus
Club." Their purpose was to censure the abuses of learning by a
fictitious Life of an infatuated Scholar. They were dispersed ;
the design was never completed ; and Warburton laments its
miscarriage as an event very disastrous to polite letters.

[181] Lyttelton supported his friend, and replied that he thought it an honour
to be received into the familiarity of so great a poet.—JOHNSON: Life of
Lyttelton.

[182] Dodsley's prosecution was intended as a hint to Pope, and he understood
it as such; and did not publish a Third Dialogue, which he certainly had designed to do: part of it now first appears in this edition.—WARTON'S Pope,
ed. 1797, i. lxi.

[183] Warburton.

[184] 'The Memoirs of Scriblerus' were first published in April, 1741, in 'The
Works of Mr. Alexander Pope, in Prose, vol. 2. London: printed for J. and
P. Knapton, C. Bathurst, and R. Dodsley,' folio and quarto.

If the whole may be estimated by this specimen, which seems to be the production of Arbuthnot,[185] with a few touches perhaps by Pope, the want of more will not be much lamented; for the follies which the writer ridicules are so little practised, that they are not known: nor can the satire be understood but by the learned; he raises phantoms of absurdity, and then drives them away.   He cures diseases that were never felt.

For this reason this joint production of three great writers has never obtained any notice from mankind; it has been little read, or when read has been forgotten, as no man could be wiser, better, or merrier by remembering it.

The design cannot boast of much originality; for besides its general resemblance to Don Quixote, there will be found in it particular imitations of the History of Mr. Ouffle.

Swift carried so much of it into Ireland as supplied him with hints for his travels; and with those the world might have been contented, though the rest had been suppressed.

Pope had sought for images and sentiments in a region not known to have been explored by many other of the English writers; he had consulted the modern writers of Latin poetry, a class of authors whom Boileau endeavoured to bring into contempt, and who are too generally neglected.   Pope, however, was not ashamed of their acquaintance, nor ungrateful for the advantages which he might have derived from it.   A small selection from the Italians who wrote in Latin had been published at London, about the latter end of the last century, by a man [186] who concealed his name, but whom his preface shows to have been well qualified for his undertaking.   This collection Pope amplified by more than half, and (1740) published it in two volumes, but injuriously omitted his predecessor's preface.

---

[185] "We have also obtained the Memoirs of Scriblerus, being the beginning of a considerable Work, undertaken so long ago as in 1713, by several great hands.   As much of it as is here published, and all the Tracts in the name, were written by our author and Dr. Arbuthnot, except the 'Essay on the Origin of Sciences,' in which Dr. Parnell had some hand, as Mr. Gay in the 'Memoirs of a Parish Clerk.'   The rest were Mr. Pope's."—*The Bookseller to the Reader,* before Pope's Works, vol. ii. fol., 1741.

[186] By Atterbury, afterwards Bishop of Rochester.

To these books, which had nothing but the mere text, no regard was paid, the authors were still neglected, and the editor was neither praised nor censured.

He did not sink into idleness; he had planned a work, which he considered as subsequent to his ' Essay on Man,' of which he has given this account to Dr. Swift:

"March 25, 1736.

" If ever I write more Epistles in verse, one of them shall be addressed to you. I have long concerted it, and begun it; but I would make what bears your name as finished as my last work ought to be, that is to say, more finished than any of the rest. The subject is large, and will divide into four Epistles, which naturally follow the ' Essay on Man,' viz.— 1. Of the Extent and Limits of Human Reason and Science. 2. A View of the Useful and therefore Attainable, and of the Unuseful and therefore Unattainable Arts. 3. Of the Nature, Ends, Application, and Use of different Capacities. 4. Of the Use of Learning, of the Science, of the World, and of Wit. It will conclude with a Satire against the misapplication of all these, exemplified by Pictures, Characters, and Examples."

This work, in its full extent, being now afflicted with an asthma, and finding the powers of life gradually declining, he had no longer courage to undertake; but, from the materials which he had provided, he added, at Warburton's request, another book to ' The Dunciad,' [187] of which the design is to ridicule such studies as are either hopeless or useless, as either pursue what is unattainable, or what, if it be attained, is of no use.

When this book was printed (March, 1742) the laurel had been for some time upon the head of Cibber; a man whom it cannot be supposed that Pope could regard with much kindness or esteem, though in one of the Imitations of Horace he has liberally enough praised ' The Careless Husband.' [188] In ' The Dunciad,' among other worthless scribblers, he had mentioned Cibber; who, in his ' Apology,' complains of the great poet's

[187] 'The New Dunciad: as it was found in the year 1741. With the Illustrations of Scriblerus and Notes Variorum. London: printed for T. Cooper, at the Globe in Paternoster Row. 1742. Price 1s. 6d.' 4to.
[188] First Epistle of Second Book. His name occurs thrice again, and not with praise, in the same Imitation.

unkindness as more injurious, " because," says he, " I never have offended him." [189]

It might have been expected that Pope should have been, in some degree, mollified by this submissive gentleness, but no such consequence appeared. Though he condescended to commend Cibber once, he mentioned him afterwards contemptuously in one of his satires, and again in his Epistle to Arbuthnot; [190] and in the fourth book of 'The Dunciad' attacked him with acrimony, to which the provocation is not easily discoverable. Perhaps he imagined that, in ridiculing the laureat, he satirised those by whom the laurel had been given, and gratified that ambitious petulance with which he affected to insult the great.

The severity of this satire left Cibber no longer any patience. He had confidence enough in his own powers to believe that he could disturb the quiet of his adversary, and doubtless did not want instigators, who, without any care about the victory, desired to amuse themselves by looking on the contest. He therefore gave the town a pamphlet, [191] in which he declares his resolution from that time never to bear another blow without returning it, and to tire out his adversary by perseverance, if he cannot conquer him by strength.

The incessant and unappeasable malignity of Pope he imputes to a very distant cause. After the ' Three Hours after Marriage' had been driven off the stage by the offence which

[189] In the same *Apology* he describes him as "our great imitator of Horace" (p. 19) ; "our most celebrated living author" (p. 31); "our most eminent author" (p. 32) ; and lastly (p. 33), "this inimitable writer :" all evident expressions of hearty admiration, or, as Cibber afterwards describes it, dealing with him as a gentleman.

[190] And has not Colley still his lord and whore?
                              Epistle to Arbuthnot, 1734.

So humble, he has knock'd at Tibbald's door,
Has drunk with Cibber, nay, has rhym'd for Moore.
                              Ibid.

[191] ' A Letter from Mr. Cibber to Mr. Pope, inquiring into the Motives that might induce him, in his Satirical Works, to be so frequently fond of Mr. Cibber's name. London: printed and sold by W. Lewis, in Russell Street, Covent Garden, 1742.' 8vo. A second edition appeared the same year.

the mummy and crocodile gave the audience, while the exploded scene was yet fresh in memory, it happened that Cibber played Bayes in 'The Rehearsal ;' and, as it had been usual to enliven the part by the mention of any recent theatrical transactions, he said that he once thought to have introduced his lovers disguised in a mummy and a crocodile. " This," says he, " was received with loud claps, which indicated contempt of the play." Pope, who was behind the scenes, meeting him as he left the stage, attacked him, as he says, with all the virulence of a " wit out of his senses;" to which he replied, " that he would take no other notice of what was said by so particular a man, than to declare, that, as often as he played that part, he would repeat the same provocation."

He shows his opinion to be, that Pope was one of the authors of the play which he so zealously defended; and adds an idle story of Pope's behaviour at a tavern.

The pamphlet was written with little power of thought or language, and, if suffered to remain without notice, would have been very soon forgotten. Pope had now been enough acquainted with human life to know, if his passion had not been too powerful for his understanding, that, from a contention like his with Cibber, the world seeks nothing but diversion, which is given at the expense of the higher character. When Cibber lampooned Pope, curiosity was excited; what Pope would say of Cibber nobody inquired, but in hope that Pope's asperity might betray his pain and lessen his dignity.

He should therefore have suffered the pamphlet to flutter and die, without confessing that it stung him. The dishonour of being shown as Cibber's antagonist could never be compensated by the victory. Cibber had nothing to lose : when Pope had exhausted all his malignity upon him, he would rise in the esteem both of his friends and his enemies. Silence only could have made him despicable ; the blow which did not appear to be felt would have been struck in vain.

But Pope's irascibility prevailed, and he resolved to tell the whole English world that he was at war with Cibber; and to show that he thought him no common adversary, he prepared

no common vengeance; he published [October, 1743] a new
edition of 'The Dunciad,' in which he degraded Theobald from
his painful pre-eminence, and enthroned Cibber in his stead.
Unhappily the two heroes were of opposite characters, and Pope
was unwilling to lose what he had already written; he has
therefore depraved his poem by giving to Cibber the old books,
the cold pedantry, and sluggish pertinacity of Theobald.

Pope was ignorant enough of his own interest to make
another change, and introduced Osborne contending for the
prize among the booksellers.   Osborne was a man entirely
destitute of shame, without sense of any disgrace but that of
poverty.   He told me, when he was doing that [192] which raised
Pope's resentment, that he should be put into 'The Dunciad;'
but he had the fate of Cassandra.   I gave no credit to his
prediction, till in time I saw it accomplished.   The shafts of
satire were directed equally in vain against Cibber and Osborne; being repelled by the impenetrable impudence of one,
and deadened by the impassive dulness of the other.[193]   Pope
confessed his own pain by his anger; but he gave no pain to
those who had provoked him.   He was able to hurt none but
himself; by transferring the same ridicule from one to another
he destroyed its efficacy; for by showing that what he had said
of one he was ready to say of another, he reduced himself to
the insignificance of his own magpie, who from his cage calls
cuckold at a venture.

Cibber, according to his engagement, repaid 'The Dunciad'
with another pamphlet,[194] which, Pope said, " would be as

---

[192] Osborne's offence was his pretending to sell the quarto subscription copies
of the 'Iliad' at half price.   He even issued advertisements, it is said, for a
year together, that he had copies in hand at the reduced charge.   He had cut
the common folio copies to subscription-quarto size, and no doubt sold many
at the lower price, though on worse paper and without the copper-plates.

[193] This was the Osborne of whom Johnson said, in reply to a question from
Boswell, "Sir, he was impertinent to me, and I beat him.   But it was not in
his shop; it was in my own chamber."—*Boswell by Croker*, p. 46.

[194] ' Another Occasional Letter from Mr. Cibber to Mr. Pope.   Wherein the
New Hero's preferment to his Throne in the Dunciad seems not to be accepted.
And the Author of that Poem his more rightful claim to it is asserted.
With an Expostulatory Address to the Reverend Mr. W[arburto]n, Author of

good as a dose of hartshorn to him;"[195] but his tongue and
his heart were at variance. I have heard Mr. Richardson relate, that he attended his father the painter on a visit, when
one of Cibber's pamphlets came into the hands of Pope, who
said, " These things are my diversion." They sat by him
while he perused it, and saw his features writhen with anguish;
and young Richardson said to his father, when they returned,
that he hoped to be preserved from such diversion as had been
that day the lot of Pope.[196]

From this time, finding his diseases more oppressive, and his
vital powers gradually declining, he no longer strained his
faculties with any original composition, nor proposed any other
employment for his remaining life than the revisal and correction
of his former works ; in which he received advice and assistance
from Warburton, whom he appears to have trusted and honoured
in the highest degree.

He laid aside his epic poem, perhaps without much loss to
mankind; for his hero was Brutus the Trojan, who, according
to a ridiculous fiction, established a colony in Britain. The
subject therefore was of the fabulous age; the actors were a
race upon whom imagination has been exhausted and attention
wearied, and to whom the mind will not easily be recalled
when it is invited in blank verse, which Pope had adopted with
great imprudence, and I think without due consideration of
the nature of our language. The sketch is, at least in part, preserved by Ruffhead;[197] by which it appears that Pope was
thoughtless enough to model the names of his heroes with terminations not consistent with the time or country in which he
places them.

He lingered through the next year; but perceived himself,
as he expresses it, " going down the hill." He had for at least

the New Preface, and Adviser in the curious Improvements of that Satire.'
London [as before], 1744.

[195] Letter to Warburton, 12th January, 1743–4.

[196] No one was ever more tender and sore to raillery than Pope, who was so
great a master of it, nor consequently more resentful; too strong a proof of
this was his long affair with Colley Cibber.—*Richardsoniana*, 8vo. 1776, p. 311.

[197] Ruffhead's ' Life of Pope,' 8vo. 1769, p. 410.

five years been afflicted with an asthma, and other disorders, which his physicians were unable to relieve. Towards the end of his life he consulted Dr. Thomson, a man who had, by large promises and free censures of the common practice of physic, forced himself up into sudden reputation. Thomson declared his distemper to be a dropsy, and evacuated part of the water by tincture of jalap, but confessed that his belly did not subside. Thomson had many enemies, and Pope was persuaded to dismiss him.

While he was yet capable of amusement and conversation, as he was one day sitting in the air with Lord Bolingbroke and Lord Marchmont, he saw his favourite Martha Blount at the bottom of the terrace, and asked Lord Bolingbroke to go and hand her up. Bolingbroke, not liking his errand, crossed his legs and sat still ; but Lord Marchmont, who was younger and less captious, waited on the lady ; who, when he came to her, asked, " What, is he not dead yet ? " She is said to have neglected him, with shameful unkindness, in the latter time of his decay ; yet, of the little which he had to leave, she had a very great part. Their acquaintance began early ; [198] the life of each was pictured on the other's mind ; their conversation therefore was endearing, for when they met, there was an immediate coalition of congenial notions. Perhaps he considered her unwillingness to approach the chamber of sickness as female weakness or human frailty ; perhaps he was conscious to himself

[198] Before the publication of his 'Essay on Criticism' in 1711, if indeed not some years earlier. She was the younger of two daughters of Lister Blount, of Mapledurham, in Oxfordshire, Esq. The elder, Theresa, was born in 1688 (in the same year with Pope), and Martha in 1690. Mr. Croker some years since observed to me that Mr. Bowles and Mr. Roscoe have mistaken these ladies for sisters of Mr. Edward Blount, of Blagdon in Devonshire, the correspondent of Pope, and built a great deal of idle scandal and controversy on that erroneous supposition, which Mr. Carruthers in his late edition (1853) has also exposed. They were Roman Catholics. Their father died in 1710, leaving a widow, who died in 1743, and an only son, who married in 1715, and died in 1739. Theresa was for some years the favourite sister of Pope. In 1717 he made a settlement in favour of Theresa of forty pounds a year for six years (Carruthers' 'Life of Pope,' p. 53); but there is no mention of her in Pope's will. Theresa died in 1759, and Martha in 1763. They were the Stella and Vanessa of Pope.

of peevishness and impatience, or, though he was offended by her inattention, might yet consider her merit as overbalancing her fault; and if he had suffered his heart to be alienated from her, he could have found nothing that might fill her place; he could have only shrunk within himself; it was too late to transfer his confidence or fondness.

In May 1744 his death was approaching; [199] on the 6th, he was all day delirious, which he mentioned four days afterwards as a sufficient humiliation of the vanity of man; he afterwards complained of seeing things as through a curtain and in false colours, and one day, in the presence of Dodsley, asked what arm it was that came out from the wall. He said that his greatest inconvenience was inability to think. [200]

Bolingbroke sometimes wept over him in this state of helpless decay; [201] and being told by Spence [202] that Pope, at the intermission of his deliriousness, was always saying something kind either of his present or absent friends, and that his humanity seemed to have survived his understanding, answered, "It has so." And added, "I never in my life knew a man that had so tender a heart for his particular friends, or a more general friendship for mankind." [203] At another time he said, "I have known Pope these thirty years, and value myself more in his friendship than"—his grief then suppressed his voice.

Pope expressed undoubting confidence of a future state. Being asked by his friend Mr. Hooke, a Papist, whether he would not die like his father and mother, and whether a priest should not be called, he answered, "I do not think it essential, but it will be very right; and I thank you for putting me in mind of it." [204]

In the morning, after the priest had given him the last sacraments, he said, "There is nothing that is meritorious but

[199] Spence.—JOHNSON. Ed. Singer, p. 319.

[200] Pope is given over with a dropsy, which is mounted into his head: in an evening he is not in his senses. The other day, at Chiswick, he said to my Lady Burlington, "Look at our Saviour there! how ill they have crucified him."—WALPOLE to Mann, May 29, 1744.

[201] Spence by Singer, p. 320.   [202] Ibid., p. 321.
[203] Ruffhead, p. 510.   [204] Spence by Singer, p. 322.

virtue and friendship; and indeed friendship itself is only a part of virtue." [205]

He died in the evening of the 30th day of May, 1744, so placidly, that the attendants did not discern the exact time of his expiration.[206]   He was buried at Twickenham, near his father [207] and mother, where a monument has been erected to him by his commentator, the Bishop of Gloucester.

He left the care of his papers to his executors; first to Lord Bolingbroke,[208] and if he should not be living to the Earl of Marchmont; undoubtedly expecting them [209] to be proud of the trust, and eager to extend his fame.   But let no man dream of influence beyond his life.   After a decent time, Dodsley the bookseller went to solicit preference as the publisher, and was told that the parcel had not been yet inspected; and whatever was the reason, the world has been disappointed of what was " reserved for the next age." [210]

He lost, indeed, the favour of Bolingbroke by a kind of posthumous offence.   The political pamphlet called ' The Patriot King' had been put into his hands that he might procure the impression of a very few copies, to be distributed, according to the author's direction, among his friends, and Pope assured him that no more had been printed than were allowed; but, soon after his death, the printer [211] brought and resigned a complete

---

[205] Spence by Singer, p. 322.   [206] Ibid., p. 322.

[207] His father was buried at Chiswick.   Johnson was misled by the monument in Twickenham Church, which Pope erected to his father and mother, and as he briefly added upon it, " et sibi."

[208] Lord Bolingbroke was not an executor.   The four executors were Lords Bathurst and Marchmont, Mr. Murray (afterwards Lord Mansfield), and Mr. George Arbuthnot.

[209] Johnson should have omitted Lord Marchmont from his censure, as Bolingbroke survived Pope upwards of seven years, within which time, no doubt, Dodsley's application was made.

[210] I am surprised Lord Burlington is unmentioned in Pope's will; on the whole, it appears to me more reasonable and less vain than I expected from him.—LADY MARY WORTLEY MONTAGU to Countess of Oxford. (' Works' by Lord Wharncliffe, iii. 213.)

> Publish the present age; but where the text
> Is vice too high, reserve it for the next.
>
> *Imitations of Horace.*   (To Fortescue.)

[211] Mr. Wright.

edition of fifteen hundred copies, which Pope had ordered him to print, and to retain in secret. He kept, as was observed,[212] his engagement to Pope better than Pope had kept it to his friend ; and nothing was known of the transaction till, upon the death of his employer, he thought himself obliged to deliver the books to the right owner, who, with great indignation, made a fire in his yard, and delivered the whole impression to the flames.[213]

Hitherto nothing had been done which was not naturally dictated by resentment of violated faith; resentment more acrimonious, as the violator had been more loved or more trusted. But here the anger might have stopped ; the injury was private, and there was little danger from the example.

Bolingbroke, however, was not yet satisfied ; his thirst of vengeance excited him to blast the memory of the man over whom he had wept in his last struggles ; and he employed Mallet, another friend of Pope, to tell the tale to the public, with all its aggravations. Warburton, whose heart was warm with his legacy, and tender by the recent separation, thought it proper for him to interpose ; and undertook,[214] not indeed to vindicate the action, for breach of trust has always something

[212] By Mallet.

[213] " I saw to-day in the ' London Evening Post' a letter which reflects upon my brother B[olingbro]ke in regard to Mr. P[o]pe's treachery to him, in which the blame seems to be thrown from him upon my brother. I have not yet seen any one thing more that has been published concerning it except a Preface in a Magazine in his favour, the truth of which I could attest; and have often wondered he could so long stifle the abominable usage he met with from P[o]pe in printing his work, which he had intrusted to him to review, intending that it should not be published till after his own death. The letters between P[o]pe and the printer, bargaining for the price, were found by Lord Marchmont, whose business it was, by P[o]pe's last *will*, to look over his papers jointly with Lord Bol[ingbro]ke ; but as to the subject of the book, I know nothing of it; nor is that to the purpose, as to P[o]pe's baseness to the best of friends, without whom he had never shone in the ' Essay on Man.' "—LADY LUXBOROUGH to Shenstone, June 24, 1749.

[214] In 'A Letter to the Editor of the Letters on the Spirit of Patriotism; the Idea of a Patriot-King, and the State of Parties, &c. Occasioned by the Editor's Advertisement.', " Is this my guide, philosopher, and friend?"—Pope to Lord P. . . 1749. The letter is reprinted in the Appendix to Ruffhead's ' Life of Pope,' 8vo. 1769.

criminal, but to extenuate it by an apology.[215] Having advanced what cannot be denied, that moral obliquity is made more or less excusable by the motives that produce it, he inquires what evil purpose could have induced Pope to break his promise. He could not delight his vanity by usurping the work, which, though not sold in shops, had been shown to a number more than sufficient to preserve the author's claim; he could not gratify his avarice, for he could not sell his plunder till Bolingbroke was dead; and even then, if the copy was left to another, his fraud would be defeated, and if left to himself, would be useless.[216]

Warburton therefore supposes, with great appearance of reason, that the irregularity of his conduct proceeded wholly from his zeal for Bolingbroke, who might perhaps have destroyed the pamphlet, which Pope thought it his duty to preserve, even without its author's approbation. To this apology an answer was written in 'A Letter to the most impudent Man living.'[217]

He brought some reproach upon his own memory by the petulant and contemptuous mention made in his will of Mr. Allen, and an affected repayment of his benefactions. Mrs. Blount, as the known friend and favourite of Pope, had been invited to the house of Allen, where she comported herself with such indecent arrogance, that she parted from Mrs. Allen in a state of irreconcileable dislike, and the door was for ever barred

---

[215] As the copies were printed at the instigation of Allen, Warburton had a double duty to perform.

[216] Lord Bathurst [the Chancellor] entertained me a good deal apart after dinner with anecdotes of his godfather Lord Bolingbroke, of Pope, his own father, and others, which, as they fell under his own eye, perhaps I could have learned from no other man living. He entirely exculpates Pope from any evil intention in printing 'The Patriot King,' which excited Bolingbroke's hatred so much after Pope's death; though I do still think it was a very unaccountable step.—HANNAH MORE (under 1783): *Life by Roberts*, i. 279.

[217] Ostensibly written by Mallet; but the original MS. is still preserved in Lord Bolingbroke's handwriting.—*Cooke's Life of Bolingbroke*, ii. 218. There cannot be a doubt that the unauthorised impression of 'The Patriot King' proceeded wholly from Pope's extreme, and I would add unaccountable, zeal for Bolingbroke.

against her. This exclusion she resented with so much bitterness as to refuse any legacy from Pope, unless he left the world
with a disavowal of obligation to Allen. Having been long
under her dominion, now tottering in the decline of life, and
unable to resist the violence of her temper, or perhaps, with the
prejudice of a lover, persuaded that she had suffered improper
treatment, he complied with her demand, and polluted [218] his
will with female resentment. [219]   Allen accepted the legacy,
which he gave to the hospital at Bath, [220] observing that Pope
was always a bad accountant, and that if to 150*l.* he had put a
cypher more, he had come nearer to the truth. [221]

[218] See note 45 in vol. i. p. 49.

[219] Johnson follows Warburton and Ruffhead; but he has overlooked an
entry in Spence of what Martha Blount herself told Spence : "I had never
read his will; but he mentioned to me the part relating to Mr. Allen, and I
advised him to omit it, but could not prevail on him to do so. I have a
letter of his by me on that subject; I sent it to Mr. Hooke."—*Spence by
Singer*, p. 357.

[220] As Pope had requested in his will, "If he refuses to take this himself,
I desire him to employ it in a way I am persuaded he will not dislike—to the
benefit of the Bath Hospital."—*Pope's Will*.

[221] Ruffhead's 'Life of Pope,' p. 547.

Nay, I have heard somewhere or other of a man [Mr. Allen] who, when his
dying friend, at the instigation and to quiet the impotent passions of another
(for what generous mind has not been deceived by ill-placed friendships?), had
inserted an unkind clause concerning him in his last will, took no other
revenge for a folly so unprovoked than by doubling the legacy which his
deceased friend had left to an old faithful servant [John Searle, his gardener],
because he, the survivor, deemed it to be too little.—*Warburton's Letter to the
Editor of the Letters, &c.*, 1749. Allen took the legacy because Mrs. Blount was
residuary legatee. He also took Searle and his family into his protection.
(Ruffhead's 'Life,' p. 547.)

The cause of Mrs. Blount's dislike to Allen is thus related by Sir John
Hawkins:—"Upon an invitation in which Mrs. Blount was included, Mr. Pope
made a visit to Mr. Allen, at Prior Park, and having occasion to go to Bristol
for a few days, left Mrs. Blount behind him. In his absence Mrs. Blount, who
was of the Romish persuasion, signified an inclination to go to the Popish
chapel at Bath, and desired of Mr. Allen the use of his chariot for the purpose;
but he being at that time mayor of the city, suggested the impropriety of
having his carriage seen at the door of a place of worship to which as a magis-
trate he was at least restrained from giving a sanction, and might be required
to suppress, and therefore desired to be excused. Mrs. Blount resented this
refusal, and told Pope of it at his return, and so infected him with her rage
that they both left the house abruptly."

The person of Pope is well known not to have been formed by the nicest model.[222] He has, in his account of the ' Little Club,' compared himself to a spider, and by another is described

[222] There are several excellent portraits of Pope. He sat to Kneller, Jervas, Richardson, Dahl, Pond, Vanloo, Roubiliac, and Rysbrack. At Nuneham is the fine Kneller which belonged to Lord Chancellor Harcourt. In the Bodleian Gallery is another excellent Kneller (that engraved in large by Vertue), a present to the Gallery in 1722 from Edward Earl of Oxford. Four portraits of him exist by Jervas: one at Lord Pembroke's, at Wilton (startled look, pen in hand); a second at Lord Mansfield's, at Caen Wood (right arm resting on his folio Homer, right hand against his forehead, fingers beneath his wig, slate-coloured dress); a third, a full length, is at Lord Lansdowne's, at Bowood; a fourth at Mapledurham, in Oxfordshire, the seat of the Blounts. Of those by Richardson, Sir William Wyndham's picture (a profile) is at Petworth; Lord Walpole's (a profile) is at Wolterton; Lord Cobham's was sold at the Stowe sale to Sir Robert Peel; and Lord Lyttelton's, with his dog Bounce, is at Hagley. Two half-lengths of him, by the same artist, were sold at Edward Earl of Oxford's sale in 1742; and a three-quarter portrait, by Richardson, was sold at Dr. Mead's sale for 15l. 4s. 6d. At Bayfordbury is the portrait by Dahl (engraved by Simon), which Pope presented to the nephew of old Jacob Tonson. His head, by Pond, is engraved by Houbraken, and was then in the possession of the artist. Where the Vanloo is, I know not: it was engraved by Faber in 1741. Mr. Rogers, the poet, has the head (I suspect by Jervas) so often engraved for his Letters and Poems: it was a present to Mr. Rogers from the poet Crabbe. Other portraits of him may be seen at Raby Castle (the Duke of Cleveland's), holding a book; at Wimpole (Lord Hardwicke's); at Elton Hall, in Huntingdonshire (Lord Carysfort's); and at Rousham a copy by Worsdale, after Jervas.

The marble of the bust by Roubiliac was bought at Mr. Watson Taylor's auction by Sir Robert Peel, and is still at Drayton Manor; it is dated 1741. Mr. Rogers has the original clay model. The Rysbrack bust was sold at Garrick's sale for 58l. 10s.

The following highly interesting letter is not included in any edition of Pope:—

To SIMON HARCOURT, FIRST VISCOUNT HARCOURT.

Aug. 22, 1723.

MY LORD,—It is a satisfaction to me to tell your Lordship, that I shall not be any way disappointed of the honour you intend me of filling a place in your library with my picture. I came to town yesterday and got admission to Sir Godfrey Kneller, who assured me the original was done for your Lordship, and that you, and no man but you, should have it. I saw the picture there afterwards, and was told then by his man that you had sent and put a seal upon it; so I am certain this affair is settled. Give me leave, my Lord, with great sincerity, to thank you for so obliging a thought, as thus to make me a sharer in the memory as well as I was in the love of a person who was justly the dearest object to you in the world, and thus to be authorized by you to be called his friend, after both of us shall be dust. I am ever, with all good wishes

as protuberant behind and before. He is said to have been beautiful in his infancy; but he was of a constitution originally feeble and weak; and as bodies of a tender frame are easily distorted, his deformity was probably in part the effect of his application. His stature was so low, that, to bring him to a level with common tables, it was necessary to raise his seat. But his face was not displeasing, and his eyes were animated and vivid.

By natural deformity, or accidental distortion, his vital functions were so much disordered, that his life was a "long disease." His most frequent assailant was the headach, which he used to relieve by inhaling the steam of coffee, which he very frequently required.[223]

Most of what can be told concerning his petty peculiarities was communicated by a female domestic of the Earl of Oxford, who knew him perhaps after the middle of life.[224] He was then so weak as to stand in perpetual need of female attendance; extremely sensible of cold, so that he wore a kind of fur doublet under a shirt of a very coarse warm linen with fine sleeves. When he rose, he was invested in bodice made of stiff canvas, being scarce able to hold himself erect till they were laced, and he then put on a flannel waistcoat. One side was contracted.

---

to your Lordship and your family (in which, too, I must do my mother the justice to join her),

My Lord,

Your most obliged and most faithful servant,

A. POPE.

(From the back of Pope's portrait at Nuneham. Printed in 'Nuneham Guide,' 12mo. 1797, p. 27.)

The best engravings of Pope are those executed in his own life-time by Smith, Faber, Vertue, and Richardson. Since his death the full-length of Jervas has been admirably engraved by J. H. Robinson.

[223] It is remarkable that the expletive Mr. Pope generally used by way of oath was "God mend me!" One day, in a dispute with a hackney coachman, he used this expression. "Mend *you!*" says the coachman, "it would not be half the trouble to make a new one."—R. OWEN CAMBRIDGE: *The World,* No. 50, for 13th Dec., 1753.

'Gent.'s Mag.,' 1775, p. 435.

[224] Johnson, I suspect, alludes to the account printed in the 'Gent.'s Mag.' for 1775, p. 435, from which many of the particulars in his narrative are certainly derived.

His legs were so slender, that he enlarged their bulk with three pair of stockings, which were drawn on and off by the maid ; for he was not able to dress or undress himself, and neither went to bed nor rose without help.   His weakness made it very difficult for him to be clean.

His hair had fallen almost all away ; and he used to dine sometimes with Lord Oxford, privately, in a velvet cap.[225]   His dress of ceremony was black, with a tye-wig and a little sword.

The indulgence and accommodation which his sickness required had taught him all the unpleasing and unsocial qualities of a valetudinary man.   He expected that everything should give way to his ease or humour, as a child whose parents will not hear her cry, has an unresisted dominion in the nursery.

> " *C'est que l'enfant toujours est homme,*
> *C'est que l'homme est toujours enfant.*"

When he wanted to sleep, he " nodded in company ;" and once slumbered at his own table while the Prince of Wales was talking of poetry.[226]

The reputation which his friendship gave procured him many invitations ; but he was a very troublesome inmate.   He brought no servant, and had so many wants that a numerous attendance was scarcely able to supply them.   Wherever he was, he left no room for another, because he exacted the attention and employed the activity of the whole family.[227]   His errands were so fre-

[225] In which he is represented in several of Richardson's portraits.   His scarlet cloak figures in Davies's ' Life of Garrick,' ii. 34.

[226] If I could receive letters from you and Mr. Pope as you had leisure, I would never come to town as long as I live.   In that way of conversing I should have all the pleasure that I can possibly propose without the disappointment when Mr. Pope falls asleep, nor the dread of your taking leave because you are weary.—SARAH DUCHESS OF MARLBOROUGH to Lord Marchmont, March 15, 1742.

I am glad you sleep better.   I sleep in company, and wake at night, which is vexatious.—POPE to Richardson, Nov. 21.

[227] Yet he wandered about during the summer and autumn months, especially after his mother's death.   Thus in the autumn of 1733 he was at Cirencester and Southampton (Lord Bathurst's and Lord Peterborough's).   In June 1734 he was at Stowe, in July of the same year at Cirencester, in August at Southampton, in September at Bath.   In August 1735 he lent his house to Mrs. Greville, and passed his time principally with Lord Peterborough at Bevis

quent and frivolous that the footmen in time avoided and neglected him ; and the Earl of Oxford discharged some of the servants for their resolute refusal of his messages. The maids, when they had neglected their business, alleged that they had been employed by Mr. Pope. One of his constant demands was of coffee in the night, and to the woman that waited on him in his chamber he was very burthensome : but he was careful to recompense her want of sleep; and Lord Oxford's servant declared, that in a house where her business was to answer his call she would not ask for wages.

He had another fault, easily incident to those who, suffering much pain, think themselves entitled to what pleasures they can snatch. He was too indulgent to his appetite; he loved meat highly seasoned and of strong taste ; and, at the intervals of the table, amused himself with biscuits and dry conserves. If he sat down to a variety of dishes, he would oppress his stomach with repletion; and though he seemed angry when a dram [228] was offered him, did not forbear to drink it. His friends, who knew the avenues to his heart, pampered him with presents of luxury, which he did not suffer to stand neglected. The death of great men is not always proportioned to the lustre of their lives. Hannibal, says Juvenal, did not perish by a javelin or a

---

Mount. It would be easy to trace him to his other favourite places—to Rousham and Middleton in Oxfordshire, and finally to Bath. His last ramble from home was to Bath.

[228] Pope and I, with my Lord Orrery and Sir Harry Bedingfield, dined with the late Earl of Burlington. After the first course Pope grew sick, and went out of the room. When the dinner was ended, and the cloth removed, my Lord Burlington said he would go out and see what was become of Pope. And soon after they returned together. But Pope, who had been casting up his dinner, looked very pale, and complained much. My Lord asked him if he would have some mulled wine or a glass of old sack, which Pope refused. I told my Lord Burlington that he wanted a *dram*. Upon which the little man expressed some resentment against me, and said he would not taste any spirits, and that he abhorred drams as much as I did. However, I persisted, and assured my Lord Burlington that he could not oblige our friend more at that instant than by ordering a large glass of cherry-brandy to be set before him. This was done, and in less than half an hour, while my Lord was acquainting us with an affair which engaged our attention, Pope had sipped up all the brandy. Pope's frame of body did not promise long life; but he certainly hastened his death by feeding much on high-seasoned dishes, and drinking spirits.—DR. KING: *Anecdotes*, p. 12.

sword ; the slaughters of Cannæ were revenged by a ring. The death of Pope was imputed by some of his friends to a silver saucepan, in which it was his delight to heat potted lampreys.

That he loved too well to eat is certain ;[229] but that his sensuality shortened his life will not be hastily concluded, when it is remembered that a conformation so irregular lasted six and fifty years, notwithstanding such pertinacious diligence of study and meditation.

In all his intercourse with mankind he had great delight in artifice, and endeavoured to attain all his purposes by indirect and unsuspected methods. " He hardly drank tea without a stratagem." If, at the house of his friends, he wanted any accommodation, he was not willing to ask for it in plain terms, but would mention it remotely as something convenient ; though, when it was procured, he soon made it appear for whose sake it had been recommended. Thus he teased Lord Orrery till he obtained a screen. He practised his arts on such small occasions, that Lady Bolingbroke used to say, in a French phrase, that " he played the politician about cabbages and turnips." His unjustifiable impression of 'The Patriot King,' as it can be imputed to no particular motive, must have proceeded from his general habit of secrecy and cunning ; he caught an opportunity of a sly trick, and pleased himself with the thought of outwitting Bolingbroke.

In familiar or convivial conversation it does not appear that he excelled. He may be said to have resembled Dryden as being not one that was distinguished by vivacity in company. It is remarkable that, so near his time, so much should be known of what he has written and so little of what he has said : traditional memory retains no sallies of raillery nor sentences of observation ; nothing either pointed or solid, either wise or merry. One apophthegm only stands upon record. When an objection raised against his inscription for Shakespeare was defended by

[229] We performed our journey hither [Shotover] with great ease, only little Pope was very ill the whole day. . . . Pope grew better at supper, and of course very irregular, and laughed at me for the care I pretended to take of him.—MR. BERKELEY to Lady Suffolk, June 19, 1734.

the authority of Patrick, he replied—"horresco referens"—
that " he would allow the publisher of a Dictionary to know the
meaning of a single word, but not of two words put together." [230]

He was fretful and easily displeased, and allowed himself to
be capriciously resentful. He would sometimes leave Lord
Oxford silently, no one could tell why, and was to be courted
back by more letters and messages than the footmen were willing
to carry. The table was indeed infested by Lady Mary Wortley, who was the friend of Lady Oxford, and who, knowing his
peevishness, could by no intreaties be restrained from contra-
dicting him, till their disputes were sharpened to such asperity
that one or the other quitted the house. [231]

He sometimes condescended to be jocular with servants or
inferiors; but by no merriment, either of others or his own, was
he ever seen excited to laughter. [232]

Of his domestic character frugality was a part eminently
remarkable. Having determined not to be dependent, he determined not to be in want, and therefore wisely and magnani-
mously rejected all temptations to expense unsuitable to his
fortune. This general care must be universally approved ; but

[230] When Dr. Mead once urged to our author the authority of Patrick, the
dictionary-maker, against the Latinity of the expression *amor publicus*, which
he had used in an inscription, he replied "that he would allow a dictionary-
maker to understand a single word, but not two words put together."—JOS.
WARTON (*Pope*, vi. 112).

[231] When Lady Bute [Lady Mary Wortley's daughter] read the 'Lives of
the Poets,' on their first publication, she pointed out this paragraph to one of
her daughters, observing "how ill Johnson must have been informed. . . I am
confident they never met at Lord Oxford's table in their lives."—LADY LOUISA
STUART (Lady Bute's daughter): Lord Wharncliffe's Lady Mary, i. 64.

[232] I never saw him laugh very heartily in all my life (MRS. RACKET, speaking
of Mr. Pope).

This is odd enough! because she was with him so much in all the first part
of his life, when he is said, by persons most intimate with him, to have been
most excessively gay and lively.—It is very true that in the latter part of his
life, when he told a story, he was always the last to laugh at it, and seldom
went beyond a particular easy smile on any occasion that I remember.—SPENCE.
Ed. Singer, p. 206.

He would occasionally joke with my Lord's domestics as well as higher company, but was never seen to laugh himself, even when he had set the whole
table in a roar at Tom Hearne, Humphrey Wanley, or any other persons
whose manners were as strongly tinctured with singularity.—*Gent's. Mag.*
1775, p. 435.

it sometimes appeared in petty artifices of parsimony, such as the practice of writing his compositions on the back of letters, as may be seen in the remaining copy of the 'Iliad,' by which perhaps in five years five shillings were saved;[233] or in a niggardly reception of his friends and scantiness of entertainment, as, when he had two guests in his house, he would set at supper a single pint upon the table; and, having himself taken two small glasses, would retire and say, "Gentlemen, I leave you to your wine."[234]   Yet he tells his friends that "he has a heart for all, a house for all, and, whatever they may think, a fortune for all."[235]

He sometimes, however, made a splendid dinner, and is said to have wanted no part of the skill or elegance which such performances require. That this magnificence should be often displayed, that obstinate prudence with which he conducted his affairs would not permit; for his revenue, certain and casual, amounted only to about eight hundred pounds a-year, of which however he declares himself able to assign one hundred to charity.

Of this fortune, which, as it arose from public approbation, was very honourably obtained, his imagination seems to have been too full: it would be hard to find a man, so well entitled to notice by his wit, that ever delighted so much in talking of his money. In his letters and in his poems, his garden and his grotto, his quincunx and his vines, or some hints of his opulence, are always to be found. The great topic of his ridicule is poverty; the crimes with which he reproaches his antagonists are their debts, their habitation in the Mint, and their want of

---

[233] Thus Swift, in his 'Advice to the Grub-street Verse-writers,' 1726—

> Lend these to paper-sparing Pope,
>   And when he sits to write,
> No letter with an envelope
>   Could give him more delight.

[234] Delany's 'Observations on Orrery,' 8vo. 1754, p. 181.
[235] Hardly. The expressions, or something like them, occur in a letter to Swift, March 23, 1737, inviting him to England, and to bring with him his old housekeeper, and two or three servants—" I have room for all, a heart for all, and (think what you will) a fortune for all."

a dinner. He seems to be of an opinion not very uncommon in the world, that to want money is to want every thing.

Next to the pleasure of contemplating his possessions seems to be that of enumerating the men of high rank with whom he was acquainted, and whose notice he loudly proclaims not to have been obtained by any practices of meanness or servility, a boast which was never denied to be true, and to which very few poets have ever aspired. Pope never set genius to sale; he never flattered those whom he did not love, or praised those whom he did not esteem. Savage however remarked, that he began a little to relax his dignity when he wrote a distich for "his Highness's dog."[236]

His admiration of the great seems to have increased in the advance of life.[237] He passed over peers and statesmen to inscribe his 'Iliad' to Congreve, with a magnanimity of which the praise had been complete, had his friend's virtue been equal to his wit. Why he was chosen for so great an honour it is not now possible to know; there is no trace in literary history of any particular intimacy between them.[238] The name of Con-

[236] And, as Savage might have added, to copy a fool at the same time. See Temple's Works, iii. 526, ed. 1770. "Mr. Grantam's fool's reply to a great man that asked whose fool he was? 'I am Mr. Grantam's fool; pray, whose fool are you?'"

[237] Pope courted with the utmost assiduity all the old men from whom he could hope a legacy—the Duke of Buckingham, Lord Peterborough, Sir G. Kneller, Lord Bolingbroke, Mr. Wycherley, Mr. Congreve, Lord Harcourt, &c.; and I do not doubt projected to sweep the Dean's [Swift's] whole inheritance, if he could have persuaded him to throw up his deanery and come to die in his house; and his general preaching against money was meant to induce people to throw it away that he might pick it up.—LADY MARY W. MONTAGU to Countess of Bute, June 23, 1752.

A testimony of friendship and good opinion has been left me by an old friend, from whom I had not the least imagination of such a thing, Mr. Jervas; but it takes no effect unless I outlive his widow, which is not very likely: however, I think him absolutely in the right in giving nothing from her, to whom he owed almost everything; and the sum is considerable, viz. a *thousand pounds*. It is the first legacy I ever had, and I hope I shall never have another at the expense of any man's life who would think so kindly of me.—POPE to Mr. Bethel (Nov. 1739). Ruffhead's *Life of Pope*, p. 190.

[238] On the back of a letter from Craggs to Pope, part of the MS. 'Iliad' in the Museum, is the following memorandum in Pope's handwriting—"Mem. End ye note with a dedication to Mr. Congreve, as a memorial of our friendship, occasioned by his translation of his last part of Homer." (Dibdin's Supplemental

greve appears in the letters among those of his other friends, but without any observable distinction or consequence.

To his latter works, however, he took care to annex names dignified with titles, but was not very happy in his choice ; for, except Lord Bathurst, none of his noble friends were such as that a good man would wish to have his intimacy with them known to posterity : he can derive little honour from the notice of Cobham, Burlington, or Bolingbroke.[239]

Of his social qualities, if an estimate be made from his letters, an opinion too favourable cannot easily be formed ; they exhibit a perpetual and unclouded effulgence of general benevolence and particular fondness.   There is nothing but liberality, gratitude, constancy, and tenderness.   It has been so long said as to be commonly believed, that the true characters of men may be found in their letters, and that he who writes to his friend lays his heart open before him.   But the truth is, that such were the simple friendships of the 'Golden Age,' and are now the friendships only of children.   Very few can boast of hearts which they dare lay open to themselves, and of which, by whatever accident exposed, they do not shun a distinct and continued view ; and, certainly, what we hide from ourselves we do not show to our friends.   There is, indeed, no transaction which offers stronger temptations to fallacy and sophistication than epistolary intercourse.   In the eagerness of conversation the first emotions of the mind often burst out before they are con-

---

vol. to Roscoe's 'Pope,' p. 28.)   And in the Preface to the 'Iliad' he says, "I must also acknowledge with infinite pleasure the many friendly offices as well as sincere criticisms of Mr. Congreve, who had led me the way in translating some parts of Homer, as I wish, for the sake of the world, ho had prevented in the rest."   Dryden publicly recommended a complete translation of the 'Iliad' to the care of Congreve, and entrusted, as he tells the public, his 'Æneid' to his revision. (See vol. ii. p. 239.)   Pope tells us in verse that Congreve loved his lays; but this Lady Mary Montagu in a letter to her daughter denies very positively.

[239] Johnson.—How foolish was it in Pope to give all his friendship to lords, who thought they honoured him by being with him; and to choose such lords as Burlington, and Cobham, and Bolingbroke!   Bathurst was negative—a pleasing man; and I have heard no ill of Marchmont.   And then always saying, "I do not value you for being a lord "—which was a sure proof that he did.—BOSWELL by Croker.   Ed. 1848, p. 614.

sidered; in the tumult of business, interest and passion have their
genuine effect; but a friendly letter is a calm and deliberate
performance, in the cool of leisure, in the stillness of solitude, and
surely no man sits down to depreciate by design his own character.

Friendship has no tendency to secure veracity; for by whom
can a man so much wish to be thought better than he is, as by
him whose kindness he desires to gain or keep? Even in writing to the world there is less constraint; the author is not
confronted with his reader, and takes his chance of approbation
among the different dispositions of mankind; but a letter is
addressed to a single mind, of which the prejudices and par-
tialities are known, and must therefore please, if not by favouring them, by forbearing to oppose them.

To charge those favourable representations which men give
of their own minds with the guilt of hypocritical falsehood,
would show more severity than knowledge. The writer commonly believes himself. Almost every man's thoughts, while
they are general, are right; and most hearts are pure while
temptation is away. It is easy to awaken generous sentiments
in privacy; to despise death when there is no danger; to glow
with benevolence when there is nothing to be given. While
such ideas are formed they are felt, and self-love does not suspect the gleam of virtue to be the meteor of fancy.

If the letters of Pope are considered merely as compositions,
they seem to be premeditated and artificial. It is one thing to
write, because there is something which the mind wishes to
discharge; and another to solicit the imagination, because
ceremony or vanity requires something to be written.[240] Pope
confesses his early letters to be vitiated with *affectation and
ambition*: to know whether he disentangled himself from these
perverters of epistolary integrity his book and his life must be
set in comparison.

[240] Pope seems to have thought that unless a sentence was well turned, and
every period pointed with some conceit, it was not worth the carriage. Accordingly he is to me, except in very few instances, the most disagreeable
maker of epistles that I ever met with.—COWPER to Unwin, June 8, 1780.

He [Gray] said of his [Pope's] letters, that they were not good letters, but
better things.—NORTON NICHOLL'S *Reminiscences of Gray*, p. 37.

One of his favourite topics is contempt of his own poetry. For this, if it had been real, he would deserve no commendation; and in this he was certainly not sincere, for his high value of himself was sufficiently observed; and of what could he be proud but of his poetry? He writes, he says, when "he has just nothing else to do;" yet Swift complains that he was never at leisure for conversation, because he "had always some poetical scheme in his head."[241] It was punctually required that his writing-box should be set upon his bed before he rose; and Lord Oxford's domestic related, that in the dreadful winter of Forty [1740] she was called from her bed by him four times in one night to supply him with paper lest he should lose a thought.

He pretends insensibility to censure and criticism, though it was observed by all who knew him that every pamphlet disturbed his quiet, and that his extreme irritability laid him open to perpetual vexation; but he wished to despise his critics, and therefore hoped that he did despise them.

As he happened to live in two reigns when the Court paid little attention to poetry, he nursed in his mind a foolish disesteem of Kings, and proclaims that "he never sees Courts." Yet a little regard shown him by the Prince of Wales melted his obduracy; and he had not much to say when he was asked by his Royal Highness, "How he could love a Prince while he disliked Kings?"[242]

---

[241] Swift to Mrs. Cæsar, July 30, 1733. (Scott's *Swift*, xviii. 151, 2nd ed.)

> I was not born for courts or great affairs;
> I pay my debts, believe, and say my prayers;
> Can sleep without a poem in my head,
> Nor know if Dennis be alive or dead.
>
> POPE: *Epistle to Arbuthnot*.

Yet in his First Satire of the Second Book of Horace he says, in reply to his friend Fortescue, that he should write no more:—

> Not write? but then I think,
> And for my soul I cannot sleep a wink.
> I nod in company, I wake at night,
> Fools rush into my head, and so I write.

Here is an inconsistency, which falsehood, as Johnson says, is always in danger of.

[242] Oh! a story of Mr. Pope and the Prince. "Mr. Pope, you don't love princes?" "Sir, I beg your pardon." "Well, you don't love kings then?"

He very frequently professes contempt of the world, and represents himself as looking on mankind, sometimes with gay indifference, as on emmets of a hillock, below his serious attention; and sometimes with gloomy indignation, as on monsters more worthy of hatred than of pity. These were dispositions apparently counterfeited. How could he despise those whom he lived by pleasing, and on whose approbation his esteem of himself was superstructed? Why should he hate those to whose favour he owed his honour and his ease? Of things that terminate in human life, the world is the proper judge; to despise its sentence, if it were possible, is not just; and if it were just, is not possible. Pope was far enough from this unreasonable temper; he was sufficiently *a fool to Fame*, and his fault was, that he pretended to neglect it. His levity and his sullenness were only in his Letters; he passed through common life, sometimes vexed, and sometimes pleased, with the natural emotions of common men.

His scorn of the Great is repeated too often to be real; no man thinks much of that which he despises; and as falsehood is always in danger of inconsistency, he makes it his boast at another time that he lives among them.

It is evident that his own importance swells often in his mind. He is afraid of writing, lest the clerks of the Post-office should know his secrets; he has many enemies; he considers himself as surrounded by universal jealousy; "after many deaths, and many dispersions, two or three of us," says he, "may still be brought together, not to plot, but to divert ourselves, and the world too, if it pleases;" and they can live together, and "show what friends wits may be, in spite of all the fools in the world." All this while it was likely that the clerks did not know his hand;[243] he certainly had no more

---

"Sir, I own I love the lion best before his claws are grown."—WALPOLE to Mann, 13th Sept. 1741. See also Ruffhead's 'Life of Pope,' p. 535; and Boswell by Croker, ed. 1848, p. 670.

Whether the Prince most loves poetry or prose, I protest I do not know; but this I dare venture to affirm, that you can give him as much satisfaction in either as I can.—POPE to Beau Nash.

[243] Such a letter as this was what might naturally be expected from Mr.

enemies than a public character like his inevitably excites; and
with what degree of friendship the wits might live, very few
were so much fools as ever to inquire.[244]

Some part of this pretended discontent he learned from Swift,
and expresses it, I think, most frequently in his correspondence
with him.   Swift's resentment was unreasonable, but it was
sincere; Pope's was the mere mimicry of his friend, a fictitious
part which he began to play before it became him.   When
he was only twenty-five years old, he related that " a glut of
study and retirement had thrown him on the world," and that
there was danger lest " a glut of the world should throw him
back upon study and retirement."   To this Swift answered
with great propriety, that Pope had not yet either acted or
suffered enough in the world to have become weary of it.   And,
indeed, it must be some very powerful reason that can drive
back to solitude him who has once enjoyed the pleasures of
society.

In the Letters both of Swift and Pope there appears such
narrowness of mind as makes them insensible of any excellence
that has not some affinity with their own, and confines their
esteem and approbation to so small a number, that whoever
should form his opinion of the age from their representation,
would suppose them to have lived amidst ignorance and bar-

Pope.   Notwithstanding the seeming modesty towards the conclusion, the
vanity of an applauded writer bursts through every line of it.   The difficulty
of concealing his hand from the clerks at the Post-Office, and the solicitude to
have his name concealed, were marks of the consciousness of his own importance.   It is probable his hand was not so very well known, nor his letters so
eagerly opened, by the clerks of the office, as he seems always to think; but
in all his letters, as well as in those of Swift, there runs a strain of pride, as if
the world talked of nothing but themselves.   " Alas," says he, in one of them,
"the day after I am dead, the sun will shine as bright as the day before, and
the world will be as merry as usual!"   Very strange that neither an eclipse
nor an earthquake should follow the loss of a poet!—GOLDSMITH: *Life of Nash.*
Compare Pulteney to Swift, Nov. 22, 1735.

[244] Compare Addison's excellent paper ('Spectator,' No. 253) on this subject.
The advice which Addison gives, in so gentlemanlike a way, to Pope in this
very paper was not forgotten when the character of Atticus was drawn.

Few characters can bear the microscopic scrutiny of wit quickened by anger;
and perhaps the best advice to authors would be, that they should keep out of
the way of one another.—JOHNSON: *Life of Rowe.*

barity, unable to find among their contemporaries either virtue
or intelligence, and persecuted by those that could not understand them.

When Pope murmurs at the world, when he professes contempt of fame, when he speaks of riches and poverty, of success
and disappointment, with negligent indifference, he certainly
does not express his habitual and settled sentiments, but either
wilfully disguises his own character, or, what is more likely,
invests himself with temporary qualities, and sallies out in the
colours of the present moment. His hopes and fears, his joys
and sorrows, acted strongly upon his mind; and if he differed
from others, it was not by carelessness; he was irritable and
resentful; his malignity to Philips, whom he had first made
ridiculous, and then hated for being angry, continued too long.
Of his vain desire to make Bentley contemptible, I never heard
any adequate reason. He was sometimes wanton in his attacks;
and, before Chandos, Lady Wortley, and Hill, was mean in
his retreat.[245]

The virtues which seem to have had most of his affection
were liberality and fidelity of friendship, in which it does not
appear that he was other than he describes himself. His fortune
did not suffer his charity to be splendid and conspicuous; but
he assisted Dodsley with a hundred pounds, that he might open
a shop; and of the subscription of forty pounds a year that he
raised for Savage, twenty were paid by himself. He was
accused of loving money, but his love was eagerness to gain,
not solicitude to keep it.[246]

In the duties of friendship he was zealous and constant; his
early maturity of mind commonly united him with men older
than himself; and therefore, without attaining any considerable
length of life, he saw many companions of his youth sink into
the grave; but it does not appear that he lost a single friend
by coldness or by injury; those who loved him once, continued
their kindness. His ungrateful mention of Allen in his will

---

[245] He was also mean in his retreat before his assistant Broome.

[246] 'Tis most certain that nobody ever loved money so little as my brother.
—MRS. RACKET in *Spence, ed. Singer*, p. 267.

was the effect of his adherence to one [247] whom he had known much longer, and whom he naturally loved with greater fondness. His violation of the trust reposed in him by Bolingbroke could have no motive inconsistent with the warmest affection ; he either thought the action so near to indifferent that he forgot it, or so laudable that he expected his friend to approve it.

It was reported, with such confidence as almost to enforce belief, that in the papers intrusted to his executors was found a defamatory Life of Swift, which he had prepared as an instrument of vengeance, to be used if any provocation should be ever given.   About this I inquired of the Earl of Marchmont, who assured me that no such piece was among his remains.[248]

The religion in which he lived and died was that of the Church of Rome, to which in his correspondence with Racine he professes himself a sincere adherent.   That he was not scrupulously pious in some part of his life, is known by many idle and indecent applications of sentences taken from the Scriptures ; a mode of merriment which a good man dreads for its profaneness, and a witty man disdains for its easiness and vulgarity.   But to whatever levities he has been betrayed, it does not appear that his principles were ever corrupted, or that he ever lost his belief of Revelation.   The positions which he transmitted from Bolingbroke he seems not to have understood, and was pleased with an interpretation that made them orthodox.

A man of such exalted superiority, and so little moderation, would naturally have all his delinquencies observed and aggravated : those who could not deny that he was excellent, would rejoice to find that he was not perfect.[249]

[247] Martha Blount.

[248] The Pope interview between Lord Marchmont and Johnson was brought about by Boswell, but not without considerable difficulty. (See ' Boswell ' by Croker, p. 630.)   When, in a previous interview, Boswell proposed to Lord Marchmont that he should revise Johnson's ' Life of Pope,' "So," said his Lordship, "you would put me in a dangerous position. You know he knocked down Osborne, the bookseller."—*Ib.* p. 613; see also note 193, p. 87.

[249] He [Warburton] had once a very full and free conversation with Mr. Pope about changing his religion : the persecution allowed and followed so much by the Church of Rome, he owned, looked like the sign of a false church. The Doctor said, "Why then should you not conform with the religion of your country?"   He seemed, in himself, not averse to it, and replied, "There were

Perhaps it may be imputed to the unwillingness with which
the same man is allowed to possess many advantages, that his
learning has been depreciated.   He certainly was, in his early
life, a man of great literary curiosity ; and when he wrote his
'Essay on Criticism' had, for his age, a very wide acquaintance
with books.   When he entered into the living world, it seems
to have happened to him as to many others, that he was less
attentive to dead masters ; he studied in the academy of Para-
celsus, and made the universe his favourite volume. He gathered
his notions fresh from reality, not from the copies of authors,
but the originals of Nature.   Yet there is no reason to believe
that literature ever lost his esteem ; he always professed to love
reading ; and Dobson, who spent some time at his house translating his 'Essay on Man,' when I asked him what learning he
found him to possess, answered, " More than I expected."   His
frequent references to history, his allusions to various kinds of
knowledge, and his images selected from art and nature, with
his observations on the operations of the mind and the modes
of life, show an intelligence perpetually on the wing, excursive,
vigorous, and diligent, eager to pursue knowledge, and attentive
to retain it.

From this curiosity arose the desire of travelling, to which he
alludes in his verses to Jervas, and which, though he never
found an opportunity to gratify it, did not leave him till his life
declined.[250]

Of his intellectual character, the constituent and fundamental
principle was good sense, a prompt and intuitive perception of
consonance and propriety.   He saw immediately, of his own

but two reasons that kept him from it: one, that the doing so would make him
a great many enemies; and the other, that it would do nobody else any good.''
—SPENCE: *ed. Singer*, p. 364.

[250] He [Pope] should have travelled, had it not been for his ill-health; and
on every occasion that offered had a desire to travel to the very end of his
life.—*Spence by Singer*, p. 8.

In earnest I would go a thousand miles by land to see you, but the sea
I dread.   My ailments are such, that I really believe a sea-sickness (considering the oppression of colical pains and the great weakness of my breast)
would kill me.— POPE to Swift, 1st Sept. 1733.   See also Letter to Swift of
27th May, 1739.

conceptions, what was to be chosen, and what to be rejected; and, in the works of others, what was to be shunned, and what was to be copied.

But good sense alone is a sedate and quiescent quality, which manages its possessions well, but does not increase them; it collects few materials for its own operations, and preserves safety, but never gains supremacy.   Pope had likewise genius; a mind active, ambitious, and adventurous, always investigating, always aspiring; in its widest searches still longing to go forward, in its highest flights still wishing to be higher; always imagining something greater than it knows, always endeavouring more than it can do.

To assist these powers, he is said to have had great strength and exactness of memory.   That which he had heard or read was not easily lost; and he had before him not only what his own meditations suggested, but what he had found in other writers, that might be accommodated to his present purpose.

These benefits of nature he improved by incessant and unwearied diligence; he had recourse to every source of intelligence, and lost no opportunity of information; he consulted the living as well as the dead; he read his compositions to his friends, and was never content with mediocrity when excellence could be attained.   He considered poetry as the business of his life; and, however he might seem to lament his occupation, he followed it with constancy; to make verses was his first labour, and to mend them was his last.

From his attention to poetry he was never diverted.   If conversation offered anything that could be improved, he committed it to paper; if a thought, or perhaps an expression more happy than was common, rose to his mind, he was careful to write it; an independent distich was preserved for an opportunity of insertion; and some little fragments have been found containing lines, or parts of lines, to be wrought upon at some other time.

He was one of those few whose labour is their pleasure:[251]

---

[251] The sense of my faults made me correct; besides that it was as pleasant to me to correct as to write.—POPE: *Preface to Works,* 4to. 1717.

he was never elevated to negligence, nor wearied to impatience ; he never passed a fault unamended by indifference, nor quitted it by despair. He laboured his works first to gain reputation and afterwards to keep it.

Of composition there are different methods. Some employ at once memory and invention, and, with little intermediate use of the pen, form and polish large masses by continued meditation, and write their productions only when, in their own opinion, they have completed them.[252] It is related of Virgil, that his custom was to pour out a great number of verses in the morning, and pass the day in retrenching exuberances and correcting inaccuracies. The method of Pope, as may be collected from his translation, was to write his first thoughts in his first words, and gradually to amplify, decorate, rectify, and refine them.

With such faculties, and such dispositions, he excelled every other writer in poetical prudence; he wrote in such a manner as might expose him to few hazards. He used almost always the same fabric of verse; and, indeed, by those few essays which he made of any other, he did not enlarge his reputation. Of this uniformity the certain consequence was readiness and dexterity. By perpetual practice, language had, in his mind, a systematical arrangement; having always the same use for words, he had words so selected and combined as to be ready at his call.[253] This increase of facility he confessed himself to have perceived in the progress of his translation.

But what was yet of more importance, his effusions were always voluntary, and his subjects chosen by himself. His independence secured him from drudging at a task, and labouring upon a barren topic : he never exchanged praise for money,

[252] This was Johnson's own practice; partly, however, induced by his own nearness of sight.

[253] This I might have done in prose; but I chose verse, and even rhyme, for two reasons. The one will appear obvious ; that principles, maxims, or precepts so written, both strike the reader more strongly at first, and are more easily retained by him afterwards; the other may seem odd, but it is true: I found I could express them more shortly this way than in prose itself.—POPE: *Pref. to Essay on Man.*

nor opened a shop of condolence or congratulation. His
poems, therefore, were scarce ever temporary. He suffered
coronations and royal marriages to pass without a song, and
derived no opportunities from recent events, nor any popularity
from the accidental disposition of his readers. He was never
reduced to the necessity of soliciting the sun to shine upon a
birth-day, of calling the Graces and Virtues to a wedding, or
of saying what multitudes have said before him. When he
could produce nothing new, he was at liberty to be silent.

His publications were for the same reason never hasty. He
is said to have sent nothing to the press till it had lain two
years under his inspection : it is at least certain that he ventured nothing without nice examination. He suffered the
tumult of imagination to subside, and the novelties of invention
to grow familiar. He knew that the mind is always enamoured
of its own productions, and did not trust his first fondness.
He consulted his friends, and listened with great willingness to
criticism ; and, what was of more importance, he consulted
himself, and let nothing pass against his own judgment.

He professed to have learned his poetry from Dryden, whom,
whenever an opportunity was presented, he praised through his
whole life with unvaried liberality ; and perhaps his character
may receive some illustration, if he be compared with his
master.

Integrity of understanding and nicety of discernment were
not allotted in a less proportion to Dryden than to Pope. The
rectitude of Dryden's mind was sufficiently shown by the dismission of his poetical prejudices, and the rejection of unnatural
thoughts and rugged numbers. But Dryden never desired to
apply all the judgment that he had. He wrote, and professed
to write, merely for the people ; and when he pleased others,
he contented himself. He spent no time in struggles to rouse
latent powers ; he never attempted to make that better which
was already good, nor often to mend what he must have
known to be faulty. He wrote, as he tells us, with very little
consideration ; when occasion or necessity called upon him, he
poured out what the present moment happened to supply, and,

when once it had passed the press, ejected it from his mind; for when he had no pecuniary interest, he had no further solicitude.

Pope was not content to satisfy; he desired to excel, and therefore always endeavoured to do his best: he did not court the candour, but dared the judgment of his reader, and, expecting no indulgence from others, he showed none to himself. He examined lines and words with minute and punctilious observation, and retouched every part with indefatigable diligence, till he had left nothing to be forgiven.

For this reason he kept his pieces very long in his hands, while he considered and reconsidered them. The only poems which can be supposed to have been written with such regard to the times as might hasten their publication were the two satires of 'Thirty-eight;' of which Dodsley told me that they were brought to him by the author, that they might be fairly copied. "Almost every line," he said, "was then written twice over; I gave him a clean transcript, which he sent some time afterwards to me for the press, with almost every line written twice over a second time."

His declaration that his care for his works ceased at their publication was not strictly true. His parental attention never abandoned them; what he found amiss in the first edition,[254] he silently corrected in those that followed. He appears to have revised the 'Iliad,' and freed it from some of its imperfections; and the 'Essay on Criticism' received many improvements after its first appearance. It will seldom be found that he altered without adding clearness, elegance, or vigour. Pope had perhaps the judgment of Dryden; but Dryden certainly wanted the diligence of Pope.[255]

[254] Mr. Pope used to tell me, that when he had anything better than ordinary to say, and yet too bold, he always reserved it for a second or third edition, and then nobody took any notice of it.—WARBURTON to Hurd, Sept. 22, 1751.

[255] It is enough for those who make poetry the business of their lives to learn that correct; yet excepting Virgil, I never met with any which was so in any language.—DRYDEN: *Defence of the Essay on Dramatic Poesy.*

A poet cannot have too great a reverence for his readers, if he expects his labours should survive him.—DRYDEN: *Dedication of the Æneid.*

In acquired knowledge, the superiority must be allowed to
Dryden, whose education was more scholastic, and who before
he became an author had been allowed more time for study,
with better means of information.   His mind has a larger
range, and he collects his images and illustrations from a more
extensive circumference of science.   Dryden knew more of
man in his general nature, and Pope in his local manners.
The notions of Dryden were formed by comprehensive speculation, and those of Pope by minute attention.   There is more
dignity in the knowledge of Dryden, and more certainty in
that of Pope.

Poetry was not the sole praise of either ; for both excelled
likewise in prose ; but Pope did not borrow his prose from his
predecessor.   The style of Dryden is capricious and varied ;
that of Pope is cautious and uniform.   Dryden observes the
motions of his own mind ; Pope constrains his mind to his own
rules of composition.   Dryden is sometimes vehement and rapid ;
Pope is always smooth, uniform, and gentle.   Dryden's page
is a natural field, rising into inequalities, and diversified by the
varied exuberance of abundant vegetation ; Pope's is a velvet
lawn, shaven by the scythe, and levelled by the roller.

Of genius, that power which constitutes a poet ; that quality
without which judgment is cold, and knowledge is inert ; that
energy which collects, combines, amplifies, and animates ; the
superiority must, with some hesitation, be allowed to Dryden.   It
is not to be inferred that of this poetical vigour Pope had only
a little, because Dryden had more ; for every other writer since
Milton must give place to Pope ; and even of Dryden it must
be said, that, if he has brighter paragraphs, he has not better
poems.   Dryden's performances were always hasty, either
excited by some external occasion, or extorted by domestic
necessity ; he composed without consideration, and published
without correction.   What his mind could supply at call, or
gather in one excursion, was all that he sought, and all that he
gave.   The dilatory caution of Pope enabled him to condense
his sentiments, to multiply his images, and to accumulate all
that study might produce or chance might supply.   If the

flights of Dryden therefore are higher, Pope continues longer
on the wing. If of Dryden's fire the blaze is brighter, of
Pope's the heat is more regular and constant. Dryden often
surpasses expectation, and Pope never falls below it. Dryden
is read with frequent astonishment, and Pope with perpetual
delight.[256]

This parallel will, I hope, when it is well considered, be
found just; and if the reader should suspect me, as I suspect
myself, of some partial fondness for the memory of Dryden, let
him not too hastily condemn me; for meditation and inquiry
may, perhaps, show him the reasonableness of my determination.

The Works of Pope are now to be distinctly examined, not
so much with attention to slight faults or petty beauties, as to
the general character and effect of each performance.

It seems natural for a young poet to initiate himself by
pastorals, which, not professing to imitate real life, require no
experience; and, exhibiting only the simple operation of un-
mingled passions, admit no subtle reasoning or deep inquiry.
Pope's pastorals are not, however, composed but with close
thought; they have reference to the time of the day, the seasons of the year, and the periods of human life. The last, that
which turns the attention upon age and death, was the author's
favourite. To tell of disappointment and misery, to thicken

[256] I am bound to acquiesce in Johnson's opinion of Pope, because it has
always been my own. I could never agree with those who preferred him to
Dryden; nor with others (I have known such, and persons of taste and discernment too), who could not allow him to be a poet at all. He was certainly
a mechanical maker of verses, and in every line he ever wrote we see indubi-
table marks of the most indefatigable industry and labour. Writers who find
it necessary to make such strenuous and painful exertions are generally as
phlegmatic as they are correct; but Pope was in this respect exempted from the
common lot of authors of that class. With the unwearied application of a
plodding Flemish painter, who draws a shrimp with the most minute exactness,
he had all the genius of one of the first masters. Never, I believe, were such
talents and such drudgery united. But I admire Dryden most, who has succeeded by mere dint of genius, and in spite of a laziness and carelessness almost
peculiar to himself. His faults are numberless, but so are his beauties. His
faults are those of a great man, and his beauties are such (at least sometimes)
as Pope, with all his touching and re-touching, could never equal.—COWPER:
Letter to Unwin, Jan. 5, 1782.

the darkness of futurity, and perplex the labyrinth of uncertainty, has been always a delicious employment of the poets. His preference was probably just. I wish, however, that his fondness had not overlooked a line in which the *Zephyrs* are made *to lament in silence.*

To charge these pastorals with want of invention, is to require what was never intended. The imitations are so ambitiously frequent, that the writer evidently means rather to show his literature than his wit. It is surely sufficient for an author of sixteen, not only to be able to copy the poems of antiquity with judicious selection, but to have obtained sufficient power of language and skill in metre to exhibit a series of versification which had in English poetry no precedent, nor has since had an imitation.[257]

The design of ' Windsor Forest ' is evidently derived from Cooper's Hill,' with some attention to Waller's poem on ' The Park ;' but Pope cannot be denied to excel his masters in variety and elegance, and the art of interchanging description, narrative, and morality. The objection made by Dennis is the want of plan, of a regular subordination of parts terminating in the principal and original design. There is this want in most descriptive poems, because as the scenes, which they must exhibit successively, are all subsisting at the same time, the order in which they are shown must by necessity be arbitrary, and more is not to be expected from the last part than from the first. The attention, therefore, which cannot be detained by suspense, must be excited by diversity, such as his poem offers to its reader.

But the desire of diversity may be too much indulged ; the parts of ' Windsor Forest ' which deserve least praise, are those

[257] He [Warton] necessarily begins with his Pastorals, which, considered as representations of any kind of life, he very justly censures; for there is in them a mixture of Grecian and English, of ancient and modern images. Windsor is coupled with Hybla, and Thames with Pactolus. He remarks, I am afraid with too much justice, that there is not a single new thought in the Pastorals; and with equal reason declares that their chief beauty consists in their correct and musical versification, which has so influenced the English ear as to render every moderate writer harmonious.—JOHNSON: *Review of Warton's Essay.*

which were added to enliven the stillness of the scene, the appearance of Father Thames, and the transformation of Lodona.
Addison had in his 'Campaign' derided the rivers that " rise
from their oozy beds " to tell stories of heroes ; and it is therefore strange that Pope should adopt a fiction not only unnatural,
but lately censured.   The story of Lodona is told with
sweetness ; but a new metamorphosis is a ready and puerile
expedient : nothing is easier than to tell how a flower was once
a blooming virgin, or a rock an obdurate tyrant.[258]

The 'Temple of Fame' has, as Steele warmly declared,
" a thousand beauties."   Every part is splendid ; there is great
luxuriance of ornaments ; the original vision of Chaucer was
never denied to be much improved ; the allegory is very skilfully
continued, the imagery is properly selected, and learnedly displayed : yet, with all this comprehension of excellence, as its
scene is laid in remote ages, and its sentiments, if the concluding paragraph be excepted, have little relation to general
manners or common life, it never obtained much notice, but is
turned silently over, and seldom quoted or mentioned with
either praise or blame.

That the 'Messiah' excels the 'Pollio' is no great praise,
if it be considered from what original the improvements are
derived.

The 'Verses on the Unfortunate Lady' have drawn much
attention by the illaudable singularity of treating suicide with
respect ; and they must be allowed to be written in some parts
with vigorous animation, and in others with gentle tenderness ;
nor has Pope produced any poem in which the sense predomi-

[258] On 'Windsor Forest,' he [Warton] declares, I think without proof, that descriptive poetry was by no means the excellence of Pope.   He draws this inference
from the few images introduced in this poem, which would not equally belong
to any other place.   He must inquire whether 'Windsor Forest' has in reality
anything peculiar.   The stag-chase is not, he says, so full, so animated, and
so circumstantiated as Somervile's.   Barely to say that one performance is not
so good as another is to criticise with little exactness.   Yet Pope has directed
that we should in every work regard the author's end.   The stag-chase is the
main subject of Somervile, and might therefore be properly dilated into all
its circumstances : in Pope it was only incidental, and was to be despatched in
a few lines.—JOHNSON : *Review of Warton's Essay.*

nates more over the diction.   But the tale is not skilfully told ;
it is not easy to discover the character of either the Lady or
her Guardian.   History relates that she was about to disparage
herself by a marriage with an inferior ; Pope praises her for the
dignity of ambition, and yet condemns the uncle to detestation
for his pride ; the ambitious love of a niece may be opposed by
the interest, malice, or envy of an uncle, but never by his pride.
On such an occasion a poet may be allowed to be obscure, but
inconsistency never can be right.

The 'Ode for St. Cecilia's Day' was undertaken at the
desire of Steele : in this the author is generally confessed to
have miscarried, yet he has miscarried only as compared with
Dryden ; for he has far outgone other competitors.   Dryden's
plan is better chosen ; history will always take stronger hold of
the attention than fable : the passions excited by Dryden are
the pleasures and pains of real life, the scene of Pope is laid in
imaginary existence ; Pope is read with calm acquiescence,
Dryden with turbulent delight ; Pope hangs upon the ear, and
Dryden finds the passes of the mind.[259]

Both the odes want the essential constituent of metrical compositions, the stated recurrence of settled numbers.   It may be
alleged, that Pindar is said by Horace to have written *numeris
lege solutis :* but as no such lax performances have been transmitted to us, the meaning of that expression cannot be fixed ;
and perhaps the like return might properly be made to a modern Pindarist, as Mr. Cobb received from Bentley, who, when
he found his criticisms upon a Greek Exercise, which Cobb had
presented, refuted one after another by Pindar's authority, cried
out at last, " Pindar was a bold fellow, but thou art an impudent one."

If Pope's ode be particularly inspected, it will be found
that the first stanza consists of sounds well chosen indeed, but
only sounds.

[259] *Ode for Music* (*Pope*).—This Ode has by many been thought equal to the
former.   As it is a repetition of Dryden's manner, it is so far inferior to him.
The whole hint of Orpheus, with many of the lines, have been taken from an
obscure ode upon music, published in Tate's Miscellanies.—GOLDSMITH.   *See
Cunningham's Goldsmith,* vol. iii. p. 436.

The second consists of hyperbolical common-places, easily to be found, and perhaps without much difficulty to be as well expressed.

In the third, however, there are numbers, images, harmony, and vigour, not unworthy the antagonist of Dryden. Had all been like this—but every part cannot be the best.

The next stanzas place and detain us in the dark and dismal regions of mythology, where neither hope nor fear, neither joy nor sorrow, can be found: the poet, however, faithfully attends us; we have all that can be performed by elegance of diction or sweetness of versification; but what can form avail without better matter?

The last stanza recurs again to common-places. The conclusion is too evidently modelled by that of Dryden; and it may be remarked that both end with the same fault; the comparison of each is literal on one side, and metaphorical on the other.[260]

Poets do not always express their own thoughts: Pope, with all this labour in the praise of music, was ignorant of its principles, and insensible of its effects.

One of his greatest, though of his earliest works, is the 'Essay on Criticism,' which, if he had written nothing else, would have placed him among the first critics and the first poets, as it exhibits every mode of excellence that can embellish or dignify didactic composition—selection of matter, novelty of arrangement, justness of precept, splendour of illustration, and propriety of digression. I know not whether it be pleasing to consider that he produced this piece at twenty, and never afterwards excelled it: he that delights himself with observing that such powers may be soon attained, cannot but grieve to think that life was ever after at a stand.

[260] He [Warton] justly commends the fourth; but without notice of the best line in that stanza or in the poem:

> Transported demi-gods stood round,
> And men grew heroes at the sound.

. . . . He observes very justly that the Odes, both of Dryden and Pope, conclude unsuitably and unnaturally with epigram.—JOHNSON: *Review of Warton's Essay*.

To mention the particular beauties of the Essay would be unprofitably tedious; but I cannot forbear to observe, that the comparison of a student's progress in the sciences with the journey of a traveller in the Alps, is perhaps the best that English poetry can show.[261]   A simile, to be perfect, must both illustrate and ennoble the subject; must show it to the understanding in a clearer view, and display it to the fancy with greater dignity; but either of these qualities may be sufficient to recommend it.   In didactic poetry, of which the great purpose is instruction, a simile may be praised which illustrates, though it does not ennoble; in heroics, that may be admitted which ennobles, though it does not illustrate.   That it may be complete, it is required to exhibit, independently of its references, a pleasing image; for a simile is said to be a short episode.   To this antiquity was so attentive, that circumstances were sometimes added, which, having no parallels, served only to fill the imagination, and produced what Perrault ludicrously called "comparisons with a long tail."   In their similes the greatest writers have sometimes failed: the ship-race, compared with the chariot-race, is neither illustrated nor aggrandised; land and water make all the difference: when Apollo, running after Daphne, is likened to a greyhound chasing a hare, there is nothing gained; the ideas of pursuit and flight are too plain to be made plainer; and a god and the daughter of a god are not represented much to their advantage by a hare and dog.   The simile of the Alps has no useless parts, yet affords a striking picture by itself; it makes the foregoing position better understood, and enables it to take faster hold on the attention; it assists the apprehension and elevates the fancy.

Let me likewise dwell a little on the celebrated paragraph in which it is directed that " the sound should seem an echo to

[261] We cannot agree with him in his censure of the comparison of a student advancing in science with a traveller passing the Alps, which is perhaps the best simile in our language; that in which the most exact resemblance is traced between things in appearance utterly unrelated to each other.   That the last line conveys no new *idea* is not true; it makes particular what before was general.—JOHNSON: *Review of Warton's Essay.*

the sense;" a precept which Pope is allowed to have observed beyond any other English poet.[262]

This notion of representative metre, and the desire of discovering frequent adaptations of the sound to the sense, have produced, in my opinion, many wild conceits and imaginary beauties. All that can furnish this representation are the sounds of the words considered singly, and the time in which they are pronounced. Every language has some words framed to exhibit the noises which they express, as *thump*, *rattle*, *growl*, *hiss*. These, however, are but few; and the poet cannot make them more, nor can they be of any use but when sound is to be mentioned. The time of pronunciation was in the dactylic measures of the learned languages capable of considerable variety; but that variety could be accommodated only to motion or duration, and different degrees of motion were perhaps expressed by verses rapid or slow, without much attention of the writer, when the image had full possession of his fancy; but our language having little flexibility, our verses can differ very little in their cadence. The fancied resemblances, I fear, arise sometimes merely from the ambiguity of words; there is supposed to be some relation between a *soft* line and *soft* couch, or between *hard* syllables and *hard* fortune.

Motion, however, may be in some sort exemplified; and yet it may be suspected that in such resemblances the mind often governs the ear, and the sounds are estimated by their meaning. One of their most successful attempts has been to describe the labour of Sisyphus:

"With many a weary step, and many a groan,
    Up the high hill he heaves a huge round stone;
    The huge round stone, resulting with a bound,
    Thunders impetuous down, and smokes along the ground."[263]

---

[262] Homer is perpetually applying the sound to the sense. This, indeed, is one of the most exquisite beauties of poetry, and attainable by very few: I know only of Homer eminent for it in the Greek, and Virgil in Latin. I am sensible it is what may sometimes happen by chance, when a writer is warm and fully possest of his image: however, it may reasonably be believed they designed this, in whose verses it so manifestly appears, in a superior degree to all others. Few readers have the ears to be judges of it, but those who have will see I have endeavoured at this beauty.—POPE: *Pref. to Homer*.

[263] *Odyssey*, xi. 733. This is from the book professedly translated by

Who does not perceive the stone to move slowly upward, and roll violently back ? But set the same numbers to another sense :

> " While many a merry tale, and many a song,
>   Cheer'd the rough road, we wish'd the rough road long ;
>   The rough road then, returning in a round,
>   Mock'd our impatient steps, for all was fairy ground."

We have now surely lost much of the delay, and much of the rapidity.

But, to show how little the greatest master of numbers can fix the principles of representative harmony, it will be sufficient to remark that the poet who tells us that

> " When Ajax strives some rock's vast weight to throw,
>   The line too labours, and the words move slow ;
>   Not so when swift Camilla scours the plain,
>   Flies o'er th' unbending corn, and skims along the main ;" [264]

when he had enjoyed for about thirty years the praise of Camilla's lightness of foot, he tried another experiment upon *sound* and *time*, and produced this memorable triplet :

> " Waller was smooth ; but Dryden taught to join
>   The varying verse, the full resounding line,
>   The long majestic march, and energy divine."

Here are the swiftness of the rapid race, and the march of slow-paced majesty, exhibited by the same poet in the same sequence of syllables, except that the exact prosodist will find the line of *swiftness* by one time longer than that of *tardiness*.

Broome. . . . . " I have loaded the verse," says Pope, " with monosyllables, and these almost begin with aspirates :

> ' Up the high hill he heaves a huge round stone.' "

[264] In these lines which mention the effort of Ajax, there is no particular heaviness, obstruction, or delay. The swiftness of Camilla is rather contrasted than exemplified ; why the verse should be lengthened to express speed will not easily be discovered. In the dactyls used for that purpose by the ancients, two short syllables were pronounced with such rapidity as to be equal only to one long ; they therefore naturally exhibit the act of passing through a long space in a short time. But the Alexandrine, by its pause in the midst, is a tardy and stately measure ; and the word *unbending,* one of the most sluggish and slow which our language affords, cannot much accelerate its motion. — JOHNSON : *The Rambler,* No. 92.

Beauties of this kind [265] are commonly fancied; and, when real, are technical and nugatory, not to be rejected, and not to be solicited.

To the praises which have been accumulated on 'The Rape of the Lock' by readers of every class, from the critic to the waiting-maid, it is difficult to make any addition. Of that which is universally allowed to be the most attractive of all ludicrous compositions, let it rather be now inquired from what sources the power of pleasing is derived.

Dr. Warburton, who excelled in critical perspicacity, has remarked that the preternatural agents are very happily adapted to the purposes of the poem. The heathen deities can no longer gain attention: we should have turned away from a contest between Venus and Diana. The employment of allegorical persons always excites conviction of its own absurdity; they may produce effects, but cannot conduct actions: when the phantom is put in motion, it dissolves: thus *Discord* may raise a mutiny; but *Discord* cannot conduct a march, nor besiege a town. Pope brought in view a new race of beings, with powers and passions proportionate to their operation. The sylphs and gnomes act at the toilet and the tea-table, what more terrific and more powerful phantoms perform on the stormy ocean or the field of battle; they give their proper help, and do their proper mischief.

Pope is said, by an objector,[266] not to have been the inventor of this petty nation; a charge which might with more justice have been brought against the author of the 'Iliad,' who doubtless adopted the religious system of his country; for what is there but the names of his agents which Pope has not invented? Has he not assigned them characters and operations never heard of before? Has he not, at least, given them their first poetical existence? If this is not sufficient to denominate his work original, nothing original ever can be written.

[265] Compare Addison's paper on Pope's 'Essay on Criticism' in 'Spectator,' No. 253.

[266] Johnson alludes to Joseph Warton. He [Pope] took the idea of those invisible beings, so proper to be employed in a poem of this nature, from a little French book entitled ' Le Compte de Gabalis.'— *Warton's Essay on Pope*, i. 227, 4th edit., 1782.

In this work are exhibited, in a very high degree, the two most engaging powers of an author. New things are made familiar, and familiar things are made new. A race of aërial people, never heard of before, is presented to us in a manner so clear and easy, that the reader seeks for no further information, but immediately mingles with his new acquaintance, adopts their interests, and attends their pursuits, loves a sylph, and detests a gnome.

That familiar things are made new, every paragraph will prove. The subject of the poem is an event below the common incidents of common life; nothing real is introduced that is not seen so often as to be no longer regarded; yet the whole detail of a female-day is here brought before us, invested with so much art of decoration, that, though nothing is disguised, every thing is striking, and we feel all the appetite of curiosity for that from which we have a thousand times turned fastidiously away.

The purpose of the poet is, as he tells us, to laugh at "the little unguarded follies of the female sex." It is therefore without justice that Dennis charges 'The Rape of the Lock' with the want of a moral, and for that reason sets it below the 'Lutrin,' which exposes the pride and discord of the clergy. Perhaps neither Pope nor Boileau has made the world much better than he found it; but, if they had both succeeded, it were easy to tell who would have deserved most from public gratitude. The freaks, and humours, and spleen, and vanity of women, as they embroil families in discord, and fill houses with disquiet, do more to obstruct the happiness of life in a year than the ambition of the clergy in many centuries. It has been well observed, that the misery of man proceeds not from any single crush of overwhelming evil, but from small vexations continually repeated.

It is remarked by Dennis likewise that the machinery is superfluous; that, by all the bustle of preternatural operation, the main event is neither hastened nor retarded. To this charge an efficacious answer is not easily made. The Sylphs cannot be said to help or to oppose, and it must be allowed to imply some want of art, that their power has not been sufficiently intermingled with the action. Other parts may likewise

be charged with want of connection; the game at *ombre* might
be spared; but if the Lady had lost her hair while she was
intent upon her cards, it might have been inferred that those
who are too fond of play will be in danger of neglecting more
important interests.   Those perhaps are faults; but what are
such faults to so much excellence?[267]

The Epistle of 'Eloisa to Abelard' is one of the most happy
productions of human wit; the subject is so judiciously chosen,
that it would be difficult, in turning over the annals of the
world, to find another which so many circumstances concur to
recommend.   We regularly interest ourselves most in the
fortune of those who most deserve our notice.   Abelard and
Eloisa were conspicuous in their days for eminence of merit.
The heart naturally loves truth.   The adventures and misfortunes of this illustrious pair are known from undisputed
history.   Their fate does not leave the mind in hopeless de-
jection, for they both found quiet and consolation in retirement
and piety.   So new and so affecting is their story, that it
supersedes invention, and imagination ranges at full liberty
without straggling into scenes of fable.

The story, thus skilfully adopted, has been diligently improved.   Pope has left nothing behind him which seems more
the effect of studious perseverance and laborious revisal.   Here
is particularly observable the *curiosa felicitas*, a fruitful soil
and careful cultivation.   Here is no crudeness of sense, nor
asperity of language.[268]

The sources from which sentiments which have so much

---

[267] *The Rape of the Lock.*—This seems to be Mr. Pope's most finished production, and is, perhaps, the most perfect in our language.   It exhibits
stronger powers of imagination, more harmony of numbers, and a greater
knowledge of the world, than any other of this poet's works; and it is probable, if our country were called upon to show a specimen of their genius to
foreigners, this would be the work fixed upon.—GOLDSMITH: *Works by Cunningham*, iii. 435.

[268] *Eloisa to Abelard.*—The harmony of numbers in this poem is very fine.   It
is rather drawn out to too tedious a length, although the passions vary with
great judgment.   It may be considered as superior to anything in the epistolary way; and the many translations which have been made of it into the
modern languages are in some measure a proof of this.—GOLDSMITH: *Works by
Cunningham*, iii. 436.

vigour and efficacy have been drawn, are shown to be the
mystic writers by the learned author of the ' Essay on the Life
and Writings of Pope ;' [269] a book which teaches how the brow
of Criticism may be smoothed, and how she may be enabled,
with all her severity, to attract and to delight.

The train of my disquisition has now conducted me to that
poetical wonder, the translation of the ' Iliad,' a performance
which no age or nation can pretend to equal. To the Greeks
translation was almost unknown ; it was totally unknown to the
inhabitants of Greece. They had no recourse to the Barbarians
for poetical beauties, but sought for everything in Homer, where
indeed there is but little which they might not find.

The Italians have been very diligent translators, but I can
hear of no version, unless perhaps Anguillara's 'Ovid' may be
excepted, which is read with eagerness. The 'Iliad' of Sal-
vini every reader may discover to be punctiliously exact ; but it
seems to be the work of a linguist skilfully pedantic, and his
countrymen, the proper judges of its power to please, reject it
with disgust.

Their predecessors the Romans have left some specimens of
translation behind them, and that employment must have had
some credit in which Tully and Germanicus engaged ; but
unless we suppose, what is perhaps true, that the plays of Te-
rence were versions of Menander, nothing translated seems ever
to have risen to high reputation. The French, in the meridian
hour of their learning, were very laudably industrious to enrich
their own language with the wisdom of the ancients ; but found
themselves reduced, by whatever necessity, to turn the Greek
and Roman poetry into prose. Whoever could read an author
could translate him. From such rivals little can be feared.

The chief help of Pope in this arduous undertaking was
drawn from the versions of Dryden. Virgil had borrowed
much of his imagery from Homer, and part of the debt was
now paid by his translator. Pope searched the pages of Dryden

---

[269] Joseph Warton. When this was written, only one of the two volumes
had been published. Johnson's review of the first volume had been reprinted
in his Works.

for happy combinations of heroic diction; but it will not be
denied that he added much to what he found. He cultivated
our language with so much diligence and art that he has left
in his 'Homer' a treasure of poetical elegances to posterity.
His version may be said to have tuned the English tongue;
for since its appearance no writer, however deficient in other
powers, has wanted melody. Such a series of lines, so elaborately corrected and so sweetly modulated, took possession of
the public ear; the vulgar was enamoured of the poem, and the
learned wondered at the translation.

But in the most general applause discordant voices will always
be heard. It has been objected by some, who wish to be numbered among the sons of learning, that Pope's version of Homer
is not Homerical; that it exhibits no resemblance of the original and characteristic manner of the father of poetry, as it
wants his awful simplicity, his artless grandeur, his unaffected
majesty.[270] This cannot be totally denied; but it must be remembered that *necessitas quod cogit defendit;* that may be
lawfully done which cannot be forborne. Time and place will
always enforce regard. In estimating this translation, consideration must be had of the nature of our language, the form of
our metre, and above all of the change which two thousand
years have made in the modes of life and the habits of thought.
Virgil wrote in a language of the same general fabric with that
of Homer, in verses of the same measure, and in an age nearer
to Homer's time by eighteen hundred years, yet he found, even
then, the state of the world so much altered, and the demand
for elegance so much increased, that mere nature would be
endured no longer; and perhaps, in the multitude of borrowed
passages, very few can be shown which he has not embellished.

[270] Bentley was one of these. He and Pope, soon after the publication of
Homer, met at Dr. Mead's at dinner; when Pope, desirous of his opinion of
the translation, addressed him thus: " Dr. Bentley, I ordered my bookseller
to send you your books; I hope you received them." Bentley, who had
purposely avoided saying any thing about Homer, pretended not to understand
him, and asked, " Books! books! what books?" "My Homer," replied Pope,
"which you did me the honour to subscribe for."—" Oh," said Bentley, " ay,
now I recollect—your translation:—it is a pretty poem, Mr. Pope; but you
must not call it Homer."—Sir John Hawkins.

There is a time when nations emerging from barbarity, and falling into regular subordination, gain leisure to grow wise, and feel the shame of ignorance and the craving pain of unsatisfied curiosity. To this hunger of the mind plain sense is grateful; that which fills the void removes uneasiness, and to be free from pain for a while is pleasure; but repletion generates fastidiousness; a saturated intellect soon becomes luxurious, and knowledge finds no willing reception till it is recommended by artificial diction. Thus it will be found, in the progress of learning, that in all nations the first writers are simple, and that every age improves in elegance. One refinement always makes way for another; and what was expedient to Virgil was necessary to Pope.

I suppose many readers of the English 'Iliad,' when they have been touched with some unexpected beauty of the lighter kind, have tried to enjoy it in the original, where, alas! it was not to be found. Homer doubtless owes to his translator many Ovidian graces not exactly suitable to his character; but to have added can be no great crime, if nothing be taken away. Elegance is surely to be desired, if it be not gained at the expense of dignity. A hero would wish to be loved as well as to be reverenced.

To a thousand cavils one answer is sufficient: the purpose of a writer is to be read, and the criticism which would destroy the power of pleasing must be blown aside. Pope wrote for his own age and his own nation; he knew that it was necessary to colour the images and point the sentiments of his author; he therefore made him graceful, but lost him some of his sublimity.

The copious notes with which the version is accompanied, and by which it is recommended to many readers, though they were undoubtedly written to swell the volumes, ought not to pass without praise: commentaries which attract the reader by the pleasure of perusal have not often appeared; the notes of others are read to clear difficulties, those of Pope to vary entertainment.

It has, however, been objected, with sufficient reason, that there is in the commentary too much of unseasonable levity

and affected gaiety; that too many appeals are made to the
ladies, and the ease which is so carefully preserved is sometimes
the ease of a trifler.   Every art has its terms, and every kind of
instruction its proper style; the gravity of common critics may
be tedious, but is less despicable than childish merriment.

Of the 'Odyssey' nothing remains to be observed : the same
general praise may be given to both translations, and a particular examination of either would require a large volume. The
notes were written by Broome, who endeavoured, not unsuccessfully, to imitate his master.

Of 'The Dunciad' the hint is confessedly taken from Dryden's
'Mac Flecknoe;' but the plan is so enlarged and diversified
as justly to claim the praise of an original, and affords perhaps
the best specimen that has yet appeared of personal satire ludicrously pompous.

That the design was moral, whatever the author might tell
either his readers or himself, I am not convinced. The first
motive [271] was the desire of revenging the contempt with which
Theobald had treated his 'Shakespeare,' and regaining the
honour which he had lost, by crushing his opponent. Theobald
was not of bulk enough to fill a poem, and therefore it was
necessary to find other enemies with other names, at whose expense he might divert the public.

In this design there was petulance and malignity enough;
but I cannot think it very criminal.   An author places himself
uncalled before the tribunal of criticism, and solicits fame at the
hazard of disgrace.   Dulness or deformity are not culpable in
themselves, but may be very justly reproached when they pretend to the honour of wit or the influence of beauty.   If bad
writers were to pass without reprehension, what should restrain
them? *impune diem consumpserit ingens Telephus;* and upon
bad writers only will censure have much effect.   The satire
which brought Theobald and Moore into contempt, dropped
impotent from Bentley like the javelin of Priam.

[271] I cannot but concur in a suspicion which Mr. Croker has communicated
to me, that Pope had planned a Dunciad long before Theobald's offence: with
Eusden, or Cibber, or some one not less notorious, for the hero of his poem.

All truth is valuable, and satirical criticism may be considered as useful when it rectifies error and improves judgment; he that refines the public taste is a public benefactor.

The beauties of this poem are well known; its chief fault is the grossness of its images. Pope and Swift had an unnatural delight in ideas physically impure, such as every other tongue utters with unwillingness, and of which every ear shrinks from the mention.

But even this fault, offensive as it is, may be forgiven for the excellence of other passages—such as the formation and dissolution of Moore, the account of the Traveller, the misfortune of the Florist, and the crowded thoughts and stately numbers which dignify the concluding paragraph.[272]

The alterations which have been made in 'The Dunciad,' not always for the better, require that it should be published, as in the present collection,[273] with all its variations.

The 'Essay on Man' was a work of great labour and long consideration, but certainly not the happiest of Pope's performances. The subject is perhaps not very proper for poetry, and the poet was not sufficiently master of his subject; metaphysical morality was to him a new study, he was proud of his acquisitions, and, supposing himself master of great secrets, was in haste to teach what he had not learned. Thus he tells us, in the first epistle, that from the nature of the Supreme Being may be deduced an order of beings such as mankind, because Infinite Excellence can do only what is best. He finds out that these beings must be " somewhere," and that " all the question

---

[272] After dinner our conversation first turned upon Pope. Johnson said his characters of men were admirably drawn; those of women not so well. He repeated to us, in his forcible, melodious manner, the concluding lines of 'The Dunciad.' While he was talking loudly in praise of those lines, one of the company [Boswell himself] ventured to say, "Too fine for such a poem; a poem on what?" Johnson (with a disdainful look), "Why, on *dunces*. It was worth while being a dunce then. Ah, Sir, hadst thou lived in those days !"—*Boswell by Croker*, p. 203.

[273] The collection for which these Lives were written. Johnson has not made any allusion to the separate publication of 'The New Dunciad, as it was found in the year 1741,' better known as the Fourth Book of the Dunciad, and to Warburton's curious note thereupon. (Note on verse 282 of 'Prologue to the Satires.')

is whether man be in a wrong place." Surely if, according to
the poet's Leibnitian reasoning, we may infer that man ought
to be, only because he is, we may allow that his place is the
right place because he has it. Supreme Wisdom is not less in-
fallible in disposing than in creating. But what is meant by
somewhere and *place*, and *wrong place*, it had been vain to ask
Pope, who probably had never asked himself.

Having exalted himself into the chair of wisdom, he tells us
much that every man knows, and much that he does not know
himself : that we see but little, and that the order of the universe is beyond our comprehension—an opinion not very uncommon ; and that there is a chain of subordinate beings
" from infinite to nothing," of which himself and his readers are
equally ignorant. But he gives us one comfort which, without
his help, he supposes unattainable, in the position " that though
we are fools, yet God is wise."

This essay affords an egregious instance of the predominance
of genius, the dazzling splendour of imagery, and the seductive
powers of eloquence. Never was penury of knowledge and
vulgarity of sentiment so happily disguised. The reader feels
his mind full, though he learns nothing ; and when he meets it
in its new array, no longer knows the talk of his mother and
his nurse. When these wonder-working sounds sink into sense,
and the doctrine of the Essay, disrobed of its ornaments, is left
to the powers of its naked excellence, what shall we discover ?
That we are, in comparison with our Creator, very weak and
ignorant—that we do not uphold the chain of existence—and
that we could not make one another with more skill than we
are made. We may learn yet more—that the arts of human
life were copied from the instinctive operations of other animals
—that if the world be made for man, it may be said that man
was made for geese. To these profound principles of natural
knowledge are added some moral instructions equally new :
that self-interest, well understood, will produce social concord—
that men are mutual gainers by mutual benefits—that evil is
sometimes balanced by good—that human advantages are un-
stable and fallacious, of uncertain duration and doubtful effect—

that our true honour is, not to have a great part, but to act it well—that virtue only is our own—and that happiness is always in our power.

Surely a man of no very comprehensive search may venture to say that he has heard all this before ; but it was never till now recommended by such a blaze of embellishments, or such sweetness of melody. The vigorous contraction of some thoughts, the luxuriant amplification of others, the incidental illustrations, and sometimes the dignity, sometimes the softness of the verses, enchain philosophy, suspend criticism, and oppress judgment by overpowering pleasure.

This is true of many paragraphs ; yet if I had undertaken to exemplify Pope's felicity of composition before a rigid critic, I should not select the ' Essay on Man ; ' for it contains more lines unsuccessfully laboured, more harshness of diction, more thoughts imperfectly expressed, more levity without elegance, and more heaviness without strength, than will easily be found in all his other works.

The ' Characters of Men and Women ' are the product of diligent speculation upon human life ; much labour has been bestowed upon them, and Pope very seldom laboured in vain. That his excellence may be properly estimated, I recommend a comparison of his ' Characters of Women ' with Boileau's Satire ; it will then be seen with how much more perspicacity female nature is investigated, and female excellence selected ; and he surely is no mean writer to whom Boileau shall be found inferior. The ' Characters of Men,' however, are written with more, if not with deeper, thought, and exhibit many passages exquisitely beautiful.   The ' Gem and the Flower ' will not easily bo equalled.   In the women's part are some defects : the character of Atossa is not so neatly finished as that of Clodio ; and some of the female characters may be found perhaps more frequently among men ; what is said of Philomede was true of Prior.[274]

[274] So Philomedé lecturing all mankind
     On the soft passion, and the taste refin'd,
     The address, the delicacy—stoops at once,
     And makes her hearty meal upon a dunce.

In the Epistles to Lord Bathurst and Lord Burlington, Dr. Warburton has endeavoured to find a train of thought which was never in the writer's head, and, to support his hypothesis, has printed that first which was published last.[275] In one, the most valuable passage is perhaps the Elegy on 'Good Sense;' and the other, the 'End of the Duke of Buckingham.'

The 'Epistle to Arbuthnot,' now arbitrarily called the 'Prologue to the Satires,' [276] is a performance consisting, as it seems, of many fragments wrought into one design, which by this union of scattered beauties contains more striking paragraphs than could probably have been brought together into an occasional work. As there is no stronger motive to exertion than self-defence, no part has more elegance, spirit, or dignity than the poet's vindication of his own character. The meanest passage is the satire upon Sporus.[277]

Of the two poems which derived their names from the year, and which are called the 'Epilogue to the Satires,' it was very justly remarked by Savage, that the second was in the whole more strongly conceived, and more equally supported, but that it had no single passages equal to the contention in the first for the dignity of Vice, and the celebration of the triumph of Corruption.

The 'Imitations of Horace' seem to have been written as relaxations of his genius. This employment became his favourite by its facility; the plan was ready to his hand, and nothing was required but to accommodate as he could the sentiments of an old author to recent [278] facts or familiar images; but what

[275] Warburton only follows the arrangement made by Pope himself in 1735, at least four years before he knew Warburton. See the 12mo. ed. of that year, where the four moral Epistles are arranged as Warburton retained them.

[276] This was one of Warburton's forced alterations.

[277] Here again we have (see p. 81) Johnson's fondness for the Herveys over-ruling his better judgment. Byron is high in his praises of the Sporus portrait.

[278] Compare p. 78. Surely Johnson's own imitation of Juvenal is an exception to this criticism. " ' London' is to me," says Gray, " one of those few imitations that have all the ease and all the spirit of an original." (Letter to Walpole.) " Imitation," says Goldsmith, "gives a much truer idea of the ancients than even translation could do."— *Works by Cunningham*, iii. 436.

is easy is seldom excellent ; such imitations cannot give pleasure to common readers ; the man of learning may be sometimes surprised and delighted by an unexpected parallel ; but the comparison requires knowledge of the original, which will likewise often detect strained applications.   Between Roman images and English manners there will be an irreconcileable dissimilitude, and the works will be generally uncouth and party-coloured ; neither original nor translated, neither ancient nor modern.[279]

Pope had, in proportions very nicely adjusted to each other, all the qualities that constitute genius.   He had *Invention*, by which new trains of events are formed, and new scenes of imagery displayed, as in ‘ The Rape of the Lock ; ’ and by which extrinsic and adventitious embellishments and illustrations are connected with a known subject, as in the ‘ Essay on Criticism.’   He had *Imagination*, which strongly impresses on the writer’s mind, and enables him to convey to the reader, the various forms of nature, incidents of life, and energies of passion, as in his ‘ Eloisa,’ ‘ Windsor Forest,’ and the ‘ Ethic Epistles.’   He had *Judgment*, which selects from life or nature what the present purpose requires, and by separating the essence of things from its concomitants, often makes the representation more powerful than the reality : and he had colours of language always before him, ready to decorate his matter with every grace of elegant expression, as when he accommodates his diction to the wonderful multiplicity of Homer’s sentiments and descriptions.

---

[279] In one of these poems [1st Sat. 2nd Book] is a couplet, to which belongs a story that I once heard the Reverend Dr. Ridley relate :—

> Slander or poison dread from Della’s rage;
> Hard words or hanging, if your judge be ****.

Sir Francis Page, a judge well known in his time, conceiving that his name was meant to fill up the blank, sent his clerk to Mr. Pope, to complain of the insult.   Pope told the young man that the blank might be supplied by many monosyllables other than the judge’s name.   “ But, Sir,” said the clerk, “ the judge says that no other word will make sense of the passage.”   “ So then, it seems,” says Pope, “ your master is not only a judge, but a poet : as that is the case, the odds are against me.   Give my respects to the judge, and tell him I will not contend with one that has the advantage of me, and he may fill up the blank as he pleases.”— SIR JOHN HAWKINS.

Poetical expression includes sound as well as meaning. " Music," says Dryden, " is inarticulate poetry ; " among the excellences of Pope, therefore, must be mentioned the melody of his metre. By perusing the works of Dryden, he discovered the most perfect fabric of English verse, and habituated himself to that only which he found the best ; in consequence of which restraint, his poetry has been censured as too uniformly musical, and as glutting the ear with unvaried sweetness. I suspect this objection to be the cant of those who judge by principles rather than perception ; and who would even themselves have less pleasure in his works, if he had tried to relieve attention by studied discords, or affected to break his lines and vary his pauses.

But though he was thus careful of his versification, he did not oppress his powers with superfluous rigour. He seems to have thought with Boileau, that the practice of writing might be refined till the difficulty should overbalance the advantage. The construction of his language is not always strictly grammatical ; with those rhymes which prescription had conjoined he contented himself, without regard to Swift's remonstrances, though there was no striking consonance ; nor was he very careful to vary his terminations, or to refuse admission, at a small distance, to the same rhymes.

To Swift's edict for the exclusion of Alexandrines and Triplets he paid little regard ; he admitted them, but, in the opinion of Fenton, too rarely ; he uses them more liberally in his translation than his poems.[280]

He has a few double rhymes ; and always, I think, unsuccessfully, except once in ' The Rape of the Lock.' [281]

Expletives he very early ejected from his verses ; but he now and then admits an epithet rather commodious than important.

[280] Mr. Pope never used them till he translated Homer, which was too long a work to be very exact in; and I think in one or two of his last poems he has, out of laziness, done the same thing, though very seldom.—SWIFT to Mr. Thomas Beach, April 12, 1735. (Scott, xviii. 298, 2nd ed.)

[281] The meeting points the sacred hair dissever
From the fair head, for ever and for ever.
                                                        Canto iii.

Each of the six first lines of the ' Iliad ' might lose two syllables
with very little diminution of the meaning; and sometimes,
after all his art and labour, one verse seems to be made for the
sake of another.   In his latter productions the diction is sometimes vitiated by French idioms, with which Bolingbroke had
perhaps infected him.

I have been told that the couplet by which he declared his
own ear to be most gratified was this :

> " Lo, where Mæotis sleeps, and hardly flows
> The freezing Tanais through a waste of snows."

But the reason of this preference I cannot discover.

It is remarked by Watts, that there is scarcely a happy combination of words, or a phrase poetically elegant in the English
language, which Pope has not inserted into his version of
Homer.   How he obtained possession of so many beauties of
speech, it were desirable to know.   That he gleaned from
authors, obscure as well as eminent, what he thought brilliant
or useful, and preserved it all in a regular collection, is not
unlikely.   When, in his last years, Hall's Satires were shown
him, he wished that he had seen them sooner.

New sentiments and new images others may produce ; but to
attempt any further improvement of versification will be dangerous.   Art and diligence have now done their best, and what
shall be added will be the effort of tedious toil and needless
curiosity.

After all this, it is surely superfluous to answer the question
that has once been asked, Whether Pope was a poet?
otherwise than by asking in return, If Pope be not a poet,
where is poetry to be found ?   To circumscribe poetry by a
definition will only show the narrowness of the definer, though
a definition which shall exclude Pope will not easily be made.
Let us look round upon the present time, and back upon the
past ; let us inquire to whom the voice of mankind has decreed
the wreath of poetry ; let their productions be examined, and
their claims stated, and the pretensions of Pope will be no more
disputed.   Had he given the world only his version, the name

of poet must have been allowed him : if the writer of the
' Iliad ' were to class his successors, he would assign a very
high place to his translator, without requiring any other evidence of Genius.

The following Letter, of which the original is in the hands of
Lord Hardwicke, was communicated to me by the kindness of
Mr. Jodrell. (See p. 27.)

" *To* Mr. Bridges, *at the Bishop of London's at Fulham.*

" Sir,—The favour of your letter, with your remarks, can never be
enough acknowledged ; and the speed with which you discharged so
troublesome a task doubles the obligation.

" I must own you have pleased me very much by the commendations
so ill-bestowed upon me ; but, I assure you, much more by the frankness
of your censure, which I ought to take the more kindly of the two, as it
is more advantageous to a scribbler to be improved in his judgment than
to be soothed in his vanity. The greater part of those deviations from the
Greek, which you have observed, I was led into by Chapman and Hobbes,
who are, it seems, as much celebrated for their knowledge of the original,
as they are decried for the badness of their translations. Chapman pretends to have restored the genuine sense of the author, from the mistakes
of all former explainers, in several hundred places ; and the Cambridge
editors of the large Homer, in Greek and Latin, attributed so much to
Hobbes, that they confess they have corrected the old Latin interpretation
very often by his version. For my part, I generally took the author's
meaning to be as you have explained it ; yet their authority, joined to the
knowledge of my own imperfectness in the language, overruled me.[282] However, Sir, you may be confident I think you in the right, because you
happen to be of my opinion (for men—let them say what they will—never
approve any other's sense but as it squares with their own). But you
have made me much more proud of and positive in my judgment, since it
is strengthened by yours. I think your criticisms, which regard the expression, very just, and shall make my profit of them : to give you some
proof that I am in earnest, I will alter three verses on your bare objection,
though I have Mr. Dryden's example for each of them. And this, I hope,
you will account no small piece of obedience, from one who values the
authority of one true poet above that of twenty critics or commentators.
But though I speak thus of commentators, I will continue to read carefully all I can procure, to make up, that way, for my own want of critical
understanding in the original beauties of Homer. Though the greatest of
them are certainly those of invention and design, which are not at all
confined to the language : for the distinguishing excellences of Homer are

---

[282] Compare Warton's note in his ' Essay on Pope,' ii. 234, ed. 1782.

(by the consent of the best critics of all nations) first in the manners (which include all the speeches, as being no other than the representations of each person's manners by his words), and then in that rapture and fire which carries you away with him with that wonderful force, that no man who has a true poetical spirit is master of himself while he reads him. Homer makes you interested and concerned before you are aware, all at once, whereas Virgil does it by soft degrees. This, I believe, is what a translator of Homer ought principally to imitate ; and it is very hard for any translator to come up to it, because the chief reason why all translations fall short of their originals is, that the very constraint they are obliged to, renders them heavy and dispirited.

" The great beauty of Homer's language, as I take it, consists in that noble simplicity which runs through all his works (and yet his diction, contrary to what one would imagine consistent with simplicity, is at the same time very copious). I don't know how I have run into this pedantry in a letter, but I find I have said too much, as well as spoken too inconsiderately ; what farther thoughts I have upon this subject I shall be glad to communicate to you (for my own improvement) when we meet, which is a happiness I very earnestly desire, as I do likewise some opportunity of proving how much I think myself obliged to your friendship, and how truly I am, Sir,

" Your most faithful, humble servant,

" A. POPE."

The criticism upon Pope's ' Epitaphs,' which was printed in ' The Universal Visitor,' [283] is placed here, being too minute and particular to be inserted in the ' Life.'

Every art is best taught by example. Nothing contributes more to the cultivation of propriety than remarks on the works of those who have most excelled. I shall therefore endeavour, at this *visit*, to entertain the young students in poetry with an examination of Pope's ' Epitaphs.'

To define an epitaph is useless ; every one knows that it is an inscription on a tomb. An epitaph, therefore, implies no particular character of writing, but may be composed in verse or prose. It is indeed commonly panegyrical, because we are seldom distinguished with a stone but by our friends ; but it has no rule to restrain or mollify it, except this, that it ought

---

[283] For 1756. Johnson also wrote an ' Essay on Epitaphs ' for the ' Gentleman's Magazine ' for 1740.

not to be longer than common beholders may be expected to have leisure and patience to peruse.

I.

On CHARLES EARL OF DORSET, *in the Church of Wythiam in Sussex.*

> " Dorset, the grace of courts, the Muses' pride,
> Patron of arts, and judge of nature, died.
> The scourge of pride, though sanctified or great,
> Of fops in learning, and of knaves in state;
> Yet soft in nature, though severe his lay,
> His anger moral, and his wisdom gay.
> Blest satirist ! who touch'd the means so true,
> As show'd Vice had his hate and pity too.
> Blest courtier ! who could king and country please,
> Yet sacred kept his friendship and his ease.
> Blest peer ! his great forefather's every grace
> Reflecting, and reflected on his race;
> Where other Buckhursts, other Dorsets shine,
> And patriots still, or poets, deck the line."

The first distich of this epitaph contains a kind of information which few would want—that the man for whom the tomb was erected *died.* There are indeed some qualities worthy of praise ascribed to the dead, but none that were likely to exempt him from the lot of man, or incline us much to wonder that he should die. What is meant by "judge of nature," is not easy to say. Nature is not the object of human judgment; for it is in vain to judge where we cannot alter. If by nature is meant, what is commonly called *nature* by the critics, a just representation of things really existing, and actions really performed, nature cannot be properly opposed to *art;* nature being, in this sense, only the best effect of *art.*

" The scourge of pride—"

Of this couplet the second line is not, what is intended, an illustration of the former. *Pride*, in the *great*, is indeed well enough connected with knaves in state, though *knaves* is a word rather too ludicrous and light; but the mention of *sanctified* pride will not lead the thoughts to *fops in learning*, but rather to some species of tyranny or oppression, something more gloomy and more formidable than foppery.[284]

" Yet soft his nature—"

This is a high compliment, but was not first bestowed on Dorset by Pope. The next verse is extremely beautiful.

" Blest satirist !—"

In this distich is another line of which Pope was not the author. I do not mean to blame these imitations with much harshness ; in long performances they are scarcely to be avoided, and in shorter they may be indulged, because the train of the composition may naturally involve them, or the scantiness of the subject allow little choice. However, what is borrowed is not to be enjoyed as our own ; and it is the business of critical justice to give every bird of the Muses his proper feather.

" Blest courtier !—"

Whether a courtier can properly be commended for keeping his *ease sacred* may perhaps be disputable. To please king and country, without sacrificing friendship to any change of times, was a very uncommon instance of prudence or felicity, and deserved to be kept separate from so poor a commendation as care of his ease. I wish our poets would attend a little more accurately to the use of the word *sacred*, which surely should never be applied in a serious composition, but where some reference may be made to a higher Being, or where some duty is exacted or implied. A man may keep his friendship sacred, because promises of friendship are very awful ties ; but methinks he cannot, but in a burlesque sense, be said to keep his ease *sacred*.

" Blest peer !—"

The blessing ascribed to the *peer* has no connection with his peerage : they might happen to any other man whose ancestors were remembered, or whose posterity were likely to be regarded.

---

[284] Johnson has passed over the awkward and unharmonious recurrence of *pride* in the first and third lines.

I know not whether this epitaph be worthy either of the writer or the man entombed.

II.

On SIR WILLIAM TRUMBULL, *one of the Principal Secretaries of State to King William III., who, having resigned his place, died in his retirement at Easthampstead, in Berkshire,* 1716.

> " A pleasing form ; a firm, yet cautious mind ;
>   Sincere, though prudent ; constant, yet resigned ;
>   Honour unchanged, a principle profest,
>   Fixed to one side, but moderate to the rest :
>   An honest courtier, yet a patriot too,
>   Just to his prince, and to his country true.
>   Filled with the sense of age, the fire of youth,
>   A scorn of wrangling, yet a zeal for truth ;
>   A generous faith, from superstition free ;
>   A love to peace, and hate of tyranny :
>   Such this man was, who, now from earth removed,
>   At length enjoys that liberty he loved."

In this epitaph, as in many others, there appears at the first view a fault which I think scarcely any beauty can compensate. The name is omitted.[285]   The end of an epitaph is to convey some account of the dead ; and to what purpose is anything told of him whose name is concealed ?   An epitaph and a history of a nameless hero are equally absurd, since the virtues and qualities so recounted in either are scattered at the mercy of fortune, to be appropriated by guess.   The name, it is true, may be read upon the stone, but what obligation has it to the poet, whose verses wander over the earth, and leave their subject behind them, and who is forced, like an unskilful painter, to make his purpose known by adventitious help ?

This epitaph is wholly without elevation, and contains nothing striking or particular ; but the poet is not to be blamed for the defects of his subject.   He said perhaps the best that could be said.   There are, however, some defects which were not made necessary by the character in which he was employed.   There

---

[285] Pope has some epitaphs without names ; which are, therefore, epitaphs to be let, occupied indeed for the present, but hardly appropriated.—JOHNSON : *Life of Cowley.*

is no opposition between an *honest courtier* and a *patriot*, for an *honest courtier* cannot but be a *patriot*.[286]

It was unsuitable to the nicety required in short compositions to close his verse with the word *too*: every rhyme should be a word of emphasis, nor can this rule be safely neglected, except where the length of the poem makes slight inaccuracies excusable, or allows room for beauties sufficient to overpower the effects of petty faults.

At the beginning of the seventh line the word *filled* is weak and prosaic, having no particular adaptation to any of the words that follow it.

The thought in the last line is impertinent, having no connexion with the foregoing character, nor with the condition of the man described. Had the epitaph been written on the poor conspirator [287] who died lately in prison, after a confinement of more than forty years, without any crime proved against him, the sentiment had been just and pathetical; but why should Trumbull be congratulated upon his liberty, who had never known restraint?

[286] Pope, it appears, has appropriated part of an epitaph, which he had previously written on John Lord Caryl, Secretary to King James's Queen (d. 1711). (See 'The Athenæum' of 15th July, 1854.)

Epitaph on John Lord Caryl.

A manly Form; a bold, yet modest mind;
Sincere, tho' prudent; constant, yet resign'd;
Honour unchang'd; a Principle profest;
Fix'd to one side, but mod'rate to the rest;
An honest Courtier, and a Patriot too;
Just to his Prince, and to his Country true:
All these were join'd in one, yet fail'd to save
The Wise, the Learn'd, the Virtuous, and the Brave;
Lost, like the common plunder of the Grave!
  Ye Few, whom better Genius does inspire,
Exalted Souls, inform'd with purer Fire!
Go now, learn all vast Science can impart;
Go fathom Nature, take the Heights of Art!
Rise higher yet: learn ev'n yourselves to know;
Nay, to yourselves alone that knowledge owe.
Then, when you seem above mankind to soar,
Look on this marble, and be vain no more!

[287] Major John Bernardi, who died in Newgate Sept. 20, 1736, after an imprisonment for forty years on an alleged conspiracy against William III.

III.

On the HON. SIMON HARCOURT, *only Son of the Lord Chancellor Harcourt,
at the Church of Stanton-Harcourt, in Oxfordshire,* 1720.

" To this sad shrine, whoe'er thou art, draw near :
　Here lies the friend most loved, the son most dear ;
　Who ne'er knew joy, but friendship might divide,
　Or gave his father grief but when he died.
　　How vain is reason, eloquence how weak,
　If Pope must tell what Harcourt cannot speak !
　Oh, let thy once-loved friend inscribe thy stone,
　And with a father's sorrows mix his own ! "

This epitaph is principally remarkable for the artful introduction of the name, which is inserted with a peculiar felicity,
to which chance must concur with genius, which no man can
hope to attain twice, and which cannot be copied but with
servile imitation.

I cannot but wish that of this inscription the two last lines
had been omitted, as they take away from the energy what
they do not add to the sense.

IV.

On JAMES CRAGGS, ESQ.　*In Westminster Abbey.*

"JACOBUS CRAGGS,

REGI MAGNAE BRITANNIAE A SECRETIS
ET CONSILIIS SANCTIORIBVS
PRINCIPIS PARITER AC POPULI AMOR ET DELICIAE :
VIXIT TITULIS ET INVIDIA MAJOR,
ANNOS HEV PAVCOS, XXXV.
OB. FEB. XVI. MDCCXX.

Statesman, yet friend to truth ! of soul sincere,
In action faithful, and in honour clear !
Who broke no promise, served no private end,
Who gained no title, and who lost no friend ;
Ennobled by himself, by all approved,
Praised, wept, and honoured by the Muse he loved."

The lines on Craggs were not originally intended for an
epitaph, and therefore some faults are to be imputed to the
violence with which they are torn from the poem that first con-

tained them.   We may, however, observe some defects.   There is a redundancy of words in the first couplet : it is superfluous to tell of him who was *sincere, true,* and *faithful,* that he was *in honour clear.*

There seems to be an opposition intended in the fourth line, which is not very obvious : where is the relation between the two positions that he *gained no title* and *lost no friend ?*

It may be proper here to remark the absurdity of joining in the same inscription Latin and English, or verse and prose.   If either language be preferable to the other, let that only be used, for no reason can be given why part of the information should be given in one tongue, and part in another, on a tomb, more than in any other place, on any other occasion ; and to tell all that can be conveniently told in verse, and then to call in the help of prose, has always the appearance of a very artless expedient, or of an attempt unaccomplished.   Such an epitaph resembles the conversation of a foreigner, who tells part of his meaning by words, and conveys part by signs.

V.

Intended for Mr. Rowe.   *In Westminster Abbey.*

" Thy relics, Rowe, to this fair urn we trust,
    And sacred, place by Dryden's awful dust :
    Beneath a rude and nameless stone he lies,
    To which thy tomb shall guide inquiring eyes.
    Peace to thy gentle shade, and endless rest !
    Blest in thy genius, in thy love too blest ;
    One grateful woman to thy fame supplies
    What a whole thankless land to his denies."

Of this inscription the chief fault is, that it belongs less to Rowe, for whom it was written, than to Dryden, who was buried near him ; and indeed gives very little information concerning either.

To wish *peace to thy shade* is too mythological to be admitted into a Christian temple : the ancient worship has infected almost all our other compositions, and might therefore be contented to spare our epitaphs. Let fiction at least cease with life, and let us be serious over the grave.[288]

VI.

On MRS. CORBET, *who died of a cancer in her breast.*[269]

" Here rests a woman, good without pretence,
  Blest with plain reason, and with sober sense ;
  No conquest she, but o'er herself desir'd ;
  No arts essay'd, but not to be admir'd.
  Passion and pride were to her soul unknown,
  Convinc'd that virtue only is our own.
  So unaffected, so compos'd a mind,
  So firm, yet soft, so strong, yet so refin'd,
  Heaven, as its purest gold, by tortures tried ;
  The saint sustain'd it, but the woman died."

I have always considered this as the most valuable of all Pope's epitaphs : the subject of it is a character not discriminated by any shining or eminent peculiarities ; yet that which really makes, though not the splendour, the felicity of life, and that which every wise man will choose for his final and lasting companion in the languor of age, in the quiet of privacy, when he departs weary and disgusted from the ostentatious, the volatile, and the vain. Of such a character, which the dull overlook, and the gay despise, it was fit that the value should be made known and the dignity established. Domestic virtue, as it is exerted without great occasions, or conspicuous consequences, in an even unnoted tenor, required the genius of Pope to display it in such a manner as might attract regard and enforce reverence. Who can forbear to lament that this amiable woman has no name in the verses?

[288] Johnson has omitted to notice an epitaph, by Pope, actually inscribed on Rowe's monument in Westminster Abbey.

[269] In the north aisle of St. Margaret, Westminster. (See Maitland's 'London,' fol. 1739.)

This epitaph was first printed in D. Lewis's 'Miscellaneous Poems,' 8vo. 1730, p. 89, where it is called "Epitaph on Mrs. Elizabeth Corbett." An attempt has been made to show that it was really written on a Mrs. Cope (a Caryl by birth, and great friend of the poet's), who died in 1728, after an operation described as one of the most terrible ever performed. ('The Athenæum' of 22nd July, 1854.) The operation was for " a cancer in her breast."

If the particular lines of this inscription be examined, it will appear less faulty than the rest. There is scarce one line taken from commonplaces, unless it be that in which *only virtue* is said to be *our own*. I once heard a lady of great beauty and excellence [290] object to the fourth line, that it contained an unnatural and incredible panegyric. Of this let the ladies judge.

VII.

On the Monument of the Hon. Robert Digby, *and of his sister* Mary, *erected by their Father the Lord Digby, in the Church of Sherborne, in Dorsetshire,* 1727.

> " Go! fair example of untainted youth,
> Of modest wisdom, and pacific truth:
> Composed in sufferings, and in joy sedate,
> Good without noise, without pretension great.
> Just of thy word, in every thought sincere,
> Who knew no wish but what the world might hear:
> Of softest manners, unaffected mind,
> Lover of peace, and friend of human kind:
> Go, live! for heaven's eternal year is thine,
> Go, and exalt thy mortal to divine.
>
> And thou, blest maid! attendant on his doom,
> Pensive hast follow'd to the silent tomb,
> Steered the same course to the same quiet shore,
> Not parted long, and now to part no more!
> Go, then, where only bliss sincere is known!
> Go, where to love and to enjoy are one!
> Yet take these tears, Mortality's relief,
> And till we share your joys, forgive our grief:
> These little rites, a stone, a verse receive,
> 'Tis all a father, all a friend can give! "

This epitaph contains of the brother only a general, indiscriminate character, and of the sister tells nothing but that she died. The difficulty in writing epitaphs is to give a particular and appropriate praise. This, however, is not always to be performed, whatever be the diligence or ability of the writer;

---

[290] Mary (or Molly) Aston, daughter of Sir Thomas Aston, Bart. Her sister Margaret was the wife of Gilbert Walmsley, so nobly and affectionately remembered by Johnson in his ' Life of Edmund Smith.' (See this edition of Johnson's ' Lives,' vol. ii. p. 57.)

for the greater part of mankind *have no character at all*, have little that distinguishes them from others equally good or bad, and therefore nothing can be said of them which may not be applied with equal propriety to a thousand more. It is indeed no great panegyric that there is inclosed in this tomb one who was born in one year and died in another; yet many useful and amiable lives have been spent, which yet leave little materials for any other memorial. These are, however, not the proper subjects of poetry; and whenever friendship, or any other motive, obliges a poet to write on such subjects, he must be forgiven if he sometimes wanders in generalities and utters the same praises over different tombs.

The scantiness of human praises can scarcely be made more apparent than by remarking how often Pope has, in the few epitaphs which he composed, found it necessary to borrow from himself. The fourteen epitaphs which he has written comprise about a hundred and forty lines, in which there are more repetitions than will easily be found in all the rest of his works. In the eight lines which make the character of Digby, there is scarce any thought, or word, which may not be found in the other epitaphs.

The ninth line, which is far the strongest and most elegant, is borrowed from Dryden. The conclusion is the same with that on Harcourt, but is here more elegant and better connected.

VIII.

On SIR GODFREY KNELLER. *In Westminster Abbey*, 1723.

" Kneller, by Heaven, and not a master taught,
  Whose Art was nature, and whose pictures thought ;
  Now for two ages, having snatched from fate
  Whate'er was beauteous, or whate'er was great,
  Lies crowned with Princes' honours, Poets' lays,
  Due to his merit, and brave thirst of praise.
    Living, great Nature feared he might outvie
  Her works ; and dying, fears herself may die."

Of this epitaph the first couplet is good, the second not bad, the third is deformed with a broken metaphor, the word *crowned* not being applicable to the *honours* or the *lays*, and the fourth is not only borrowed from the epitaph on Raphael, but of a very harsh construction.

IX.

On GENERAL HENRY WITHERS. *In Westminster Abbey*, 1729.

" Here, Withers, rest! thou bravest, gentlest mind,
　Thy country's friend, but more of human kind.
　O! born to arms! O! worth in youth approved!
　O! soft humanity in age beloved!
　For thee the hardy veteran drops a tear,
　And the gay courtier feels the sigh sincere.

　　Withers, adieu! yet not with thee remove
　Thy martial spirit, or thy social love!
　Amidst corruption, luxury, and rage,
　Still leave some ancient virtues to our age:
　Nor let us say (those English glories gone)
　The last true Briton lies beneath this stone."

The epitaph on Withers affords another instance of common-places, though somewhat diversified by mingled qualities and the peculiarity of a profession.

The second couplet is abrupt, general, and unpleasing; exclamation seldom succeeds in our language; and I think it may be observed that the particle O! used at the beginning of a sentence always offends.

The third couplet is more happy: the value expressed for him, by different sorts of men, raises him to esteem; there is yet something of the common cant of superficial satirists, who suppose that the insincerity of a courtier destroys all his sensations, and that he is equally a dissembler to the living and the dead.

At the third couplet I should wish the epitaph to close, but that I should be unwilling to lose the two next lines, which yet are dearly bought if they cannot be retained without the four that follow them.

X.

On Mr. Elijah Fenton. *At Easthampstead, in Berkshire*, 1730.

" This modest stone, what few vain marbles can,
    May truly say, Here lies an honest man :
    A poet, blest beyond the poet's fate,
    Whom Heaven kept sacred from the Proud and Great :
    Foe to loud praise, and friend to learned ease,
    Content with science in the vale of peace.
    Calmly he looked on either life ; and here
    Saw nothing to regret, or there to fear ;
    From Nature's temperate feast rose satisfied,
    Thanked Heaven that he lived, and that he died."

The first couplet of this epitaph is borrowed from Crashaw.[291]
The four next lines contain a species of praise peculiar, original,
and just.   Here, therefore, the inscription should have ended,
the latter part containing nothing but what is common to every
man who is wise and good.   The character of Fenton was so
amiable, that I cannot forbear to wish for some poet or biographer to display it more fully for the advantage of posterity.   If
he did not stand in the first rank of genius, he may claim a
place in the second ; and, whatever criticism may object to his
writings, censure could find very little to blame in his life.

XI.

On Mr. Gay. *In Westminster Abbey*, 1732.

" Of manners gentle, of affections mild ;
    In wit, a man ; simplicity, a child :
    With native humour tempering virtuous rage,
    Formed to delight at once and lash the age :
    Above temptation, in a low estate,
    And uncorrupted, ev'n among the Great :
    A safe companion, and an easy friend,
    Unblamed through life, lamented in thy end.

---

[291] The modest front of this small floor,
        Believe me, Reader, can say more
        Than many a braver marble can :
        Here lies a truly honest man.

Crashaw: *An Epitaph upon Mr. Ashton, a conformable citizen.*

> These are thy honours ! not that here thy bust
> Is mixed with heroes, or with kings thy dust ;
> But that the Worthy and the Good shall say,
> Striking their pensive bosoms—Here lies GAY."

As Gay was the favourite of our author, this epitaph was probably written with an uncommon degree of attention ; yet it is not more successfully executed than the rest, for it will not always happen that the success of a poet is proportionate to his labour. The same observation may be extended to all works of imagination, which are often influenced by causes wholly out of the performer's power, by hints of which he perceives not the origin, by sudden elevations of mind which he cannot produce in himself, and which sometimes rise when he expects them least.

The two parts of the first line are only echoes of each other ; *gentle manners* and *mild affections*, if they mean anything, must mean the same.

That Gay was a *man in wit* is a very frigid commendation ; to have the wit of a man is not much for a poet. The *wit of man*, and the *simplicity of a child*, make a poor and vulgar contrast, and raise no ideas of excellence, either intellectual or moral.[292]

In the next couplet *rage* is less properly introduced after the mention of *mildness* and *gentleness*, which are made the constituents of his character ; for a man so *mild* and *gentle* to *temper* his *rage*, was not difficult.

The next line is inharmonious in its sound, and mean in its conception ; the opposition is obvious, and the word *lash*, used absolutely and without any modification, is gross and improper.

To be *above temptation* in poverty and *free from corruption among the great*, is indeed such a peculiarity as deserved notice. But to be a *safe companion* is a praise merely negative, arising not from possession of virtue, but the absence of vice, and that one of the most odious.

[292] Pope had Dryden in his eye:

> Her wit was more than man, her innocence a child.
> *On Mrs. Killigrew.*

As little can be added to his character by asserting that he was *lamented in his end.* Every man that dies is, at least by the writer of his epitaph, supposed to be lamented, and therefore this general lamentation does no honour to Gay.

The first eight lines have no grammar; the adjectives are without any substantive, and the epithets without a subject.

The thought in the last line, that Gay is buried in the bosoms of the *worthy* and the *good*, who are distinguished only to lengthen the line, is so dark that few understand it; and so harsh when it is explained, that still fewer approve.

XII.

Intended for SIR ISAAC NEWTON.　*In Westminster Abbey.*

" ISAACUS NEWTONIUS :

Quem Immortalem
Testantur, *Tempus, Naturâ, Cœlum :*
Mortalem
Hoc marmor fatetur.

Nature, and Nature's laws, lay hid in night :
God said, *Let Newton be !* and all was light."

Of this epitaph, short as it is, the faults seem not to be very few. Why part should be Latin and part English, it is not easy to discover. In the Latin the opposition of *Immortalis* and *Mortalis* is a mere sound or a mere quibble; he is not *immortal* in any sense contrary to that in which he is *mortal.*

In the verses the thought is obvious, and the words *night* and *light* are too nearly allied.

XIII.

On EDMUND DUKE OF BUCKINGHAM,[293] *who died in the* 19*th year of his age,*
1735.

" If modest youth, with cool reflection crowned,
　And every opening virtue blooming round,
　Could save a parent's justest pride from fate,
　Or add one patriot to a sinking state ;

---

[293] Only son of John Sheffield, Duke of Buckingham, the subject of one of Johnson's " little Lives." (See vol. ii. p. 189.)

This weeping marble had not asked thy tear,
Or sadly told how many hopes lie here !
The living virtue now had shone approved,
The senate heard him, and his country loved.
Yet softer honours, and less noisy fame,
Attend the shade of gentle Buckingham :
In whom a race, for courage famed and art,
Ends in the milder merit of the heart :
And, chiefs or sages long to Britain given,
Pays the last tribute of a saint to heaven."

This epitaph Mr. Warburton prefers to the rest, but I know
not for what reason. To *crown* with *reflection* is surely a mode
of speech approaching to nonsense. *Opening virtues blooming
round* is something like tautology ; the six following lines are
poor and prosaic. *Art* is in another couplet used for *arts*, that
a rhyme may be had to *heart*. The last six lines are the best,
but not excellent.

The rest of his sepulchral performances hardly deserve the
notice of criticism. The contemptible 'Dialogue' between
HE and SHE should have been suppressed for the author's
sake.

In his last epitaph, 'On Himself,' in which he attempts to be
jocular upon one of the few things that make wise men serious,
he confounds the living man with the dead :

" Under this stone, or under this sill,
    Or under this turf," &c.

When a man is once buried, the question under what he is
buried is easily decided. He forgot that though he wrote the
epitaph in a state of uncertainty, yet it could not be laid over
him till his grave was made. Such is the folly of wit when it is
ill employed.

The world has but little new ; even this wretchedness seems
to have been borrowed from the following tuneless lines :

" Ludovici Ariosti humantur ossa
    Sub hoc marmore, vel sub hac humo, seu
    Sub quicquid voluit benignus hæres
    Sive hærede benignior comes, seu

> Opportunius incidens Viator :
> Nam scire haud potuit futura, sed nec
> Tanti erat vacuum sibi cadaver
> Ut utnam cuperet parare vivens,
> Vivens ista tamen sibi paravit.
> Quæ inscribi voluit suo sepulchro
> Olim siquod haberetis sepulchrum."

Surely Ariosto did not venture to expect that his trifle would have ever had such an illustrious imitator.

> In Pope I cannot read a line
> But with a sigh I wish it mine;
> When he can in one couplet fix
> More sense than I can do in six.
>
> SWIFT: *On Poetry. A Rhapsody.*

No one ever threw so much sense, together with so much ease, into a couplet, as Pope.—SHENSTONE.

JONATHAN SWIFT.

SWIFT.

1667–1745.

Born in Dublin of English Parents — Educated at Dublin and Oxford — Enters the service of Sir William Temple — Becomes acquainted with Stella — Is introduced to William III. — Is left Sir William Temple's Literary Executor — His unpromising appearance as a Poet — Dryden's Criticism on his Odes — Publishes ' The Tale of a Tub ' — Sides with the Whigs under Somers and Godolphin — Seeks the patronage of Halifax — Introduced to Harley and St. John — Sides with the Tories — His Political Influence — Is made Dean of St. Patrick's — His Church Prospects ruined by the Death of Queen Anne — His two Visits to England — Publishes 'Gulliver's Travels' — Supposed to have been married to Stella — Stella and Vanessa — His Services to Ireland — Disappointments and Idiotcy — Death and Burial in St. Patrick's Cathedral — Works and Character.

An account of Dr. Swift has been already collected, with great diligence and acuteness, by Dr. Hawkesworth, according to a scheme which I laid before him in the intimacy of our friendship. I cannot therefore be expected to say much of a life concerning which I had long since communicated my thoughts to a man capable of dignifying his narrations with so much elegance of language and force of sentiment.

Jonathan Swift was, according to an account said to be written by himself,[1] the son of Jonathan Swift, an attorney, and was born at Dublin on St. Andrew's Day, 1667: according to his own report, as delivered by Pope to Spence,[2] he was born at Leicester, the son of a clergyman, who was minister of a parish in Herefordshire.[3] During his life the place of his birth was undetermined. He was contented to be called an Irishman by the Irish ; but would occasionally call himself an Englishman.

[1] This account, the original MS. of which, in his own hand, was presented to the University Library of Dublin by Deane Swift, was first printed in Deane Swift's Essay, &c. 8vo. 1755.
[2] Spence by Singer, p. 161.
[3] Goodrich.

The question may, without much regret, be left in the obscurity in which he delighted to involve it.[4]

Whatever was his birth, his education was Irish. He was sent at the age of six to the school at Kilkenny, and in his fifteenth year (1682) was admitted into the University of Dublin.

In his academical studies he was either not diligent or not happy. It must disappoint every reader's expectation, that when at the usual time he claimed the Bachelorship of Arts, he was found by the examiners too conspicuously deficient for regular admission, and obtained his degree at last by *special favour*;[5] a term used in that university to denote want of merit.

Of this disgrace it may be easily supposed that he was much ashamed, and shame had its proper effect in producing reformation. He resolved from that time to study eight hours a-day, and continued his industry for seven years, with what improvement is sufficiently known. This part of his story well deserves to be remembered ; it may afford useful admonition and powerful encouragement to men whose abilities have been made for a time useless by their passions or pleasures, and who, having lost one part of life in idleness, are tempted to throw away the remainder in despair.

[4] As to my native country, I happened indeed by a perfect accident to be born here; my mother being left here from returning to her house at Leicester; and I was a year old before I was sent to England; and thus I am a Teague, or an Irishman, or what people please, although the best part of my life was in England.—SWIFT to Mr. Grant, Dublin, March 23, 1733-4 (Scott, xviii. 203).

I loved my Lord your father better than any other man in the world, although I had no obligation to him on the score of preferment, having been driven to this wretched kingdom, to which I was almost a stranger, by his want of power to keep me in what I ought to call my own country, although I happened to be dropped here, and was a year old before I left it; and to my sorrow did not die before I came back to it again.—SWIFT to Edward Earl of Oxford, June 14, 1737. (Scott, xix. 76.)

In 'An Examination of certain Abuses, Corruptions, and Enormities in the City of Dublin,' written in 1732, Swift observes that he had always been watchful over the interests of the city of Dublin—"that renowned city where (*absit invidia*) I had the honour to draw my first breath."—(*Swift's Works by Scott*, 2nd ed. vii. 337.)

His mother was Abigail Erick, of a good family in Leicestershire. She died at Leicester, 24th April, 1710, and is affectionately remembered by Swift. (*Scott*, xv. 355, 2nd ed.)

[5] *Speciali gratia* is the entry in the Register.

In this course of daily application he continued three years longer at Dublin; and in this time, if the observation of an old companion may be trusted, he drew the first sketch of his 'Tale of a Tub.' [6]

When he was about one-and-twenty (1688), being by the death of Godwin Swift his uncle, who had supported him, left without subsistence, he went to consult his mother, who then lived at Leicester, about the future course of his life, and by her direction solicited the advice and patronage of Sir William Temple, who had married one of Mrs. Swift's relations, and whose father Sir John Temple, Master of the Rolls in Ireland, had lived in great familiarity of friendship with Godwin Swift, by whom Jonathan had been to that time maintained.

Temple received with sufficient kindness the nephew of his father's friend, with whom he was, when they conversed together, so much pleased, that he detained him two years in his house. Here [7] he became known to King William, who sometimes visited Temple when he was disabled by the gout, and, being attended by Swift in the garden, showed him how to cut asparagus in the Dutch way. [8]

King William's notions were all military; and he expressed his kindness to Swift by offering to make him a captain of horse. [9]

When Temple removed to Moor Park, [10] he took Swift with him; and when he was consulted by the Earl of Portland about the expedience of complying with a bill then depending for making parliaments triennial, against which King William was strongly prejudiced, after having in vain tried to show the Earl that the proposal involved nothing dangerous to royal power, he sent Swift for the same purpose to the King. Swift, who pro-

[6] This fact Swift's companion, Mr. Waryng, often mentioned to Mr. Whiteway.—SCOTT.

[7] At Sheen, near Richmond, in Surrey.

[8] In their evening conversations, among other bagatelles, the King, as I have heard from the Doctor's own mouth, offered to make him a captain of horse, and gave him instructions, so great was the freedom of their conversation, how to cut asparagus (a vegetable which his Majesty was extremely fond of) in the Dutch manner.—DEANE SWIFT: *Essay*, 8vo. 1755, p. 108.

[9] Orrery's 'Remarks,' 12mo. 1753, p. 13.

[10] Moor Park, near Farnham, in Surrey.

bably was proud of his employment, and went with all the confidence of a young man, found his arguments, and his art of displaying them, made totally ineffectual by the predetermination of the King; and used to mention this disappointment as his first antidote against vanity.

Before he left Ireland he contracted a disorder, as he thought, by eating too much fruit. The original of diseases is commonly obscure. Almost every boy eats as much fruit as he can get, without any great inconvenience. The disease of Swift was giddiness with deafness, which attacked him from time to time, began very early, pursued him through life, and at last sent him to the grave, deprived of reason.

Being much oppressed at Moor Park by this grievous malady, he was advised to try his native air, and went to Ireland; but, finding no benefit, returned to Sir William, at whose house he continued his studies, and is known to have read, among other books, 'Cyprian' and 'Irenæus.' He thought exercise of great necessity, and used to run half a mile up and down a hill every two hours.[11]

[11] The original of the following letter is in the rich collection of John Young, Esq., of Vanbrugh Fields, Blackheath, and is now published for the first time by his kind permission:—

SIR WILLIAM TEMPLE TO SIR ROBERT SOUTHWELL.

S^r,—I was lately acquainted by Mr Hanbury with the favor of y^r remembrance and inquirys after mee and my family, by w^h wee are all obliged, and returne you all our wishes for y^r good health and good fortunes wch way soever you turne them. This afternoon I hear, though by a common hande, that you are going over into Irelande, Secretary of State for that Kingdome, upon wch I venture to make you the offer of a servant, in case you may have occasion for such a one as this bearer. Hee was borne and bred there (though of a good family in Herefordshire), was neer seven years in the colledge of Dublyn, and ready to take his degree of Master of Arts, when hee was forced away by the desertion of that colledge upon the calamitys of the country. Since that time hee has lived in my house, read to mee, writt for mee, and kept all accounts as farr as my small occasions required. Hee has latine and greek, some french, writes a very good and current hand, is very honest and diligent, and has good friends, though they have for the present lost their fortunes, in Irelande, and his whole family having been long known to mee obliged mee thus farr to take care of him. If you please to accept him into your service, either as a Gentleman to waite on you, or as Clarke to write under you, and either to use him so if you like his service, or upon any establishment of the Colledge, to recommend him to a fellowship there, wch hee

It is easy to imagine that the mode in which his first degree was conferred left him no great fondness for the University of Dublin, and therefore he resolved to become a Master of Arts at Oxford. In the testimonial which he produced, the words of disgrace were omitted; and he took his Master's degree (July 5, 1692) with such reception and regard as fully contented him.

While he lived with Temple, he used to pay his mother at Leicester a yearly visit. He travelled on foot, unless some violence of weather drove him into a waggon, and at night he would go to a penny lodging, where he purchased clean sheets for sixpence. This practice Lord Orrery imputes to his innate love of grossness and vulgarity : [12] some may ascribe it to his desire of surveying human life through all its varieties; and others, perhaps with equal probability, to a passion which seems to have been deep fixed in his heart, the love of a shilling. [13]

In time he began to think that his attendance at Moor Park deserved some other recompence than the pleasure, however mingled with improvement, of Temple's conversation; [14] and grew so impatient, that (1694) he went away in discontent.

Temple, conscious of having given reason for complaint, is said to have made him Deputy Master of the Rolls in Ireland;

has a just pretence to, I shall acknowledge it as a great obligation to mee, as well as to him, and endeavour to deserve it by the constancy of my being alwaies,

S[r], y[r] most faithfull and most humble servant,

W. TEMPLE,

Moor Parke, neer Farnham, May 29, 1690.

    Addressed
       For S[r] Robert Southwell.

[12] Orrery's ' Remarks,' ed. 1753, p. 21.

[13] If he walked an hour or two on any occasion, instead of taking a coach or a chair, he then cried out that he had earned a shilling or eighteenpence.— DELANY, p. 13.

I persuade myself that it is shilling weather as seldom as possible; and have found out that there are few court visits that are worth a shilling.—GAY to Swift, March 20, 1730-1.

[14] I am not to take orders till the King [William III.] gives me a prebend, and Sir William Temple, though he promises me the certainty of it, yet is less forward than I could wish, because (I suppose) he believes I shall leave him, and, upon some accounts, he thinks me a little necessary to him.—SWIFT to Mr. William Swift (Moor Park, Nov. 29, 1692). *Scott*, xv. 257.

which, according to his kinsman's[15] account, was an office which he knew him not able to discharge. Swift therefore resolved to enter into the Church, in which he had at first no higher hopes than of the chaplainship to the Factory at Lisbon ; but being recommended to Lord Capel [then Lord Lieutenant of Ireland], he obtained the prebend of Kilroot in Connor, of about a hundred pounds a year.

But the infirmities of Temple made a companion like Swift so necessary, that he invited him back, with a promise to procure him English preferment in exchange for the prebend, which he desired him to resign. With this request Swift complied, having perhaps equally repented their separation, and they lived on together with mutual satisfaction ; and, in the four years that passed between his return and Temple's death, it is probable that he wrote 'The Tale of a Tub' and 'The Battle of the Books.'[16]

Swift began early to think, or to hope, that he was a poet, and wrote Pindaric Odes to Temple, to the King, and to the Athenian Society, a knot of obscure men, who published a periodical pamphlet of answers to questions sent, or supposed to be sent, by letters. I have been told that Dryden, having perused these verses, said, "Cousin Swift, you will never be a poet ;" and that this denunciation was the motive of Swift's perpetual malevolence to Dryden.[17]

In 1699 Temple died and left a legacy with his manuscripts to Swift, for whom he had obtained from King William a pro-

[15] Deane Swift in his Essay, 8vo. 1755, Appendix, p. 49.

[16] Mr. Temple, nephew to Sir William Temple, and brother to Lord Palmerston, who lately died at Bath, declared to a friend of mine, that Sir William hired Swift, at his first entrance into the world, to read to him, and sometimes to be his amanuensis, at the rate of 20l. a year and his board, which was then high preferment to him; but that Sir William never favoured him with his conversation, because of his ill qualities, nor allowed him to sit down at table with him.—RICHARDSON (the Novelist) to Lady Bradshaigh, April 22, 1752.

[17] " I remember to have heard my father say that Mr. Elijah Fenton, who was his intimate friend, and had been his master, informed him that Dryden, upon seeing some of Swift's earliest verses, said to him, 'Young man, you will never be a poet :' and that this was the cause of Swift's rooted aversion to Dryden."—JOS. WARTON: Essay on Pope, ii. 312. (See also Note 5, in Malone's Life of Dryden, p. 241.)

mise of the first prebend that should be vacant at Westminster or Canterbury.

That this promise might not be forgotten, Swift dedicated to the King the posthumous works with which he was intrusted; but neither the dedication nor tenderness for the man whom he once had treated with confidence and fondness revived in King William the remembrance of his promise. Swift awhile attended the Court, but soon found his solicitations hopeless.

He was then invited by the Earl of Berkeley [18] to accompany him into Ireland as his private secretary; but after having done the business till their arrival at Dublin, he then found that one Bushe had persuaded the Earl that a clergyman was not a proper secretary, and had obtained the office for himself. In a man like Swift such circumvention and inconstancy must have excited violent indignation.

But he had yet more to suffer. Lord Berkeley had the disposal of the deanery of Derry, and Swift expected to obtain it, but by the secretary's influence, supposed to have been secured by a bribe, it was bestowed on somebody else; and Swift was dismissed with the livings of Laracor and Rathbeggan, in the diocese of Meath, which together did not equal half the value of the deanery. [19]

At Laracor he increased the parochial duty by reading prayers on Wednesdays and Fridays, and performed all the offices of his profession with great decency and exactness.

Soon after his settlement at Laracor he invited to Ireland the unfortunate Stella, [20] a young woman whose name was Johnson,

---

[18] Newly appointed one of the Lords Justices of Ireland. He died in 1710. One of his daughters, Lady Betty Germaine, was an able and favourite correspondent of Swift's.

[19] Laracor is about twenty miles from Dublin, in the neighbourhood of Trim. "The first of these," says Lord Orrery, p. 20, "was worth about two hundred, and the latter about sixty pounds a year, and they were the only church preferments he enjoyed till he was appointed Dean of St. Patrick's in the year 1713." It was at Laracor that the willows were of which we read so often in the Journal to Stella.

[20] She [Esther Johnson] was born at Richmond in Surrey, on the 13th day of March, in the year 1681. Her father was a younger brother of a good family in Nottinghamshire, her mother of a lower degree; and indeed she

the daughter of the steward of Sir William Temple, who, in
consideration of her father's virtues, left her a thousand pounds.
With her came Mrs. Dingley,[21] whose whole fortune was twenty-
seven pounds a year for her life.   With these ladies he passed
his hours of relaxation, and to them he opened his bosom ; but
they never resided in the same house, nor did he see either
without a witness.   They lived at the Parsonage when Swift
was away ; and when he returned, removed to a lodging or to
the house of a neighbouring clergyman.

Swift was not one of those minds which amaze the world
with early pregnancy : his first work, except his few poetical
Essays, was the 'Dissensions in Athens and Rome,' published
(1701) in his thirty-fourth year.   After its appearance, paying
a visit to some bishop, he heard mention made of the new
pamphlet that Burnet had written, replete with political knowledge.   When he seemed to doubt Burnet's right to the work,
he was told by the Bishop that he was " a young man ;" and
still persisting to doubt, that he was " a very positive young
man."

Three years afterwards (1704) was published ' The Tale of
a Tub :' of this book charity may be persuaded to think that
it might be written by a man of a peculiar character, without
ill intention ; but it is certainly of dangerous example.   That
Swift was its author, though it be universally believed, was
never owned by himself, nor very well proved by any evidence ;
but no other claimant can be produced, and he did not deny
it when Archbishop Sharp and the Duchess of Somerset, by
showing it to the Queen, debarred him from a bishopric.[22]

had little to boast of her birth. I knew her from six years old, and had some
share in her education, &c.—SWIFT: *Works by Scott*, ix. 281, sec. ed.

Her mother is described in Stella's will as " my dear mother, Mrs. Bridget
Mose, of Farnham in Surrey;" and her only sister as " my dear sister, Ann
Johnson *alias* Filby."   Swift disliked Stella's mother.   Ann Johnson was bap-
tized at Richmond in Surrey, in 1683.

[21] Rebecca Dingley, who died unmarried in July, 1743.

[22] Lord Bolingbroke told me last Friday that he would reconcile you to
Lady Somerset, and then it would be easy to set you right with the Queen;
and that you should be made easy here and never go over.—BARBER to Swift,
Aug. 3, 1714.   "Dr.

When this wild work first raised the attention of the public, Sacheverell, meeting Smalridge, tried to flatter him, seeming to think him the author ; but Smalridge answered with indignation, " Not all that you and I have in the world, nor all that ever we shall have, should hire me to write ' The Tale of a Tub.' " [23]

The digressions relating to Wotton and Bentley must be confessed to discover want of knowledge, or want of integrity ; he did not understand the two controversies, or he willingly misrepresented them. But wit can stand its ground against truth only a little while. The honours due to learning have been justly distributed by the decision of posterity.

' The Battle of the Books ' is so like the ' Combat des Livres,' which the same question concerning the ancients and moderns had produced in France, that the improbability of such a coincidence of thoughts without communication is not, in my opinion, balanced by the anonymous protestation [24] prefixed, in which all knowledge of the French book is peremptorily disowned.

For some time after Swift was probably employed in solitary

" Dr. Swift was always persuaded that the Archbishop of York [Sharp] had made impressions on Queen Anne to his disadvantage, and by that means had obstructed his preferment in England; and he has hinted this in his 'Apology for the Tale of the Tub,' and in other parts of his works; and yet my Lord Bolingbroke, who must have been well informed of this particular, told me that he had been assured by the Queen herself that she never had received any unfavourable character of Dr. Swift, nor had the Archbishop, or any other person, endeavoured to lessen him in her esteem. My Lord Bolingbroke added, that this tale was invented by the Earl of Oxford to deceive Swift, and make him contented with his Deanery in Ireland; which, although his native country, he always looked on as a place of banishment. If Lord Bolingbroke had hated the Earl of Oxford less, I should have been readily inclined to believe him."—DR. KING: *Anecdotes*, p. 60.

Swift was never introduced to Queen Anne.—SCOTT, xv. 403.

[23] I am of your opinion as to 'The Tale of a Tub.' I am not alone in the opinion, as you are there; but I am pretty near it, having but very few on my side; but those few are worth a million. However, I have never spoke my sentiments, not caring to contradict a multitude. Bottom admires it, and cannot bear my saying I confess I was diverted with several passages when I read it, but I should not care to read it again.—CONGREVE to Keally, Oct. 28, 1704. (Berkeley's ' Literary Relics,' 8vo., 1789, p. 340.)

[24] The *anonymous* protestation was, however, the work of Swift.

study, gaining the qualifications requisite for future eminence.
How often he visited England, and with what diligence he
attended his parishes, I know not. It was not till about four
years afterwards that he became a professed author ; and then
one year (1708) produced 'The Sentiments of a Church of
England Man,' the ridicule of astrology, under the name of
' Bickerstaff,' the ' Argument against Abolishing Christianity,'
and the defence of the ' Sacramental Test.'

' The Sentiments of a Church of England Man ' is written
with great coolness, moderation, ease, and perspicuity. The
'Argument against Abolishing Christianity' is a very happy
and judicious irony. One passage in it deserves to be
selected.

" If Christianity were once abolished, how could the freethinkers, the strong reasoners, and the men of profound learning be able to find another subject so calculated, in all points,
whereon to display their abilities? What wonderful productions of wit should we be deprived of from those whose genius
by continual practice has been wholly turned upon raillery and
invectives against religion, and would therefore never be able
to shine, or distinguish themselves, upon any other subject ! We
are daily complaining of the great decline of wit among us, and
would we take away the greatest, perhaps the only topic we
have left ? Who would ever have suspected Asgill for a wit, or
Toland for a philosopher, if the inexhaustible stock of Christianity
had not been at hand to provide them with materials ? What
other subject, through all art or nature, could have produced
Tindal for a profound author, or furnished him with readers?
It is the wise choice of the subject that alone adorns and distinguishes the writer ; for had a hundred such pens as these
been employed on the side of religion, they would have immediately sunk into silence and oblivion."

The reasonableness of a *test* is not hard to be proved ; but
perhaps it must be allowed that the proper test has not been
chosen.

The attention paid to the papers published under the name
of ' Bickerstaff' induced Steele, when he projected ' The

Tatler,' to assume an appellation which had already gained possession of the reader's notice.

In the year following [1709] he wrote a 'Project for the Advancement of Religion,' addressed to Lady Berkeley,[25] by whose kindness it is not unlikely that he was advanced to his benefices. To this project, which is formed with great purity of intention, and displayed with sprightliness and elegance, it can only be objected that, like many projects, it is, if not generally impracticable, yet evidently hopeless, as it supposes more zeal, concord, and perseverance than a view of mankind gives reason for expecting.

He wrote likewise this year [1709] a 'Vindication of Bickerstaff,' and an explanation of an 'Ancient Prophecy,' part written after the facts, and the rest never completed, but well planned to excite amazement.

Soon after began the busy and important part of Swift's life. He was employed (1710) by the primate of Ireland [26] to solicit the Queen for a remission of the First Fruits and Twentieth parts to the Irish clergy. With this purpose he had recourse to Mr. Harley, to whom he was mentioned as a man neglected and oppressed by the last ministry because he had refused to co-operate with some of their schemes. What he had refused has never been told ; what he had suffered was, I suppose, the exclusion from a bishopric by the remonstrances of Sharp, whom he describes as " the harmless tool of others' hate," and whom he represents as afterwards " suing for pardon." [27]

Harley's designs and situation were such as made him glad of an auxiliary so well qualified for his service ; he therefore soon admitted him to familiarity—whether ever to confidence some have made a doubt ; but it would have been difficult to excite his zeal without persuading him that he was trusted, and not very easy to delude him by false persuasions.

He was certainly admitted to those meetings in which the

[25] Daughter of Noel, Earl of Gainsborough, and wife of Charles, Lord Berkeley, before referred to.

[26] Dr. Narcissus Marsh.

[27] 'The Author, upon himself.' ('Works,' by Scott, xii. 317 ; and to Delany, p. 271.)

first hints and original plan of action are supposed to have been formed, and was one of the sixteen ministers, or agents of the ministry, who met weekly at each other's houses, and were united by the name of 'Brother.' [28]

Being not immediately considered as an obdurate Tory, he conversed indiscriminately with all the wits, and was yet the friend of Steele, who, in 'The Tatler,' which began in April, 1709, confesses the advantage of his conversation, and mentions something contributed by him to his paper. But he was now immerging into political controversy; for the year 1710 produced 'The Examiner,' of which Swift wrote thirty-three papers. In argument he may be allowed to have the advantage; for where a wide system of conduct, and the whole of a public character, is laid open to inquiry, the accuser, having the choice of facts, must be very unskilful if he does not prevail; but with regard to wit, I am afraid none of Swift's papers will be found equal to those by which Addison opposed him.[29]

He wrote in the year 1711 a 'Letter to the October Club,' a number of Tory gentlemen sent from the country to Parliament, who formed themselves into a club to the number of about a hundred, and met to animate the zeal and raise the expectations of each other. They thought, with great reason, that the ministers were losing opportunities; that sufficient use was not made of the ardour of the nation; they called loudly for more changes and stronger efforts; and demanded the punishment of part, and the dismission of the rest, of those whom they considered as public robbers.

Their eagerness was not gratified by the Queen or by Harley. The Queen was probably slow because she was afraid, and Harley was slow because he was doubtful: he was a Tory only by necessity, or for convenience; and, when he had power in

[28] For the *sixteen*, see note 35, vol. ii. p. 216. They met oftener at taverns than at each other's houses. The number was afterwards enlarged.

[29] Here is an error already referred to (see vol. ii. p. 142). Addison had retired before Swift began to write. Swift's first 'Examiner' was " No. XIII., Thursday, Nov. 2, 1710," and Addison's last 'Whig Examiner' is dated Thursday, Oct. 12, 1710—exactly three weeks before Swift commenced writing in 'The Examiner.'

his hands, had no settled purpose for which he should employ it ; forced to gratify to a certain degree the Tories who supported him, but unwilling to make his reconcilement to the Whigs utterly desperate, he corresponded at once with the two expectants of the Crown, and kept, as has been observed, the succession undetermined. Not knowing what to do, he did nothing ; and, with the fate of a double dealer, at last he lost his power, but kept his enemies.

Swift seems to have concurred in opinion with the 'October Club,' but it was not in his power to quicken the tardiness of Harley, whom he stimulated as much as he could, but with little effect. He that knows not whither to go is in no haste to move. Harley, who was perhaps not quick by nature, became yet more slow by irresolution ; and was content to hear that dilatoriness lamented as natural, which he applauded in himself as politic.

Without the Tories, however, nothing could be done ; and as they were not to be gratified they must be appeased, and the conduct of the minister, if it could not be vindicated, was to be plausibly excused.

Early in the next year [1712] he published a 'Proposal for Correcting, Improving, and Ascertaining the English Tongue,' in a letter to the Earl of Oxford, written without much knowledge of the general nature of language, and without any accurate inquiry into the history of other tongues. The certainty and stability which, contrary to all experience, he thinks attainable, he proposes to secure by instituting an academy ; the decrees of which every man would have been willing, and many would have been proud to disobey, and which, being renewed by successive elections, would in a short time have differed from itself.[30]

Swift now attained the zenith of his political importance : he published (1712) 'The Conduct of the Allies,' ten days before the parliament assembled. The purpose was to persuade the nation to a peace, and never had any writer more success. The

[30] This was the only work of his many writings to which Swift put his name.

people, who had been amused with bonfires and triumphal pro-
cessions, and looked with idolatry on the General [Marlborough]
and his friends, and who, as they thought, had made England
the arbitress of nations, were confounded between shame and
rage when they found that " mines had been exhausted and
millions destroyed " to secure the Dutch or aggrandize the
Emperor, without any advantage to ourselves ; that we had been
bribing our neighbours to fight their own quarrel, and that
amongst our enemies we might number our allies.

That is now no longer doubted, of which the nation was then
first informed, that the war was unnecessarily protracted to fill
the pockets of Marlborough ; and that it would have been continued without end if he could have continued his annual
plunder.   But Swift, I suppose, did not yet know what he has
since written, that a commission was drawn which would have
appointed him General for life, had it not become ineffectual by
the resolution of Lord Cowper, who refused the seal.[31]

" Whatever is received," say the schools, " is received in
proportion to the recipient."   The power of a political treatise
depends much upon the disposition of the people ; the nation
was then combustible, and a spark set it on fire.   It is boasted,
that between November and January eleven thousand were
sold ; a great number at that time, when we were not yet a
nation of readers.   To its propagation certainly no agency of
power or influence was wanting.   It furnished arguments for
conversation, speeches for debate, and materials for parliamentary resolutions.

Yet surely whoever surveys this wonder-working pamphlet
with cool perusal, will confess that its efficacy was supplied by
the passions of its readers ; that it operates by the mere weight
of facts, with very little assistance from the hand that produced
them.

This year (1712) he published his ' Reflections on the Barrier
Treaty,' which carries on the design of his ' Conduct of the
Allies,' and shows how little regard in that negotiation had

[31] See vol. ii. p. 137, note 53.

been shown to the interest of England, and how much of the conquered country had been demanded by the Dutch.

This was followed by 'Remarks on the Bishop of Sarum's Introduction to his Third Volume of the History of the Reformation;' a pamphlet which Burnet published as an alarm, to warn the nation of the approach of Popery. Swift, who seems to have disliked the Bishop with something more than political aversion, treats him like one on whom he is glad of an opportunity to insult.

Swift being now [1712-14] the declared favourite and supposed confidant of the Tory ministry, was treated by all that depended on the Court with the respect which dependents know how to pay. He soon began to feel part of the misery of greatness; he that could say that he knew him, considered himself as having fortune in his power. Commissions, solicitations, remonstrances, crowded about him; he was expected to do every man's business, to procure employment for one, and to retain it for another. In assisting those who addressed him, he represents himself as sufficiently diligent; and desires to have others believe, what he probably believed himself, that by his interposition many Whigs of merit, and among them Addison and Congreve, were continued in their places.[32] But every man of known influence has so many petitions which he cannot grant, that he must necessarily offend more than he gratifies, because the preference given to one affords all the rest reason for complaint. " When I give away a place," said Louis XIV., " I make a hundred discontented, and one ungrateful."

Much has been said of the equality and independence which he preserved in his conversation with the ministers, of the frankness of his remonstrances, and the familiarity of his friendship. In accounts of this kind a few single incidents are set against the general tenor of behaviour. No man, however, can pay a more servile tribute to the great than by suffering his liberty in their presence to aggrandize him in his own esteem. Between different ranks of the community there is

[32] 'History of the Four Last Years.'—*Swift's Works, by Scott*, v. 15, second edition.

necessarily some distance : he who is called by his superior to
pass the interval, may properly accept the invitation ; but petulance and obtrusion are rarely produced by magnanimity, nor
have often any nobler cause than the pride of importance and
the malice of inferiority.   He who knows himself necessary may
set, while that necessity lasts, a high value upon himself ; as, in
a lower condition, a servant eminently skilful may be saucy ;
but he is saucy only because he is servile.   Swift appears to
have preserved the kindness of the great when they wanted him
no longer ; and therefore it must be allowed that the childish
freedom, to which he seems enough inclined, was overpowered
by his better qualities.

His disinterestedness has been likewise mentioned ; a strain
of heroism which would have been in his condition romantic
and superfluous.   Ecclesiastical benefices, when they become
vacant, must be given away ; and the friends of power may, if
there be no inherent disqualification, reasonably expect them.
Swift accepted (April 1713) the deanery of St. Patrick, the
best preferment that his friends could venture to give him.
That ministry was in a great degree supported by the clergy,
who were not yet reconciled to the author of ' The Tale of a
Tub,' and would not, without much discontent and indignation,
have borne to see him installed in an English cathedral.[33]

He refused, indeed, fifty pounds from Lord Oxford ; but he
accepted afterwards a draft of a thousand upon the Exchequer, which was intercepted by the Queen's death, and which
he resigned, as he says himself, " *multa gemens*, with many a
groan." [34]

[33] I have had two or three projects on foot for making such an establishment
here as might tempt you to quit Ireland.   One of them would have succeeded,
&c. . . . Another of them cannot take place without the consent of those who
would rather have you a Dean in Ireland than a parish priest in England, and
who are glad to keep you where your sincere friend, my late Lord Oxford, sent
you.—BOLINGBROKE to Swift, Aug. 2, 1731.

What Swift sought from Lord Oxford was the Deanery of Wells. (See
' Journal to Stella,' 21st March, 1711–12, 23rd April, 1713 ; also Ballad in
Scott's ' Swift,' ii. 72.)

[34] Tell him [Archdeacon Wall] that I never asked for my 1000*l.*, which he
hears I have got, though I mentioned it to the Princess [afterwards Queen

In the midst of his power and his politics [1710-13] he kept a Journal of his visits, his walks, his interviews with ministers, and quarrels with his servant, and transmitted it to Mrs. Johnson and Mrs. Dingley, to whom he knew that whatever befel him was interesting, and no accounts could be too minute. Whether these diurnal trifles were properly exposed to eyes which had never received any pleasure from the presence of the Dean, may be reasonably doubted ; [35] they have, however, some odd attraction ; the reader, finding frequent mention of names which he has been used to consider as important, goes on in hope of information ; and, as there is nothing to fatigue attention, if he is disappointed he can hardly complain. It is easy to perceive from every page that though ambition pressed Swift into a life of bustle, the wish for a life of ease was always returning.

He went [June, 1713] to take possession of his deanery as soon as he had obtained it ; but he was not suffered to stay in Ireland more than a fortnight before he was recalled to England, that he might reconcile Lord Oxford and Lord Bolingbroke, who began to look on one another with malevolence, which every day increased, and which Bolingbroke appeared to retain in his last years.[36]

Swift contrived an interview, from which they both departed discontented : he procured a second, which only convinced him that the feud was irreconcileable ; he told them his opinion, that all was lost.   This denunciation was contradicted by Oxford ; but Bolingbroke whispered that he was right.[37]

Caroline] the last time I saw her ; but I bid her tell Walpole I scorned to ask him for it.—SWIFT to Sheridan, London, July 8, 1726.

[35] The 'Journal to Stella' was first published in 1766. Swift, it appears, had given it to his friend Dr. Lyons, from whom it was obtained with other papers by Mr. Thomas Wilkes, of Dublin, and sold to the booksellers. This characteristic Journal has been edited in the most slovenly manner.

[36] And of which he has left many striking proofs in his letters to Swift, who retained to the last his partiality for Lord Oxford. " He distinguished and chose me above all other men," says Swift, " while he was great, and his letter to me the t'other day was the most moving imaginable."— *To Vanessa*, Aug. 1, 1714.   (Scott, xix. 340.)

[37] In May before the Queen died, I had my last meeting with them at my Lord Masham's.   He left us together, and therefore I spoke very freely to them

Before this violent dissension had shattered the ministry,
Swift had published, in the beginning of the year 1714, ' The
Public Spirit of the Whigs,' in answer to 'The Crisis,' a pamphlet
for which Steele was expelled from the House of Commons.
Swift was now so far alienated from Steele as to think him no
longer entitled to decency, and therefore treats him sometimes
with contempt, and sometimes with abhorrence.[38]

In this pamphlet the Scotch were mentioned in terms so pro-
voking to that irritable nation, that, resolving " not to be
offended with impunity," the Scotch Lords in a body demanded an audience of the Queen, and solicited reparation. A
proclamation was issued, in which three hundred pounds was
offered for discovery of the author. From this storm he was,
as he relates, " secured by a sleight;" of what kind, or by
whose prudence, is not known ; and such was the increase of
his reputation, that the Scottish " Nation applied again that he
would be their friend."

He was become so formidable to the Whigs, that his familiarity with the ministers was clamoured at in Parliament, particularly by two men afterwards of great note, Aislabie and
Walpole.

But, by the disunion of his great friends, his importance and
designs were now at an end ; and seeing his services at last
useless, he retired about June (1714) into Berkshire,[39] where,
in the house of a friend, he wrote what was then suppressed,

both, and told them " I would retire, for I found all was gone." Lord Bolingbroke whispered me, " I was in the right." Your father said, " All would do
well." I told him that I would go to Oxford on Monday, since I found it was
impossible to be of any use. I took coach to Oxford on Monday; went to a
friend [at Letcombe] in Berkshire ; there staid until the Queen's death, and
then to my station here, where I staid twelve years [1714–26], and never
saw my Lord your father afterwards.—SWIFT to Edward Earl of Oxford, June
14, 1737.

I have seen in Mr. Croker's hands ' the comical account' of the visit to Letcombe, made by Pope and Parnell, and described by Pope to Arbuthnot in the
manner of a news-letter. This unpublished letter, in Pope's best vein, is
alluded to in Arbuthnot's letter to Swift of July 17, 1714.

[38] Mr. Steele might have been safe enough, if his continually repeated indis-
cretions, and a zeal mingled with scurrilities, had not forfeited all title to
lenity.—SWIFT: *Four Last Years* (Works by Scott, v. 16, second edition).

[39] To Letcombe, in Berkshire, the living of the Rev. Mr. Gery.

but has since appeared under the title of ' Free Thoughts on the present State of Affairs.'

While he was waiting in his retirement for events which time or chance might bring to pass, the death of the Queen [1 Aug., 1714] broke down at once the whole system of Tory politics; and nothing remained but to withdraw from the implacability of triumphant Whiggism, and shelter himself in unenvied obscurity.

The accounts of his reception in Ireland, given by Lord Orrery and Dr. Delany,[40] are so different, that the credit of the writers, both undoubtedly veracious, cannot be saved but by supposing, what I think is true, that they speak of different times.   When Delany says that he was received with respect, he means for the first fortnight, when he came to take legal possession ; and when Lord Orrery tells that he was pelted by the populace, he is to be understood of the time when, after the Queen's death, he became a settled resident.

The Archbishop of Dublin[41] gave him at first some disturbance in the exercise of his jurisdiction ; but it was soon discovered that between prudence and integrity he was seldom in the wrong ; and that, when he was right, his spirit did not easily yield to opposition.[42]

Having so lately quitted the tumults of a party and the intrigues of a court, they still kept his thoughts in agitation, as the sea fluctuates a while when the storm has ceased.   He therefore filled his hours with some historical attempts, relating to the " Change of the Ministers," and " the Conduct of the Ministry."   He likewise is said to have written a ' History of the Four last Years of Queen Anne,' which he began in her lifetime, and afterwards laboured with great attention, but never published.   It was after his death in the hands of Lord Orrery and Dr. King.[43]   A book under that title was published [1758], with Swift's name, by Dr. Lucas ; of which I can only

<hr />

[40] Delany's ' Observations,' 8vo., 1754, p. 87.
[41] Archbishop King.   He was rather troublesome to Swift.
[42] Delany, p. 88.
[43] Author of ' The Toast,' and better still, of a volume of ' Anecdotes.'

say, that it seemed by no means to correspond with the notions
that I had formed of it from a conversation which I once heard
between the Earl of Orrery and old Mr. Lewis.[44]

Swift now, much against his will, commenced Irishman for
life, and was to contrive how he might be best accommodated
in a country where he considered himself as in a state of exile.
It seems that his first recourse was to piety. The thoughts of
death rushed upon him at this time with such incessant impor-
tunity, that they took possession of his mind, when he first
waked, for many years together.

He opened his house by a public table two days a week, and
found his entertainments gradually frequented by more and
more visitants of learning among the men, and of elegance
among the women. Mrs. Johnson had left the country and
lived in lodgings not far from the deanery. On his public days
she regulated the table, but appeared at it as a mere guest, like
other ladies.[45]

On other days he often dined, at a stated price, with Mr.
Worrall, a clergyman of his cathedral, whose house was recommended by the peculiar neatness and pleasantry of his wife.[46]
To this frugal mode of living he was first disposed by care to
pay some debts which he had contracted, and he continued it
for the pleasure of accumulating money. His avarice, however,
was not suffered to obstruct the claims of his dignity; he was
served in plate, and used to say that he was the poorest gentleman in Ireland that eat upon plate, and the richest that lived
without a coach.

How he spent the rest of his time, and how he employed his
hours of study, has been inquired with hopeless curiosity. For
who can give an account of another's studies? Swift was not
likely to admit any to his privacies, or to impart a minute
account of his business or his leisure.

[44] Erasmus Lewis.

[45] Deane Swift's 'Essay,' 8vo. 1755, p. 91.

[46] Delany's 'Observations,' 8vo. 1754, p. 91. Mrs. Worrall was with Swift's
mother at the period of her death. (See Scott's 'Swift,' xv. 355.) Worrall
left part of his money to public charities, and to Swift's Hospital in particular.
(Delany, p. 92.)

Soon after (1716), in his forty-ninth year, he was privately married to Mrs. Johnson, by Dr. Ashe, Bishop of Clogher, as Dr. Madden [47] told me, in the garden. The marriage made no change in their mode of life ; they lived in different houses, as before ; nor did she ever lodge in the deanery but when Swift was seized with a fit of giddiness. " It would be difficult," says Lord Orrery, " to prove that they were ever afterwards together without a third person." [48]

The Dean of St. Patrick's lived in a private manner, known and regarded only by his friends, till, about the year 1720, he, by a pamphlet, recommended to the Irish the use, and consequently the improvement, of their manufacture. For a man to use the productions of his own labour is surely a natural right, and to like best what he makes himself is a natural passion. But to excite this passion, and enforce this right, appeared so criminal to those who had an interest in the English trade, that the printer was imprisoned ; and, as Hawkesworth justly observes, the attention of the public being by this outrageous resentment turned upon the proposal, the author was by consequence made popular.

In 1723 died [at Celbridge, near Dublin] Mrs. [Esther] Van Homrigh,[49] a woman made unhappy by her admiration of wit, and ignominiously distinguished by the name of Vanessa, whose conduct has been already sufficiently discussed, and whose his-

---

[47] Dr. Samuel Madden, died 31st Dec. 1765 :—confirmed by Orrery's ' Remarks,' 12mo., 1753, p. 14.

[48] Orrery's ' Remarks,' 12mo., 1753, p. 16. That Swift was married to Stella is, I think, disproved by her will, in which she describes herself as "Esther Johnson, spinster;" and signs her name "Esther Johnson." Her will is dated within a month of her death. She had money to leave; and her will had been vitiated if she had described herself wrongly.

"The general rule, I think, between him and Mrs. Johnson was this : when the Doctor was absent from home she lived at his house; but when he was at home she lodged either somewhere at Trim, or was resident at the house of Dr. Raymond, the vicar of Trim, a gentleman of great hospitality, a friend of Dr. Swift, a man of learning and fine address, with the advantage of a tall, handsome, and graceful person."—DEANE SWIFT : Essay, 8vo., 1755, p. 90.

Lord Orrery says, ed. 1753, p. 14, she was "the concealed but undoubted wife" of Swift; and his kinsman, Deane Swift, was "thoroughly persuaded" that they were married in 1716 (' Essay,' 1755, p. 92).

[49] Pronounced Vannummery.

tory is too well known to be minutely repeated.[50]   She was a
young woman fond of literature, whom Decanus the Dean,
called Cadenus by transposition of the letters, took pleasure in
directing and instructing ; till, from being proud of his praise, she
grew fond of his person. Swift was then about forty-seven, at an
age when vanity is strongly excited by the amorous attention of
a young woman.[51]   If it be said that Swift should have checked
a passion which he never meant to gratify, recourse must be had
to that extenuation which he so much despised, " men are but
men :" perhaps, however, he did not at first know his own
mind, and, as he represents himself, was undetermined. For
his admission of her courtship, and his indulgence of her hopes
after his marriage to Stella, no other honest plea can be found,
than that he delayed a disagreeable discovery from time to
time, dreading the immediate bursts of distress, and watching
for a favourable moment. She thought herself neglected, and
died of disappointment ; having ordered by her will the poem
to be published, in which Cadenus had proclaimed her excellence, and confessed his love.[52]   The effect of the publication
upon the Dean and Stella is thus related by Delany :

" I have good reason to believe that they both were greatly
shocked and distressed (though it may be differently) upon this
occasion. The Dean made a tour to the south of Ireland, for
about two months, at this time, to dissipate his thoughts, and
give place to obloquy ; and Stella retired (upon the earnest
invitation of the owner) to the house of a cheerful, generous,

[50] Johnson alludes to Lord Orrery's ' Remarks,' 12mo., 1753, pp. 75-7.

[51] Swift, when neither young, nor handsome, nor rich, nor even amiable,
inspired the two most extraordinary passions upon record, Vanessa's and
Stella's :—

> Vanessa, aged scarce a score,
> Sighs for a gown of forty-four.

He requited them bitterly; for he seems to have broken the heart of the
one, and worn out that of the other; and he had his reward, for he died a
solitary idiot in the hands of servants.—BYRON: *A Second Letter on Bowles.*

It is charitable to think that the malady that drove him mad affected his
heart long before it overthrew his intellect.

[52] Johnson follows Delany (p. 122); but there is no such order in Vanessa's
will, nor even an allusion to Swift in it. See the will in Scott's ' Swift,' xix.
379, 2nd ed.

good-natured friend of the Dean's, whom she also much loved and honoured.   There my informer often saw her ; and, I have reason to believe, used his utmost endeavours to relieve, support, and amuse her, in this sad situation.

" One little incident he told me of, on that occasion, I think I shall never forget.   As her friend was an hospitable, open-hearted man, well-beloved, and largely acquainted, it happened one day that some gentlemen dropt in to dinner, who were strangers to Stella's situation ; and as the poem of ' Cadenus and Vanessa' was then the general topic of conversation, one of them said, 'Surely that Vanessa must be an extraordinary woman, that could inspire the Dean to write so finely upon her.' Mrs. Johnson smiled, and answered, ' that she thought that point not quite so clear ; for it was well known the Dean could write finely upon a broomstick.' " [53]

The great acquisition of esteem and influence was made by the ' Drapier's Letters ' in 1724.   One Wood, of Wolverhampton in Staffordshire, a man enterprising and rapacious, had, as is said, by a present to the Duchess of Munster,[54] obtained a patent, empowering him to coin one hundred and eighty thousand pounds of halfpence and farthings for the kingdom of Ireland, in which there was a very inconvenient and embarrassing scarcity of copper coin ; so that it was impossible to run in debt upon the credit of a piece of money ; for the cook or

[53] Delany's ' Observations,' 8vo., 1754, p. 57.
Near twenty years ago I heard from a gentleman now living, with whom Vanessa lived or lodged in England, an account of the Dean's behaviour to the unhappy woman, much less to his reputation than the account my Lord [Orrery] gives of that affair.   According to this gentleman's account she was not the creature that she became when she was in Ireland, whither she followed him, and, in hopes to make herself an interest with his vanity, threw herself into glare and expense ; and at last by disappointment into a habit of drinking, till grief and the effects of that vice destroyed her.   You may gather from that really pretty piece of his, ' Cadenus and Vanessa,' how much he flattered her, and that he took great pains to gloss over that affair.   I remember once to have seen a little collection of letters and poetical scraps of Swift's, which passed between him and Mrs. Van Homrigh, this same Vanessa, which the bookseller then told me were sent him to be published from the originals, by this lady, in resentment of his perfidy.—RICHARDSON (the novelist) to Lady Bradshaigh, April 22, 1752.
[54] Better known as Duchess of Kendal, the German mistress of George I.

keeper of an alehouse could not refuse to supply a man that had
silver in his hand, and the buyer would not leave his money
without change.

The project was therefore plausible. The scarcity, which
was already great, Wood took care to make greater, by agents
who gathered up the old halfpence; and was about to turn his
brass into gold, by pouring the treasures of his new mint upon
Ireland, when Swift, finding that the metal was debased to an
enormous degree, wrote Letters, under the name of *M. B.
Drapier*, to show the folly of receiving, and the mischief that
must ensue by giving, gold and silver for coin worth perhaps
not a third part of its nominal value.

The nation was alarmed; the new coin was universally refused; but the governors of Ireland considered resistance to the
King's patent as highly criminal; and one Whitshed, then
Chief Justice, who had tried the printer of the former pamphlet,
and sent out the jury nine times, till by clamour and menaces
they were frightened into a special verdict, now presented
the *Drapier*, but could not prevail on the grand jury to find the
bill.

Lord Carteret[55] and the Privy Council published [1724] a
proclamation, offering three hundred pounds for discovering the
author of the Fourth Letter.[56] Swift had concealed himself
from his printers, and trusted only his butler, who transcribed
the paper. The man, immediately after the appearance of the
proclamation, strolled from the house, and stayed out all night

---

[55] Lord Carteret was then Lord Lieutenant of Ireland.

[56] This was the second sum of the same amount offered for his detection:—

> Fair Liberty was all his cry:
> For her he stood prepared to die;
> For her he boldly stood alone;
> For her he oft exposed his own.
> Two kingdoms, just as faction led,
> Had set a price upon his head;
> But not a traitor could be found
> To sell him for six hundred pound.
>
> SWIFT: *Verses on his own Death.*

What I did for this country was from perfect hatred of tyranny and oppression, for which I had a proclamation against me of 300*l.*, which my old friend
Lord Carteret was forced to consent to, the very first or second night of his
arrival hither.—SWIFT to Mr. Grant, March 23, 1733–4.

and part of the next day. There was reason enough to fear
that he had betrayed his master for the reward ; but he came
home, and the Dean ordered him to put off his livery and leave
the house ; " for," says he, " I know that my life is in your
power, and I will not bear, out of fear, either your insolence or
negligence." The man excused his fault with great submission,
and begged that he might be confined in the house while it was
in his power to endanger his master ; but the Dean resolutely
turned him out, without taking farther notice of him, till the
term of information had expired, and then received him again.
Soon afterwards he ordered him and the rest of the servants
into his presence, without telling his intentions, and bade them
take notice that their fellow-servant was no longer Robert the
butler, but that his integrity had made him Mr. Blakeley, verger
of St. Patrick's ; an officer whose income was between thirty and
forty pounds a year : yet he still continued for some years to
serve his old master as his butler.[57]

Swift was known from this time by the appellation of *The
Dean*. He was honoured by the populace as the champion,
patron, and instructor of Ireland ; and gained such power as,
considered both in its extent and duration, scarcely any man has
ever enjoyed without greater wealth or higher station.

He was from this important year the oracle of the traders,
and the idol of the rabble, and by consequence was feared and
courted by all to whom the kindness of the traders or the
populace were necessary. The *Drapier* was a sign ; the *Drapier* was a health ;[58] and which way soever the eye or the ear
was turned, some tokens were found of the nation's gratitude to
the *Drapier*.[59]

[57] Deane Swift's ' Essay,' 8vo., 1755, p. 191.
[58] Bumpers were poured forth to the Drapier as large and as frequent as to
the glorious and immortal memory of King William III. —ORRERY : *Remarks*,
ed. 1753, p. 47.

> [59] O thou, whatever title please thine ear,
>   Dean, Drapier, Bickerstaff, or Gulliver !
>   Whether thou choose Cervantes' serious air,
>   Or laugh and shake in Rabelais' easy-chair,
>   Or praise the Court, or magnify mankind,
>   Or thy griev'd country's copper-chains unbind.
>   POPE : *The Dunciad*, B. i.

The benefit was indeed great : he had rescued Ireland from
a very oppressive and predatory invasion ; and the popularity
which he had gained he was diligent to keep, by appearing
forward and zealous on every occasion where the public interest
was supposed to be involved.   Nor did he much scruple to
boast his influence ; for when, upon some attempts to regulate
the coin, Archbishop Boulter, then one of the justices, accused
him of exasperating the people, he exculpated himself by saying,
" If I had lifted up my finger, they would have torn you to
pieces."

But the pleasure of popularity was soon interrupted by domestic misery.   Mrs. Johnson, whose conversation was to him
the great softener of the ills of life, began in the year of the
Drapier's triumph to decline ; and two years afterwards [1726]
was so wasted with sickness, that her recovery was considered
as hopeless.

Swift was then [1726] in England, and had been invited
by Lord Bolingbroke to pass the winter with him in France ;
but this call of calamity hastened him to Ireland, where perhaps his presence contributed to restore her to imperfect and
tottering health.

He was now so much at ease, that (1727) he returned to
England, where he collected three volumes of Miscellanies in
conjunction with Pope, who prefixed a querulous and apologetical Preface.[60]

This important year [1727][61] sent likewise into the world
' Gulliver's Travels,' a production so new and strange, that it
filled the reader with a mingled emotion of merriment and
amazement.   It was received with such avidity, that the price
of the first edition was raised before the second could be made ;
it was read by the high and the low, the learned and illiterate.
Criticism was for a while lost in wonder ; no rules of judgment
were applied to a book written in open defiance of truth and
regularity.   But when distinctions came to be made, the part

[60] See vol. iii. p. 51.
[61] No : the previous year.   See Gay to Swift, 16th Nov. 1726, and Swift to
the Countess of Suffolk, 27th Nov. 1726.

which gave the least pleasure was that which describes the Flying Island, and that which gave most disgust must be the history of the Houyhnhnms.

While Swift was enjoying the reputation of his new work, the news of the King's death [June, 1727] arrived; and he kissed the hands of the new King and Queen [George II. and Queen Caroline] three days after their accession.

By the Queen, when she was Princess, he had been treated with some distinction, and was well received by her in her exaltation ; [62] but whether she gave hopes which she never took care to satisfy, or he formed expectations which she never meant to raise, the event was, that he always afterwards thought on her with malevolence, and particularly charged her with breaking her promise of some medals which she engaged to send him.[63]

I know not whether she had not in her turn some reason for complaint. A letter was sent her, not so much entreating as requiring her patronage of Mrs. Barber, an ingenious Irish-woman, who was then begging subscriptions for her poems. To this letter was subscribed the name of Swift, and it has all the appearances of his diction and sentiments; but it was not written in his hand, and had some little improprieties. When he was charged with this letter, he laid hold of the inaccuracies and urged the improbability of the accusation, but never denied it:

---

[62] It is six years last spring since I first went to visit my friends in England, after the Queen's death. Her present Majesty heard of my arrival, and sent at least nine times to command my attendance before I would obey her, for several reasons not hard to guess; and among others, because I heard her character from those who knew her well. At last I went, and she received me very graciously. I told her the first time " That I was informed she loved to see odd persons; and that having sent for a wild boy from Germany, she had a curiosity to see a wild Dean from Ireland!"—SWIFT to Lady Betty Germaine, January 8, 1732-3.

[63] The King, it is true, had little propensity to refined pleasures; but Queen Caroline was ever ready to reward merit, and wished to have their reign illustrated by monuments of genius. . . . Pope might have enjoyed her favour, and Swift had it at first, till, insolent under the mask of independence, and not content without domineering over her politics, she abandoned him to his ill-humour, and to the vexation of that misguided and disappointed ambition that perverted and preyed on his excellent genius.—HORACE WALPOLE : *Anec. of Painters,* chap. xix.

he shuffles between cowardice and veracity, and talks big when he says nothing.[64]

He seemed desirous enough of recommencing courtier, and endeavoured to gain the kindness of Mrs. Howard, remembering what Mrs. Masham had performed in former times; but his flatteries were, like those of other wits, unsuccessful; the lady either wanted power or had no ambition of poetical immortality.[65]

He was seized not long afterwards by a fit of giddiness, and again heard of the sickness and danger of Mrs. Johnson. He then left [Sept. 1727] the house of Pope, as it seems, with very little ceremony, finding "that two sick friends cannot live together;" and did not write to him till he found himself at Chester.

He returned to a home of sorrow : poor Stella was sinking into the grave, and, after a languishing decay of about two months, died in her forty-fourth year, on January 28, 1727-8. How much he wished her life his papers show ; nor can it be doubted that he dreaded the death of her whom he loved most, aggravated by the consciousness that himself had hastened it.

Beauty and the power of pleasing, the greatest external advantages that woman can desire or possess, were fatal to the unfortunate Stella. The man whom she had the misfortune to love was, as Delany observes, fond of singularity and desirous to make a mode of happiness for himself, different from the general course of things and order of Providence. From the time of her arrival in Ireland he seems resolved to keep her in his power, and therefore hindered a match sufficiently advantageous by accumulating unreasonable demands and prescribing conditions that could not be performed. While she was at her

[64] The mystery which Swift's editors have found in this affair of Mrs. Barber's letters is easily solved by supposing that Mrs. Barber forged them for her own purposes; which, as they were violently recommendatory of her and her objects, she, who was by no means a scrupulous person, probably did.— CROKER: *Suffolk Letters*, ii. 12. See the letter itself in Scott's ' Swift,' xviii. 379, 2nd ed.

[65] It is now clear that Mrs. Howard had every inclination, but wanted the power, to assist the Dean and Gay.—See Lord Hervey's 'Memoirs,' 2 vols. 8vo., 1848; and Mrs. Howard's own ' Correspondence,' 2 vols. 8vo. 1824.

own disposal he did not consider his possession as secure; resentment, ambition, or caprice might separate them; he was therefore resolved to make " assurance doubly sure," and to appropriate her by a private marriage, to which he had annexed the expectation of all the pleasures of perfect friendship without the uneasiness of conjugal restraint.   But with this state poor Stella was not satisfied ; she never was treated as a wife, and to the world she had the appearance of a mistress.   She lived sullenly on, in hope that in time he would own and receive her ; but the time did not come till the change of his manners and depravation of his mind made her tell him, when he offered to acknowledge her, that " it was too late."   She then gave up herself to sorrowful resentment, and died under the tyranny of him by whom she was in the highest degree loved and honoured.

What were her claims to this eccentric tenderness, by which the laws of nature were violated to retain her, curiosity will inquire ; but how shall it be gratified?   Swift was a lover ; his testimony may be suspected.   Delany and the Irish saw with Swift's eyes, and therefore add little confirmation.   That she was virtuous, beautiful, and elegant, in a very high degree, such admiration from such a lover makes it very probable ; but she had not much literature, for she could not spell her own language ; and of her wit, so loudly vaunted, the smart sayings which Swift himself has collected afford no splendid specimen.[66]

The reader of Swift's ' Letter to a Lady on her Marriage ' may be allowed to doubt whether his opinion of female excellence ought implicitly to be admitted ; for if his general thoughts on women were such as he exhibits, a very little sense in a lady would enrapture and a very little virtue would astonish him. Stella's supremacy therefore was perhaps only local ; she was great because her associates were little.

In some remarks lately published on the Life of Swift,[67] his

---

[66] Of these *bons mots* the reader will probably think some flat and others coarse; but enough will remain to vindicate the praises of Stella's wit.— WALTER SCOTT (ed. Swift, ix. 296).

[67] Johnson alludes, I suspect, to a paper of remarks by Dr. Lyons, printed by Nichols, in 1779, in a supplemental volume to Swift's Works.

marriage is mentioned as fabulous or doubtful; but, alas! poor
Stella, as Dr. Madden told me, related her melancholy story to
Dr. Sheridan when he attended her as a clergyman to prepare
her for death; and Delany mentions it not with doubt, but only
with regret. Swift never mentioned her without a sigh.[68]

The rest of his life [1728–45] was spent in Ireland—in a
country to which not even power almost despotic, nor flattery
almost idolatrous, could reconcile him. He sometimes wished
to visit England, but always found some reason to delay. He
tells Pope, in the decline of life, that he hopes once more to see
him; "but if not," says he, "we must part as all human beings
have parted."

After the death of Stella his benevolence was contracted and
his severity exasperated; he drove his acquaintance from his
table and wondered why he was deserted. But he continued his
attention to the public, and wrote from time to time such directions, admonitions, or censures, as the exigency of affairs, in his
opinion, made proper; and nothing fell from his pen in vain.

In a short poem on the Presbyterians, whom he always regarded
with detestation, he bestowed [1733-4] one stricture upon Bettesworth,[69] a lawyer eminent for his insolence to the clergy, which,
from very considerable reputation, brought him into immediate
and universal contempt. Bettesworth, enraged at his disgrace
and loss, went to Swift and demanded whether he was the author
of that poem? "Mr. Bettesworth," answered he, "I was in my
youth acquainted with great lawyers, who, knowing my disposition to satire, advised me that if any scoundrel or blockhead
whom I had lampooned should ask, 'Are you the author of this
paper?' I should tell him that I was not the author; and therefore I tell you, Mr. Bettesworth, that I am not the author of
these lines." [70]

[68] Orrery's ' Remarks,' 12mo., 1753, p. 18.

" To these terms Stella readily acceded; and in 1716 they were married by
the Bishop of Clogher, who himself related the circumstance to Bishop
Berkeley, by whose relict the story was communicated to me."—G. M. BERKE-
LEY: *Literary Relics*, 8vo., 1789, p. xxxvi.

[69] Thus at the bar the booby Bettesworth,
    Though half a crown o'erpays his sweat's worth.

[70] I should have believed Burke to be Junius, because I know no man but

Bettesworth was so little satisfied with this account that he publicly professed his resolution of a violent and corporal revenge ; but the inhabitants of St. Patrick's district embodied themselves in the Dean's defence. Bettesworth declared in Parliament that Swift had deprived him of twelve hundred pounds a-year.

Swift was popular awhile by another mode of beneficence. He set aside some hundreds to be lent in small sums to the poor, from five shillings, I think, to five pounds. He took no interest, and only required that, at repayment, a small fee should be given to the accountant : but he required that the day of promised payment should be exactly kept. A severe and punctilious temper is ill qualified for transactions with the poor ; the day was often broken, and the loan was not repaid. This might have been easily foreseen ; but for this Swift had made no provision of patience or pity. He ordered his debtors to be sued. A severe creditor has no popular character ; what then was likely to be said of him who employs the catchpoll under the appearance of charity ? The clamour against him was loud, and the resentment of the populace outrageous ; he was therefore forced to drop his scheme and own the folly of expecting punctuality from the poor.[71]

His asperity continually increasing condemned him to solitude ; and his resentment of solitude sharpened his asperity. He was not, however, totally deserted ; some men of learning and some women of elegance often visited him ;[72] and he wrote from time to time either verse or prose ; of his verses he willingly gave copies, and is supposed to have felt no discontent when he saw them printed. His favourite maxim was "Vive

Burke who is capable of writing these letters; but Burke spontaneously denied it to me. The case would have been different, had I asked him if he was the author; a man so questioned as to an anonymous publication may think he has a right to deny it.—JOHNSON, in Boswell by Croker, p. 625.

[71] Dr. Johnson, no friend to Swift's fame, has represented this circumstance in an unfavourable view, as if he " employed the catchpoll under the appearance of charity;" yet no one knew better than Dr. Johnson the uselessness of vague and indiscriminate bounty, or the advantage of awaking the needy to habits of regular economy.—SIR WALTER SCOTT: *Life of Swift* (Miscellaneous Prose Works, i. 424).

[72] More wrote to him, and his correspondence with his early female friends in England says much for the persuasive and attractive nature of his manners.

la bagatelle :" he thought trifles a necessary part of life, and perhaps found them necessary to himself. It seems impossible to him to be idle, and his disorders made it difficult or dangerous to be long seriously studious or laboriously diligent. The love of ease is always gaining upon age, and he had one temptation to petty amusements peculiar to himself: whatever he did he was sure to hear applauded; and such was his predominance over all that approached, that all their applauses were probably sincere. He that is much flattered soon learns to flatter himself: we are commonly taught our duty by fear or shame, and how can they act upon the man who hears nothing but his own praises?

As his years increased, his fits of giddiness and deafness grew more frequent, and his deafness made conversation difficult: they grew likewise more severe, till in 1736, as he was writing a poem called 'The Legion Club,' he was seized with a fit so painful and so long continued that he never after thought it proper to attempt any work of thought or labour.[73]

He was always careful of his money, and was therefore no liberal entertainer; but was less frugal of his wine than of his meat. When his friends of either sex came to him in expectation of a dinner, his custom was to give every one a shilling that they might please themselves with their provision. At last his avarice grew too powerful for his kindness; he would refuse a bottle of wine, and in Ireland no man visits where he cannot drink.

Having thus excluded conversation and desisted from study, he had neither business nor amusement; for, having by some ridiculous resolution or mad vow determined never to wear spectacles, he could make little use of books in his later years: his ideas therefore, being neither renovated by discourse nor increased by reading, wore gradually away and left his mind vacant to the vexations of the hour, till at last his anger was heightened into madness.

---

[73] Orrery's 'Remarks,' 12mo., 1753, p. 169.

Years and infirmities have quite broke me; I mean that odious continual disorder in my head. I neither read, nor write, nor remember, nor converse. All I have left is to walk and ride.—SWIFT to Pope, Dec. 2, 1736.

He however permitted one book to be published, which had been the production of former years, 'Polite Conversation,' which appeared in 1738. The 'Directions for Servants' was printed soon after his death. These two performances show a mind incessantly attentive, and, when it was not employed upon great things, busy with minute occurrences. It is apparent that he must have had the habit of noting whatever he observed; for such a number of particulars could never have been assembled by the power of recollection.

He grew more violent; and his mental powers declined, till (1741) it was found necessary that legal guardians should be appointed of his person and fortune. He now lost distinction. His madness was compounded of rage and fatuity. The last face that he knew was that of Mrs. Whiteway;[74] and her he ceased to know in a little time. His meat was brought him cut into mouthfuls; but he would never touch it while the servant stayed, and at last, after it had stood perhaps an hour, would eat it walking; for he continued his old habit, and was on his feet ten hours a-day.

Next year (1742) he had an inflammation in his left eye, which swelled it to the size of an egg, with boils in other parts; he was kept long waking with the pain, and was not easily restrained by five attendants from tearing out his eye.

The tumour at last subsided; and a short interval of reason ensuing, in which he knew his physician and his family, gave hopes of his recovery; but in a few days he sunk into lethargic stupidity, motionless, heedless, and speechless. But it is said, that, after a year of total silence, when his housekeeper, on the 30th of November, told him that the usual bonfires and illuminations were preparing to celebrate his birth-day, he answered, " It is all folly; they had better let it alone." [75]

It is remembered, that he afterwards spoke now and then, or gave some intimation of a meaning; but at last sunk into a

[74] His near kinswoman (Delany, p. 130).

[75] I hope things will be better on Thursday [his birthday], else I shall be full of the spleen, because it is a day you seem to regard, although I detest it, and I read the third chapter of Job that morning.—SWIFT to Mrs. Whiteway, Nov. 27, 1738.

perfect silence, which continued till about the end of October, 1745,[76] when, in his seventy-eighth year, he expired without a struggle.

When Swift is considered as an author, it is just to estimate his powers by their effects. In the reign of Queen Anne he turned the stream of popularity against the Whigs, and must be confessed to have dictated for a time the political opinions of the English nation. In the succeeding reign he delivered Ireland from plunder and oppression ; and showed that wit, confederated with truth, had such force as authority was unable to resist. He said truly of himself, that Ireland " was his debtor." [77] It was from the time when he first began to patronize the Irish that they may date their riches and prosperity. He taught them first to know their own interest, their weight, and their strength, and gave them spirit to assert that equality with their fellow-subjects to which they have ever since been making vigorous advances, and to claim those rights which they have at last established. Nor can they be charged with ingratitude to their benefactor ; for they reverenced him as a guardian and obeyed him as a dictator.[78]

In his works he has given very different specimens both of sentiments and expression. His ' Tale of a Tub ' has little resemblance to his other pieces. It exhibits a vehemence and rapidity of mind, a copiousness of images, and vivacity of diction, such as he afterwards never possessed or never exerted. It is of a mode so distinct and peculiar, that it must be considered by itself; what is true of that, is not true of any thing else which he has written.

---

[76] All the editions of Johnson read 1744. " Unless I am misinformed, he died worth about twelve thousand pounds."—ORRERY : *Remarks*, ed. 1753, p. 171.

> [77] That kingdom he had left his debtor,
> I wish it soon may have a better.
>
> SWIFT: *Verses on his own Death*, Nov. 1731.

[78] When people ask me how I governed Ireland, I say that I pleased Dr. Swift.—LORD CARTERET to Swift, March 24, 1736-7 (Scott, xix. 51).

In his other works is found an equable tenor of easy language, which rather trickles than flows. His delight was in simplicity. That he has in his works no metaphor, as has been said, is not true; but his few metaphors seem to be received rather by necessity than choice.[79] He studied purity; and though perhaps all his strictures are not exact, yet it is not often that solecisms can be found; and whoever depends on his authority may generally conclude himself safe. His sentences are never too much dilated or contracted; and it will not be easy to find any embarrassment in the complication of his clauses, any inconsequence in his connections, or abruptness in his transitions.

His style was well suited to his thoughts, which are never subtilised by nice disquisitions, decorated by sparkling conceits, elevated by ambitious sentences, or variegated by far-sought learning. He pays no court to the passions; he excites neither surprise nor admiration; he always understands himself, and his readers always understand him: the peruser of Swift wants little previous knowledge; it will be sufficient that he is acquainted with common words and common things; he is neither required to mount elevations nor to explore profundities; his passage is always on a level, along solid ground, without asperities, without obstruction.

This easy and safe conveyance of meaning it was Swift's desire to attain, and for having attained he deserves praise, though perhaps not the highest praise. For purposes merely didactic, when something is to be told that was not known before, it is the best mode; but against that inattention by which known truths are suffered to lie neglected, it makes no provision; it instructs, but does not persuade.

By his political education he was associated with the Whigs; but he deserted them when they deserted their principles, yet without running into the contrary extreme; he continued throughout his life to retain the disposition which he assigns to

[79] Johnson said once to me, speaking of the simplicity of Swift's style, "The rogue never hazards a metaphor."—Jos. WARTON: *Pope's Works*, viii. 130.

the " Church-of-England Man," of thinking commonly with
the Whigs of the State and with the Tories of the Church.[80]

He was a churchman rationally zealous; he desired the
prosperity and maintained the honour of the clergy; of the
dissenters he did not wish to infringe the toleration, but he
opposed their encroachments.

To his duty as dean he was very attentive. He managed
the revenues of his church with exact economy; and it is said
by Delany [81] that more money was, under his direction, laid out
in repairs than had ever been in the same time since its first
erection.   Of his choir he was eminently careful; and, though
he neither loved nor understood music, took care that all the
singers were well qualified, admitting none without the testimony of skilful judges.[82]

In his church he restored the practice of weekly communion,
and distributed the sacramental elements in the most solemn
and devout manner with his own hand. He came to church
every morning, preached commonly in his turn, and attended
the evening anthem, that it might not be negligently performed.

He read the service " rather with a strong, nervous voice
than in a graceful manner; [83] his voice was sharp and high-
toned, rather than harmonious."

He entered upon the clerical state with hope to excel in
preaching; but complained, that, from the time of his political
controversies, " he could only preach pamphlets." This censure
of himself, if judgment be made from those sermons which have
been printed, was unreasonably severe.

The suspicions of his irreligion proceeded in a great measure
from his dread of hypocrisy; instead of wishing to seem better,
he delighted in seeming worse than he was.   He went in

[80] I was a common advocate for those they called the Whigs, to a degree
that a certain great minister told me I had always a Whig in my sleeve.—
SWIFT to King, Archbishop of Dublin, Dec. 22, 1716.

Of Swift, while a Whig, two remarkable letters, addressed to Lord Halifax,
have been discovered since Scott wrote. See them in the Appendix to this
Life.

[81] Delany, p. 201.   [82] Delany, p. 189.

[83] Orrery's ' Remarks,' 12mo. 1753, p. 3.

London to early prayers, lest he should be seen at church;[84] he read prayers to his servants every morning with such dexterous secrecy, that Dr. Delany was six months in his house before he knew it.[85]   He was not only careful to hide the good which he did, but willingly incurred the suspicion of evil which he did not. He forgot what himself had formerly asserted, that hypocrisy is less mischievous than open impiety.   Dr. Delany, with all his zeal for his honour, has justly condemned this part of his character.

The person of Swift had not many recommendations.   He had a kind of muddy complexion, which, though he washed himself with Oriental scrupulosity, did not look clear.[86]   He had a countenance sour and severe, which he seldom softened by any appearance of gaiety.   He stubbornly resisted any tendency to laughter.

To his domestics he was naturally rough;[87] and a man of a rigorous temper, with that vigilance of minute attention which his works discover, must have been a master that few could bear.   That he was disposed to do his servants good, on important occasions, is no great mitigation ; benefaction can be but rare, and tyrannic peevishness is perpetual.   He did not spare the servants of others.   Once, when he dined alone with the Earl of Orrery, he said of one that waited in the room, " That man has, since we sat to the table, committed fifteen faults."   What the faults were, Lord Orrery, from whom I heard the story, had not been attentive enough to discover. My number may perhaps not be exact.

[84] Delany's ' Observations,' 8vo. 1754, p. 44.   [85] Delany, p. 44.

[86] The best portraits of Swift are by Jervas and Bindon. The fine Jervas (of Swift during the last four years of Queen Anne) was presented by Alderman Barber, in 1739, to the Bodleian Library. He has a prim, but able and insolent look. The witty Lord Chesterfield had a portrait of Swift by Jervas. The Bindon (done at the request and expense of the Chapter of the Cathedral) is at the Deanery House, St. Patrick's, and a duplicate is at Howth Castle.—(See Scott's Swift, xix. 191, xvii. 457, xvi. 480.)

Edward Lord Oxford had his portrait by Jervas drawn in Ireland. "It is very like you, and is a very good picture." (Oxford to Swift, Aug. 30, 1725.)

[87] To his domestics he was passionate and churlish; to his equals and superiors rather an entertaining than a desirable companion.— ORRERY: Remarks, 12mo. 1753, p. 146.

In his economy he practised a peculiar and offensive parsimony, without disguise or apology. The practice of saving
being once necessary, became habitual, and grew first ridiculous,
and at last detestable. But his avarice, though it might
exclude pleasure, was never suffered to encroach upon his
virtue. He was frugal by inclination, but liberal by principle;
and if the purpose to which he destined his little accumulations
be remembered, with his distribution of occasional charity, it
will perhaps appear that he only liked one mode of expense
better than another, and saved merely that he might have
something to give. He did not grow rich by injuring his
successors, but left both Laracor and the Deanery more valuable
than he found them.—With all this talk of his covetousness
and generosity, it should be remembered that he was never
rich. The revenue of his Deanery was not much more than
seven hundred a year.[88]

His beneficence was not graced with tenderness or civility;
he relieved without pity, and assisted without kindness; so that
those who were fed by him could hardly love him.

He made a rule to himself to give but one piece at a time,
and therefore always stored his pocket with coins of different
value.[89]

Whatever he did, he seemed willing to do in a manner
peculiar to himself, without sufficiently considering that singularity, as it implies a contempt of the general practice, is a
kind of defiance which justly provokes the hostility of ridicule;
he, therefore, who indulges peculiar habits is worse than others,
if he be not better.

Of his humour, a story told by Pope may afford a specimen.

---

[88] Delany, p. 200. He always kept three horses, and but one groom.—
DELANY: *Observations*, p. 6.

To live in England half as tolerably as I do here would ruin me. I must
have two servants and three horses, and dare drink nothing but wine; and my
ragged church-rents would never be paid in my absence.—SWIFT to Mrs.
Cæsar, July 30, 1733.

Although my own lands, as Dean, be let for four-fifths under their value,
I have not raised them a sixth part in twenty-three years, and took very moderate fines.—SWIFT to Barber, March 30, 1737.

[89] Delany, p. 13.

"Dr. Swift has an odd, blunt way, that is mistaken, by strangers, for ill-nature.—'Tis so odd, that there's no describing it but by facts. I'll tell you one that just comes into my head. One evening, Gay and I went to see him: you know how intimately we were all acquainted. On our coming in, ' Hey-day, gentlemen (says the Doctor), what's the meaning of this visit? How come you to leave all the great Lords, that you are so fond of, to come hither to see a poor Dean?'—' Because we would rather see you than any of them.'—' Ay, any one that did not know you so well as I do, might believe you. But since you are come, I must get some supper for you, I suppose.'—' No, Doctor, we have supped already.'—' Supped already? that's impossible! why, 'tis not eight o'clock yet.'— ' Indeed, we have.'—' That's very strange; but, if you had not supped, I must have got something for you. Let me see, what should I have had? A couple of lobsters; ay, that would have done very well; two shillings—tarts a shilling: but you will drink a glass of wine with me, though you supped so much before your usual time only to spare my pocket?'— ' No, we had rather talk with you than drink with you.'—' But if you had supped with me, as in all reason you ought to have done, you must have drank with me.—A bottle of wine, two shillings—two and two is four, and one is five: just two-and-sixpence a-piece. There, Pope, there's half a crown for you, and there's another for you, Sir; for I won't save anything by you, I am determined.'—This was all said and done with his usual seriousness on such occasions; and, in spite of everything we could say to the contrary, he actually obliged us to take the money." [90]

In the intercourse of familiar life, he indulged his disposition to petulance and sarcasm, and thought himself injured if the licentiousness of his raillery, the freedom of his censures, or the petulance of his frolics, was resented or repressed. He predominated over his companions with very high ascendency, and probably would bear none over whom he could not predominate.

[90] Spence by Singer, p. 19.

To give him advice was, in the style of his friend Delany, " to
venture to speak to him." [91]   This customary superiority soon
grew too delicate for truth ; and Swift, with all his penetration,
allowed himself to be delighted with low flattery.

On all common occasions, he habitually affects a style of
arrogance, and dictates rather than persuades.[92]   This authori-
tative and magisterial language he expected to be received as
his peculiar mode of jocularity : but he apparently flattered his
own arrogance by an assumed imperiousness, in which he was
ironical only to the resentful, and to the submissive sufficiently
serious.

He told stories with great felicity, and delighted in doing
what he knew himself to do well ; he was therefore captivated
by the respectful silence of a steady listener, and told the same
tales too often.[93]

He did not, however, claim the right of talking alone ; for it
was his rule, when he had spoken a minute, to give room by a
pause for any other speaker.   Of time, on all occasions, he was
an exact computer, and knew the minutes required to every
common operation.[94]

It may be justly supposed that there was in his conversation,
what appears so frequently in his letters, an affectation of
familiarity with the great, an ambition of momentary equality
sought and enjoyed by the neglect of those ceremonies which
custom has established as the barriers between one order of
society and another.   This transgression of regularity was by
himself and his admirers termed greatness of soul.   But a great
mind disdains to hold anything by courtesy, and therefore
never usurps what a lawful claimant may take away.   He that
encroaches on another's dignity, puts himself in his power ; he

[91] Swift had a mixture of insolence in his conversation.—Dr. Young: *Spence
by Singer*, p. 334.
[92] He assumed more the air of a patron than of a friend.   He affected rather
to dictate than advise.—Orrery: *Remarks*, ed. 1753, p. 29.
[93] Delany, p. 218.
[94] His hours of walking and reading never varied.   His motions were guided
by his watch, which was so constantly held in his hand, or placed before him
on his table, that he seldom deviated many minutes in the daily revolution of
his exercises and employments.—Orrery: *Remarks*, p. 44.

is either repelled with helpless indignity, or endured by clemency and condescension.

Of Swift's general habits of thinking, if his letters can be supposed to afford any evidence, he was not a man to be either loved or envied. He seems to have wasted life in discontent, by the rage of neglected pride, and the languishment of unsatisfied desire. He is querulous and fastidious, arrogant and malignant; he scarcely speaks of himself but with indignant lamentations, or of others but with insolent superiority when he is gay, and with angry contempt when he is gloomy. From the letters that pass between him and Pope, it might be inferred that they, with Arbuthnot and Gay, had engrossed all the understanding and virtue of mankind; that their merits filled the world, or that there was no hope of more. They show the age involved in darkness, and shade the picture with sullen emulation.

When [1714] the Queen's death drove him into Ireland, he might be allowed to regret for a time the interception of his views, the extinction of his hopes, and his ejection from gay scenes, important employment, and splendid friendships; but when time had enabled reason to prevail over vexation, the complaints, which at first were natural, became ridiculous because they were useless. But querulousness was now grown habitual, and he cried out when he probably had ceased to feel. His reiterated wailings persuaded Bolingbroke that he was really willing to quit his deanery for an English parish; and Bolingbroke procured an exchange, which was rejected; and Swift still retained the pleasure of complaining.[95]

The greatest difficulty that occurs in analysing his character is to discover by what depravity of intellect he took delight in revolving ideas from which almost every other mind shrinks with disgust. The ideas of pleasure, even when criminal, may solicit the imagination; but what has disease, deformity, and filth, upon which the thoughts can be allured to dwell? Delany

---

[95] The living was that of Burfield, in Berkshire (Warton's Pope, vi. 15); but it does not appear that the exchange was procured. Bolingbroke, who suggested the exchange, offered to interest himself in effecting it.

is willing to think that Swift's mind was not much tainted with
this gross corruption before his [first] long visit to Pope.[96] He
does not consider how he degrades his hero by making him at
fifty-nine the pupil of turpitude, and liable to the malignant
influence of an ascendant mind. But the truth is, that Gulliver
had described his Yahoos before the visit; and he that had
formed those images had nothing filthy to learn.

I have here given the character of Swift as he exhibits himself to my perception; but now let another be heard who knew
him better.   Dr. Delany, after long acquaintance, describes
him to Lord Orrery in these terms:—

" My Lord, when you consider Swift's singular, peculiar, and
most variegated vein of wit, always rightly intended (although
not always so rightly directed), delightful in many instances,
and salutary even where it is most offensive ; when you consider
his strict truth, his fortitude in resisting oppression and arbitrary power ; his fidelity in friendship, his sincere love and zeal
for religion, his uprightness in making right resolutions, and his
steadiness in adhering to them ; his care of his church, its choir,
its economy, and its income ; his attention to all those that
preached in his cathedral, in order to their amendment in pronunciation and style ; as also his remarkable attention to the
interest of his successors, preferably to his own present emolu-
ments ; his invincible patriotism, even to a country which he
did not love ; his very various, well-devised, well-judged, and
extensive charities, throughout his life, and his whole fortune (to
say nothing of his wife's) conveyed to the same Christian purposes at his death ; charities from which he could enjoy no
honour, advantage, or satisfaction of any kind in this world ;
when you consider his ironical and humorous, as well as his
serious schemes, for the promotion of true religion and virtue,
his success in soliciting for the First Fruits and Twentieths, to
the unspeakable benefit of the Established Church of Ireland ;
and his felicity (to rate it no higher) in giving occasion to the
building of fifty new churches in London :

" All this considered, the character of his life will appear

96 Delany's ' Observations,' 8vo. 1754, p. 75.

like that of his writings; they will both bear to be re-considered and re-examined with the utmost attention, and always discover new beauties and excellences upon every examination.

" They will bear to be considered as the sun, in which the brightness will hide the blemishes; and whenever petulant ignorance, pride, malignity, or envy interposes to cloud or sully his fame, I will take upon me to pronounce that the eclipse will not last long.

" To conclude—No man ever deserved better of his country than Swift did of his.   A steady, persevering, inflexible friend ; a wise, a watchful, and a faithful counsellor, under many severe trials and bitter persecutions, to the manifest hazard both of his liberty and fortune.

" He lived a blessing, he died a benefactor, and his name will ever live an honour to Ireland." [97]

In the poetical works of Dr. Swift there is not much upon which the critic can exercise his powers.   They are often humorous, almost always light, and have the qualities which recommend such compositions, easiness and gaiety.   They are, for the most part, what their author intended.   The diction is correct, the numbers are smooth, and the rhymes exact.   There seldom occurs a hard-laboured   expression,   or a redundant

[97] Delany's 'Observations,' 8vo. 1754, p. 291.

My breakfast is that of a sickly man, rice-gruel; and I am wholly a stranger to tea and coffee, the companions of bread and butter.—SWIFT to Miss Hoadly, June 4, 1734.

My chief support is French wine, which, although not equal to yours, I drink a bottle to myself every day.   I keep three horses, two men, and an old woman, in a large empty house, and dine half the week like a king by myself.— SWIFT to Barber, March 1, 1734-5.

I very seldom go to church for fear of being seized with a fit of giddiness in the midst of the service.—SWIFT to Barber, Sept. 3, 1735.

I dine constantly at home in my chamber, with a grave housekeeper [Mrs. Brent], whom I call Sir Robert [Walpole]; and sometimes receive one or two friends, and a female cousin [Mrs. Whiteway], with strong, high, tenor voices.— SWIFT to Erasmus Lewis, July 23, 1737.

When he rode he wore strong spatterdashes, which he could slip off as soon as he alighted from his horse; and to match these spatterdashes, he had shoes strong in proportion to bear the dirt and weather; but he never wore boots.— DEANE SWIFT (note on Letter to Sheridan, of June, 1735).

epithet; all his verses exemplify his own definition of a good
style—they consist of " proper words in proper places."

To divide this collection into classes, and show how some
pieces are gross, and some are trifling, would be to tell the
reader what he knows already, and to find faults of which the
author could not be ignorant, who certainly wrote not often to
his judgment, but his humour.

It was said, in a preface to one of the Irish editions, that
Swift had never been known to take a single thought from any
writer, ancient or modern.[98] This is not literally true; but
perhaps no writer can easily be found that has borrowed so
little, or that in all his excellences and all his defects has so
well maintained his claim to be considered as original.

---

[98] Copied from the ' Verses on his own Death:'

> To steal a hint was never known,
> But what he writ was all his own.

But the last line is stolen from Denham's verses on Cowley:

> To him no author was unknown,
> Yet what he wrote was all his own.

The ' Life of Swift,' by Hawkesworth, has been superseded by Sir Walter
Scott's able and ample account of Swift, prefixed to the second edition of
Swift's Works (19 vols. 8vo. 1824).

The first to write about Swift were three Irishmen: Lord Orrery in 1752,
Dr. Delany in 1754, and Deane Swift in 1755. Lord Orrery abused Swift,
Delany abused Orrery, and Deane Swift abused Orrery and Delany. Soon
after Johnson wrote (this too-imperfect memoir), a fourth Irishman, Thomas
Sheridan, appeared with a new Life of Swift, in a thick octavo volume. Sheri-
dan, in a dull book, laboured to abuse everybody. All that has been written
by Irishmen of Swift, reminds one of a saying preserved by Swift himself:—
" I heard King William say, that if the people of Ireland could be believed in
what they said of each other, there was not an honest man in the kingdom."
(Swift to Tickell, 18th Sept. 1735.)

A fear of overlaying Johnson's *Life* has been my sole reason for not extract-
ing some masterly passages from Lord Jeffrey's able review of Scott's *Life of
Swift*.

APPENDIX.

SWIFT TO CHARLES LORD HALIFAX.

[Addit. MS. Brit. Mus. 7121, fol. 71, *Orig.*]

Leicester, January 13, 1709.

MY LORD,—Before I leave this place (where ill-health has detained me longer than I intended) I thought it my duty to return your Lordship my acknowledgments for all your favours to me while I was in town ; and, at the same time, to beg some share in your Lordship's memory, and the continuance of your protection. You were pleased to promise me your good offices upon occasion ; which I humbly challenge in two particulars : one is, that you will sometimes put my Lord President in mind of me ; the other is, that your Lordship will duly once every year wish me removed to England. In the mean time, I must take leave to reproach your Lordship for a most inhuman piece of cruelty ; for I can call your extreme good usage of me no better, since it has taught me to hate the place where I am banished, and raised my thoughts to an imagination that I might live to be some way useful or entertaining if I were permitted to live in town, or (which is the highest punishment on Papists) anywhere within ten miles round it. You remember very well, my Lord, how another person of quality in Horace's time used to serve a sort of fellows who had disobliged him ; how he sent them fine clothes and money, which raised their thoughts and their hopes, till those were worn out and spent, and then they were ten times more miserable than before. *Hac ego si compellar imagine, cuncta resigno.* I could cite several other passages from the same author, to my purpose ; and whatever is applied to Mæcenas I will not thank your Lordship for accepting, because it is what you have been condemned to these twenty years by every one of us, *qui se mêlent d'avoir de l'esprit.* I have been studying how to be revenged of your Lordship, and have found out the way. They have in Ireland the same idea with us of your Lordship's generosity, magnificence, wit, judgment, and knowledge of the enjoyment of life. But I shall quickly undeceive them, by letting them plainly know that you have neither interest nor fortune which you can call your own ; both having been long made over to the corporation of deserving men in want, who have appointed you their advocate and steward, which the world is pleased to call patron and protector. I shall inform them, that myself and about a dozen others kept the best table in England, to which because we admitted your Lordship in common with us, made you our manager, and sometimes allowed you to bring a friend, therefore ignorant people would needs take you to be the owner. And lastly, that you are the most injudicious person alive ; because, though you have fifty times more wit than all of us together, you never discover the least value for it, but are perpetually countenancing and encouraging that of others. I could add a great deal more, but shall reserve the rest of my threatenings till further provoca-

tion. In the mean time I demand of your Lordship the justice of believing
me to be with the greatest respect,

My Lord, your Lordship's most obedient and
most obliged humble servant,   JON. SWIFT.

Pray, my Lord, desire Dr. South to die about the fall of the leaf, for he
has a prebend of Westminster, which will make me your neighbour, and a
sinecure in the country, both in the Queen's gift, which my friends have
often told me would fit me extremely : and forgive me one word, which I
know not what extorts from me ; that if my Lord President would in
such a juncture think me worth laying any worth of his credit, you
cannot think me persuaded that it would be a very easy matter to
compass ; and I have some sort of pretence, since the late King promised
me a prebend of Westminster, when I petitioned him in pursuance of a
recommendation I had from Sir William Temple.[99]

SWIFT TO CHARLES LORD HALIFAX.
[Addit. MS. Brit. Mus. 7121, fol. 73, *Orig.*]

Dublin, November 13, 1709.

MY LORD,—I cannot but pity your Lordship's misfortune in being a
great man, by which disadvantage you are never qualified to receive such
letters as you write ; but instead of them, only tedious expressions of
respect and gratitude ; wherein you are generally deceived too : for I
believe it is with gratitude as with love, the more a man has of it at heart,
he is but the worse at expressing it. Such reflections as these were occasioned by your Lordship's letter ; and what is yet worse, I am afraid I
have discovered through all your Lordship's civilities, that I have some
share in your favour, and God knows what deductions a man may draw
from thence, though he had no vanity to assist him. I ever thought it a
mighty oversight in Courts to let the *honnête homme*, the *homme d'esprit*,
and *homme de bien* gain ground among them, because those qualities will
be sure to predominate over business and greatness, as they now do with
your Lordship, who against all forms is pleased to remember a useless
man at so great a distance, where it would be pardonable for his idlest
friends, and of his own level, to forget him. I join with your Lordship in
one compliment, because it is grounded on so true a knowledge of the
taste of this country, where I can assure you, and I call Mr. Addison for
my witness, I pass as undistinguished in every point that is merit with
your Lordship as any man in it. But then I do them impartial justice ;
for, except the Bishop of Clogher and perhaps one or two more, my opinion
is extremely uniform of the whole kingdom. However, I retire into
myself with great satisfaction, and remembering I have had the honour to
converse with your Lordship, I say as Horace did when he meant your
predecessor, *Cum magnis vixisse invita fatebitur usque invidia.*

Yet for all this, if I had a mind to be malicious, I could make a vanity

---

[99] Halifax's answer was preserved by Swift with this endorsement :—" I
kept this letter as a true original of courtiers and court promises." Scott's
Swift, xv. 348.

at your Lordship's expense, by letting people here know that I have some share in your esteem.   For I must inform you, to your great mortification, that your Lordship is universally admired by this tasteless people.   But not to humble you too much, I find that it is for no other reason than that for which women are so fond of those they call the wits, merely for their reputation.   They have heard wonderful things of your Lordship, and they presently imagine you to possess those qualities they most esteem in themselves, as the asses did when they discoursed about Socrates.   For if your Lordship were here in disguise, perhaps it would be just as if you sent your pictures and statues to a country fair ; where one would offer half a crown for a piece of Titian to stick on a sign-post, another a shilling for a Grecian statue to fright away the crows.   Which thought I have a mind to make into a fable, and put it on Mr. Addison for an old one, in revenge for his putting that of Socrates and the asses upon me, because it scaped his reading.

Can your Lordship pardon so tedious a letter in Parliament time ?   Put it under your couch, I advise you, my Lord, as I remember you use to do the dull poems and pamphlets that come out, till the end of the Sessions. Otherwise I shall be tempted to laugh with pride when I consider my own power, how I was able at this distance to put a stop to the whole course of public business ; how I deferred some new scheme for supplying the war in all these exigencies without burthening the subject ; how I suspended some law wherein the welfare of ten millions was concerned ; and how I withheld the peace of Europe for four minutes together.

Yet all these are trifles in comparison of having such a solicitor as your Lordship, of which I will make this use, that if you think this gentle winter will not carry off Dr. South,[100] or that his reversion is not to be compassed, your Lordship would please to use your credit that, as my Lord Somers thought of me last year for the Bishopric of Waterford, so my Lord President may now think on me for that of Cork, if the incumbent dies of the spotted fever he is now under ; and then I shall be sure of the honour to pass some winters at your Lordship's Levee ; though not with equal satisfaction, as in the former case.

> I am, with the greatest respect, my Lord,
>> Your Lordship's most obedient, most obliged,
>>> and most humble servant,   J. SWIFT.

SWIFT TO ARBUTHNOT.   [Now first published.]

[Letcombe,] June 16, 1714.

DEAR BROTHER,—My stomach is prouder than you imagine, and I scorned to write till I was writ to.   I have already half lost the ideas of Courts and Ministers.   I dine between 12 and 1, and the whole house is abed by 10 and up at 6.   I drink no wine, and see but one dish of meat. I pay a guinea a week for dieting and lodging myself and man with an

---

[100] South lingered on till 1716, and Halifax lost political power in 1710, when Swift went over to the Tories.   Compare note 11, vol. ii. p. 84.

honest clergyman of my old acquaintance, and my paying is forced, for he
has long invited me. I did not know till last night that the Princess Sophia
was dead, when my landlord and I chanced to pay a visit to a farmer in a
neighbouring village, and was told so over a mug of ale, by a brisk young
fellow just come from London, who talked big and looked on us with great
contempt. I thank you for your kindness to poor Gay : was the money
paid, or put off till the day after he went ? I reckon by what you tell me
that it is now a high season to be very merry in Lady   lodgings.
I heartily pity you in particular. Look after your mistress and yourself,
grow rich, and since nothing better can be done, let the world   . I
have a mind to live in Yorkshire for a year, in order to put myself out of
memory and debt. The fashion of this world passeth away : however, I am
angry at those who disperse us sooner than these may need. I have a mind
to be very angry, and to let my anger break out in some manner that will not
please them at the end of a pen. I wish you could get Lady M[asham]
to give you these hints we have often spoke of, and to muster up your own :
for the Dragon [Oxford], I despair he will do that any more than anything
else, and indeed you are all of you Dragons more or less, for I am sure it
is above 3 years since I have spoke to Lady M. and you about this. My
humble service to my Lord and her, whom I love as much as you do,
though I have greater obligations to them, and my humble services and
thanks to the Qu— of Prudes for remembering me. You are a set of
people drawn almost to the dregs ; you must try another game ; this is at
an end. Your ministry is fourscore and ten years old, and all you can
endeavour at is an Euthanasia, or rather it is in a deep consumption at
five-and-twenty. I approve Lady M[asham]'s conduct, and think all she
can do in relation to the Dragon is to be passive ; for the rest to cultivate
her own credit to the utmost. Writing to you much would make me stark
mad. Judge his condition who has nothing to keep him from being miserable
but endeavouring to forget those for whom he has the greatest value, love,
and friendship. But you are a Philosopher and a Physician, and can
overcome by your wisdom and your faculty those weaknesses which other
men are forced to reduce by not thinking on them. Adieu, and love me
half so well as I do you.

SWIFT TO ARBUTHNOT.   [Now first published.]

[Letcombe,] July 25, 1714.

YOU are every way too kind. As to the Historiographer's place, I now
hear it has been disposed of these 3 weeks to one Madocks. I wonder Lord
Bol— knew nothing of it. So there is an end of that, and of twenty
reflections one might make upon it. If the Qu— is indifferent in those
matters, I may well be so too. I was 3 days last week in Oxford with
Lord and Lady H, and Dr. Str—d. Our talk was of the Dragon's being
out, as a thing done ; so no more reflections on that neither :—Qu'est que
l'homme. And so you will lend me all your money. The mischief
is I never borrow money of a friend. You are mightily mistaken : all your
honour, generosity, good nature, good sense, wit, and every other praiseworthy quality, will never make me think one jot the better of you. That

time is now some years past, and you will never mend in my opinion. But really, Brother, you have a sort of shuffle in your gait; and now I have said the worst that your most mortal enemy would say of you with truth.   I defy Pope and his burning glasses.[101]   A man cannot amuse himself 50 miles from London, after four years jading himself with Ministers of State, but all the town must hear of it.   However, if Pope makes the right use of your hint for an epigram, or a longer copy, I shall not be angry.   It was a malicious satire of yours upon Whiston, that what you intended as a ridicule, should be any way struck upon by him for a reality.   Go on for the sake of wit and humour, and cultivate that vein which no man alive possesses but yourself, and which lay like a mine in the earth, which the owner for a long time never knew of.   Lady M——m, who talked of writing to me, but yet has not answered my letter : put her not in mind, I beg you.   I believe she has heard of my letter to the Dragon, and dislikes it as partial.   I hear he has shown it to every living soul, and I believe has done so in *malice*, as the French understand that word.   My humble service to Lord and Lady M— and Mrs. Hill.   By what I heard at Oxford Lord Trevor is fallen off with the rest ; and indeed the circle of the Dragon's friends seemed very narrow, by the loss they were at for healths :—we came to yours six glasses before the usual time.

SWIFT TO ARBUTHNOT.   [Now first published.]

[Dublin, 1733 ?]

MY DEAR FRIEND,—I never once suspected your forgetfulness or want of friendship, but very often dreaded your want of health, to which alone I imputed every delay longer than ordinary in hearing from you.   I should be very ungrateful indeed if I acted otherwise to you, who are pleased to take such generous constant care of my health, my interests, and my reputation, who represented me so favourably to that blessed Queen your mistress, as well as to her Ministers, and to all your friends. The letters you mention which I did not answer, I cannot find, and yet I have all that ever came from you, for I constantly endorse yours and those of a few other friends, and date them ; only if there be anything particular, though of no consequence, when I go to the country I send them to some friends among other papers for fear of accidents in my absence.   I thank you kindly for your favour to the young man who was bred in my quire.   The people of skill in music represent him to me as a lad of virtue, and hopeful and endeavouring in his way.   It is your own fault if I give you trouble, because you never refused me anything in your life.   You tear my heart with the ill account of your health ; yet if it should please God to call you away before me, I should not pity you in the least, except on the account of what pains you might feel before you passed into a better life.   I should pity none but your friends, and among them chiefly myself, although I never can hope to have health enough to leave this country till I leave the world.   I do not know among mankind any person more prepared to depart from us than yourself, not even the

---

[101] Swift alludes to a news-letter (as yet unpublished) from Pope to Arbuthnot.

Bishop of Marseilles,[102] if he be still alive ; for among all your qualities that have procured you the love and esteem of the world, I ever most valued your moral and Christian virtues, which were not the product of years or sickness, but of reason and religion, as I can witness after above five-and-twenty years' acquaintance.   I except only the too little care of your fortune ; upon which I have been so free as sometimes to examine and to chide you, and the consequence of which hath been to confine you to London, when you are under a disorder for which I am told, and know, that the clear air of the country is necessary.   The great reason that hinders my journey to England, is the same that drives you from Highgate : I am not in circumstances to keep horses and servants in London.   My revenues by the miserable oppressions of this kingdom are sunk 300*l.* a year, for tithes are become a drug, and I have but little rents from the Deanery lands, which are my only sure payments.   I have here a large convenient house ; I live at two-thirds cheaper here than I could there ; I drink a bottle of French wine myself every day, though I love it not; but it is the only thing that keeps me out of pain.   I ride every fair day a dozen miles, on a large strand or turnpike road.   You in London have no such advantages.   I can buy a chicken for a groat, and entertain three or four friends, with as many dishes, and two or three bottles of French wine, for 10 shillings.   When I dine alone, my pint and chicken with the appendices cost me about 15 pence.   I am thrifty in everything but wine, of which though I be not a constant housekeeper, I spend between five and six hogsheads a year.   When I ride to a friend a few miles off, if he be not richer than I, I carry my bottle, my bread and chicken, that he may be no loser.   I talk thus foolishly to let you know the reasons which, joined to my ill-health, make it impossible for me to see you and my other friends.   And perhaps this domestic tattle may excuse me, and amuse you.   I could not live with my Lord Bo— or Mr. Pope : they are both too temperate and too wise for me, and too profound and too poor.   And how could I afford horses ?   And how could I ride over their cursed roads in winter, and be turned into a ditch by every carter or hackney coach ?   Every parish minister of this city is governor of all carriages, and so are the two Deans, and every carter, &c., makes way for us at their peril. Therefore, like Cæsar, I will be one of the first here rather than the last among you.   I forget that I am so near the bottom.   I am now with one of my Prebendaries five miles in the country, for five days.   I brought with me 8 bottles of wine, with bread and meat for three days, which is my club : he is a bachelor, with 300*l.* a year.   Pray God preserve you, my dear friend.   Entirely yours,   J. SWIFT.[103]

Dr. John Arbuthnot, at his house, Cork
Street, Burlington Gardens.

---

[102] The Bishop immortalized by Pope.

[103] Lord Mahon has published for the first time an able character of Arbuthnot by no less an observer than Lord Chesterfield.   (Letters, vol. ii. p. 446.)

WILLIAM BROOME.

BROOME.

1689 ?–1745.

Born at Haslington, in Cheshire — Educated at Eton and Cambridge — Enters into Holy Orders — Introduced to Pope — Assists Pope in the Notes to the Iliad — Assists him in translating the Odyssey — His Quarrel with Pope — His Miscellany Poems — Marries — Death and Burial in Bath Abbey Church — Works and Character.

WILLIAM BROOME was born in Cheshire, as is said, of very mean parents. Of the place of his birth, or the first part of his life, I have not been able to gain any intelligence.[1] He was educated upon the foundation at Eton, and was captain of the school a whole year, without any vacancy, by which he might have obtained a scholarship at King's College. Being by this delay, such as is said to have happened very rarely,[2] superannuated, he was sent to St. John's College [Cambridge] by the contributions of his friends, where he obtained a small exhibition.[3]

At his College he lived for some time in the same chamber with the well-known Ford,[4] by whom I have formerly heard him described as a contracted scholar and a mere versifier, unacquainted with life, and unskilful in conversation. His addiction

---

[1] He was born at Haslington, in the parish of Barthomley and county of Chester, about the year 1689. His father (Randle Broome) was a farmer. See Barlow's 'Memoir of Broome,' 12mo., 1854, p. 7. On his portrait before his 'Poems'—D. Heins, p. 1725, G. Vertue, sculp.—is this inscription: "William Broome, ætat. xxxvii. 1726." He was therefore born in 1688 or 1689, and consequently of the same age as Pope.

[2] It happened but four times in 160 years, viz., in 1619, 1653, 1707, 1756.—*Gent.'s Mag.* for 1780, p. 269.

[3] He was matriculated a sizar the 10th of July, 1708, took his B.A. degree in January, 1711-12, and his A.M. degree in 1716.—BARLOW'S *Broome*, p. 7.

[4] See Johnson's Life of Fenton, vol. ii. p. 276, and Mr. Croker's note in Boswell, ed. 1847, p. 9.

to metre was then such, that his companions familiarly called
him Poet. When he had opportunities of mingling with mankind, he cleared himself, as Ford likewise owned, from great
part of his scholastic rust.

He appeared early in the world as a translator of the 'Iliads'
into prose, in conjunction with Ozell and Oldisworth. How
their several parts were distributed is not known. This is the
translation of which Ozell boasted [5] as superior, in Toland's
opinion, to that of Pope : it has long since vanished, and is now
in no danger from the critics.

He was introduced to Mr. Pope, who was then visiting Sir
John Cotton at Madingley near Cambridge, and gained so
much of his esteem, that he was employed, I believe, to make
extracts from Eustathius for the notes to the translation of the
'Iliad ;' and in the volumes of poetry published by Lintot,
commonly called ' Pope's Miscellanies,' many of his early pieces
were inserted. [6]

Pope and Broome were to be yet more closely connected.
When the success of the 'Iliad' gave encouragement to a
version of the 'Odyssey,' Pope, weary of the toil, called Fenton
and Broome to his assistance ; and taking only half the work
upon himself, divided the other half between his partners, giving
four books to Fenton, and *eight* to Broome. Fenton's books I
have enumerated in his Life ; to the lot of Broome fell the second,
sixth, eighth, eleventh, twelfth, sixteenth, eighteenth, and twenty-
third, together with the burthen of writing all the notes. [7]

[5] In an advertisement of 20th September, 1729, in a paper called 'The
Weekly Medley.' Pope transferred the advertisement to his edition of 'The
Dunciad,' 1736, 12mo. p. 111.

[6] In the first ed., 1 vol. 8vo., 1712, he has five poems. In the fourth ed.,
2 vols. 12mo., 1722, he has twelve poems. In the sixth ed., 2 vols. 12mo.,
1732, his former poems are omitted, and two new ones (those to Pope) inserted
instead.

[7] Before Broome's ' Poems,' 8vo., 1739, is the following ' Advertisement :'—
" The author has not inserted into this collection any part of his Translation of
the eight books of the Odyssey published by Mr. Pope: he thought it an im-
position on the public to swell this volume with verses taken from a work that
is in the hands of almost every reader." And in the Preface to the same
volume he describes himself, p. xii., as " The Annotator in part upon the
Iliad, and entirely upon the Odyssey."

As this translation is a very important event in poetical history, the reader has a right to know upon what grounds I establish my narration.   That the version was not wholly Pope's, was always known : he had mentioned the assistance of two friends in his Proposals,[8] and at the end of the work some account is given by Broome of their different parts, which, however, mentions only *five* books as written by the coadjutors ; the fourth and twentieth by Fenton ; the sixth, the eleventh, and eighteenth by himself ; though Pope, in an advertisement prefixed afterwards to a new volume of his works, claimed only twelve.[9]   A natural curiosity, after the real conduct of so great an undertaking, incited me once to inquire of Dr. Warburton, who told me, in his warm language, that he thought the relation given in the note [10] " a lie ;" but that he was not able to ascertain the several shares.   The intelligence which Dr. Warburton could not afford me, I obtained from Mr. Langton, to whom Mr. Spence had imparted it.[11]

The price at which Pope purchased this assistance was three hundred pounds paid to Fenton, and five hundred to Broome,[12] with as many copies as he wanted for his friends, which amounted to one hundred more.   The payment made to Fenton I know not but by hearsay ; Broome's is very distinctly told by Pope in the notes to ' The Dunciad.' [13]

[8] Dated 10th January, 1724-5.   " The benefit of this Proposal is not solely for my own use, but for that of two of my friends, who have assisted me in this work.   One of them enjoins me to conceal his name ; the other is the Reverend Mr. Broome, whose assistance I have formerly acknowledged in many of the notes and extracts annexed to my translation of the Iliad."

[9] Advertisement to the second volume of his Works in folio, quarto, and duodecimo, 1735.

[10] By the note Johnson means the Postscript to ' The Odyssey,' in which the statement there made by Pope is certainly a lie.

[11] See Johnson's Letter to Joseph Warton on this subject in Boswell by Croker, p. 647, ed. 1848.

[12] The only statement on this subject in Spence is, that Fenton had 240*l.*, and Broome 600*l.* (' Spence by Singer,' p. 326.)   Broome, in a letter to Pope, of 29th October, 1735, says, " You paid me 500*l.* ; that is, 100*l.* for the notes, and 400*l.* for eight books of the verse translation, and Mr. Fenton in proportion for his four books."—(Unpublished Letter in Mr. Croker's possession.) From this it would appear that Broome believed that Fenton's remuneration was the same as his own, which it appears now was not the case.

[13] And also in his famous letter to Lord Hervey. " What he gave him

It is evident that, according to Pope's own estimate, Broome was unkindly treated. If four books could merit three hundred pounds, eight and all the notes, equivalent at least to four, had certainly a right to more than six.

Broome probably considered himself as injured, and there was for some time more than coldness between him and his employer. He always spoke of Pope as too much a lover of money, and Pope pursued him with avowed hostility; for he not only named him disrespectfully in 'The Dunciad,' [14] but quoted him more than once in the 'Bathos,' as a proficient in the "Art of Sinking;" and in his enumeration of the different kinds of poets distinguished for the profound, he reckons Broome among "the parrots who repeat another's words in such a hoarse odd voice as makes them seem their own." [15]   I have been told

was five hundred pounds: his receipt can be produced to your Lordship." Sir Henry Bunbury has large extracts, in Broome's handwriting, from his portion of the 'Odyssey,' and from his poem on the 'War in Flanders,' which he had probably sent to Sir Thomas [Hanmer] for approbation and patronage. Sir Henry also possesses "a memorandum of the respective shares borne by Pope, Fenton, and Broome in the translation of the 'Odyssey,' which corresponds with the statements already published."—*Hanmer Correspondence*, 8vo., 1838, p. 213.

[14] Johnson should have said in the early editions of 'The Dunciad.'

> Hibernian politics, O Swift, thy doom;
> And Pope's, translating three whole years with Broome.

Where also this note occurs: "He concludes his irony with a stroke upon himself; for whoever imagines this a sarcasm on the other ingenious person is surely mistaken." Broome, however, was not satisfied, and in the edition 12mo., 1736, we read:

> Hibernian politics, O Swift, thy fate;
> And Pope's, *whole* years to comment and translate.

Subsequently altered to *ten*. The leaf of the edition of 1736 in which the alteration occurs was sent by Pope to Broome in a letter, dated 12th Jan., 1735–6, and is now in Mr. Croker's possession.

[15] But the passage in 'The Art of Sinking' which occasioned the greatest annoyance to Broome is that in Chapter VII.: "Another author [there are no initials], describing a poet that shines forth amidst a circle of critics—

> Thus Phœbus through the Zodiac takes his way,
> And amid monsters rises into day.

What a peculiarity is here of invention!" &c. This couplet is by Broome, and Broome wrote to Fenton and to Pope himself about it. Pope, in his reply,

that they were afterwards reconciled; but I am afraid their peace was without friendship.[16]

He afterwards [1739] published a Miscellany of Poems, which is inserted, with corrections,[17] in the late compilation.

He never rose to a very high dignity in the church. He was some time rector of Sturston in Suffolk, where he married [1716][18] a wealthy widow; and afterwards, when the King[19] visited Cambridge (1728), became Doctor of Laws. He was (1733) presented by the Crown to the rectory of Pulham in Norfolk, which he held with Oakley Magna in Suffolk, given him by the Lord Cornwallis, to whom he was chaplain, and who added the vicarage of Eye in Suffolk; he then resigned Pulham, and retained the other two.[20]

Towards the close of his life he grew again poetical, and amused himself with translating Odes of Anacreon, which he

says that it was neither his doing nor Dr. Arbuthnot's, but was inserted by a friend.—(Unpublished Letters in Mr. Croker's possession.)

An Epigram, occasioned by P—'s abuse of Mr. Broome, Author of the Dissertation and Notes upon Homer.

> By Pope's applause, Broome gain'd a Critic's fame,
>   And by his envy lost the Poet's name.
> (Thus does the moon in feeble radiance bright
>   Eclipse the sun to whom she owes her light.)
> How vile the Instruments which Heaven employs
>   To swell our sorrows or exalt our joys!
> So Rome's fam'd Capitol, devoid of aid,
>   A Goose once sav'd, a strumpet once betray'd.

The Daily Journal, Oct. 2, 1728.

[16] Their reconciliation took place in 1735, on Broome's transmitting to Pope a letter of the 22nd July, 1735, from Curll, applying for any letter he might wish to publish, addressed to him by Pope. Broome did not even answer Curll's letter. (Unpublished Letters in Mr. Croker's possession.)

[17] " The second Edition, with large alterations and additions," was published in 8vo., 1750, "for Henry Lintot." In Bernard Lintot's Book of Accounts, under the name Broome, is the following entry :—

Feb. 22, 1726-7 . . . Misc. Poems, £35.

[18] 1716. William Broome, clerk and rector of this parish, and Mrs. Elizabeth Clarke, widow, were married with license July y[e] 22d, by me, James Oldfield, rector of Brome.—*Parish Register of Sturston* (Barlow's Broome, p. 11).

[19] George II.

[20] This is not the case. He died rector of Pulham, and so describes himself in his will, dated a month before he died.

published [1739-40] in 'The Gentleman's Magazine,' under the name of Chester.[21]

He died at Bath, November 16, 1745, and was buried in the Abbey Church.[22]

Of Broome, though it cannot be said that he was a great poet, it would be unjust to deny that he was an excellent versifier; his lines are smooth and sonorous, and his diction is select and elegant.[23]   His rhymes are sometimes unsuitable : in his 'Melancholy,' he makes *breath* rhyme to *birth* in one place, and to *earth* in another.   Those faults occur but seldom ; and he had such power of words and numbers as fitted him for translation ; but, in his original works, recollection seems to have been his business more than invention.   His imitations are so apparent, that it is part of his reader's employment to recall the verses of some former poet.   Sometimes he copies the most popular writers, for he seems scarcely to endeavour at concealment ; and sometimes he picks up fragments in obscure corners. His lines to Fenton, ·

> " Serene, the sting of pain thy thoughts beguile,
>   And make afflictions objects of a smile,"

brought to my mind some lines on the death of Queen Mary, written by Barnes, of whom I should not have expected to find an imitator :

> " But thou, O Muse, whose sweet nepenthean tongue
>   Can charm the pangs of death with deathless song ;
>   Canst *stinging plagues* with easy *thoughts beguile*,
>   *Make* pains and tortures *objects of a smile*."

To detect his imitations were tedious and useless.   What he takes he seldom makes worse ; and he cannot be justly thought a mean man whom Pope chose for an associate, and whose

[21] That is, Charles Chester, M.D.

[22] Dr. Gooch, Bishop of Norwich, read the service. His grave is not marked, and the date of his burial in the register is the date of his death. He left an only son, Charles John Broome, who died 1747, an under-graduate of St. John's College, Cambridge. The poet's widow died in 1750.

[23] Christopher Pitt, the poet, who has a right to be heard on a poetical question, praises particularly "the charming translation of the Eleventh Book of the 'Odyssey.'"—*MS. Letter to Broome.*

co-operation was considered by Pope's enemies as so important, that he was attacked by Henley with this ludicrous distich :

"Pope came off clean with Homer ; but they say
Broome went before, and kindly swept the way." [24]

APPENDIX.

BROOME'S WILL. [*From Barlow's ' Broome,'* 12mo. 1854.]

"In the name of the most High and Adorable God, Amen. I, William Broome, Rector of Pulham, in yᵉ County of Norfolk, make my Will and Testament, in yᵉ manner following : First, I give to Elizabeth Broome, my Wife, all my Lands and Tenements whatsoever lying in Mindlesham, Brockford, Thwaite, or any other Parish adjoining, as also yᵉ Marshes in Sudborne, the House in Dickleburgh, and likewise all that Estate, now in yᵉ occupation of Samuel Weavers, yᵉ younger, rented at forty-four pounds yearly, whether yᵉ premises ly in Sturston, Thrandiston, Brome, in Suffolk, or any Parish adjoining ; and my Will is, that she hold and enjoy yᵉ same during yᵉ term of her natural life, upon this express condition, that she contracts no future marriage, but continues a Widow during life. Also I give unto yᵉ said Elizabeth Broome, my Wife, all my Bills, Bonds, Notes, Plate, Household Goods, and all Furniture within doors and without, during yᵉ term of her natural life, if she shall continue unmarried to yᵉ day of her death ; but if she shall marry again, then my Will is, that all yᵉ aforesaid premises, personal or real, of what kind soever, immediately descend to my only Son, Charles John Broome, as if yᵉ said Elizabeth were naturally extinct. Item I give to yᵉ said Charles John Broome, all my Estates lying in Mindlesham, Brockford, Thwaite, or any Parish adjoining, as also yᵉ Marshes in Sudborne, all lying in Suffolk, to him and his heirs, lawfully begotten, for ever, as also all my Plate, Moneys, Furniture, Stock and Household Goods of all kinds, after yᵉ decease of his Mother. Item I give to yᵉ said Charles John Broome, all that Estate in yᵉ occupation of Samuel Weavers, yᵉ younger, rented of me at forty-four pounds yearly, during yᵉ term of his natural life, whether

---

[24] A couplet like this had been applied before to Richard Brome, the dramatic poet and servant of Ben Jonson :—

Sent by Ben Jonson, as some authors say,
Broom went before, and kindly swept the way.
Choyce Drollery : Songs and Sonnets, 12mo., London, 1656.

yᵉ premises ly in Sturston, Thrandiston, or any other Parish adjoining, but if yᵉ said Charles John Broome shall have Heir or Heirs, lawfully begotten, then I give yᵉ said premises to him and his Heirs for ever; but my Will and intent is, that if yᵉ said Charles John Broome shall decease without Heirs or Heir, lawfully begotten, that then all yᵉ said Estate, now occupied by Samuel Weavers, shall descend to yᵉ Right Honourable Charles Lord Cornwallis, my patron and constant friend, and to his Heirs for ever, as a testimony of my gratitude to my great Benefactor, and to be possessed by him or them in full right of any of the Estates of theirs, in Brome or Culford. And whereas, my Brother, Richard Broome, of Dagenham, in Essex, stands indebted to me, in a note of twenty pounds, bearing date October yᵉ 5th, 1737, or thereabouts; as also in a Bond of £240, bearing date March yᵉ 25th, 1737, or thereabouts; as also in another Bond of four-score pounds, bearing date June yᵉ 25th, or thereabouts. And Whereas all yᵉ interest of both yᵉ Bonds, remaining entirely unpaid, I give and bequeath to my four Sisters, Elizabeth Cook, of Bank Hall, Lancashire; and to my three other Sisters, Margaret, Anne, and Sarah, the sum of one hundred pounds, to be paid by yᵉ said Richard Broome, within yᵉ space of one year after my decease, to be equally divided amongst them, and if he, yᵉ said Richard Broome, shall fail of discharging this my Legacy, within yᵉ time mention'd, I give to my said four Sisters yᵉ above named note and bonds for their own proper use and property; but if yᵉ said Richard Broome shall perform this my intent and will, I hereby discharge him of yᵉ above debt and give it him as a Legacy. Lastly I nominate and appoint Elizabeth Broome my wife sole Executrix of this my last Will and Testament. And now, O my God, Thou Father of all comforts and fountain of all mercies, I recommend my soul to thy infinite goodness for pardon and forgiveness of all my sins, trusting entirely in thy infinite mercies and yᵉ infinite merits of Christ Jesus my Saviour. Amen. Amen.

(SEAL.)

" WILLIAM BROOME.

" Signed, sealed, and delivered as my last Will and Testament in yᵉ presence of us the underwritten, Octr. 22, 1745, the words ' personal or real ' being first interlined.

" JOHN COLLET.
" BENJ. MARTIN.
" MARY MARTIN.

" Proved 31st December, 1745, by the Oath
  of the Sole Executrix within named."

CHRISTOPHER PITT.

P I T T.

1699-1748.

Born at Blandford in Dorsetshire — Educated at Winchester and Oxford — Presented to the Rectory of Pimpern in Dorsetshire — Translates Vida's 'Art of Poetry,' and Virgil's 'Æneid' — His Miscellany of Poems — Death and Burial at Blandford.

CHRISTOPHER PITT, of whom whatever I shall relate, more than has been already published, I owe to the kind communication of Dr. Warton, was born in 1699, at Blandford, the son of a physician much esteemed.

He was, in 1714, received as a scholar into Winchester College, where he was distinguished by exercises of uncommon elegance, and, at his removal to New College in 1719, presented to the electors, as the product of his private and voluntary studies, a complete version of Lucan's poem, which he did not then know to have been translated by Rowe.

This is an instance of early diligence which well deserves to be recorded. The suppression of such a work, recommended by such uncommon circumstances, is to be regretted. It is indeed culpable to load libraries with superfluous books; but incitements to early excellence are never superfluous, and from this example the danger is not great of many imitations.

When he had resided at his college three years, he was presented to the rectory of Pimpern, in Dorsetshire (1722), by his relation, Mr. Pitt of Stratfieldsaye, in Hampshire;[1] and, resigning his Fellowship, continued at Oxford two years longer, till he became Master of Arts (1724).

He probably about this time translated 'Vida's Art of Poetry,'[2] which Tristram's splendid edition had then made

---

[1] To whom he afterwards dedicated his 'Poems and Translations,' 1727.

[2] 'Vida's Art of Poetry, Translated into English Verse by the Reverend Mr. Christoph. Pitt, A.M., late Fellow of New College in Oxford, Rector of

popular. In this translation he distinguished himself, both by its general elegance and by the skilful adaptation of his numbers to the images expressed —a beauty which Vida has with great ardour enforced and exemplified.

He then retired to his living,[3] a place very pleasing by its

Pimpern in Dorsetshire, and Chaplain to the Right Honourable Philip Earl Stanhope,' &c. London: printed by Sam. Palmer, for A. Bettesworth, at the Red Lion, in Paternoster Row, 1725. 12mo. A new edition, corrected, was printed, in an Elzevir type, by Dodsley, in 1743, price 2s. 6d.

[3] I had never any thoughts of leaving Pimpern, nor would I change it for a benefice of three times the value in a bad country. If I may quote the end of one of these *Epistles*, you will find it so :—

> When to delicious Pimpern I retire,
> What greater bliss (my Spence) can I desire?
> Contented there my easy hours I spend
> With maps, books, globes, a bottle, and a friend.
> There I can live upon my income still,
> Ev'n tho' the House should pass the Quakers' Bill;
> Yet to my share should some good prebend fall,
> I think myself of size to fill a stall.
> For life or wealth let Heaven my lot assign,
> A firm and even soul shall still be mine.
>
>   CHR. PITT to Broome, the poet, 2nd May, 1740, (MS.)

Of these *Epistles* he gives, in the same letter to Broome, the following account:—" You are pleased to think I shall scarce ever be unemployed in something or other in the Poetical Way. The only things I have writ of that nature of late are some Imitations of Horace's Satires and Epistles, which are not touched upon by Mr. Pope, which I never designed to publish, because I thought 'em too Particular in some passages as to Times, Places, and Persons; but Mr. Pope told me, just before I left the town (for he had read 'em over), he saw no reason why they should not be published; that if in some parts they were a little too Particular (as I objected), 'twas what was unavoidable in modernizing Horace, and that he thought they might appear when I judged it a proper time." In another letter to the same correspondent he supplies an anecdote of Spence and Lord Bathurst that merits preservation:—" In one of my Imitations there is a blank in a lord's name. It was Lord Bathurst: on this occasion applied to *Quid de quoque viro*. Mr. Spence told Lord Bathurst (who you know was one of the *twelve*) that he thought the making *twelve* Peers at a dash was the worst transaction in the Queen's reign. You may guess, as soon as he recollected himself, he was in no small confusion, which my Lord dissipated in a very candid manner by joining in his opinion."

Mr. Christopher Pitt has imitated the Seventh Satire of Horace, Book II., the Nineteenth Epistle of Book II., the Fourth Epistle of Book I., and the Tenth and Eighteenth of Book I., with a *freedom* and a facility of versification truly Horatian,—JOS. WARTON (Pope, ed. 1797, i. liii.; see also vi. 3).

"I gave your service, Sir, to Mr. Dobson. He has just left me, and is going to Winchester. He finished the largest part of the 7th book [of ' Paradise

situation, and therefore likely to excite the imagination of a poet, where he passed the rest of his life, reverenced for his virtue, and beloved for the softness of his temper and the easiness of his manners.   Before strangers he had something of the scholar's timidity or distrust ; but when he became familiar he was in a very high degree cheerful and entertaining.   His general benevolence procured general respect, and he passed a life placid and honourable, neither too great for the kindness of the low, nor too low for the notice of the great.

At what time he composed his miscellany, published in 1727,[4] it is not easy nor necessary to know ; those which have dates appear to have been very early productions, and I have not observed that any rise above mediocrity.

The success of his 'Vida' animated him to a higher undertaking ; and in his thirtieth year he published a version of the first book of the ' Æneid.'   This being, I suppose, commended by his friends, he some time afterwards added three or four more, with an advertisement, in which he represents himself as translating with great indifference, and with a progress of which himself was hardly conscious.   This can hardly be true, and, if true, is nothing to the reader.

At last, without any further contention with his modesty, or any awe of the name of Dryden, he gave us [5] a complete English 'Æneid,' which I am sorry not to see joined in this publication with his other poems.   It would have been pleasing to have an opportunity of comparing the two best translations that perhaps were ever produced by one nation of the same author.

Lost'] at Pimpern.   I read one or two of the books, and think 'em very happy in the variety of the periods and harmony of the numbers, the want of which, you know, is the chief fault of Ovid and Claudian.—PITT to Broome, the poet, July 29, 1740.

[4] 'Poems and Translations,' by Christopher Pitt, M.A., late Fellow of New College in Oxford.   London: printed for Bernard Lintot, &c. 1727, 8vo. p. 192.

Under Pitt's name in Lintot's book of accounts is the following entry:—

Oct. 13, 1726.   His Misc. Poems   .   .   .   .   £21.

[5] April, 1740, in 2 vols. 4to. price 21s.

Pitt engaging as a rival with Dryden naturally observed his failures, and avoided them; and as he wrote after Pope's ' Iliad,' he had an example of an exact, equable, and splendid versification. With these advantages, seconded by great diligence, he might successfully labour particular passages, and escape many errors. If the two versions are compared, perhaps the result would be, that Dryden leads the reader forward by his general vigour and sprightliness, and Pitt often stops him to contemplate the excellence of a single couplet—that Dryden's faults are forgotten in the hurry of delight, and that Pitt's beauties are neglected in the languor of a cold and listless perusal—that Pitt pleases the critics, and Dryden the people—that Pitt is quoted, and Dryden read.[6]

He did not long enjoy the reputation which this great work deservedly conferred, for he left the world in 1748, and lies buried under a stone at Blandford, on which is this inscription:

> " In memory of
> CHR. PITT, clerk, M.A.
> Very eminent
> for his talents in poetry;
> and yet more
> for the universal candour of
> his mind, and the primitive
> simplicity of his manners.
> He lived innocent,
> and died beloved,
> Apr. 13, 1748,
> aged 48."[7]

---

[6] Warton's translation [of the ' Georgics '] may in many instances be found more faithful and concise than Dryden's; but it wants that elastic and idiomatic freedom by which Dryden reconciles us to his faults, and exhibits rather the diligence of a scholar than the spirit of a poet.—T. CAMPBELL: *Specimens*, p. 664.

[7] Pitt's father translated the ' Plague of Athens,' in Creech's ' Lucretius ' ('Spence by Singer,' p. 332). He had a brother also who was a poet.

"I had an elder brother, Fellow of Wadham, who translated the first five books [of Milton] on his first going to Oxford, which upon the whole I believe were well executed, for he had a vast command of Virgil's phraseology, and could apply it very happily on some occasions."—PITT to Broome, the poet.

Whoever is curious to know more about Christopher Pitt should turn to his letters in Hughes's Correspondence.

JAMES THOMSON.

THOMSON.

1700–1748.

Born at Ednam in Roxburghshire — Educated at Edinburgh, and designed for the Church — Starts for London — His Poverty — Publishes his 'Winter,' 'Summer,' 'Spring,' and other Poems — Writes for the Stage — Is made Tutor to the Son of Lord Chancellor Talbot — Visits Italy — Made Secretary of the Briefs — Loses his office at Lord Talbot's death — Patronized by the Prince of Wales and Mr. Lyttelton — Writes 'Agamemnon' and other Tragedies — Publishes 'Liberty,' a Poem — Death and Burial at Richmond in Surrey — Works and Character.

JAMES THOMSON, the son of [the Rev. Thomas Thomson] a minister well esteemed for his piety and diligence, was born September 11, 1700, at Ednam, in the shire of Roxburgh, of which his father was pastor. His mother, whose name was Trotter,[1] inherited as co-heiress a portion of a small estate.[2] The revenue of a parish in Scotland is seldom large ; and it was probably in commiseration of the difficulty with which Mr. Thomson supported his family, having nine children, that Mr. Riccaltoun, a neighbouring minister,[3] discovering in James un-

---

[1] Johnson, following the first edition of Murdoch's 'Life,' had given the maiden name as Hume; but Murdoch discovered his error, and corrected it, as I have here corrected Johnson's. Compare Boswell to Johnson, June 18th, 1778.

[2] Widehope, in Roxburghshire.

[3] He was a poet himself. (See 'Gent.'s Mag.' for April 1853, p. 369.) "Nature delights me in every form. I am just now painting her in her most lugubrious dress for my own amusement, describing Winter as it presents itself. After my first proposal of the subject,

> I sing of Winter and his gelid reign,
> Nor let a rhyming insect of the Spring
> Deem it a barren theme. To me 'tis full
> Of manly charms; to me, who court the shade,
> Whom the gay Seasons suit not, and who shun[s]
> The glare of Summer. Welcome, kindred glooms!
> Drear, awful, wintry horrors, welcome all! &c.

"Mr. Rickleton's poem on Winter, which I still have, first put the design into my head. In it are some masterly strokes that awakened me."—THOMSON to Cranston (*cir.* Sept. 1725).

common promises of future excellence, undertook to superintend
his education and provide him books.

He was taught the common rudiments of learning at the
school of Jedburgh, a place which he delights to recollect in his
poem of ' Autumn;' but was not considered by his master as
superior to common boys, though in those early days he amused
his patron and his friends with poetical compositions; with
which, however, he so little pleased himself, that on every new-
year's day he threw into the fire all the productions of the foregoing year.

From the school he was removed to Edinburgh, where he
had not resided two years when his father died, and left all his
children to the care of their mother, who raised upon her little
estate what money a mortgage could afford, and, removing
with her family to Edinburgh, lived to see her son rising into
eminence.[4]

The design of Thomson's friends was to breed him a
minister. He lived at Edinburgh, as at school, without distinction or expectation, till, at the usual time, he performed a pro-
bationary exercise by explaining a psalm.[5] His diction was so
poetically splendid that Mr. Hamilton, the Professor of
Divinity, reproved him for speaking language unintelligible to
a popular audience; and he censured one of his expressions as
indecent, if not profane.

This rebuke is reported to have repressed his thoughts of an
ecclesiastical character, and he probably cultivated with new
diligence his blossoms of poetry, which, however, were in some
danger of a blast; for, submitting his productions to some who
thought themselves qualified to criticise, he heard of nothing but
faults; but, finding other judges more favourable, he did not
suffer himself to sink into despondence.

He easily discovered that the only stage on which a poet
could appear, with any hope of advantage, was London; a

---

[4] His father died in 1720; his mother in 1725.

[5] The prescribed exercise was an illustration of the 10th section of the 119th
Psalm. It was delivered in the Divinity Hall on the 27th October, 1724.—
CORNEY: *The Seasons, with Life by Murdoch*, p. vii.

place too wide for the operation of petty competition and
private malignity, where merit might soon become conspicuous,
and would find friends as soon as it became reputable to be-
friend it.   A lady,[6] who was acquainted with his mother,
advised him to the journey, and promised some countenance or
assistance, which at last he never received; however, he justified his adventure by her encouragement, and came [1725] to
seek in London patronage and fame.

At his arrival he found his way to Mr. Mallet, then tutor to
the sons of the Duke of Montrose.   He had recommendations
to several persons of consequence, which he had tied up carefully in his handkerchief; but as he passed along the street,
with the gaping curiosity of a new-comer, his attention was upon
every thing rather than his pocket, and his magazine of credentials was stolen from him.[7]

His first want was a pair of shoes.[8]   For the supply of all his
necessities his whole fund was his ' Winter,' which for a time
could find no purchaser; till, at last [1726], Mr. Millan was
persuaded to buy it at a low price;[9] and this low price he had
for some time reason to regret; but, by accident, Mr. Whatley,[10]
a man not wholly unknown among authors, happening to turn
his eye upon it, was so delighted that he ran from place to
place celebrating its excellence.   Thomson obtained likewise
the notice of Aaron Hill, whom, being friendless and indigent,
and glad of kindness, he courted with every expression of servile
adulation.[11]

---

[6] Lady Grisel Baillie (d. 1746), daughter of Sir Patrick Hume, afterwards
Earl of Marchmont, and wife of George Baillie of Jerviswood, Esq., then member for Berwickshire.

[7] One at least of his letters was delivered.   See his letter to Cranston, dated
London, 3rd April, 1725.

[8] This is in some measure confirmed by his letter dated Barnet, Sept. 1725.

[9] Three guineas.   John Millan died 15th Feb. 1784.

[10] Cibber's 'Lives of the Poets,' v. 195.   Rev. Robert Whatley, afterwards
Prebendary of York.

[11] When Thomson published his ' Winter,' 1726, it lay a long time neglected,
till Mr. Spence made honourable mention of it in his ' Essay on the Odyssey,'
which, becoming a popular book, made this poem universally known.   Thomson always acknowledged the use of this recommendation; and from this circumstance an intimacy commenced between the critic and the poet, which

' Winter' was dedicated to Sir Spencer Compton,[12] but attracted no regard from him to the author; till Aaron Hill awakened his attention by some verses addressed to Thomson, and published in one of the newspapers, which censured the great for their neglect of ingenious men. Thomson then received a present of twenty guineas, of which he gives this account to Mr. Hill:

" I hinted to you in my last that on Saturday morning I was with Sir Spencer Compton. A certain gentleman, without my desire, spoke to him concerning me : his answer was that I had never come near him. Then the gentleman put the question, If he desired that I should wait on him? He returned, he did. On this the gentleman gave me an introductory letter to him. He received me in what they commonly call a civil manner; asked me some common-place questions ; and made me a present of twenty guineas. I am very ready to own that the present was larger than my performance deserved; and shall ascribe it to his generosity, or any other cause, rather than the merit of the address." [13]

The poem, which, being of a new kind, few would venture at first to like, by degrees gained upon the public; and one edition was very speedily succeeded by another.[14]

Thomson's credit was now high, and every day brought him new friends ; among others Dr. Rundle,[15] a man afterwards unfortunately famous, sought his acquaintance, and found his

lasted till the lamented death of the latter, who was of a most amiable and benevolent temper.—JOS. WARTON: *on Pope,* i. 154, ed. 1782.

'Winter' was in a *fourth* edition, and therefore well enough known, before Spence's 'Essay' appeared.

[12] Afterwards (1730) Earl of Wilmington. The Dedication was written by Mallet.—SPENCE: *ed. Singer,* p. 327.

[13] 'Letters to Mr. Hill,' 12mo., 1751.

[14] Three editions of 'Winter' appeared during the year in which it was first published. The first consisted of only 413 lines; the second of 463; and the third of 464. No further additions were made, I believe, till Millar (1730) printed the first edition of 'The Seasons,' when 'Winter' was enlarged to 781 lines. As left by its author, it consists of 1069 lines.

[15] Afterwards Bishop of Derry, and commended by Pope:

Secker is decent; Rundle has a heart.

He died in 1743. (See vol. ii. p. 401.)

qualities such, that he recommended him to the Lord Chancellor Talbot.

'Winter' was accompanied, in many editions, not only with a preface and dedication, but with poetical praises by Mr. Hill, Mr. Mallet (then Malloch), and Mira, the fictitious name of a lady once too well known.[16] Why the dedications are to 'Winter' and the other Seasons, contrarily to custom, left out in the collected works, the reader may inquire.[17]

The next year (1727) he distinguished himself by three publications[18]—of 'Summer,' in pursuance of his plan; of 'A Poem on the Death of Sir Isaac Newton,' which he was enabled to perform as an exact philosopher by the instruction of Mr. Gray ;[19] and of 'Britannia,' a kind of poetical invective against the Ministry, whom the nation then thought not forward enough in resenting the depredations of the Spaniards. By this piece he declared himself an adherent to the Opposition, and had therefore no favour to expect from the Court.

Thomson, having been some time entertained in the family of the Lord Binning, was desirous of testifying his gratitude by making him the patron of his 'Summer ;' but the same kindness which had first disposed Lord Binning to encourage him, determined him to refuse the dedication, which was by his advice addressed to Mr. Dodington,[20] a man who had more power to advance the reputation and fortune of a poet.

[16] Mira's verses were written at the request of Mallet.

[17] The three prose dedications to which Johnson alludes (for 'Autumn' was published without a dedication in prose) were omitted because the poet supplied their places with dedications in verse, which still remain, though Smollett tells us ('Dedication of Ferdinand Count Fathom') that Thomson intended to have withdrawn the whole of the dedications he had made, and to have stigmatised his unworthy patrons by their names.

[18] No; 'Britannia' was not published till 1729, and was then published anonymously. A *third* publication of the year 1729 was a 'Poem on the Death of Congreve,' addressed to Henrietta, Duchess of Marlborough, recovered by the Rev. H. F. Cary, and reprinted by me for the Percy Society in 1843.

[19] John Gray, Esq., F.R.S.; died 1769.

[20] The 'Bubo' of Pope, the patron of Young, and afterwards (1761) Lord Melcombe (d. 1762). Johnson wrote from the information of Lord Hailes, derived from Lady Murray, a near relative of Lord Binning's.—MALONE: *Life of Dryden*, p. 518.

'Spring' was published next year [June 1728] with a dedication to the Countess of Hertford,[21] whose practice it was to invite every summer some poet into the country, to hear her verses and assist her studies.[22] This honour was one summer conferred on Thomson, who took more delight in carousing with Lord Hertford and his friends than assisting her Ladyship's poetical operations, and therefore never received another summons.[23]

'Autumn,' the season to which the 'Spring' and 'Summer' are preparatory, still remained unsung, and was delayed till he published (May, 1730) his works collected.[24]

He produced in 1729[25] the tragedy of 'Sophonisba,' which raised such expectation, that every rehearsal was dignified with a splendid audience, collected to anticipate the delight that was preparing for the public. It was observed, however, that nobody was much affected, and that the company rose as from a moral lecture.

It had upon the stage no unusual degree of success. Slight accidents will operate upon the taste of pleasure. There is a feeble line in the play :

" O Sophonisba, Sophonisba, O ! "

This gave occasion to a waggish parody :

" O, Jemmy Thomson, Jemmy Thomson, O ! "

which for a while was echoed through the town.[26]

I have been told by Savage that of the Prologue to 'Sopho-

---

[21] Afterwards Duchess of Somerset. See vol. ii. p. 368.

[22] She wrote under the name of *Eusebia*. See her letter to Dr. Watts in Milner's 'Watts,' p. 504.

[23] 'Spring' was published by Andrew Millar (died 1768), who continued Thomson's publisher, and contributed largely to the handsome quarto edition of 1762, the profits of which were spent on the poet's monument in Westminster Abbey. For 'Spring' he received fifty guineas.

[24] In quarto, by subscription. Three hundred and eighty-seven subscribers took 454 copies. Pope subscribed for three copies.

[25] First acted at Drury Lane, 28th Feb. 1729-30. Mrs. Oldfield played Sophonisba; and this was her last new part in tragedy. It ran ten nights. The third, sixth, and ninth nights were for the benefit of the author.

[26] Johnson follows Cibber's 'Lives' (v. 209). The author of the parody was " a smart from the pit."

nisba,' the first part was written by Pope, who could not be persuaded to finish it ; and that the concluding lines were added by Mallet.

Thomson was not long afterwards, by the influence of Dr. Rundle, sent [1730] to travel with Mr. Charles Talbot, the eldest son of the Chancellor. He was yet young enough to receive new impressions, to have his opinions rectified, and his views enlarged ; nor can he be supposed to have wanted that curiosity which is inseparable from an active and comprehensive mind. He may therefore now be supposed to have revelled in all the joys of intellectual luxury ; he was every day feasted with instructive novelties ; he lived splendidly without expense, and might expect when he returned home a certain establishment.

At this time a long course of opposition to Sir Robert Walpole had filled the nation with clamours for liberty, of which no man felt the want, and with care for liberty, which was not in danger. Thomson, in his travels on the Continent, found or fancied so many evils arising from the tyranny of other governments, that he resolved to write a very long poem, in five parts, upon Liberty.[27]

While he was busy on the first book, Mr. Talbot died,[28] and Thomson, who had been rewarded for his attendance by the place of Secretary of the Briefs, pays in the initial lines a decent tribute to his memory.

Upon this great poem two years were spent, and the author congratulated himself upon it as his noblest work ; but an author and his reader are not always of a mind. Liberty called in vain upon her votaries to read her praises, and reward her encomiast : her praises were condemned to harbour spiders, and to gather dust : none of Thomson's performances were so little regarded.

The judgment of the public was not erroneous ; the recur-

---

[27] The pupil seems to have held sentiments similar to his tutor ; for Rundle writes to Mrs. Sandys, 30th January, 1730-1 : "His [Sir Charles Talbot's] eldest son is at Paris, and behaves as one would wish he should behave. His rough English love for liberty disdains the embroidered slavery that glitters in that trifling court. He hates chains, though made of gold."

[28] Mr. Talbot died 27th Sept. 1733.

rence of the same images must tire in time ; an enumeration of examples to prove a position which nobody denied, as it was from the beginning superfluous, must quickly grow disgusting.

The poem of 'Liberty' does not now appear in its original state ; but, when the author's works were collected after his death, was shortened by Sir George Lyttelton, with a liberty which, as it has a manifest tendency to lessen the confidence of society, and to confound the characters of authors, by making one man write by the judgment of another, cannot be justified by any supposed propriety of the alteration, or kindness of the friend : I wish to see it exhibited as its author left it.[29]

Thomson now lived in ease and plenty, and seems for a while to have suspended his poetry ; but he was soon called back to labour by the death [1737] of the Chancellor, for his place then became vacant ; and though the Lord Hardwicke delayed for some time to give it away, Thomson's bashfulness, or pride, or some other motive perhaps not more laudable, withheld him from soliciting ; and the new Chancellor would not give him what he would not ask.

He now relapsed to his former indigence ; but the Prince of Wales was at that time [1737] struggling for popularity, and by the influence of Mr. Lyttelton professed himself the patron of wit ; to him Thomson was introduced, and being gaily interrogated about the state of his affairs, said, " that they were in a more poetical posture than formerly ;" and had a pension allowed him of one hundred pounds a year.

Being now obliged to write, he produced (1738) the tragedy of 'Agamemnon,'[30] which was much shortened in the representa-

[29] This was done by Murdoch in the subscription quarto of 1762. (See Murdoch's letter to Millar in Wooll's ' Warton,' p. 252.)

Lord Lyttelton reduced the *five* parts of ' Liberty' to three, and made the ' Fox Chase,' inserted by its author in ' Autumn,' a separate poem. Murdoch (his dear friend and biographer) made some slight alterations in ' The Seasons,' which Mr. Bolton Corney was the first to point out publicly and to restore. (Corney's ed. of ' Thomson's Seasons,' 8vo. 1843.)

[30] Produced at Drury Lane. The first night was 6th April, 1738. Quin played Agamemnon, and Mrs. Porter Clytemnestra. The third, sixth, and ninth were for the benefit of the author. The seventh was by command of the Prince and Princess of Wales, who were present.

tion. It had the fate which most commonly attends mythological stories, and was only endured, but not favoured. It
struggled with such difficulty through the first night, that
Thomson, coming late to his friends with whom he was to sup,
excused his delay by telling them how the sweat of his distress
had so disordered his wig, that he could not come till he had
been refitted by a barber.

He so interested himself in his own drama, that, if I remember right,[31] as he sat in the upper gallery, he accompanied the
players by audible recitation, till a friendly hint frighted him
to silence. Pope countenanced ' Agamemnon' by coming to
it the first night, and was welcomed to the theatre by a general
clap ; he had much regard for Thomson, and once expressed it
in a poetical Epistle sent to Italy, of which, however, he abated
the value by transplanting some of the lines into his ' Epistle to
Arbuthnot.'[32]

About this time [1737] the Act[33] was passed for licensing
plays, of which the first operation was the prohibition of ' Gus-
tavus Vasa,' a tragedy of Mr. Brooke, whom the public recompensed by a very liberal subscription ; the next was the refusal

---

[31] Johnson arrived in London in 1737. *Theo* Cibber tells the story of Sophonisba.

[32] Pope did more for ' Agamemnon' than countenance the first night. He
assisted Thomson in making certain necessary *cuttings*. (See Victor's letter,
vol. i.) But this, it is said (' Gent's. Mag.' for Dec. 1841, p. 570), was not Pope's
only service to Thomson. A copy of ' The Seasons' is in the possession of the Rev.
John Mitford, with numerous corrections in the handwriting (as some believe)
of Pope himself. These corrections were in very many cases adopted by Thomson; but I cannot help thinking that the writing bears a greater resemblance
to Lord Lyttelton's handwriting than to Pope's. The edition is that of 1736.
    " Though ' Agamemnon' is not a capital play on the whole, and abounds in
languid and long declamatory speeches, yet parts of it are striking, particularly
Melisander's account of the desert island to which he was banished, copied
from the ' Philoctetes' of Sophocles; and the prophetic speeches of Cassandra
during the moment of Agamemnon's being murdered, well calculated to fill
the audience with alarm, astonishment, and suspense at an awful event, ob-
scurely hinted at in very strong imagery. These speeches are closely copied
from the ' Agamemnon' of Eschylus, as is a striking scene in his ' Eleonora '
from the ' Alcestis' of Euripides. Thomson was well acquainted with the
Greek tragedies, on which I heard him talk learnedly when I was once introduced to him by my friend Mr. W. Collins."—Jos. WARTON: *Pope*, vii. 10.

[33] 10th George II. cap. 28. It received the royal assent 21st June, 1737.

of 'Edward and Eleonora,' offered by Thomson. It is hard
to discover why either play should have been obstructed.
Thomson likewise endeavoured to repair his loss by a subscription, of which I cannot now tell the success.[34]

When the public murmured at the unkind treatment of
Thomson, one of the ministerial writers remarked, that " he
had taken a *Liberty* which was not agreeable to *Britannia* in
any *Season*."

He was soon after employed, in conjunction with Mr. Mallet,
to write the masque of 'Alfred,' which was acted before the
Prince at Cliefden House.[35]

His next work (1745) was 'Tancred and Sigismunda,'[36] the
most successful of all his tragedies; for it still keeps its turn
upon the stage. It may be doubted whether he was, either by
the bent of nature or habits of study, much qualified for tragedy.
It does not appear that he had much sense of the pathetic;
and his diffusive and descriptive style produced declamation
rather than dialogue.

His friend Mr. Lyttelton was now in power, and conferred
upon him the office of surveyor-general of the Leeward Islands;
from which, when his deputy was paid, he received about three
hundred pounds a year.

[34] Speedily will be published, by subscription, EDWARD AND ELEONORA, a
Tragedy, by Mr. Thomson. The representation of this tragedy on the stage
has been prohibited by AUTHORITY, for what reason the author knows not.
He is conscious that he had no other intention but to paint Virtue and Vice
in their proper colours; and he hopes there is neither sentiment nor reflection
introduced that does not flow naturally from the subject. The characters in
the play cannot offend those whom they may be thought to resemble; they are
virtuous. If they displease, they can displease those alone to whom they
were never intended to be applied. And how moral reflections and sentiments
of Liberty should offend in a free nation he will not inquire. He is only solicitous to approve himself to all who judge impartially an honest man and a
lover of his country. For his success he trusts to that candour and indulgence which he has already met with from the public on other occasions.
—'The Daily Post,' April 7, 1739.

[35] In this masque is the national anthem 'Rule Britannia.'

[36] First acted at Drury Lane, 18th March, 1745. Garrick played Tancred.
At its revival, long after the author's death, Mrs. Siddons played Sigismunda.
"The two great statesmen Pitt and Lyttelton attended the rehearsal of
'Tancred and Sigismunda' with great assiduity; they had a sincere value for
the amiable author."—T. DAVIES: *Life of Garrick*, i. 79.

The last piece that he lived to publish [1748] was the 'Castle of Indolence,' which was many years under his hand, but was at last finished with great accuracy. The first canto opens a scene of lazy luxury that fills the imagination.

He was now at ease, but was not long to enjoy it; for, by taking cold on the water between London and Kew, he caught a disorder, which, with some careless exasperation, ended in a fever that put an end to his life, August 27, 1748. He was buried in the church of Richmond, without an inscription; [37] but a monument has been erected to his memory in Westminster Abbey. [38]

Thomson was of stature above the middle size, and " more fat than bard beseems," [39] of a dull countenance, and a gross, unanimated, uninviting appearance; silent in mingled company, but cheerful among select friends, and by his friends very tenderly and warmly beloved.

He left behind him the tragedy of 'Coriolanus,' which was, by the zeal of his patron, Sir George Lyttelton, brought upon the stage for the benefit of his family, and recommended by a Prologue, which Quin, who had long lived with Thomson in fond intimacy, spoke in such a manner as showed him " to be," on that occasion, " no actor." [40] The commencement of this benevolence is very honourable to Quin; who is reported to

[37] His grave, in 1792, was marked by a mural brass by the eccentric Earl of Buchan, and this is still (1854) his only memorial in Richmond Church.

[38] He died intestate; and administration of his effects was granted to Mr. Lyttelton (afterwards Lord Lyttelton) and to Andrew Mitchell, Esq., afterwards Sir Andrew Mitchell, in trust for Mary Craig, the lawful sister, and next of kin.

[39] 'Castle of Indolence,' canto ii. The best portrait of Thomson is that by Aikman, still at Hagley, in Worcestershire, the seat of Lord Lyttelton. The great Lord Chatham said of this picture, that it was "beastly like." (Letter to Editor from Lord Lyttelton, d. 1837.) A chalk drawing of him by the same artist is in the Library of the University of Edinburgh, part of a strange gift to the University made by the Earl of Buchan. The drawing of him by Paton, engraved by Basire for his Works, 1762, 4to., is at Culloden House. He sat to Slaughter. ('Gent's. Mag.' 1736, p. 743.)

[40] Murdoch. (Ed. Corney, i. p. xxvi.)
Quin spoke the prologue (and it is a fine one) in mourning. 'Coriolanus' was produced at Covent-Garden, Friday, 13th Jan. 1748–9, and ran ten nights. The third, sixth, and ninth nights were for the benefit of the poet's sister.

have delivered Thomson, then known to him only for his genius, from an arrest by a very considerable present; and its continuance is honourable to both; for friendship is not always the sequel of obligation. By this tragedy a considerable sum was raised, of which part discharged his debts, and the rest was remitted to his sisters, whom, however removed from them by place or condition, he regarded with great tenderness, as will appear by the following letter, which I communicate with much pleasure, as it gives me at once an opportunity of recording the fraternal kindness of Thomson, and reflecting on the friendly assistance of Mr. Boswell, from whom I received it.

" Hagley, in Worcestershire,
October the 4th, 1747.

" My dear Sister,—I thought you had known me better than to interpret my silence into a decay of affection, especially as your behaviour has always been such as rather to increase than diminish it. Don't imagine, because I am a bad correspondent, that I can ever prove an unkind friend and brother. I must do myself the justice to tell you that my affections are naturally very fixed and constant ; and if I had ever reason of complaint against you (of which, by the bye, I have not the least shadow), I am conscious of so many defects in myself, as dispose me to be not a little charitable and forgiving.

" It gives me the truest heart-felt satisfaction to hear you have a good, kind husband, and are in easy, contented circumstances ; but, were they otherwise, that would only awaken and heighten my tenderness towards you. As our good and tender-hearted parents did not live to receive any material testimonies of that highest human gratitude I owed them (than which nothing could have given me equal pleasure), the only return I can make them now is by kindness to those they left behind them. Would to God poor Lizy had lived longer, to have been a farther witness of the truth of what I say, and that I might have had the pleasure of seeing once more a sister who so truly deserved my esteem and love ! But she is happy, while we must toil a little longer here below ; let us, however, do it cheerfully and gratefully, supported by the pleasing hope of meeting yet again on a safer shore, where to recollect the storms and difficulties of life will not perhaps be inconsistent with that blissful state.[41] You did right to call your daughter by her name ; for you must needs have had a particular tender friendship for one another, endeared as you were by nature, by having passed the affectionate years of your youth together, and by that great softener and engager of hearts—mutual hardship. That it was in my power to ease it a little, I account one of the most exquisite pleasures of my life. But enough of this melancholy though not unpleasing strain.

---

[41] Compare his beautiful verses on Aikman's death.

" I esteem you for your sensible and disinterested advice to Mr. Bell, as you will see by my letter to him : as I approve entirely of his marrying again, you may readily ask me why I don't marry at all. My circumstances have hitherto been so variable and uncertain in this fluctuating world, as induce to keep me from engaging in such a state ; and now, though they are more settled, and of late (which you will be glad to hear) considerably improved, I begin to think myself too far advanced in life for such youthful undertakings, not to mention some other petty reasons that are apt to startle the delicacy of difficult old bachelors. I am, however, not a little suspicious that, was I to pay a visit to Scotland (which I have some thought of doing soon), I might possibly be tempted to think of a thing not easily repaired if done amiss. I have always been of opinion that none make better wives than the ladies of Scotland ; [42] and yet, who more forsaken than they, while the gentlemen are continually running abroad all the world over ? Some of them, it is true, are wise enough to return for a wife. You see I am beginning to make interest already with the Scots ladies. But no more of this infectious subject. Pray let me hear from you now and then ; and, though I am not a regular correspondent, yet perhaps I may mend in that respect. Remember me kindly to your husband, and believe me to be

" Your most affectionate brother,
" JAMES THOMSON."

(Addressed)   " To Mrs. Thomson in Lanark."

The benevolence of Thomson was fervid, but not active : he would give on all occasions what assistance his purse would supply ; but the offices of intervention or solicitation he could not conquer his sluggishness sufficiently to perform. The affairs of others, however, were not more neglected than his own. He had often felt the inconveniences of idleness, but he never cured it ; and was so conscious of his own character, that he talked of writing an Eastern Tale ' of the Man who Loved to be in Distress.' [43]

[42] As Thomson never returned to Scotland (which *you* will think very wise), his sister can speak of her own knowledge only as to the early part of his life. —BOSWELL to Johnson, July 9, 1777.

[43] MY DEAR JOHN,—God grant you the continuance of your health, and may you prosper in everything while you live. It comforts me not a little, that, besides your natural right to outlive me, there are other circumstances in your favour ; for of all mortifications, the loss of a dear friend with whom one has been often happy is to me the most insupportable. The loss of such an agreeable friend as poor Thomson is so much the more shocking that it was unexpected by everybody. He died of a malignant nervous fever, that came upon the back of a tertian ; and I had no notice of his being in any danger till I saw it in the most formidable shapes. It is certain nature was oppressed in him with a great load of materials for a disease, not to be easily thrown off by

Among his peculiarities was a very unskilful and inarticulate manner of pronouncing any lofty or solemn composition. He was once reading to Dodington, who being himself a reader eminently elegant, was so much provoked by his odd utterance, that he snatched the paper from his hands, and told him that he did not understand his own verses.[44]

The biographer of Thomson [45] has remarked, that an author's life is best read in his works: his observation was not well timed. Savage, who lived much with Thomson, once told me how he heard a lady remarking that she could gather from his works three parts of his character: that he was a "great lover, a great swimmer, and rigorously abstinent;" but, said Savage, he knows not any love but that of the sex; he was perhaps never in cold water in his life; and he indulges himself in all the luxury that comes within his reach. Yet Savage always spoke with the most eager praise of his social qualities, his warmth and constancy of friendship, and his adherence to his first acquaintance when the advancement of his reputation had left them behind him.[46]

a constitution so much worn as his was; and if he had struggled through that fever, there are many reasons to believe that it must almost unavoidably have been followed by some lingering disease, much worse than a speedy death. This is the most comfortable light in which I can view this shocking loss. We are to be pitied that are left behind; and if it was not for a very few friends whom I have still remaining, and who, I have reason to hope, will live as long as I, life would soon become too tedious and melancholy to be supported."—ARMSTRONG (the poet) to John Forbes.   London, Sept. 3, 1748. *Culloden Papers*, 4to., 1815.

[44] Johnson had this from Lord Hailes.   "You booby," was the exclamation, "you do not understand your own verses!"—MALONE: *Life of Dryden*, p. 518.

Tom Davies, in his 'Dramatic Miscellanies,' tells a somewhat similar story of Thomson's reading his 'Agamemnon' to the managers of Drury Lane.

[45] The Rev. Patrick Murdoch (d. 1774).

[46] Have the farmers found out that you cannot distinguish rye from barley, or an oak from a crab-tree? You are sensible that I know the full extent of your country-skill is in fishing for roaches or gudgeons at the highest.—SWIFT to Gay, May 4, 1732.

We still agree on Tuesday; and I think we shall see Claremont, as we did Canons, and then come to dine at Richmond. Had I best send Mr. Thomson word that we shall be at such an inn at Richmond by noon, his hour of rising?—CAVE, the bookseller, to Dr. Birch, 12th Aug. 1738.

Thomson, with the most benevolent heart that ever warmed the human breast, maintained a perpetual war with the difficulties of a narrow fortune.—SMOLLETT: *History of England*.

As a writer, he is entitled to one praise of the highest kind: his mode of thinking, and of expressing his thoughts, is original. His blank verse is no more the blank verse of Milton, or of any other poet, than the rhymes of Prior are the rhymes of Cowley. His numbers, his pauses, his diction, are of his own growth, without transcription, without imitation. He thinks in a peculiar train, and he thinks always as a man of genius; he looks round on Nature and on life with the eye which Nature bestows only on a poet; the eye that distinguishes, in everything presented to its view, whatever there is on which imagination can delight to be detained, and with a mind that at once comprehends the vast and attends to the minute. The reader of ' The Seasons ' wonders that he never saw before what Thomson shows him, and that he never yet has felt what Thomson impresses.

His is one of the works in which blank verse seems properly used. Thomson's wide expansion of general views, and his enumeration of circumstantial varieties, would have been obstructed and embarrassed by the frequent intersections of the sense, which are the necessary effects of rhyme.

His descriptions of extended scenes and general effects bring before us the whole magnificence of Nature, whether pleasing or dreadful. The gaiety of Spring, the splendour of Summer, the tranquillity of Autumn, and the horror of Winter, take in their turns possession of the mind. The poet leads us through the appearances of things as they are successively varied by the vicissitudes of the year, and imparts to us so much of his own enthusiasm, that our thoughts expand with his imagery, and kindle with his sentiments. Nor is the naturalist without his part in the entertainment; for he is assisted to recollect and to combine, to arrange his discoveries, and to amplify the sphere of his contemplation.

The great defect of ' The Seasons ' is want of method; but for this I know not that there was any remedy. Of many appearances subsisting all at once, no rule can be given why one should be mentioned before another; yet the memory wants the help of order, and the curiosity is not excited by suspense or expectation.

His diction is in the highest degree florid and luxuriant, such as may be said to be to his images and thoughts " both their lustre and their shade ;" such as invest them with splendour, through which perhaps they are not always easily discerned. It is too exuberant, and sometimes may be charged with filling the ear more than the mind.

These poems, with which I was acquainted at their first appearance, I have since found altered and enlarged by subsequent revisals, as the author supposed his judgment to grow more exact, and as books or conversation extended his knowledge and opened his prospects.[47] They are, I think, improved in general; yet I know not whether they have not lost part of what Temple calls their " race ;" a word which, applied to wines in its primitive sense, means the flavour of the soil.[48]

' Liberty,' when it first appeared, I tried to read, and soon desisted. I have never tried again, and therefore will not hazard either praise or censure.

The highest praise which he has received ought not to be suppressed : it is said by Lord Lyttelton, in the Prologue to his posthumous play, that his works contained

" No line which, dying, he could wish to blot."

---

[47] See Appendix.

[48] *Race ;* a particular strength or taste of wine, applied by Temple to any extraordinary natural force of intellect.—JOHNSON: *Dictionary.*

You must know that all my earlier love-songs were the breathings of ardent passion; and though it might have been easy in after times to have given them a polish, yet that polish, to me, whose they were, and who perhaps alone cared for them, would have defaced the legend of my heart, which was so faithfully inscribed on them. Their uncouth simplicity was, as they say of wines, their race.—BURNS to Geo. Thomson.

My friend Mr. William Collins, author of the ' Persian Eclogues and Odes,' assured me that Thomson informed him that he took the first hint and idea of writing his ' Seasons' from the titles of Pope's four Pastorals.—JOS. WARTON.

Autumn I think the most pleasing and the most poetical season of the year. The spirits are not then dissipated with the gaiety of Spring, and the glaring light of Summer, but composed into a serious and tempered joy. The year is perfect.—THOMSON to Lyttelton, London, July 14, 1743.

The amplest and ablest account of Thomson is contained in a Memoir by Allan Cunningham, prefixed to an edition of ' The Seasons,' &c. published in 1841. The ' Life' by Sir Harris Nicolas, prefixed to the Aldine edition of Thomson in 1847, contains the largest series of Thomson's Letters.

APPENDIX.

THREE editions of 'Winter' appeared during the year in which it was first printed. The *first* consisted of only 413 lines, the *second* of 463, and the *third* of 464. No further additions or even corrections were, I believe, made till Millar printed the first edition of 'The Seasons' (the subscription edition), when 'Winter' was enlarged to 781 lines. In 1744, the year in which a thousand lines were added to 'The Seasons,' 'Winter' was made to contain 1069 lines. Of this length Thomson left it, and thus it is always printed. The chief additions after the first three impressions were printed, are the picture of the man perishing among the snows, and the reflections on the wants and miseries of human life, the view of Winter within the Polar Circle, the passage relative to the Jail Committee, the eulogies on Hammond, Pope, and Chesterfield, the descriptions of a winter evening in the country and in the city, and the happiness of Russia under Peter the Great.

Between 'Summer' as originally printed, and as Thomson left it, there is a difference of 658 lines. The gradual progress of the poem to its present length will be best shown by the following table of lines in various editions :—

						Lines.
First Ed.	1727	..	..	..	..	1146
	1730	..	..	..	..	1206
	1744	..	..	..	..	1796
	1746	..	..	..	..	1805
Murdoch	1762	..	..	..	..	1804
Corney	1843	..	..	..	..	1805

It would be difficult to show by what additions, alterations, and expansion of passages, the poem of 'Summer' reached its present state. He alone who has collated (as I have done) the various editions of 'The Seasons' which passed under the author's own eye, can form any exact notion of the number of these changes and additions. In his 'Autumn,' he says that, wherever he went, the subject of his poem was ever in his mind :—

"My pleasing theme continual prompts my thought."

And this the numerous texts of his poem satisfactorily prove. He was always bettering it; yet in these changes he at times omitted lines of superior beauty to some that he inserted.

One passage that appeared originally in 'Summer' is now in 'Autumn;' and another, originally in 'Spring,' is now in 'Summer.' But transfers of this kind were not common with him—indeed, I have traced no others.

The story of Damon and Musidora is not in the first edition of 'Summer.' I find it for the first time in the subscription quarto of 1730, where it is told in a way almost wholly different from the settled text.

The beautiful allusion to Miss Stanley is an after-insertion. The Panegyric on Great Britain was altered and enlarged as his sentiments changed
and his views expanded. I am not aware of his reasons for rejecting from
his list of worthies the names of Tillotson and Barrow, when once they
had been admitted, and admitted for the strength and elegance of their
truths.

The first edition of ' Spring ' consists of 1082 lines. In 1730 it was
enlarged to 1087, in 1744 to 1173, in 1746 to 1176. The chief additions
are the passage on fishing, the ensuing digression, and the part relating to
Lyttelton and Hagley.

' Autumn ' contained, in the first edition, 1269 lines. In 1744 it was
enlarged to 1375, and in 1746 it was reduced to 1373.

The first edition of the ' Hymn ' consists of 121 lines; Thomson himself
reduced it to its present number, 118.

The original DAMON AND MUSIDORA *of ' Summer,' as now printed,*
l. 1268 to 1370.

" 'Twas then beneath a secret waving shade,
    Where winded into lovely solitudes
    Runs out the rambling dale, that Damon sat,
    Thoughtful, and fix'd in philosophic muse :
    Damon, who still, amid the savage woods
    And lonely lawns, the force of beauty scorn'd,
    Firm, and to false philosophy devote.
    The brook ran babbling by; and sighing weak,
    The breeze among the bending willows play'd,
    When Sacharissa to the cool retreat
    With Amoret and Musidora stole.
    Warm in their cheek the sultry season glow'd;
    And, rob'd in loose array, they came to bathe
    Their fervent limbs in the refreshing stream.
    Tall, and majestic, Sacharissa rose,
    Superior treading, as on Ida's top
    (So Grecian bards in wanton fable sung)
    High-shone the sister and the wife of Jove.
    Another Pallas Musidora seem'd,
    Meek-ey'd, sedate, and gaining every look
    A surer conquest of the sliding heart;
    While, like the Cyprian goddess, Amoret,
    Delicious dress'd in rosy-dimpled smiles,
    And all one softness, melted on the sense.
    Nor Paris panted stronger, when aside
    The rival goddesses the veil divine
    Cast unconfin'd, and gave him all their charms,
    Than, Damon, thou; the stoic now no more,
    But man deep-felt, as from the snowy leg,
    And slender foot, th' inverted silk they drew;

As the soft touch dissolv'd the virgin-zone;
And, thro' the parting robe, th' alternate breast,
With youth wild-throbbing, on thy lawless gaze
Luxuriant rose.   Yet more enamour'd still,
When from their naked limbs, of glowing white,
In folds loose-floating fell the fainter lawn;
And fair expos'd they stood, shrunk from themselves;
With fancy blushing; at the doubtful breeze
Arous'd, and starting like the fearful fawn.
So stands the statue that enchants the world,
Her full proportions such, and bashful so
Bends ineffectual from the roving eye.
Then to the flood they rush'd; the plunging fair
The parted flood with closing waves receiv'd;
And, every beauty softening, every grace
Flushing afresh, a mellow lustre shed:
As shines the lily thro' the crystal mild;
Or as the rose amid the morning-dew
Puts on a warmer glow.   In various play,
While thus they wanton'd; now beneath the waves,
But ill-conceal'd; and now with streaming locks
That half-embrac'd them in a humid veil,
Rising again; the latent Damon drew
Such draughts of love and beauty to the soul,
As put his harsh philosophy to flight,
The joyless search of long-deluded years;
And Musidora fixing in his heart,
Inform'd and humanis'd him into man."

From ' Summer,' ed. 1730, l. 980 to 1038.

Specimen of ' THE SEASONS,' as altered by POPE.[49]
(See note 32, p. 233.)

" Thoughtless of beauty, she was Beauty's self,
Recluse among the woods: if city dames
Will deign their faith; and thus she went compell'd
By strong Necessity, with as serene
And pleas'd a look as Patience e'er put on,
To glean Palæmon's fields."

These lines Pope erased, and wrote the following in their place, which
now stand in the subsequent editions :

" Thoughtless of beauty, she was Beauty's self.
Recluse among the *close* embowering woods.
                              deep
As in the hollow breast of Apennine,

---

[49] From Gray's Works, by Mitford, vol. ii. p. viii. (ed. 1836).

> Beneath the shelter of encircling hills,
> A myrtle rises far from human eyes,
> And breathes its balmy fragrance o'er the wild:
> So flourish'd, blooming and unseen by all,
> The sweet Lavinia; till at length compell'd
> By strong Necessity's supreme command,
> With smiling Patience in her looks, she went
> To glean Palæmon's fields."

The 259th line of this episode now stands :

> " And as he view'd her ardent o'er and o'er."

But in the edition of 1736 it is somewhat comically expressed :

> " Then blaz'd his smother'd flame, avow'd and bold,
> And as he *run*[50] her ardent o'er and o'er," &c.

This, however, Thomson himself altered.

---

[50] This very awkward and improper expression is from ' The Conscious Lovers' of Sir Richard Steele, a comedy commended by Thomson in his poem of ' Winter' :

" *Cimberton.* I say, madam, her impatience, while we are looking at her, throws out all attractions: her arms, her neck—what a spring in her step!

" *Lucinda.* Don't you run me over thus, you strange unaccountable——"

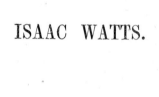

ISAAC WATTS.

W A T T S.

1674–1748.

Born at Southampton — Educated among the Independents — Becomes
Tutor to the Son of Sir John Hartopp — Is received into Sir Thomas
Abney's Family — Popularity of his preaching — His Work on ' The
Improvement of the Mind ' — Death and Burial at Bunhill Fields in
London.

THE Poems of Dr. Watts were by my recommendation
inserted in the late Collection; the readers of which are to
impute to me whatever pleasure or weariness they may find in
the perusal of Blackmore, Watts, Pomfret, and Yalden.[1]

Isaac Watts was born July 17, 1674, at Southampton, where
his father, of the same name, kept a boarding-school for young
gentlemen, though common report makes him a shoemaker.[2]
He appears, from the narrative of Dr. Gibbons, to have been
neither indigent nor illiterate.

Isaac, the eldest of nine children, was given to books from
his infancy; and began, we are told, to learn Latin when he
was four years old, I suppose at home. He was afterwards
taught Latin, Greek, and Hebrew by Mr. Pinhorne, a clergy-

---

[1] Johnson was willing to have said still more about Watts:—

TO MR. W. SHARP.

Bolt Court, July 7, 1777.

SIR,—To the collection of English poets I have recommended the volume of
Dr. Watts to be added: his name has long been held by me in veneration, and
I would not willingly be reduced to tell of him only that he was born and died.
Yet of his life I know very little, and therefore must pass him in a manner
very unworthy of his character, unless some of his friends will favour me with
the necessary information. Many of them must be known to you; and by your
influence perhaps I may obtain some instruction. My plan does not exact
much; but I wish to distinguish Watts, a man who never wrote but for a good
purpose. Be pleased to do for me what you can.

I am, Sir, &c.,

SAM. JOHNSON.

(*Boswell by Croker*, ed. 1847, p. 536.)

[2] Common report is here in error.

man, master of the free-school at Southampton, to whom the
gratitude of his scholar afterwards inscribed a Latin ode.

His proficiency at school was so conspicuous that a subscription was proposed for his support at the university ; but he
declared his resolution of taking his lot with the Dissenters.[3]
Such he was as every Christian Church would rejoice to have
adopted.

He therefore repaired in 1690 to an academy taught by Mr.
Rowe,[4] where he had for his companions and fellow-students
Mr. Hughes the poet, and Dr. Horte, afterwards Archbishop of
Tuam.[5]   Some Latin Essays, supposed to have been written as
exercises at this academy, show a degree of knowledge, both
philosophical and theological, such as very few attain by a
much longer course of study.

He was, as he hints in his ' Miscellanies,' a maker of verses
from fifteen to fifty, and in his youth he appears to have paid
attention to Latin poetry.   His verses to his brother, in the
glyconic measure, written when he was seventeen, are remarkably easy and elegant.   Some of his other odes are deformed
by the Pindaric folly then prevailing, and are written with such
neglect of all metrical rules as is without example among the
ancients ; but his diction, though perhaps not always exactly
pure, has such copiousness and splendour as shows that he was
but at a very little distance from excellence.

His method of study was to impress the contents of his books
upon his memory by abridging them, and by interleaving them
to amplify one system with supplements from another.

With the congregation of his tutor, Mr. Rowe, who were, I
believe, Independents, he communicated in his nineteenth year.[6]

At the age of twenty he left the academy, and spent two

---

[3] His father was a non-conformist, and in the reign of Charles II. was imprisoned for non-conformity, and on his release was, as his son records,
" forced to leave his family, and live privately in London for two years."—
MILNER: *Life of Watts*, 8vo. 1834, p. 60.

[4] Mr. Thomas Rowe died in August, 1705 (Milner, p. 89).

[5] Also Daniel Neale, author of 'The History of the Puritans.'

[6] He was " admitted to Mr. T. Rowe's church" in Dec. 1693, as he states
himself in some brief notes of his life, printed in Milner, p. 137.   Mr. Rowe
died in Aug. 1705.

years in study and devotion at the house of his father, who
treated him with great tenderness; and had the happiness,
indulged to few parents, of living to see his son eminent for
literature and venerable for piety.[7]

He was then entertained by Sir John Hartopp[8] five years, as
domestic tutor to his son; and in that time particularly devoted
himself to the study of the Holy Scriptures; and being chosen
assistant to Dr. Chauncy, preached the first time on the birth-
day that completed his twenty-fourth year;[9] probably considering that as the day of a second nativity, by which he entered
on a new period of existence.

In about three years, 8 March, 1701-2, he succeeded Dr.
Chauncy; but, soon after his entrance on his charge, he was
seized by a dangerous illness, which sunk him to such weakness
that the congregation thought an assistant necessary, and [June,
1703] appointed Mr. Price.[10]   His health then returned gradually; and he performed his duty, till (1712) he was seized
by a fever of such violence and continuance, that from the
feebleness which it brought upon him, he never perfectly recovered.

This calamitous state made the compassion of his friends
necessary, and drew upon him the attention of Sir Thomas
Abney,[11] who received him into his house; where, with a constancy of friendship and uniformity of conduct not often to be
found, he was treated for thirty-six years with all the kindness
that friendship could prompt, and all the attention that respect
could dictate.   Sir Thomas died about eight years afterwards;
but he continued with the lady and her daughters to the end
of his life.   The lady died about a year after him.[12]

[7] His father died 10th Feb. 1736–7.

[8] At Stoke Newington.   He went there for the first time (as his notes
record) 15th Oct. 1696.

[9] 17th July, 1698.   Dr. Chauncy preached in Mark Lane, London.

[10] Samuel Price, died 1756, and buried in Bunhill Fields, where on his grave
is recorded, at his own request, that he was assistant and co-partner to the
truly Reverend Dr. Watts for forty-five years.

[11] A dissenter and Lord Mayor of London in 1700, died 1722, in his 83rd
year.

[12] Mary Gunston, eldest daughter of John Gunston, Esq., of Stoke Newington,

A coalition like this, a state in which the notions of patronage
and dependence were overpowered by the perception of reciprocal benefits, deserves a particular memorial ; and I will not
withhold from the reader Dr. Gibbons's representation, to
which regard is to be paid as to the narrative of one who writes
what he knows, and what is known likewise to multitudes
besides.

" Our next observation shall be made upon that remarkably
kind Providence which brought the Doctor into Sir Thomas
Abney's family, and continued him there till his death, a period
of no less than thirty-six years.   In the midst of his sacred
labours for the glory of God and good of his generation, he is
seized with a most violent and threatening fever, which leaves
him oppressed with great weakness, and puts a stop at least to
his public services for four years.   In this distressing season,
doubly so to his active and pious spirit, he is invited to Sir
Thomas Abney's family, nor ever removes from it till he had
finished his days.   Here he enjoyed the uninterrupted demon-
strations of the truest friendship.   Here, without any care of his
own, he had everything which could contribute to the enjoyment
of life, and favour the unwearied pursuits of his studies.   Here
he dwelt in a family which, for piety, order, harmony, and every
virtue, was a house of God.   Here he had the privilege of a
country recess, the fragrant bower, the spreading lawn, the
flowery garden, and other advantages, to soothe his mind and
aid his restoration to health ; to yield him, whenever he chose
them, most grateful intervals from his laborious studies, and
enable him to return to them with redoubled vigour and delight.
Had it not been for this most happy event, he might, as to
outward view, have feebly, it may be painfully, dragged on
through many more years of languor, and inability for public
service, and even for profitable study, or perhaps might have
sunk into his grave under the overwhelming load of infirmities
in the midst of his days ; and thus the church and world would

and second wife of Sir Thomas Abney.   Sir Thomas's first wife was the
daughter of the Rev. Joseph Caryl, known by his voluminous 'Commentary
on the Book of Job.'

have been deprived of those many excellent sermons and works which he drew up and published during his long residence in this family.   In a few years after his coming hither Sir Thomas Abney dies; but his amiable consort survives, who shows the Doctor the same respect and friendship as before, and most happily for him and great numbers besides; for, as her riches were great, her generosity and munificence were in full proportion; her thread of life was drawn out to a great age, even beyond that of the Doctor's; and thus this excellent man, through her kindness and that of her daughter, the present Mrs. Elizabeth Abney, who in a like degree esteemed and honoured him, enjoyed all the benefits and felicities he experienced at his first entrance into this family, till his days were numbered and finished; and, like a shock of corn in its season, he ascended into the regions of perfect and immortal life and joy."

If this quotation has appeared long, let it be considered that it comprises an account of six-and-thirty years, and those the years of Dr. Watts.

From the time of his reception into this family his life was no otherwise diversified than by successive publications.   The series of his works I am not able to deduce; their number and their variety show the intenseness of his industry and the extent of his capacity.

He was one of the first authors that taught the Dissenters to court attention by the graces of language.   Whatever they had among them before, whether of learning or acuteness, was commonly obscured and blunted by coarseness and inelegance of style.   He showed them that zeal and purity might be expressed and enforced by polished diction.

He continued to the end of his life the teacher of a congregation, and no reader of his works can doubt his fidelity or diligence.   In the pulpit, though his low stature, which very little exceeded five feet, graced him with no advantages of appearance, yet the gravity and propriety of his utterance made his discourses very efficacious.   I once mentioned the reputation which Mr. Foster [13] had gained by his proper delivery to my

[13] Pope's "modest Foster."

friend Dr. Hawkesworth, who told me that in the art of pronunciation he was far inferior to Dr. Watts.

Such was his flow of thoughts, and such his promptitude of
language, that in the latter part of his life he did not precom-
pose his cursory sermons, but having adjusted the heads, and
sketched out some particulars, trusted for success to his extem-
porary powers.

He did not endeavour to assist his eloquence by any gesticula-
tions ; for, as no corporeal actions have any correspondence with
theological truth, he did not see how they could enforce it.

At the conclusion of weighty sentences he gave time, by a
short pause, for the proper impression.

To stated and public instruction he added familiar visits and
personal application, and was careful to improve the opportunities which conversation offered of diffusing and increasing
the influence of religion.

By his natural temper he was quick of resentment ; but by his
established and habitual practice he was gentle, modest, and
inoffensive.   His tenderness appeared in his attention to children
and to the poor.   To the poor, while he lived in the family of
his friend, he allowed the third part of his annual revenue,
though the whole was not a hundred a-year ; and for children
he condescended to lay aside the scholar, the philosopher, and
the wit, to write little poems of devotion, and systems of instruction, adapted to their wants and capacities, from the dawn of
reason through its gradations of advance in the morning of life.
Every man acquainted with the common principles of human
action will look with veneration on the writer who is at one
time combating Locke, and at another making a catechism for
children in their fourth year.   A voluntary descent from the
dignity of science is perhaps the hardest lesson that humility
can teach.

As his mind was capacious, his curiosity excursive, and his
industry continual, his writings are very numerous, and his
subjects various.   With his theological works I am only enough
acquainted to admire his meekness of opposition and his mildness of censure.   It was not only in his book but in his mind
that *orthodoxy* was *united* with *charity*.

Of his philosophical pieces, his Logic [1724] has been received into the universities, and therefore wants no private recommendation : if he owes part of it to Le Clerc, it must be considered that no man who undertakes merely to methodise or illustrate a system, pretends to be its author.

In his metaphysical disquisitions, it was observed by the late learned Mr. Dyer,[14] that he confounded the idea of *space* with that of *empty space*, and did not consider that though space might be without matter, yet matter being extended could not be without space.

Few books have been perused by me with greater pleasure than his 'Improvement of the Mind,' of which the radical principles may indeed be found in Locke's ' Conduct of the Understanding,' but they are so expanded and ramified by Watts, as to confer upon him the merit of a work in the highest degree useful and pleasing. Whoever has the care of instructing others, may be charged with deficience in his duty if this book is not recommended.

I have mentioned his treatises of Theology as distinct from his other productions, but the truth is, that whatever he took in hand was, by his incessant solicitude for souls, converted to Theology. As piety predominated in his mind, it is diffused over his works : under his direction it may be truly said, *Theologiæ Philosophia ancillatur*, philosophy is subservient to evangelical instruction ; it is difficult to read a page without learning, or at least wishing, to be better. The attention is caught by indirect instruction, and he that sat down only to reason is on a sudden compelled to pray.

It was therefore with great propriety that, in 1728, he received from Edinburgh and Aberdeen an unsolicited diploma, by which he became a Doctor of Divinity. Academical honours would have more value, if they were always bestowed with equal judgment.

He continued many years to study and to preach, and to do good by his instruction and example ; till at last the infirmities of age disabled him from the more laborious part of his minis-

---

[14] Samuel Dyer (died 1772), thought by some to have been 'Junius.' (See an account of him in Malone's ' Life of Dryden,' p. 181.)

terial functions, and being no longer capable of public duty, he offered to remit the salary appendant to it; but his congregation would not accept the resignation.

By degrees his weakness increased, and at last confined him to his chamber and his bed; where he was worn gradually away without pain, till he expired Nov. 25, 1748, in the seventy-fifth year of his age.[15]

Few men have left behind such purity of character or such monuments of laborious piety. He has provided instruction for all ages, from those who are lisping their first lessons to the enlightened readers of Malbranche and Locke; he has left neither corporeal nor spiritual nature unexamined; he has taught the Art of Reasoning and the Science of the Stars.

His character, therefore, must be formed from the multiplicity and diversity of his attainments, rather than from any single performance; for it would not be safe to claim for him the highest rank in any single denomination of literary dignity; yet perhaps there was nothing in which he would not have excelled, if he had not divided his powers to different pursuits.

As a poet,[16] had he been only a poet, he would probably have

---

[15] He was buried in Bunhill Fields burial-ground, where a monument to his memory, erected by his pupil Sir John Hartopp and his true friend Lady Abney, is still to be seen. The modest inscription which it bears was written by himself :—

ISAAC WATTS, D.D.,
Pastor of a Church of Christ in London,
Successor to
The Rev. JOSEPH CARYL, Dr. JOHN OWEN, Mr. DAVID CLARKSON,
and Dr. ISAAC CHAUNCY;
After fifty years of feeble labours in the Gospel,
Interrupted by four years of tiresome sickness,
Was at last dismissed to his rest.

In uno Jesu omnia.

2 Cor. v. 8.   Absent from the body, and present with the Lord.
Col. iii. 4.   When Christ, who is my life, shall appear, then shall
I also appear with him in glory.

His will is printed in Milner's 'Life,' p. 729.

[16] Watts's first publication was his 'Horæ Lyricæ,' in December, 1705, of which a second edition appeared in 1709, a seventh in 1736, and a ninth in 1751. The first edition of his Psalms has this title: 'The Psalms of David, imitated in the language of the New Testament, and applyd to the Christian

stood high among the authors with whom he is now associated. For his judgment was exact, and he noted beauties and faults with very nice discernment; [17] his imagination, as the 'Dacian Battle' proves, was vigorous and active, and the stores of knowledge were large by which his fancy was to be supplied. His ear was well-tuned, and his diction was elegant and copious. But his devotional poetry is, like that of others, unsatisfactory. The paucity of its topics enforces perpetual repetition, and the sanctity of the matter rejects the ornaments of figurative diction. It is sufficient for Watts to have done better than others what no man has done well. [18]

His poems on other subjects seldom rise higher than might be expected from the amusements of a Man of Letters, and have different degrees of value as they are more or less laboured, or as the occasion was more or less favourable to invention.

He writes too often without regular measures, and too often in blank-verse : the rhymes are not always sufficiently correspondent. He is particularly unhappy in coining names expressive of characters. His lines are commonly smooth and easy, and his thoughts always religiously pure ; but who is there that, to so much piety and innocence, does not wish for a greater measure of sprightliness and vigour ? He is at least one of the few poets with whom youth and ignorance may be safely pleased ;

State and Worship. By I. Watts. London, 1719,' 12mo. A first edition of his 'Hymns' is rarer than a first edition of the 'Pilgrim's Progress,' of which only one copy is known.

[17] Where was this judgment and this nice discernment when he professed his admiration of Sir Richard Blackmore, and went for an example of English heroic verse in his Grammar to that Knight's "excellent poem called King Arthur"?—SOUTHEY: *Life of Watts*, 12mo., 1834.

[18] When Johnson asserts that devotional poetry is unsatisfactory, because the paucity of its topics enforces perpetual repetition, and the sanctity of the matter rejects the ornaments of figurative diction, it seems as if he had taken a most contracted and short-sighted view of the subject, and as if he had forgotten that, of all poetry, inspired poetry is the most figurative.—SOUTHEY : *Life of Watts,* p. lxxv.

This, I think, is a just censure on the greatest part of those who have written religious books in English verse; but I except from this number the ingenious Mr. Watts, whose Divine poetry is very laudable, and much superior to all that have gone before him in the lyric kind.—SIR RICHARD BLACKMORE: *Preface to a Collection of Poems*, 8vo., 1718.

and happy will be that reader whose mind is disposed by his
verses, or his prose, to imitate him in all but his non-conformity,
to copy his benevolence to man, and his reverence to God.[19]

[19] I am glad to be undeceived respecting the opinion I had been erroneously
led into on the subject of Johnson's criticism on Watts. Nothing can be more
judicious or more characteristic of a distinguishing taste than his observations
upon that writer; though I think him a little mistaken in his notion that
Divine subjects have never been poetically treated with success. A little more
Christian knowledge and experience would perhaps enable him to discover
excellent poetry upon spiritual themes in the aforesaid little Doctor.—
COWPER: *Letter to Newton*, Oct. 4, 1781.

AMBROSE PHILIPS.

AMBROSE PHILIPS.

1675–1749.

A Native of Shropshire — Educated at Cambridge — Encouraged by the
Earl of Dorset — Sides with the Whigs — His friendship with Addison
and Steele — Produces ' The Distressed Mother,' a Tragedy — The
famous Epilogue to his Tragedy — Publishes his Pastorals — His Quarrel
with Pope — Joins in ' The Freethinker ' — Is patronised by Archbishop Boulter — Death and Burial in Audley Chapel, South Audley
Street, London.

Of the birth or early part of the life of Ambrose Philips I
have not been able to find any account.[1] His academical education he received at St. John's College in Cambridge, where he
first solicited the notice of the world by some English verses, in
the collection published by the University on the death of Queen
Mary.

From this time how he was employed, or in what station he
passed his life, is not yet discovered. He must have published
his Pastorals before the year 1708, because they are evidently
prior to those of Pope.[2]

[1] Ambrosius Philips, filius Ambrosii P. pannicularii natus infra Salopiam
ibidemq; literis institutus sub M[ro] Lloyd, annum agens 18 admissus est sub-
sizator pro M[ro] Conway, Tutore & fidejussore M[ro] Nourse. Junii 25. 1693.

Nov. 6. 1693. Ego Ambrosius Phillips Salopiensis juratus et admissus sum
in discipulum hujus collegii pro Dominâ Fundatrice decessore Gandy.

Electio sociorum Martii 27. 1699.
Admissio Martii 28. 1699.

Ego Ambrosius Phillips Salopiensis juratus & admissus in perpetuum socium
hujus Collegii pro Dominâ Fundatrice decessore M[ro] Apperly.—*Register of St.
John's College, Cambridge.*

In the ' Graduati Cantabrigienses ' his degrees are given:—B.A. 1696 (*i.e.*
1696-7), M.A. 1700.

[2] This is inaccurate. (See ' Life of Pope,' iii. 11.) Philips's ' Pastorals '
appeared simultaneously with those of Pope in the sixth and concluding
volume of Tonson's ' Miscellany.' The volume (8vo., 1709) begins with the
' Pastorals ' of Philips, and ends with those of Pope.

He afterwards (1709) addressed to the universal patron, the Duke of Dorset,[3] a 'Poetical Letter from Copenhagen,' which was published in 'The Tatler' (No. 12), and is by Pope in one of his first letters mentioned with high praise, as the production of a man "who could write very nobly." [4]

Philips was a zealous Whig, and therefore easily found access to Addison and Steele; but his ardour seems not to have procured him anything more than kind words; since he was reduced to translate the 'Persian Tales' for Tonson,[5] for which he was afterwards reproached, with this addition of contempt, that he worked for half-a-crown. The book is divided into many sections, for each of which if he received half-a-crown, his reward, as writers then were paid, was very liberal; but half-a-crown had a mean sound.

He was employed in promoting the principles of his party, by epitomising Hacket's 'Life of Archbishop Williams.' The original book is written with such depravity of genius, such mixture of the fop and pedant, as has not often appeared. The epitome is free enough from affectation, but has little spirit or vigour.

In 1712 he brought upon the stage 'The Distressed Mother,' almost a translation of Racine's 'Andromaque.' Such a work requires no uncommon powers, but the friends of Philips exerted every art to promote his interest. Before the appearance of the play, a whole 'Spectator,'[6] none indeed of the best, was devoted to its praise; while it yet continued to be acted, another 'Spectator' was written, to tell what impression it made upon Sir

[3] This is a mistake; the witty Lord Dorset was only an Earl. His son Lionel was the first Duke.

[4] Compare Pope to Cromwell, Oct. 28, 1710. I cannot find the words quoted by Johnson in any letter to Cromwell.

Philips went to Copenhagen with Lord Mark Kerr, and Mr. Mitford has printed in the Aldine edition of Swift two interesting letters from Swift to Philips while abroad. They are very Whiggish. "I wish," says Swift, "the victory we have got, and the scenes you pass through, would put you into humour of writing a Pastoral to celebrate the Duke of Marlborough, who, I hope, will soon be your General."

[5] The Thousand and One Days, 'Persian Tales,' vol. i. 8vo.: London, 1714. —*Bodleian Catalogue.*

[6] 'Spectator,' No. 290, Feb. 1, 1712.

Roger ;[7] and on the first night [8] a select audience, says Pope,[9] was called together to applaud it.

It was concluded with the most successful Epilogue that was ever yet spoken on the English theatre.   The three first nights it was recited twice ; and not only continued to be demanded through the run, as it is termed, of the play, but whenever it is recalled to the stage, where by peculiar fortune, though a copy from the French, it yet keeps its place, the Epilogue is still expected, and is still spoken.[10]

The propriety of Epilogues in general, and consequently of this, was questioned by a correspondent of ‘ The Spectator,’[11] whose letter was undoubtedly admitted for the sake of the answer, which soon followed,[12] written with much zeal and acrimony.   The attack and the defence equally contributed to stimulate curiosity and continue attention.   It may be discovered in the defence, that Prior’s Epilogue to ‘ Phædra ’ had a little excited jealousy ; and something of Prior’s plan may be discovered in the performance of his rival.

Of this distinguished Epilogue the reputed author was the wretched Budgell, whom Addison used to denominate [13] “ the

[7] ‘ Spectator,’ No. 335, March 25, 1712.   “ But pray,” says Sir Roger, “ you that are a critic, is this play according to your dramatic rules, as you call them? Should your people in tragedy always talk to be understood?   Why, there is not a single sentence in this play that I do not know the meaning of.”—*Spec.* No. 335.

[8] It was acted at Drury Lane, and for the first time on the 17th March, 1712. It ran nine nights.

[9] Spence.—JOHNSON.   Ed. Singer, p. 46.

[10] The Epilogue to ‘ The Distressed Mother ’ was spoke no less than nine times by Mrs. Oldfield the three first nights ‘ The Distressed Mother ’ was acted, and is still constantly called for by the audience whenever that play is represented on the stage.   Lord Halifax sent for Mr. Budgell, then a stranger to him, and told him that from thenceforward he must be acquainted with him, and desired to be ranked among the number of his friends.—BUDGELL: *Bee,* vol. ii. p. 855.

Till then it was usual to discontinue an epilogue after the sixth night.   But this was called for by the audience, and continued for the whole run of this play.   Budgell did not scruple to sit in the pit and call for it himself.— CIBBER: *Lives of the Poets,* v. 3.

[11] ‘ Spectator,’ No. 338, March 28, 1712.

[12] ‘ Spectator,’ No. 341, April 1, 1712.

[13] Spence.—JOHNSON.   Ed. Singer, p. 161.

man who calls me cousin;" and when he was asked how such a silly fellow could write so well, replied, "The Epilogue was quite another thing when I saw it first." [14] It was known in Tonson's family, and told to Garrick, that Addison was himself the author of it, and that, when it had been at first printed with his name, he came early in the morning, before the copies were distributed, and ordered it to be given to Budgell, that it might add weight to the solicitation which he was then making for a place.[15]

Philips was now high in the ranks of literature. His play was applauded; his translations from Sappho had been published in 'The Spectator;' [16] he was an important and distinguished associate of clubs witty and political; and nothing was wanting to his happiness but that he should be sure of its continuance.

The work which had procured him the first notice from the public was his Six Pastorals, which, flattering the imagination with Arcadian scenes, probably found many readers, and might have long passed as a pleasing amusement, had they not been unhappily too much commended.

The rustic poems of Theocritus were so highly valued by the Greeks and Romans, that they attracted the imitation of Virgil, whose Eclogues seem to have been considered as precluding all attempts of the same kind; for no shepherds were taught to sing by any succeeding poet, till Nemesian and Calphurnius ventured their feeble efforts in the lower age of Latin literature.

At the revival of learning in Italy, it was soon discovered that

[14] Pope in Spence by Singer, p. 257.

[15] He [Johnson] told us [26th April, 1776] that Addison wrote Budgell's papers in 'The Spectator,' at least mended them so much that he made them almost his own; and that Draper, Tonson's partner, assured Mrs. Johnson that the much-admired Epilogue to 'The Distressed Mother,' which came out in Budgell's name, was in reality written by Addison.—*Boswell by Croker*, ed. 1847, p. 509.

I have heard Mr. Garrick say that Addison wrote the celebrated Epilogue published in the name of Budgell; that this was a fact he received from some of the Tonsons.—WARTON: *Essay on Pope*, vol. ii. p. 240.

[16] 'Spectator,' No. 223, of Nov. 15, 1711, and 'Spectator,' No. 229, Nov. 22, 1711. Joseph Warton was of opinion that in these exquisite fragments Philips received assistance from Addison.—*Essay on Pope*, i. 300.

a dialogue of imaginary swains might be composed with little
difficulty ; because the conversation of shepherds excludes profound or refined sentiment ; and, for images and descriptions,
satyrs and fauns, and naiads and dryads, were always within
call ; and woods and meadows, and hills and rivers, supplied
variety of matter, which, having a natural power to soothe the
mind, did not quickly cloy it.

Petrarch entertained the learned men of his age with the
novelty of modern Pastorals in Latin.   Being not ignorant of
Greek, and finding nothing in the word *Eclogue* of rural meaning, he supposed it to be corrupted by the copiers, and therefore called his own productions *Æglogues*, by which he meant
to express the talk of goatherds, though it will mean only the
talk of goats.   This new name was adopted by subsequent
writers, and amongst others by our Spenser.

More than a century afterwards (1498) Mantuan published
his Bucolics with such success, that they were soon dignified
by Badius with a comment, and, as Scaliger complained, received
into schools, and taught as classical ; his complaint was vain, and
the practice, however injudicious, spread far, and continued
long.   Mantuan was read, at least in some of the inferior
schools of this kingdom, to the beginning of the present century.
The speakers of Mantuan carried their disquisitions beyond the
country, to censure the corruptions of the Church ; and from him
Spenser learned to employ his swains on topics of controversy.

The Italians soon transferred Pastoral Poetry into their own
language : Sannazaro wrote ' Arcadia ' in prose and verse ;
Tasso and Guarini wrote ' Favole Boschareccie,' or Sylvan
Dramas ; and all nations of Europe filled volumes with Thyrsis
and Damon, and Thestylis and Phyllis.

Philips thinks it " somewhat strange to conceive how, in an
age so addicted to the Muses, Pastoral Poetry never comes to
be so much as thought upon."   His wonder seems very unseasonable : there had never, from the time of Spenser, wanted
writers to talk occasionally of Arcadia and Strephon ; and half
the book in which he first tried his powers consists of dialogues
on Queen Mary's death, between Tityrus and Corydon, or

Mopsus and Menalcas.   A series or book of Pastorals, however, I know not that any one had then lately published.[17]

Not long afterwards [18] Pope made the first display of his powers in four Pastorals, written in a very different form. Philips had taken Spenser, and Pope took Virgil for his pattern. Philips endeavoured to be natural, Pope laboured to be elegant.

Philips was now favoured by Addison, and by Addison's companions, who were very willing to push him into reputation. 'The Guardian' gave [April 1713] an account of Pastoral, partly critical, and partly historical; in which, when the merit of the modern is compared, Tasso and Guarini are censured for remote thoughts and unnatural refinements; and, upon the whole, the Italians and French are all excluded from rural poetry; and the pipe of the pastoral muse is transmitted by lawful inheritance from Theocritus to Virgil, from Virgil to Spenser, and from Spenser to Philips.

With this inauguration of Philips his rival Pope was not much delighted; he therefore drew a comparison of Philips's performance with his own, in which, with an unexampled and unequalled artifice of irony, though he has himself always the advantage, he gives the preference to Philips.   The design of aggrandizing himself he disguised with such dexterity, that, though Addison discovered it, Steele was deceived, and was afraid of displeasing Pope by publishing his paper.[19]   Published, however, it was ('Guard. 40'): and from that time Pope and Philips lived in a perpetual reciprocation of malevolence.[20]

In poetical powers, of either praise or satire, there was no

[17] Whoever wishes to pursue the subject of Pastoral Poetry still further, may read with advantage Johnson's two papers in 'The Rambler,' Nos. 36 and 37.

[18] At the same time.   (See Note 2, p. 259.)

[19] Of 27th April, 1713.

[20] His [Pope's] malignity to Philips, whom he had first made ridiculous, and then hated for being angry, continued too long.—JOHNSON: Life of Pope.

The secret grounds of Philips's malignity to Pope are said to be the ridicule and laughter he met with from all the Hanover Club, of which he was secretary, for mistaking the incomparable ironical paper in 'The Guardian' for a serious criticism on pastoral poetry.   The learned Heyne also mistook this irony.—WARTON: Essay on Pope, ii. 234.

proportion between the combatants; but Philips, though he could not prevail by wit, hoped to hurt Pope with another weapon, and charged him, as Pope thought,[21] with Addison's approbation, as disaffected to the Government.

Even with this he was not satisfied; for, indeed, there is no appearance that any regard was paid to his clamours.   He proceeded to grosser insults, and hung up a rod at Button's,[22] with which he threatened to chastise Pope, who appears to have been extremely exasperated; for in the first edition of his Letters he calls Philips " rascal,"[23] and in the last still charges him with detaining in his hands the subscriptions for Homer delivered to him by the Hanover Club.[24]

I suppose it was never suspected that he meant to appropriate the money; he only delayed, and with sufficient meanness, the gratification of him by whose prosperity he was pained.

Men sometimes suffer by injudicious kindness; Philips became ridiculous, without his own fault, by the absurd admiration of his friends, who decorated him with honorary garlands, which the first breath of contradiction blasted.

When upon the succession of the House of Hanover [1st Aug. 1714] every Whig expected to be happy, Philips seems to have obtained too little notice: he caught few drops of the golden shower, though he did not omit what flattery could perform. He was only made a Commissioner of the Lottery (1717), and, what did not much elevate his character, a Justice of the Peace.[25]

---

[21] His constant cry was, that Mr. P. was an *enemy to the Government*; and in particular he was the avowed author of a report very industriously spread, that he had a hand in a party-paper called the *Examiner*: a falsehood well known to those yet living, who had the direction and publication of it.—*Note to Dunciad*, 8vo., 1729, p. 167.   The note was afterwards omitted.

[22] Cibber's 'Letter to Pope,' 8vo., 1742, p. 65.   The same story is told in ' Pope Alexander's Supremacy and Infallibility examined,' 1728, and is confirmed by an unpublished letter, in Mr. Croker's hands, from Broome to Fenton, of 3rd May, 1729.

[23] No; "scoundrel."—*Letters*, 12mo., 1735, p. 161.   In his own quarto ed., p. 121, he omits the sentence in which the word appears.

[24] Pope's ' Letters,' 4to., 1737, p. 121.

[25] He was made Paymaster of the Lottery in the place of John Morley, Esq., by Treasury Warrant of 25th January, 1715, with a yearly fee or salary of 500*l*. for the service of himself, clerks, and others.

The success of his first play must naturally dispose him to turn his hopes towards the stage: he did not, however, soon commit himself to the mercy of an audience, but contented himself with the fame already acquired, till after nine years he produced [26] (1722) 'The Briton,' a tragedy which, whatever was its reception, is now neglected; though one of the scenes, between Vanoc the British Prince and Valens the Roman General, is confessed to be written with great dramatic skill, animated by spirit truly poetical.

He had not been idle, though he had been silent; for he exhibited another tragedy the same year,[27] on the story of 'Humphry Duke of Gloucester.' This tragedy is only remembered by its title.

His happiest undertaking was [1711] of a paper, called 'The Freethinker,' in conjunction with associates, of whom one was Dr. Boulter, who, then only minister of a parish in Southwark, was of so much consequence to the Government that he was made first Bishop of Bristol, and afterwards Primate of Ireland, where his piety and his charity will be long honoured.[28]

It may easily be imagined that what was printed under the direction of Boulter would have nothing in it indecent or licentious; its title is to be understood as implying only freedom from unreasonable prejudice. It has been reprinted in

[26] At Drury Lane, 19th Feb., 1721-2. 'The Briton' ran eight nights.

[27] At Drury Lane, and acted, for the first time, 15th Feb., 1722-3. 'Humphry Duke of Gloucester' ran nine nights.

[28] Johnson was fond of repeating, in his "best manner," the following lines from a poem entitled 'Boulter's Monument, written by Dr. Madden, and corrected by himself:'—

> Some write their wrongs in marble: he, more just,
> Stoop'd down serene and wrote them in the dust;
> Trod under foot, the sport of every wind,
> Swept from the earth, and blotted from his mind.
> There, secret in the grave, he bade them lie,
> And griev'd they could not 'scape the Almighty's eye.

He also introduced them into the last edition of his 'Dictionary,' under the word "SPORT."—*Boswell by Croker*, ed. 1847, p. 830.

volumes, but is little read; nor can impartial criticism recommend it as worthy of revival.

Boulter was not well qualified to write diurnal essays; but he knew how to practise the liberality of greatness and the fidelity of friendship. When he was advanced to the height of ecclesiastical dignity, he did not forget the companion of his labours. Knowing Philips to be slenderly supported, he took him to Ireland, as partaker of his fortune; and, making him his secretary, added such preferments as enabled him to represent the county of Armagh in the Irish Parliament.[29]

In December, 1726, he was made Secretary to the Lord Chancellor; and in August, 1733, became Judge of the Prerogative Court.[30]

After the death of his patron[31] he continued some years in Ireland; but at last longing, as it seems, for his native country, he returned (1748) to London, having doubtless survived most of his friends and enemies, and among them his dreaded antagonist Pope. He found, however, the Duke of Newcastle still living, and to him he dedicated his poems collected into a volume.

Having purchased an annuity of four hundred pounds, he now certainly hoped to pass some years of life in plenty

[29]   B[enson] sole judge of architecture sit,
    And Namby Pamby be preferred for wit.

                The Dunciad, Book iii., 1729.

    On poets' tombs see Benson's titles writ:
    Lo! Ambrose Philips is preferred for wit.

                The Dunciad, Book iii.

    Whom have I hurt? has poet yet or peer
    Lost the arch'd eyebrow or Parnassian sneer?
            .   .   .   .   .   .
    Does not one table Bavius still admit?
    Still to one Bishop, Philips seem a wit?

                POPE, in 1734: *Epistle to Arbuthnot.*

[30]   He was Registrar, and not Judge, and obtained his appointment in September, 1734.

[31]   Boulter died 28th September, 1742.

and tranquillity; but his hope deceived him: he was struck with a palsy, and died June 18, 1749, in his seventy-eighth year.[32]

Of his personal character all that I have heard is, that he was eminent for bravery and skill in the sword, and that in conversation he was solemn and pompous.[33] He had great sensibility of censure, if judgment may be made by a single story which I heard long ago from Mr. Ing, a gentleman of great eminence in Staffordshire. " Philips," said he, " was once at table, when I asked him, How came thy king of Epirus to drive oxen, and to say ' I'm goaded on by love?' After which question he never spoke again."

Of ' The Distressed Mother ' not much is pretended to be his own, and therefore it is no subject of criticism: his other two tragedies, I believe, are not below mediocrity, nor above it. Among the Poems comprised in the late Collection,[34] the ' Letter from Copenhagen ' [35] may be justly praised; the Pastorals, which by the writer of ' The Guardian ' were ranked as one of the four genuine productions of the rustic Muse, cannot surely be despicable. That they exhibit a mode of life which did not exist, nor ever existed, is not to be objected: the supposition of such a state is allowed to Pastoral. In his other poems he cannot be denied the praise of lines sometimes elegant; but he has seldom much force, or much comprehension. The pieces that please best are those which, from Pope and Pope's adherents, procured him the name of *Namby Pamby*, the poems of short lines, by which he paid his court to all ages and characters, from Walpole the " steerer of the realm," to Miss Pulteney in the nursery.[36] The numbers are smooth and sprightly, and the

---

[32] He died "at his lodgings near Vauxhall." (*Cibber's Lives*, v. 142), or, as I have seen elsewhere stated, in Hanover-square, and was buried in the chapel in South Audley-street.

[33] We gather from Spence (ed. Singer, p. 375) that Ambrose Philips was a neat dresser, very vain, of lean make, and about five feet seven inches high.

[34] The collection for which these 'Lives' were written.

[35] The opening of this poem is incomparably fine. The latter part is tedious and trifling.—GOLDSMITH: *Beauties of English Poesy*.

[36] The name " Namby Pamby" occurs in ' The Dunciad ' of 1729, with this note: "an author whose eminence in the infantine style obtained him this

diction is seldom faulty. They are not loaded with much thought, yet, if they had been written by Addison, they would have had admirers : little things are not valued but when they are done by those who cannot do greater.

In his translations from Pindar he found the art of reaching all the obscurity of the Theban bard, however he may fall below his sublimity; he will be allowed, if he has less fire, to have more smoke.

He has added nothing to English poetry, yet at least half his book deserves to be read : perhaps he valued most himself that part which the critic would reject.[37]

name." The name was given, if we may trust Cibber's 'Lives' (v. 139), by Harry Carey. One of the earliest of these attacks occurs in the 'Gentleman's Magazine' for October, 1733: "To an infant expiring the second day of its birth. Written by its mother in imitation of Namby Pamby." The excellent imitation in the 'Pipe of Tobacco' of the infantine style of Philips was not written by Hawkins Browne, "but sent to him by an ingenious friend."— (Browne's 'Poems,' 1768: To the Reader.)

[37] To Pope's character of 'Macer,' first printed in the volume of 'Miscellanies' (1728, 8vo.), containing the celebrated Preface signed by Swift, and the still more celebrated *Art of Sinking in Poetry*, there is this note:

"He requested, by publick Advertisements, the aid of the Ingenious to make up a Miscellany in 1713 " (p. 134).

That 'Macer' was meant for Philips, I can now additionally prove by the following 'Advertisement:'

" There is now preparing for the Press, a Collection of Original Poems and Translations by the most Eminent Hands, to be published by Mr. Philips. Such gentlemen, therefore, who are willing to appear in this Miscellany, are desired to communicate the same, directed to Jacob Tonson, Bookseller, in the Strand."—*The London Gazette*, 4-8 January, 1714-15.

The Miscellany never appeared.

MACER.

" When simple *Macer*, now of high Renown,
First sought a Poet's Fortune in the Town:
'Twas all th' Ambition his high Soul could feel,
To wear red Stockings, and to dine with St[eele]. [38]
Some Ends of Verse his Betters might afford,
And gave the harmless Fellow a good Word.
Set up with these, he ventur'd on the Town,
And in a borrow'd Play, out-did poor Cr[ow]n.

There

[38] At a Blacksmith's shop in the Friars, a Pindaric writer in red stockings.— POPE: *An Account of the Condition of E. Curll.*

There he stopt short, nor since has writ a tittle,
But has the Wit to make the most of little :
Like stunted hide-bound Trees, that just have got
Sufficient Sap, at once to bear and rot.
Now he begs Verse, and what he gets commends,
Not of the Wits his Foes, but Fools his Friends.

So some coarse Country Wench, almost decay'd,
Trudges to Town, and first turns Chambermaid;
Awkward and supple, each Devoir to pay,
She flatters her good Lady twice a Day;
Thought wond'rous honest, tho' of mean Degree,
And strangely lik'd for her *Simplicity :*
In a translated Suit, then tries the Town,
With borrow'd Pins, and Patches not her own;
But just endur'd the Winter she began,
And in four Months, a batter'd Harridan.
Now nothing's left, but, wither'd, pale, and shrunk,
To bawd for others, and go Shares with Punk."

GILBERT WEST.

W E S T.

1700 ?–1756.

Educated at Eton and Oxford — Marries, and retires to Wickham in Kent — Translates Pindar, and publishes 'Observations on the Resurrection' — His Friendship with Lyttelton and Pitt — Death and Burial at Wickham — Works and Character.

GILBERT WEST is one of the writers of whom I regret my inability to give a sufficient account; the intelligence which my inquiries have obtained is general and scanty.

He was the son of the Reverend Dr. West; perhaps him who published 'Pindar' at Oxford about the beginning of this century.[1] His mother was sister to Sir Richard Temple, afterwards Lord Cobham. His father purposing to educate him for the Church, sent him first to Eton, and afterwards to Oxford; but he was seduced to a more airy mode of life, by a commission in a troop of horse procured him by his uncle.

He continued some time in the army; though it is reasonable to suppose that he never sunk into a mere soldier, nor ever lost the love or much neglected the pursuit of learning; and afterwards, finding himself more inclined to civil employment, he laid down his commission, and engaged in business under the Lord Townshend, then Secretary of State, with whom he attended the King to Hanover.

His adherence to Lord Townshend ended in nothing but a nomination (May, 1729) to be Clerk-Extraordinary of the Privy Council, which produced no immediate profit; for it

---

[1] His father, Richard West (d. 1716), *was* with Robert Welsted the joint editor of an edition of Pindar, published at Oxford in 1697, folio. The same Richard West, I suspect, described by Wood as the son of Richard West, of Creiton, in Northamptonshire, Clerk. His mother was living in 1749 with his sister Hetty, at Meres-Ashby, in Northamptonshire. His brother, Admiral Temple West, has a monument in Westminster Abbey.

only placed him in a state of expectation and right of succession, and it was very long before a vacancy admitted him to profit.

Soon afterwards he married,[2] and settled himself in a very pleasant house at Wickham, in Kent, where he devoted himself to learning and to piety. Of his learning the late Collection[3] exhibits evidence, which would have been yet fuller, if the dissertations which accompany his version of 'Pindar' had not been improperly omitted. Of his piety the influence has, I hope, been extended far by his 'Observations on the Resurrection,' published in 1747, for which the University of Oxford created him a Doctor of Laws by Diploma (March 30, 1748), and would doubtless have reached yet further had he lived to complete what he had for some time meditated, the Evidences of the Truth of the New Testament. Perhaps it may not be without effect to tell that he read the prayers of the public liturgy every morning to his family, and that on Sunday evening he called his servants into the parlour, and read to them first a sermon, and then prayers. Crashaw is now not the only maker of verses to whom may be given the two venerable names of *Poet and Saint.*[4]

He was very often visited by Lyttelton[5] and Pitt, who, when they were weary of faction and debates, used at Wickham to find books and quiet, a decent table, and literary conversation. There is at Wickham a walk made by Pitt; and, what is of far more importance, at Wickham Lyttelton received that conviction which produced [1748] his 'Observations on St. Paul.'[6]

These two illustrious friends had for a while listened to the

---

[2] His wife's Christian name was Catherine. Who she was I know not.

[3] Of English Poets, for which Johnson's 'Prefaces' or 'Lives' were written.

[4]   Poet and Saint! to thee alone are given
      The two most sacred names of Earth and Heaven.

                    COWLEY: *On the Death of Mr. Crashaw.*

[5] Who was his first cousin.

[6] Observations on the Conversion and Apostleship of St. Paul. In a Letter to Gilbert West, Esq. Dodsley, 1748, 8vo. It was written to convince the poet of 'The Seasons.'

blandishments of infidelity; and when West's book was published, it was bought by some who did not know his change of opinion, in expectation of new objections against Christianity; and as infidels do not want malignity, they revenged the disappointment by calling him a Methodist.

Mr. West's income was not large; and his friends endeavoured, but without success, to obtain an augmentation. It is reported that the education of the young Prince [7] was offered to him, but that he required a more extensive power of superintendence than it was thought proper to allow him. [8]

In time, however, his revenue was improved; he lived to have one of the lucrative clerkships of the Privy Council (1752); and Mr. Pitt at last had it in his power to make him treasurer of Chelsea Hospital. [9]

He was now sufficiently rich; but wealth came too late to be long enjoyed; nor could it secure him from the calamities of life: he lost (1755) his only son; and the year after (March 26) a stroke of the palsy brought to the grave one of the few poets to whom the grave might be without its terrors. [10]

Of his translations [11] I have only compared the first Olympic ode with the original, and found my expectation surpassed both by its elegance and its exactness. He does not confine himself to his author's train of stanzas; for he saw that the difference of the languages required a different mode of versification. The first strophe is eminently happy; in the second he has a little strayed from Pindar's meaning, who says, " If thou, my soul, wishest to speak of games, look not in the desert sky for a planet hotter than the sun, nor shall we tell of nobler

---

[7] Afterwards George III.

[8] Pope left him 200*l.*, and 5*l.* to buy "a ring or any memorial of me."

[9] West was *Under* Treasurer. The Paymaster of the Forces was Treasurer.

[10] He had long suffered from the gout. He was buried at West Wickham, by his request in his will, in the same grave with his son. His brother, Admiral West, was his executor. His wife survived him, enjoyed a pension from the Crown, after his death, of 200*l.* a year, and died 29th Sept., 1757. Mrs. Montagu has left a charming account of her in her 'Letters' (iii. 105). There is a good portrait of West at Hagley, artist unknown. He was handsome.

[11] 'Odes of Pindar, with several other Poems, in prose and verse, translated from the Greek; to which is prefixed a Dissertation on the Olympick Games,

games than those of Olympia.'' He is sometimes too para-
phrastical. Pindar bestows upon Hiero an epithet, which, in
one word, signifies *delighting in horses;* a word which, in the
translation, generates these lines :

> " Hiero's royal brows, whose care
> Tends the courser's noble breed,
> Pleas'd to nurse the pregnant mare,
> Pleas'd to train the youthful steed."

Pindar says of Pelops, that " he came alone in the dark to the
White Sea ;" and West,

> " Near the billow-beaten side
> Of the foam-besilver'd main,
> Darkling, and alone, he stood :"

which, however, is less exuberant than the former passage.

A work of this kind must, in a minute examination, discover
many imperfections; but West's version, so far as I have considered it, appears to be the product of great labour and great
abilities.

by Gilbert West, LL.D.' Dodsley [May], 1749. 4to. *Other Editions*, 2 vols.
12mo. 1753; 3 vols. 12mo. 1766. The dedication is particularly elegant :—

To
The Right Honourable
WILLIAM PITT, Esq.
Paymaster General of His Majesty's Forces,
One of His Majesty's most Honourable Privy Council,
and to the Honourable
Sir GEORGE LYTTELTON, Bart.
One of the Lords Commissioners of the Treasury,
These Volumes
Are Inscribed by the Author,
who is desirous that the Friendship,
With which they have for many years honoured him,
And the sincere affection and high esteem,
Which he hath conceived for them,
From a long and intimate knowledge
of their Worth and Virtue,
May be known
Wherever the Publication of the ensuing pieces
Shall make known the name of
GILBERT WEST.

His ' Institution of the Garter' (1742) [12] is written with sufficient knowledge of the manners that prevailed in the age to which it is referred, and with great elegance of diction; but for want of a process of events, neither knowledge nor elegance preserve the reader from weariness.

His ' Imitations of Spenser ' [13] are very successfully performed, both with respect to the metre, the language, and the fiction; and being engaged at once by the excellence of the sentiments and the artifice of the copy, the mind has two amusements together. But such compositions are not to be reckoned among the great achievements of intellect, because their effect is local and temporary; they appeal not to reason or passion, but to memory, and pre-suppose an accidental or artificial state of mind. An imitation of Spenser is nothing to a reader, however acute, by whom Spenser has never been perused. Works of this kind may deserve praise, as proofs of great industry and great nicety of observation, but the highest praise, the praise of genius, they cannot claim. The noblest beauties of art are those of which the effect is co-extended with rational nature, or at least with the whole circle of polished life; what is less than this can be only pretty, the plaything of fashion and the amusement of a day. [14]

[12] ' The Institution of the Order of the Garter. A Dramatick Poem.' [Anonymous.] Dodsley [February], 1742. 4to.

[13] Such as his ' Canto of the Fairy Queen,' 1739, folio, and his 'Education, a Poem, in two Cantos,' of which the first appeared in March, 1751.

" Now I talk of verses, Mr. Walpole and I have frequently wondered you should never mention a certain imitation of Spenser, published last year [May, 1739], by a namesake of yours, with which we are all enraptured and enmarvailed."—GRAY to Richard West, July 16, 1740.

[14] With all his faults, no poet enlarges the imagination more than Spenser. Cowley was formed into poetry by reading him; and many of our modern writers, such as Gray, Akenside, and others, seem to have studied his manner with the utmost attention: from him their compounded epithets, and solemn flow of numbers, seem evidently borrowed; and the verses of Spenser may, perhaps, one day be considered the standard of English poetry. It were happy indeed if his beauties were the only objects of modern imitation; but many of his words, justly fallen into disuse among his successors, have been of late revived, and a language already too copious has been augmented by an unnecessary reinforcement. Learning and language are ever fluctuating, either rising to perfection or retiring into primeval barbarity: perhaps the point of English perfection is already passed, and every intended improvement may

There is in 'The Adventurer' a paper of verses given to one of the authors as Mr. West's, and supposed to have been written by him. It should not be concealed, however, that it is printed with Mr. Jago's name in Dodsley's Collection, and is mentioned as his in a letter of Shenstone's. Perhaps West gave it without naming the author, and Hawkesworth, receiving it from him, thought it his ; for his he thought it, as he told me, and as he tells the public.

now be only deviation. This at least is certain, that posterity will perceive a strong similitude between the poets of the sixteenth and those of the latter end of the eighteenth century.—GOLDSMITH: *Works by Cunningham*, iv. 203.

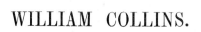

WILLIAM COLLINS.

COLLINS.

1720–1759.

Born at Chichester — Educated at Winchester and Oxford — Publishes
' Oriental Eclogues ' and Odes on several Descriptive and Allegoric
subjects — Publishes Proposals for a ' History of the Revival of Learning '
— Publishes a Poem on Thomson's Death — Dies insane, and Buried
in St. Andrew's Church, Chichester — Works and Character.

WILLIAM COLLINS was born at Chichester on the 25th day of
December, 1720. His father was a hatter of good reputation. He was in 1733, as Dr. Warton has kindly informed
me, admitted scholar of Winchester College, where he was
educated by Dr. Burton. His English exercises were better
than his Latin.

He first courted the notice of the public by some verses to a
' Lady weeping,' published in ' The Gentleman's Magazine.' [1]

In 1740 he stood first in the list of the scholars to be received
in succession at New College, but unhappily there was no vacancy. He became a Commoner of Queen's College, probably
with a scanty maintenance; but was, in about half a year,
elected a *Demy* of Magdalen College, where he continued till
he had taken a Bachelor's degree, and then suddenly left the
University, for what reason I know not that he told.

He now (about 1744) came to London a literary adventurer,
with many projects in his head, and very little money in his
pocket. He designed many works; but his great fault was
irresolution, or the frequent calls of immediate necessity broke
his schemes, and suffered him to pursue no settled purpose. A
man doubtful of his dinner, or trembling at a creditor, is not

---

[1] For January, 1739. They are signed ' Amasius.' The other Amasius of
the Magazine at that time was Dr. Swan, the translator of Sydenham. (See
' Gent.'s Mag.' for January 1739, p. 43, and Johnson's note to Nichols in
' Gent.'s Mag.' for January 1785.)

much disposed to abstracted meditation, or remote inquiries. He published proposals for a History of the Revival of Learning ; and I have heard him speak with great kindness of Leo the Tenth,[2] and with keen resentment of his tasteless successor. But probably not a page of his history was ever written. He planned several tragedies, but he only planned them. He wrote now and then odes and other poems, and did something, however little.[3]

About this time I fell into his company. His appearance was decent and manly ;[4] his knowledge considerable, his views extensive, his conversation elegant, and his disposition cheerful. By degrees I gained his confidence ; and one day was admitted to him when he was immured by a bailiff that was prowling in the street. On this occasion recourse was had to the booksellers, who, on the credit of a translation of Aristotle's ' Poetics,' which he engaged to write with a large commentary, advanced as much money as enabled him to escape into the country. He showed me the guineas safe in his hand. Soon afterwards his uncle, Mr. Martin, a lieutenant-colonel,[5] left him about two thousand pounds ; a sum which Collins could scarcely think exhaustible, and which he did not live to exhaust. The guineas were then repaid, and the translation neglected.

But man is not born for happiness. Collins, who, while he *studied to live*, felt no evil but poverty, no sooner *lived to study*[6] than his life was assailed by more dreadful calamities, disease and insanity.

[2] See Warton's ' Essay on Pope,' i. 186.

[3] Only one gentleman, Mr. Collins, who had lived some time at Richmond, but forsook it when Mr. Thomson died, wrote an ode to his memory.—MURDOCH: *Life of Thomson*.

This fine ode was printed in folio, " London: R. Manby and H. S. Cox, 1749 " [June], and " inscribed " by the author to " George Lyttelton, Esq."

[4] Mr. Collins was in stature somewhat above the middle size; of a brown complexion; keen, expressive eyes; and a fixed, sedate aspect, which, from intense thinking, had contracted an habitual frown.—LANGHORNE.

[5] Lieutenant-Colonel Martin Bladen, stigmatised, it is said, by Pope in ' The Dunciad,' Book iv. 560. (See Warton's ' Pope,' v. 284.) Colonel Martin Bladen died 15th Feb. 1745-6, and was buried at Stepney.

[6] For we that live to please, must please—to live.

JOHNSON: *Prologue on opening Drury Lane Theatre.*

Having formerly written his character,[7] while perhaps it was yet more distinctly impressed upon my memory, I shall insert it here.

" Mr. Collins was a man of extensive literature, and of vigorous faculties. He was acquainted not only with the learned tongues, but with the Italian, French, and Spanish languages. He had employed his mind chiefly upon works of fiction, and subjects of fancy ; and, by indulging some peculiar habits of thought, was eminently delighted with those flights of imagination which pass the bounds of nature, and to which the mind is reconciled only by a passive acquiescence in popular traditions. He loved fairies, genii, giants, and monsters ; he delighted to rove through the meanders of enchantment, to gaze on the magnificence of golden palaces, to repose by the water-falls of Elysian gardens.

" This was, however, the character rather of his inclination than his genius ; the grandeur of wildness, and the novelty of extravagance, were always desired by him, but were not always attained. Yet, as diligence is never wholly lost, if his efforts sometimes caused harshness and obscurity, they likewise produced in happier moments sublimity and splendour. This idea which he had formed of excellence led him to Oriental fictions and allegorical imagery ; and perhaps, while he was intent upon description, he did not sufficiently cultivate sentiment. His poems are the productions of a mind not deficient in fire, nor unfurnished with knowledge either of books or life, but somewhat obstructed in its progress by deviation in quest of mistaken beauties.

" His morals were pure, and his opinions pious ; in a long continuance of poverty, and long habits of dissipation, it cannot be expected that any character should be exactly uniform. There is a degree of want by which the freedom of agency is almost destroyed ; and long association with fortuitous companions will at last relax the strictness of truth, and abate the fervour of sincerity. That this man, wise and virtuous as he

[7] In Fawkes and Woty's ' Poetical Calendar,' vol. xii. p. 110.

was, passed always unentangled through the snares of life, it would be prejudice and temerity to affirm; but it may be said that at least he preserved the source of action unpolluted, that his principles were never shaken, that his distinctions of right and wrong were never confounded, and that his faults had nothing of malignity or design, but proceeded from some unexpected pressure, or casual temptation.

" The latter part of his life cannot be remembered but with pity and sadness. He languished some years under that depression of mind which enchains the faculties without destroying them, and leaves reason the knowledge of right without the power of pursuing it. These clouds which he perceived gathering on his intellects, he endeavoured to disperse by travel, and passed into France; but found himself constrained to yield to his malady, and returned. He was for some time confined in a house of lunatics, and afterwards retired to the care of his sister in Chichester,[8] where death, in 1759,[9] came to his relief.

" After his return from France, the writer of this character paid him a visit at Islington, where he was waiting for his sister, whom he had directed to meet him: there was then nothing of disorder discernible in his mind by any but himself; but he had withdrawn from study, and travelled with no other book than an English Testament, such as children carry to the school: when his friend took it into his hand, out of curiosity to see what companion a man of letters had chosen, ' I have but one book,' said Collins, ' but that is the best.' "

Such was the fate of Collins, with whom I once delighted to converse, and whom I yet remember with tenderness.[10]

He was visited at Chichester in his last illness by his learned

[8] Afterwards married to the Rev. Dr. Durnford. She died at Chichester in Nov. 1789.

[9] Collins died on the 12th June, 1759, and on the 15th was buried in the church of St. Andrew's, Chichester. There is a mural monument to his memory in Chichester Cathedral, with a fine bas-relief by Flaxman.

[10] But how little can we venture to exult in any intellectual powers or literary attainments when we consider the condition of poor Collins! I knew him a few years ago full of hopes and full of projects, versed in many languages, high in fancy and strong in retention. This busy and forcible mind is now under the government of those who lately would not have been able to com-

friends Dr. Warton and his brother, to whom he spoke with disapprobation of his Oriental Eclogues, as not sufficiently expressive of Asiatic manners, and called them his Irish Eclogues.[11] He showed them, at the same time, an ode inscribed to Mr. John Home, on the superstitions of the Highlands; which they thought superior to his other works, but which no search has yet found.[12]

His disorder was not alienation of mind, but general laxity and feebleness, a deficiency rather of his vital than intellectual powers. What he spoke wanted neither judgment nor spirit; but a few minutes exhausted him, so that he was forced to rest upon the couch, till a short cessation restored his powers, and he was again able to talk with his former vigour.

The approaches of this dreadful malady he began to feel soon after his uncle's death; and with the usual weakness of men so diseased, eagerly snatched that temporary relief with which the table and the bottle flatter and seduce. But his health

prehend the least and most narrow of its designs. What do you hear of him? —are there hopes of his recovery?—or is he to pass the remainder of his life in misery and degradation, perhaps with complete consciousness of his calamity ?—JOHNSON to Joseph Warton, March 8, 1754.

Poor dear Collins! Let me know whether you think it would give him pleasure if I should write to him. I have often been near his state, and therefore have it in great commiseration.—JOHNSON to Joseph Warton, Dec. 24, 1754.

What becomes of poor dear Collins? I wrote him a letter, which he never answered. I suppose writing is very troublesome to him. That man is no common loss. The moralists all talk of the uncertainty of fortune, and the transitoriness of beauty; but it is yet more dreadful to consider that the powers of the mind are equally liable to change—that understanding may make its appearance and depart—that it may blaze and expire.—JOHNSON to Joseph Warton, April 15, 1756.

[11] Mr. Collins wrote his Eclogues when he was about seventeen years old, at Winchester School, and, as I well remember, had been just reading that volume of Salmon's Modern History which described Persia; which determined him to lay the scene of these pieces, as being productive of new images and sentiments. In his maturer years he was accustomed to speak very contemptuously of them, calling them his Irish Eclogues, and saying they had not in them one spark of Orientalism; and desiring me to erase a motto he had prefixed to them in a copy he gave me:

—quos primus equis oriens afflavit anhelis.—VIRG.

He was greatly mortified that they found more readers and admirers than his Odes.—JOS. WARTON: *Pope's Works*, i. 61. (See also Warton's 'Pope,' ii. 346.)

[12] It has since been discovered, and was first printed in 1788, 4to.

continually declined, and he grew more and more burthensome to himself.

To what I have formerly said of his writings may be added, that his diction was often harsh, unskilfully laboured, and injudiciously selected. He affected the obsolete [13] when it was not worthy of revival; and he puts his words out of the common order, seeming to think, with some later candidates for fame, that not to write prose is certainly to write poetry. His lines commonly are of slow motion, clogged and impeded with clusters of consonants. As men are often esteemed who cannot be loved, so the poetry of Collins may sometimes extort praise when it gives little pleasure.

Mr. Collins's first production is added here from 'The Gentleman's Magazine.' [14]

To Miss Aurelia C——r,

On her Weeping at her Sister's Wedding.

" Cease, fair Aurelia, cease to mourn ;
    Lament not Hannah's happy state ;
You may be happy in your turn,
    And seize the treasure you regret.
With Love united Hymen stands,
    And softly whispers to your charms,
' Meet but your lover in my bands,
    ' You 'll find your sister in his arms.' "

---

[13] Spenser himself affects the obsolete,
        And Sidney's verse halts ill on Roman feet.—Pope.

[14] Collins's Odes, the volume which endears his name to every reader of true poetry, is a small octavo of fifty-two pages, dated 1747, and published by Andrew Millar in Dec. 1746.

"Have you seen the works of two young authors, a Mr. [Joseph] Warton and Mr. Collins, both writers of odes? It is odd enough, but each is the half of a considerable man, and one the counterpart of the other. The first has but little invention, very poetical choice of expression, and a good ear: the second, a fine fancy, modelled upon the antique; a bad ear; a great variety of words and images, with no choice at all. They both deserve to last some years, but will not."—Gray to Wharton, Dec. 27, 1746.

How little did Gray foresee that Collins's name, as a poet, would hereafter be linked inseparably with his own!

Collins's first separate publication was his Oriental Eclogues, published in 1742, under the title of 'Persian Eclogues;' his second was his Verses to Sir Thomas Hanmer; and the third was his volume of Odes. The best edition of Collins is that by Mr. Dyce, 8vo. 1827.

JOHN   DYER.

D Y E R.

1700–1758.

Second Son of Robert Dyer, of Aberglasney, in Caermarthenshire — Edu-
cated at Westminster — Studies Poetry and Painting — Publishes
' Grongar Hill,' a Poem — Enters into Holy Orders — Publishes ' The
Ruins of Rome,' ' The Fleece,' &c. — Made Rector of Coningsby, in
Lincolnshire — Death and Burial at Coningsby.

JOHN DYER, of whom I have no other account to give than his
own letters, published with Hughes's correspondence, and the
notes added by the editor, have afforded me, was born in 1700,[1]
the second son of Robert Dyer, of Aberglasney, in Caermarthenshire, a solicitor of great capacity and note.

He passed through Westminster School under the care of
Dr. Freind, and was then called home to be instructed in his
father's profession. But his father died soon, and he took no
delight in the study of the law, but having always amused himself with drawing, resolved to turn painter, and became pupil to
Mr. Richardson, an artist then of high reputation, but now
[1780] better known by his books than by his pictures.

Having studied a while under his master, he became, as he
tells his friend, an itinerant painter, and wandered about South
Wales and the parts adjacent;[2] but he mingled poetry with
painting, and about 1727 [in 1726] printed ' Grongar Hill ' in
Lewis's Miscellany.[3]

---

[1] Rather in 1698 or 1699, as I am informed by Mr. W. Hylton Dyer Longstaff, who has the papers of the poet. The poet's mother was Catherine Cocks,
of Comins, Worcestershire, by Elizabeth, daughter and heiress of Edmond
Bennet, of Mapleton, Herefordshire. The father died between 1716 and 1720.

[2] The altarpiece at Newtown in Monmouthshire : ' The Last Supper' is said
to be by Dyer. Mr. Dyer Longstaff has a portrait of the poet in the day-cap
of the period and a green robe.

[3] ' Miscellaneous Poems, by several hands.' Published by D. Lewis. London: printed by J. Watts, 1726, 8vo. A different and, as I take it, an earlier

Being, probably, unsatisfied with his own proficiency, he, like other painters, travelled to Italy; and coming back in 1740, published [4] 'The Ruins of Rome.'

If his poem was written soon after his return, he did not make much use of his acquisitions in painting, whatever they might be; for decline of health and love of study determined him to the church. He therefore entered into orders; and, it seems, married about the same time a lady of the name of Ensor, " whose grandmother," says he, " was a Shakespeare, descended from a brother of everybody's Shakespeare;" by her, in 1756, he had a son and three daughters living.

His ecclesiastical provision was a long time but slender. His first patron, Mr. Harper, gave him, in 1741, Calthorp, in Leicestershire, of eighty pounds a year, on which he lived ten years, and then exchanged it for Belchford, in Lincolnshire, of seventy-five. His condition now began to mend. In 1751 Sir John Heathcote gave him Coningsby [in Lincolnshire], of one hundred and forty pounds a year; and in 1755 the Chancellor [5] added Kirkby, of one hundred and ten. He complains that the repair of the house at Coningsby, and other expenses, took away the profit. In 1757 he published 'The Fleece,' his greatest poetical work, [6] of which I will not suppress a ludicrous story. Dodsley, the bookseller, [7] was one day mentioning it to a critical visitor, with more expectation of success than the other could easily admit. In the conversation the author's age was asked; and being represented as advanced in life, " He will," said the critic, " be buried in woollen." [8]

version appeared the same year in 'Miscellaneous Poems and Translations, by several Hands.' Published by Richard Savage, son of the late Earl Rivers, London, 1726, 8vo. 'The Country Walk,' and five other poems by Dyer ('Grongar Hill' included), are printed in Savage's Miscellany, with Dyer's name to them.

[4] Anonymously. In March 1740, 'The Ruins of Rome, a Poem.' London: printed for Lawton Gilliver, at Homer's Head in Fleet Street, 1740, 4to.

[5] Lord Hardwicke.

[6] 'The Fleece; a Poem in Four Books,' by John Dyer, LL.B. London: printed for R. and J. Dodsley in Pall-Mall, 1757, 4to.

[7] *i. e.* Robert Dodsley.

[8] " Odious! in woollen! 'twould a saint provoke!"—
Were the last words that poor Narcissa spoke.—POPE.

He did not indeed long survive that publication, nor long enjoy the increase of his preferments; for in 1758 he died.[9]

Dyer is not a poet of bulk or dignity sufficient to require an elaborate criticism. ' Grongar Hill ' is the happiest of his productions : it is not indeed very accurately written ; but the scenes which it displays are so pleasing, the images which they raise so welcome to the mind, and the reflections of the writer so consonant to the general sense or experience of mankind, that when it is once read, it will be read again.[10]

The idea of ' The Ruins of Rome ' strikes more, but pleases less, and the title raises greater expectation than the performance gratifies. Some passages, however, are conceived with the mind of a poet ; as when, in the neighbourhood of dilapidating edifices, he says,

> " —— The Pilgrim oft,
> At dead of night, mid his orison hears
> Aghast the voice of time, disparting tow'rs,
> Tumbling all precipitate down dash'd,
> Rattling around, loud thund'ring to the moon."

Of ' The Fleece,' which never became popular, and is now universally neglected, I can say little that is likely to recall it to attention. The woolcomber and the poet appear to me such discordant natures, that an attempt to bring them together is to *couple the serpent with the fowl.*[11] When Dyer, whose mind was not unpoetical, has done his utmost, by interesting his reader in our native commodity, by interspersing rural imagery and

[9] 24th July, 1758. His brothers were Robert (died 1752), Thomas, some time perpetual curate of Paddington (died 1780), and a third whose name is unknown, (' Gent.'s Mag.' for Aug. 1847, p. 114.) The youngest and last surviving daughter, a Mrs. Hewit, died, in May 1830, at Coventry.

[10] Of English poets, perhaps none have excelled the ingenious Mr. Dyer in this oblique instruction, into which he frequently steals imperceptibly in his little descriptive poem entitled ' Grongar Hill,' where he disposes every object so as it may give occasion for some observation on human life. Denham himself is not superior to Mr. Dyer in this particular.—JOS. WARTON: *Essay on Pope*, i. 35, ed. 1782.

[11] He [Johnson] spoke slightly of Dyer's ' Fleece.' " The subject, Sir, cannot be made poetical. How can a man write poetically of serges and druggets? Yet you will hear many people talk to you gravely of that excellent poem ' The Fleece.' "—*Boswell by Croker*, ed. 1848, p. 485.

incidental digressions, by clothing small images in great words, and by all the writer's arts of delusion, the meanness naturally adhering, and the irreverence habitually annexed to trade and manufacture, sink him under insuperable oppression ; and the disgust which blank verse, encumbering and encumbered, super-adds to an unpleasing subject, soon repels the reader, however willing to be pleased.[12]

Let me, however, honestly report whatever may counter-balance this weight of censure. I have been told that Aken-side, who, upon a poetical question, has a right to be heard, said, "That he would regulate his opinion of the reigning taste by the fate of Dyer's ' Fleece ;' for, if that were ill received, he should not think it any longer reasonable to expect fame from excellence." [13]

[12] In 'The Gent.'s Mag.' for January 1835, p. 47, is a letter from Dyer to Dodsley, dated 12th May, 1757, sending some corrections for a future edition of ' The Fleece.'

[13] His ' Fleece,' which I had the pleasure of reading in manuscript with Dr. Akenside, is written in a pure and classical taste, and with many happy imita-tions of Virgil.—Jos. WARTON : *Essay on Pope*, i. 36, ed. 1782.

Mr. Dyer (here you will despise me highly) has more of poetry in his imagi-nation than almost any of our number; but rough and injudicious.—GRAY to Walpole, n. d.   (He is criticising Dodsley's Collection.)

Dyer has found warm admirers in our own time in Bowles and Wordsworth. "In blank verse I would mention a striking passage in Dyer's ' Fleece ':—

> ' The pilot steers
> Steady; with eye intent upon the steel
> Steady before the breeze the pilot steers.' "

W. L. BOWLES.

WILLIAM SHENSTONE.

SHENSTONE.

1714–1763.

Born at the Leasowes, in Shropshire — Educated at Hales-Owen and Ox-
ford — Publishes a small Miscellany of Poems without his name —
Publishes 'The Judgment of Hercules,' 'The Schoolmistress,' and other
Poems — His Ferme ornée — His pecuniary difficulties — Death and
Burial in Hales-Owen Churchyard, Shropshire — Works and Character.

WILLIAM SHENSTONE, the son of Thomas Shenstone and Anne
Penn, was born in November 1714, at the Leasowes in Hales-
Owen, one of those insulated districts which, in the division of
the kingdom, was appended, for some reason not now discoverable, to a distant county ; and which, though surrounded
by Warwickshire and Worcestershire, belongs to Shropshire,
though perhaps thirty miles distant from any other part of it.[1]

He learned to read of an old dame, whom his poem of 'The
Schoolmistress' has delivered to posterity ; and soon received
such delight from books, that he was always calling for fresh
entertainment, and expected that, when any of the family went
to market, a new book should be brought him, which, when it
came, was in fondness carried to bed and laid by him. It is
said, that when his request had been neglected, his mother
wrapped up a piece of wood of the same form, and pacified him
for the night.

As he grew older, he went for a while to the Grammar-school
in Hales-Owen, and was placed afterwards with Mr. Crumpton,
an eminent schoolmaster at Solihull, where he distinguished
himself by the quickness of his progress.

---

[1] He was the elder of the two sons of Thomas Shenstone by Anne Penn,
the eldest of the three daughters of William Penn, of Harborough, Gent. His
brother Joseph was bred an attorney at Bridgnorth, but never practised, and
died, 1757, at the Leasowes.

When he was young (June 1724) he was deprived of his father, and soon after (August 1726) of his grandfather; and was, with his brother, who died afterwards unmarried, left to the care of his grandmother, who managed the estate.[2]

From school he was sent in 1732 to Pembroke College in Oxford, a society which for half a century has been eminent for English poetry and elegant literature.[3] Here it appears that he found delight and advantage; for he continued his name in the book ten years, though he took no degree. After the first four years he put on the civilian's gown, but without showing any intention to engage in the profession.

About the time when he went to Oxford, the death of his grandmother devolved his affairs to the care of the Rev. Mr. Dolman, of Brome in Staffordshire, whose attention he always mentioned with gratitude.

At Oxford he employed himself upon English poetry; and in 1737 published a small Miscellany, without his name.[4]

He then for a time wandered about, to acquaint himself with life, and was sometimes at London, sometimes at Bath, or any other place of public resort; but he did not forget his poetry. He published in 1741[5] his 'Judgment of Hercules,' addressed to Mr. Lyttelton, whose interest he supported with great warmth at an election: this was next year [May 1742] followed by 'The Schoolmistress.'[6]

[2] His mother died in 1732.

[3] This was Johnson's own college.

[4] 'Poems upon Various Occasions. Written for the Entertainment of the Author, and printed for the Amusement of a few Friends prejudiced in his favour. *Contentus paucis Lectoribus.*—Hor. Oxford, 1737.' The volume contains a complimentary poem 'To Mr. Pope on his Dunciad,' and what Mr. D'Israeli has omitted to notice ('Curios. of Lit.'), the first sketch of 'The Schoolmistress.' There are twelve stanzas—but twelve of no ordinary merit. He sought in after-life to suppress the volume, and so successfully that it is now very rare.

[5] April, 1741, anonymously. 'The Judgment of Hercules, a Poem, inscribed to George Lyttelton, Esq. Dodsley, 1741.' 8vo. "I never inquire," he writes, "how my poem takes, and am afraid to do so. However, I find some do allow it to be Mallet's."

[6] 'The School-Mistress, a Poem. In Imitation of Spenser. Dodsley, 1742.' 8vo. Before the first stanza, and under the half title, occurs, "Written at College, 1736." The poem, as here printed, contains twenty-eight stanzas; as it at

Mr. Dolman, to whose care he was indebted for his ease and leisure, died in 1745,[7] and the care of his own fortune now fell upon himself. He tried to escape it awhile, and lived at his house with his tenants, who were distantly related; but, finding that imperfect possession inconvenient, he took the whole estate into his own hands, more to the improvement of its beauty than the increase of its produce.

Now was excited his delight in rural pleasures, and his ambition of rural elegance : he began from this time to point his prospects, to diversify his surface, to entangle his walks, and to wind his waters; which he did with such judgment and such fancy as made his little domain the envy of the great and the admiration of the skilful; a place to be visited by travellers, and copied by designers. Whether to plant a walk in undulating curves, and to place a bench at every turn where there is an object to catch the view ; to make water run where it will be heard, and to stagnate where it will be seen ; to leave intervals where the eye will be pleased, and to thicken the plantation where there is something to be hidden ; demands any great powers of mind, I will not inquire : perhaps a sullen and surly speculator may think such performances rather the sport than the business of human reason. But it must be at least confessed that to embellish the form of nature is an innocent amusement ; and some praise must be allowed, by the most supercilious observer, to him who does best what such multitudes are contending to do well.

This praise was the praise of Shenstone ; but like all other modes of felicity, it was not enjoyed without its abatements. Lyttelton was his neighbour and his rival, whose empire, spacious and opulent, looked with disdain on the *petty State* that *appeared behind it.* For a while the inhabitants of Hagley affected to

---

present stands, it consists of thirty-five. In the first edition are two poor stanzas, afterwards omitted. The alterations from the first edition are highly judicious.

[7] I was at Birmingham on Tuesday morning, from whence I saw the remains of Ligonier's Horse march with vast spirits and alacrity. They wish to have, what they call, the *refusal* of the Highlanders.—SHENSTONE to Miss Winny Fletcher. Leasowes, Nov. 28, 1745 (unpublished letter).

tell their acquaintance of the little fellow that was trying to make himself admired ; but when by degrees the Leasowes forced themselves into notice, they took care to defeat the curiosity which they could not suppress, by conducting their visitants perversely to inconvenient points of view, and introducing them at the wrong end of a walk to detect a deception ; injuries of which Shenstone would heavily complain. Where there is emulation there will be vanity ; and where there is vanity there will be folly.[8]

The pleasure of Shenstone was all in his eye ; he valued what he valued merely for its looks ; nothing raised his indignation more than to ask if there were any fishes in his water.

His house was mean, and he did not improve it ; his care was of his grounds. When he came home from his walks, he might find his floors flooded by a shower through the broken roof ; but could spare no money for its reparation.[9]

[8] If your expostulations with Mr. Lyttelton were *brusques,* his visit was as much so; and upon such occasions I never love to be behind-hand with great people.—LADY LUXBOROUGH to Shenstone, Oct. 16, 1748.

" The truth of the case, I believe, was, that the Lyttelton family went so frequently with their company to the Leasowes, that they were unwilling to break in upon Mr. Shenstone's retirement on every occasion, and therefore often went to the principal points of view without waiting for any one to conduct them regularly through the whole walks. Of this Mr. Shenstone would sometimes peevishly complain ; though I am persuaded he never really suspected any ill-natured intention in his worthy and much-valued neighbours."—GRAVES ; *Recollections of some particulars in the Life of William Shenstone, Esq.*

[9] Johnson had committed great mistakes with respect to Shenstone, which you have very properly rectified on the authority of Graves. He grossly misrepresented both his circumstances and his house, which was small, but elegant, and displayed a great deal of taste in the alteration and accommodation of the apartments, &c. On his side-board he had a neat marble cistern, which, by turning a cock, was fed with living water; and he had many other little elegant contrivances which displayed his genius, and made me regret that this little temple of the Muses was pulled down for the larger building of the house. This you may, if you please, mention in your new edition. That Johnson should have no conception of the value or merit of what is now called *picturesque gardening* we cannot wonder, as he was so extremely short-sighted that he never saw a rural landscape in his life; and in his ' Travels through Scotland' pronounces that one mountain must be like another. But you have sufficiently corrected his mistake on this subject. Among Shenstone's ' Levities and Songs' are many which he himself regretted to me had ever been committed to the press. But when Dodsley was printing that volume of his

In time his expenses brought clamours about him, that over-powered the lamb's bleat and the linnet's song ; and his groves were haunted by beings very different from fauns and fairies.[10] He spent his estate in adorning it, and his death was probably hastened by his anxieties.   He was a lamp that spent its oil in blazing.   It is said that if he had lived a little longer, he would have been assisted by a pension : such bounty could not have been ever more properly bestowed ; but that it was ever asked is not certain ; it is too certain that it never was enjoyed.[11]

He died at the Leasowes of a putrid fever, about five on Friday morning, February 11, 1763 ; and was buried by the side of his brother in the churchyard of Hales-Owen.[12]

'Miscellanies' in which they first appeared, Mr. S. was ill of a fever, and being unable to make any selection, ordered his whole portfolio to be sent to him, relying on his care to make a proper choice of what were fit to be published. But he obtruded the *whole* into his volume, and afterwards said that as a plea for inserting them in his works.   In the value of purchase, how much Mr. Shenstone's estate was improved by his taste, will be judged from the price it fetched when sold by auction in 1795, being 17,000*l*. sterling; though, when it descended to him, it was only valued at 300*l*. a year.   This, I think, will deserve mention, &c.—BISHOP PERCY to Dr. Anderson.

For views of the Leasowes, as left by Shenstone, see Gent.'s Mag. for Aug., 1823, and the cuts in Dodsley's editions of Shenstone's works.

I have heard Mr. Rogers (the poet) speak most highly of the beauty of the Leasowes, as he in his youth remembered the 'ferme ornée.'

[10] " Mr. Shenstone was too much respected in the neighbourhood to be treated with rudeness : and though his works (frugally as they were managed), added to his manner of living, must necessarily have made him exceed his income, and, of course, he might sometimes be distressed for money, yet he had too much spirit to expose himself to insults from trifling sums, and guarded against any great distress by anticipating a few hundreds; which his estate could very well bear, as appeared by what remained to his executors after the payment of his debts, and his legacies to his friends, and annuities of thirty pounds a year to one servant, and six pounds to another: for his will was dictated with equal justice and generosity."—GRAVES (the friend of Shenstone).

[11] Sept. 19, 1774.—In the way we visited the Leasowes.   It was rain, yet we visited all the waterfalls.   There are in one place fourteen falls in a short line.   It is the next place to Ham Gardens.   Poor Shenstone never tasted his pension.   It is not very well proved that any pension was obtained for him. I am afraid that he died of misery.—JOHNSON: *Journal of Tour in Wales*.

[12] He was no economist; the generosity of his temper prevented him from paying a proper regard to the use of money: he exceeded, therefore, the bounds of his paternal fortune, which, before he died, was considerably encumbered.   But when one recollects the perfect paradise he had raised around

He was never married, though he might have obtained the lady, whoever she was, to whom his 'Pastoral Ballad' was addressed. He is represented by his friend Dodsley as a man of great tenderness and generosity, kind to all that were within his influence ; but, if once offended, not easily appeased ; inattentive to economy, and careless of his expenses : in his person he was larger than the middle size, with something clumsy in his form ; very negligent of his clothes, and remarkable for wearing his grey hair in a particular manner; for he held that the fashion was no rule of dress, and that every man was to suit his appearance to his natural form.[13]

His mind was not very comprehensive, nor his curiosity active ; he had no value for those parts of knowledge which he had not himself cultivated.

His life was unstained by any crime : the Elegy on Jesse, which has been supposed to relate an unfortunate and criminal amour of his own, was known by his friends to have been suggested by the story of Miss Godfrey in Richardson's 'Pamela.'

What Gray thought of his character, from the perusal of his letters, was this :

"I have read too an octavo volume of Shenstone's Letters. Poor man ! he was always wishing for money, for fame, and other distinctions ; and his whole philosophy consisted in living against his will in retirement, and in a place which his taste had

him, the hospitality with which he lived, his great indulgence to his servants, his charities to the indigent, and all done with an estate not more than three hundred pounds a year, one should rather be led to wonder that he left any thing behind him than to blame his want of economy. He left, however, more than sufficient to pay his debts; and by his will appropriated his whole estate for that purpose.—R. DODSLEY: *Pref. to Shenstone's Works*.

[13] Johnson has new-worded Dodsley's account of him in his Preface to Shenstone's Works.

He sat for his portrait to Edward Alcock, and also to Bond, a painter in Birmingham. Dodsley had the former, and Hull the latter (Hull's Letters, i. 172). At Mr. Watt's sale at Aston Hall, near Birmingham, in April, 1849, a portrait of Shenstone (painter unknown) brought 33*l*. 12*s*. 6*d*. In Harding's 'Biographical Mirror' is an engraving of Shenstone "from an original picture" (painter unknown), then in the possession of W. G. Waldron.

Shenstone's conversation afforded me more pleasure than even the Leasowes, though that I esteem an earthly paradise.—GRAINGER, the Poet : *Letter to Bishop Percy*.

adorned ; but which he only enjoyed when people of note came
to see and commend it : his correspondence is about nothing
else but this place and his own writings, with two or three neighbouring clergymen, who wrote verses too." [14]

His poems consist of elegies, odes, and ballads, humorous
sallies, and moral pieces.

His conception of an elegy he has in his Preface very judiciously and discriminately explained. It is, according to his
account, the effusion of a contemplative mind, sometimes
plaintive, and always serious, and therefore superior to the
glitter of slight ornaments. His compositions suit not ill to
this description. His topics of praise are the domestic virtues,
and his thoughts are pure and simple ; but, wanting combination, they want variety. The peace of solitude, the innocence of
inactivity, and the unenvied security of an humble station, can
fill but a few pages. That of which the essence is uniformity
will be soon described : his Elegies have therefore too much
resemblance of each other.

The lines are sometimes, such as Elegy requires, smooth and
easy ; but to this praise his claim is not constant : his diction is
often harsh, improper, and affected ; his words ill-coined or ill-
chosen, and his phrase unskilfully inverted.

The Lyric Poems are almost all of the light and airy kind,
such as trip lightly and nimbly along, without the load of any
weighty meaning. From these, however, ' Rural Elegance ' has
some right to be excepted. I once heard it praised by a very
learned lady ; and though the lines are irregular, and the
thoughts diffused with too much verbosity, yet it cannot be denied
to contain both philosophical argument and poetical spirit.

Of the rest I cannot think any excellent ; 'The Skylark'
pleases me best, which has, however, more of the epigram than
of the ode.

But the four parts of his ' Pastoral Ballad ' demand particular
notice. I cannot but regret that it is pastoral : an intelligent
reader, acquainted with the scenes of real life, sickens at the

---

[14] Gray to Mr. Nicholls, June 24, 1769.

mention of the *crook*, the *pipe*, the *sheep*, and the *kids,* which it is not necessary to bring forward to notice, for the poet's art is selection, and he ought to show the beauties without the grossness of the country life.   His stanza seems to have been chosen in imitation of Rowe's ' Despairing Shepherd.' [15]

In the first part are two passages, to which if any mind denies its sympathy, it has no acquaintance with love or nature :

> " I priz'd every hour that went by,
>   Beyond all that had pleas'd me before ;
> But now they are past, and I sigh,
>   And I grieve that I priz'd them no more.[16]
> When forc'd the fair nymph to forego,
>   What anguish I felt in my heart !
> Yet I thought—but it might not be so—
>   'Twas with pain that she saw me depart.
> She gaz'd as I slowly withdrew,
>   My path I could hardly discern ;
> So sweetly she bade me adieu,
>   I thought that she bade me return."

In the second this passage has its prettiness, though it be not equal to the former :

> " I have found out a gift for my fair ;
>   I have found where the wood-pigeons breed :
> But let me that plunder forbear,
>   She will say 'twas a barbarous deed :
> For he ne'er could be true, she averr'd,
>   Who could rob a poor bird of its young ;
> And I lov'd her the more when I heard
>   Such tenderness fall from her tongue."

In the third he mentions the common-places of amorous poetry with some address :

---

[15] Rowe imitated Tusser (d. 1580).

> What look ye, I pray you show what?
>   Scenes painted with rhetorick fine?
> Good husbandry seeketh not that,
>   Nor is 't any meaning of mine.—TUSSER.

[16] How much soever I valued him [Levett], I now wish that I had valued him more.—JOHNSON to Langton, March 20, 1782.

> " 'T is his with mock passion to glow !
>   'T is his in smooth tales to unfold,
> How her face is as bright as the snow,
>   And her bosom, be sure, is as cold :
> How the nightingales labour the strain,
>   With the notes of his charmer to vie ;
> How they vary their accents in vain,
>   Repine at her triumphs, and die."

In the fourth I find nothing better than this natural strain of
Hope :

> " Alas ! from the day that we met,
>   What hope of an end to my woes ?
> When I cannot endure to forget
>   The glance that undid my repose.
> Yet Time may diminish the pain :
>   The flower, and the shrub, and the tree,
> Which I rear'd for her pleasure in vain,
>   In time may have comfort for me."

His ' Levities ' are by their title exempted from the severities
of criticism ; yet it may be remarked in a few words, that his
humour is sometimes gross, and seldom sprightly.

Of the Moral Poems the first is ' The Choice of Hercules,'
from Xenophon.   The numbers are smooth, the diction elegant,
and the thoughts just ; but something of vigour is still to be
wished, which it might have had by brevity and compression.
His ' Fate of Delicacy ' has an air of gaiety, but not a very
pointed and general moral.   His blank verses, those that can
read them may probably find to be like the blank verses of his
neighbours.   ' Love and Honour ' is derived from the old
ballad, ' Did you not hear of a Spanish Lady ?'—I wish it well
enough to wish it were in rhyme.

' The Schoolmistress,' of which I know not what claim it has
to stand among the Moral Works, is surely the most pleasing
of Shenstone's performances.[17]   The adoption of a particular

---

[17] This was Dodsley's blunder; for Shenstone in the first edition added an
" Index," " a *ludicrous* Index," as he tells us in his letters, " to show (fools)
that I am in jest."   His motto,

> O, quà Sol habitabiles
> Illustrat Oras, maxima Principum.—HOR.

was designed for the same purpose.   Mr. D'Israeli has printed the Index in
his ' Curiosities of Literature.'   " When

style, in light and short compositions, contributes much to the increase of pleasure : we are entertained at once with two imitations, of nature in the sentiments, of the original author in the style, and between them the mind is kept in perpetual employment.[18]

The general recommendation of Shenstone is easiness and simplicity; his general defect is want of comprehension and variety. Had his mind been better stored with knowledge, whether he could have been great, I know not; he could certainly have been agreeable.[19]

" When I bought him [Spenser] first, I read a page or two of 'The Faerie Queene,' and cared not to proceed. After that Pope's *Alley* made me consider him ludicrously; and in that light I think one may read him with pleasure."—SHENSTONE.

[18] 'The Schoolmistress' is excellent of its kind, and masterly.—GRAY: *Letter to Walpole* (Works by Mitford, iii. 89).

This poem [The Schoolmistress] is one of those happinesses in which a poet excels himself, as there is nothing in all Shenstone which any way approaches it in merit; and though I dislike the imitations of our old English poets in general, yet on this minute subject the antiquity of the style produces a very ludicrous solemnity.—GOLDSMITH: *Works by Cunningham*, iii. 436.

[19] A man of a merely argumentative cast will read poetry as prose; will only regard the quantum it contains of solid reasoning.—SHENSTONE: *Works*, ii. 231, ed. 1773.

EDWARD YOUNG.

YOUNG.

1681–1765.

Born at Upham, in Hampshire — Educated at Winchester and Oxford —
His first Poetry — Is patronised by the Duke of Wharton — Publishes
his ' Universal Passion' — Writes for the Stage — Enters into Holy
Orders — Receives a Pension of 200*l.* a-year from George I. — Marries
— Death of his Wife — Publishes ' The Complaint, or Night Thoughts'
— Presented to the Living of Welwyn, in Hertfordshire — His only
Son — Death and Burial at Welwyn — Works and Character.

THE following Life was written, at my request, by a gentleman [1]
who had better information than I could easily have obtained;
and the public will perhaps wish that I had solicited and obtained more such favours from him.

" DEAR SIR,—In consequence of our different conversations
about authentic materials for the Life of Young, I send you the
following detail:—

Of great men, something must always be said to gratify
curiosity. Of the illustrious author of the ' Night Thoughts'
much has been told of which there never could have been
proofs; and little care appears to have been taken to tell
that of which proofs, with little trouble, might have been
procured.

EDWARD YOUNG was born at Upham, near Winchester, in
June, 1681. He was the son of Edward Young, at that time
Fellow of Winchester College and rector of Upham; [2] who was

---

[1] Mr. (afterwards Sir Herbert) Croft. He died at Paris after a fifteen years'
residence in that city, April 27, 1816.
" This ' Life ' of Young was written by a friend of his son. What is crossed
with black is expunged by the author; what is crossed with red is expunged
by me. If you find anything more that can be well omitted, I shall not be
sorry to see it yet shorter."—JOHNSON to Nichols.
[2] Of the house in which Young was born (now no longer standing) there is
a view in the ' Gentleman's Magazine ' for March, 1829. When Joseph Warton

the son of Jo. Young of Woodhay in Berkshire, styled by Wood *gentleman*. In September, 1682, the poet's father was collated to the prebend of Gillingham Minor, in the church of Sarum, by Bishop Ward. When Ward's faculties were impaired through age, his duties were necessarily performed by others. We learn from Wood that, at a visitation of Sprat's, July the 12th, 1686, the prebendary preached a Latin sermon, afterwards published, with which the bishop was so pleased, that he told the chapter he was concerned to find the preacher had one of the worst prebends in their church. Some time after this, in consequence of his merit and reputation, or of the interest of Lord Bradford, to whom, in 1702, he dedicated two volumes of sermons, he was appointed chaplain to King William and Queen Mary, and preferred to the deanery of Sarum. Jacob, who wrote in 1720,[3] says, "He was chaplain and clerk of the closet to the late Queen [Anne], who honoured him by standing godmother to the poet." His Fellowship of Winchester he resigned in favour of a gentleman of the name of Harris, who married his only daughter. The dean died at Sarum, after a short illness, in 1705, in the sixty-third year of his age.[4] On the Sunday after his decease Bishop Burnet preached at the cathedral, and began his sermon with saying, " Death has been of late walking round us, and making breach upon breach upon us, and has now carried away the head of this body with a stroke ; so that he, whom you saw a week ago distributing the holy mysteries, is now laid in the dust. But he still lives in the many excellent directions he has left us, both how to live and how to die."

The dean placed his son upon the foundation at Winchester College, where he had himself been educated. At this school

had the living of Upham, he placed the following inscription in the room in which the poet was born:—"In hoc cubiculo natus erat eximius ille Poeta Edvardus Young, 1681." This inscription is preserved in the new rectory.

[3] 'The Poetical Register,' 8vo., 1723, vol. ii. p. 241.

[4] And was buried in Salisbury Cathedral, where a monument to his memory is still to be seen. On a stone in Chiddingfold Church, in Surrey, is this inscription:—"Here lyeth the body of Judeth, widow of the Rev. Edward Young, late Dean of Sarum, who dyed Dec. ye 8th, in the 69th year of her age, Anno Dom^{ni} 1714." This was the poet's mother.

Edward Young remained till the election after his eighteenth birth-day, the period at which those upon the foundation are superannuated.   Whether he did not betray his abilities early in life, or his masters had not skill enough to discover in their pupil any marks of genius for which he merited reward, or no vacancy at Oxford afforded them an opportunity to bestow upon him the reward provided for merit by William of Wykeham, certain it is that to an Oxford fellowship our poet did not succeed.   By chance, or by choice, New College cannot claim the honour of numbering among its fellows him who wrote the 'Night Thoughts.'

On the 13th of October, 1703, he was entered an independent member of New College, that he might live at little expense in the warden's lodgings, who was a particular friend of his father's, till he should be qualified to stand for a fellowship at All Souls. In a few months the warden of New College died.   He then removed to Corpus College.   The president of this society, from regard also for his father, invited him thither, in order to lessen his academical expenses.   In 1708 he was nominated to a law fellowship at All Souls by Archbishop Tenison, into whose hands it came by devolution.   Such repeated patronage, while it justifies Burnet's praise of the father, reflects credit on the conduct of the son.   The manner in which it was exerted seems to prove that the father did not leave behind him much wealth.

On the 23rd of April, 1714, Young took his degree of Bachelor of Civil Laws, and his Doctor's degree on the 10th of June, 1719.

Soon after he went to Oxford, he discovered, it is said, an inclination for pupils.   Whether he ever commenced tutor is not known.   None has hitherto boasted to have received his academical instruction from the author of the 'Night Thoughts.'

It is probable that his college was proud of him no less as a scholar than as a poet; for in 1716, when the foundation of the Codrington Library was laid, two years after he had taken his Bachelor's degree, Young was appointed to speak the Latin oration. This is at least particular for being dedicated in English " To the Ladies of the Codrington Family." To these ladies he says, " that he was unavoidably flung into a singularity, by being obliged to write an epistle dedicatory void of common-place, and such an one as was never published before by any author whatever : that this practice absolved them from any obligation of reading what was presented to them ; and that the bookseller approved of it, because it would make people stare, was absurd enough, and perfectly right."

Of this oration there is no appearance in his own edition of his works ; and prefixed to an edition by Curll and Tonson, in 1741, is a letter from Young to Curll, if we may credit Curll, dated December the 9th, 1739, wherein he says that he has not leisure to review what he formerly wrote, and adds, " I have not the ' Epistle to Lord Lansdown.' If you will take my advice, I would have you omit that, and the oration on Codrington. I think the collection will sell better without them."

There are who relate that, when first Young found himself independent, and his own master at All Souls, he was not the ornament to religion and morality which he afterwards became.

The authority of his father, indeed, had ceased some time before by his death ; and Young was certainly not ashamed to be patronized by the infamous Wharton. But Wharton befriended in Young, perhaps, the poet, and particularly the tragedian. If virtuous authors must be patronized only by virtuous peers, who shall point them out ?

Yet Pope is said by Ruffhead [5] to have told Warburton, that " Young had much of a sublime genius, though without common sense ; so that his genius, having no guide, was perpetually liable to degenerate into bombast. This made him pass a *foolish youth*, the sport of peers and poets : but his having a very good heart enabled him to support the clerical character when he assumed it, first with decency, and afterwards with honour."

[5] Ruffhead's ' Life of Pope,' p. 291.

They who think ill of Young's morality in the early part of his life, may perhaps be wrong; but Tindal could not err in his opinion of Young's warmth and ability in the cause of religion. Tindal used to spend much of his time at All Souls. "The other boys," said the atheist, "I can always answer, because I always know whence they have their arguments, which I have read a hundred times; but that fellow Young is continually pestering me with something of his own." [6]

After all, Tindal and the censurers of Young may be reconcileable. Young might, for two or three years, have tried that kind of life, in which his natural principles would not suffer him to wallow long. If this were so, he has left behind him not only his evidence in favour of virtue, but the potent testimony of experience against vice.

We shall soon see that one of his earliest productions was more serious than what comes from the generality of unfledged poets.

Young perhaps ascribed the good fortune of Addison to the 'Poem to his Majesty,' presented, with a copy of verses, to Somers; and hoped that he also might soar to wealth and honours on wings of the same kind. His first poetical flight was when Queen Anne called up to the House of Lords the sons of the Earls of Northampton and Aylesbury, and added, in one day, ten others to the number of peers. In order to reconcile the people to one, at least, of the new lords, he published, in 1713, 'An Epistle to the Right Honourable the Lord Lansdown.' [7] In this composition the poet pours out his panegyric with the extravagance of a young man, who thinks his present stock of wealth will never be exhausted.

The poem seems intended also to reconcile the public to the late peace. This is endeavoured to be done by showing that men

---

[6] As my great friend is now become the subject of biography, it should be told that every time I called upon Johnson during the time I was employed in collecting materials for this Life and putting it together, he never suffered me to depart without some such farewell as this: "Don't forget that rascal Tindal, Sir: be sure to hang up the Atheist;" alluding to this anecdote, which Johnson had mentioned to me.—HERBERT CROFT.

[7] Printed in folio, 1713, for Bernard Lintot.

are slain in war, and that in peace " harvests wave, and commerce swells her sail." If this be humanity, for which he meant it, is it politics? Another purpose of this epistle appears to have been to prepare the public for the reception of some tragedy he might have in hand. His Lordship's patronage, he says, will not let him " repent his passion for the stage ;" and the particular praise bestowed on ' Othello' and ' Oroonoko' looks as if some such character as Zanga was even then in contemplation. The affectionate mention of the death of his friend Harrison of New College, at the close of this poem, is an instance of Young's art, which displayed itself so wonderfully some time afterwards in the ' Night Thoughts,' of making the public a party in his private sorrow.

Should justice call upon you to censure this poem, it ought at least to be remembered that he did not insert it in his works ; and that in the letter to Curll, as we have seen, he advises its omission. The booksellers, in the late body of English poetry, should have distinguished what was deliberately rejected by the respective authors.[8] This I shall be careful to do with regard to Young. " I think," says he, " the following pieces in *four* volumes to be the most excusable of all that I have written ; and I wish *less apology* was needful for these. As there is no recalling what is got abroad, the pieces here republished I have revised and corrected, and rendered them as *pardonable* as it was in my power to do."

Shall the gates of repentance be shut only against literary sinners?

When Addison published ' Cato' in 1713, Young had the honour of prefixing to it a recommendatory copy of verses. This is one of the pieces which the author of the ' Night Thoughts' did not republish.

On the appearance of his poem on ' The Last Day' Addison did not return Young's compliment ; but ' The Englishman' of October 29, 1713, which was probably written by Addison, speaks handsomely of this poem. ' The Last Day' was pub-

---

[8] Dr. Johnson, in many cases, thought and directed differently, particularly in Young's Works.—JOHN NICHOLS. (Note in Johnson's Lives.)

lished soon after the peace.   The vice-chancellor's *imprimatur* (for it was first printed at Oxford)[9] is dated May the 19th, 1713. From the exordium Young appears to have spent some time on the composition of it.   While other bards " with Britain's hero set their souls on fire," he draws, he says, a deeper scene. Marlborough *had been* considered by Britain as her *hero ;* but, when 'The Last Day' was published, female cabal had blasted for a time the laurels of Blenheim.   This serious poem was finished by Young as early as 1710, before he was thirty ; for part of it is printed in ' The Tatler.'   It was inscribed to the Queen [Anne], in a dedication which, for some reason, he did not admit into his works.   It tells her that his only title to the great honour he now does himself is the obligation which he formerly received from her royal indulgence.

Of this obligation nothing is now known, unless he alluded to her being his godmother.   He is said indeed to have been engaged at a settled stipend as a writer for the Court.   In Swift's ' Rhapsody on Poetry' are these lines, speaking of the Court :

> " Whence Gay was banish'd in disgrace,
> Where Pope will never show his face,
> Where Y——— must torture his invention
> To flatter knaves, or lose his pension."

That Y——— means Young seems clear from four other lines in the same poem :

> " Attend, ye Popes and Youngs and Gays,
> And tune your harps and strew your bays ;
> Your panegyrics here provide ;
> You cannot err on flattery's side."

Yet who shall say with certainty that Young was a pensioner ?   In all modern periods of this country have not the writers on one side been regularly called hirelings, and on the other patriots ?[10]

---

[9] In 8vo.   "Oxford: printed at the Theatre, for Edward Whistler, 1713."

[10] I can say with certainty Young had a pension of 200*l.* a-year, from 1725 till his death in 1765.   The Royal Sign-Manual Warrant of George I. which

Of the dedication the complexion is clearly political. It speaks in the highest terms of the late peace; it gives her Majesty praise indeed for her victories, but says that the author is more pleased to see her rise from this lower world, soaring above the clouds, passing the first and second heavens, and leaving the fixed stars behind her; nor will he lose her there, he says, but keep her still in view through the boundless spaces on the other side of creation, in her journey towards eternal bliss, till he behold the heaven of heavens open, and angels receiving and conveying her still onward from the stretch of his imagination, which tires in her pursuit, and falls back again to earth.

The Queen was soon called away from this lower world to a place where human praise or human flattery, even less general than this, are of little consequence. If Young thought the dedication contained only the praise of truth, he should not have omitted it in his works. Was he conscious of the ex-aggeration of party? Then he should not have written it. The poem itself is not without a glance towards politics, not-withstanding the subject. The cry that the Church was in danger had not yet subsided. 'The Last Day,' written by a layman, was much approved by the Ministry and their friends.

Before the Queen's death, 'The Force of Religion, or Vanquished Love,' [11] was sent into the world. This poem is

gave him the pension was first printed by me in the 'Gentleman's Magazine' for July 1850:—

"GEORGE R.—Our will and pleasure is, and we do hereby direct and require, that an annual pension of Two Hundred Pounds be established and paid by you from Lady Day, 1725, unto Edward Young, Doctor of Laws, during Our Pleasure, by quarterly payments, in such and the like manner, &c. &c.

"Given at our Court at St. James's, the 3rd day of May, 1726, in the 12th year of our reign.

"By His Majesty's Command,

"R. WALPOLE.
"WILL. YONGE.
"WM. STRICKLAND.

"To our trusty and well-beloved Walter Chetwynd, Esq."

—*Audit-Office Enrolments*, M., p. 529.

[11] 'The Force of Religion; or Vanquish'd Love. A Poem. In two Books. By Edward Young, Fellow of All Souls College, Oxon. London: printed for E. Curll and J. Pemberton, against St. Dunstan's Church, in Fleet Street, 1714.'

founded on the execution of Lady Jane Grey and her husband
Lord Guildford, 1554; a story chosen for the subject of a
tragedy by Edmund Smith, and wrought into a tragedy by
Rowe. The dedication of it to the Countess of Salisbury [12] does
not appear in his own edition. He hopes it may be some
excuse for his presumption that the story could not have been
read without thoughts of the Countess of Salisbury, though it
had been dedicated to another. " To behold," he proceeds,
" a person *only* virtuous, stirs in us a prudent regret ; to behold
a person *only* amiable to the sight, warms us with a religious
indignation ; but to turn our eyes on a Countess of Salisbury,
gives us pleasure and improvement : it works a sort of miracle,
occasions the bias of our nature to fall off from sin, and makes
our very senses and affections converts to religion, and pro-
moters of our duty." His flattery was as ready for the other
sex as for ours, and was at least as well adapted.

August the 27th, 1714, Pope writes to his friend Jervas, that
he is just arrived from Oxford ; that every one is much concerned for the Queen's death, but that no panegyrics are ready
yet for the King. Nothing like friendship had yet taken
place between Pope and Young ; for, soon after the event
which Pope mentions, Young published a poem on the Queen's
death, and his Majesty's accession to the throne. It is inscribed to Addison, then secretary to the Lords Justices. Whatever were the obligations which he had formerly received from
Anne, the poet appears to aim at something of the same sort
from George. Of the poem the intention seems to have been.
to show that he had the same extravagant strain of praise for a
King as for a Queen. To discover, at the very outset of a
foreigner's reign, that the gods bless his new subjects in such
a King, is something more than praise. Neither was this
deemed one of his *excusable pieces*. We do not find it in his
Works.[13]

Young's father had been well acquainted with Lady Anne
Wharton, the first wife of Thomas Wharton, Esq., afterwards

---

[12] Anne Tufton, daughter of Thomas Tufton, Earl of Thanet.
[13] That is, in the edition of his Works published by the poet himself in
1762, 4 vols. 12mo.

Marquis of Wharton ; a lady celebrated for her poetical talents
by Burnet and by Waller.

To the Dean of Sarum's visitation sermon, already mentioned, were added some verses " by that excellent poetess
Mrs. Anne Wharton," upon its being translated into English,
at the instance of Waller, by Atwood. Wharton, after he
became ennobled, did not drop the son of his old friend. In
him, during the short time he lived, Young found a patron,
and in his dissolute descendant a friend and a companion. The
Marquis died in April 1715. In the beginning of the next
year the young Marquis set out upon his travels, from which he
returned in about a twelvemonth. The beginning of 1717
carried him to Ireland, where, says the Biographia, " on the
score of his extraordinary qualities, he had the honour done
him of being admitted, though under age, to take his seat in
the House of Lords."

With this unhappy character it is not unlikely that Young
went to Ireland. From his letter to Richardson on 'Original
Composition,' it is clear he was, at some period of his life, in
that country. " I remember," says he, in that letter, speaking
of Swift, " as I and others were taking with him an evening
walk, about a mile out of Dublin, he stopped short ; we passed
on ; but perceiving he did not follow us, I went back, and
found him fixed as a statue, and earnestly gazing upward at a
noble elm, which in its uppermost branches was much withered
and decayed. Pointing at it, he said, ' I shall be like that
tree, I shall die at top.' " Is it not probable that this visit to
Ireland was paid when he had an opportunity of going thither
with his avowed friend and patron ?

From ' The Englishman ' it appears that a tragedy by Young
was in the theatre so early as 1713. Yet ' Busiris ' was not
brought upon Drury-Lane stage till 1719.[14] It was inscribed
to the Duke of Newcastle,[15] because " the late instances he had

---

[14] The first night was the 7th March, 1718-19. It ran nine nights ; and
Lintot, on the 14th Feb. 1718-19, paid Young 42l. for " a half share " in its
publication. It was printed for Tonson, in 8vo., price 1s. 6d.

[15] Afterwards Prime Minister ; died 1768.

received of his Grace's undeserved and uncommon favour, in an affair of some consequence (foreign to the theatre), had taken from him the privilege of choosing a patron." The dedication he afterwards suppressed.

'Busiris' was followed in the year 1721 by 'The Revenge.' He dedicated this famous tragedy to the Duke of Wharton. "Your Grace," says the dedication, "has been pleased to make yourself accessary to the following scenes, not only by suggesting the most beautiful incident in them, but by making all possible provision for the success of the whole." [16]

That his Grace should have suggested the incident to which he alludes, whatever that incident might have been, is not unlikely. The last mental exertion of the superannuated young man, in his quarters at Lerida, in Spain, was some scenes of a tragedy on the story of Mary Queen of Scots.

Dryden dedicated 'Marriage à la Mode' to Wharton's infamous relation Rochester, whom he acknowledges not only as the defender of his poetry, but as the promoter of his fortune. Young concludes his address to Wharton thus—" My present fortune is his bounty, and my future his care, which I will venture to say will be always remembered to his honour, since he, I know, intended his generosity as an encouragement to merit, though, through his very pardonable partiality to one who bears him so sincere a duty and respect, I happen to receive the benefit of it." That he ever had such a patron as Wharton, Young took all the pains in his power to conceal from the world, by excluding this dedication from his works. He should have remembered that he at the same time concealed his obligation to Wharton for *the most beautiful incident* in what is surely not his least beautiful composition. The passage just quoted is, in a poem afterwards addressed to Walpole, literally copied:—

> " Be this thy partial smile from censure free ;
> 'T was meant for merit, though it fell on me."

---

[16] Young, in 1721, sold the copyright of 'The Revenge' for 50*l*. (Malone's Shakespeare by Boswell, iii. 164.)

While Young, who, in his ' Love of Fame,' complains grievously how often ' dedications wash an Æthiop white,' was painting an amiable Duke of Wharton in perishable prose, Pope was, perhaps, beginning to describe the " scorn and wonder of his days " in lasting verse.

To the patronage of such a character, had Young studied men as much as Pope, he would have known how little to have trusted.   Young, however, was certainly indebted to it for something material ; and the Duke's regard for Young, added to his ' Lust of Praise,' procured to All Souls College a donation, which was not forgotten by the poet when he dedicated ' The Revenge.'

It will surprise you to see me cite second Atkins, Case 136, Stiles *versus* the Attorney-General, 14th March, 1740, as authority for the life of a poet.   But biographers do not always find such certain guides as the oaths of the persons whom they record.   Chancellor Hardwicke was to determine whether two annuities, granted by the Duke of Wharton to Young, were for legal considerations.   One was dated the 24th of March, 1719, and accounted for his Grace's bounty in a style princely and commendable, if not legal—" considering that the public good is advanced by the encouragement of learning and the polite arts, and being pleased therein with the attempts of Dr. Young, in consideration thereof, and of the love I bear him," &c.   The other was dated the 10th of July, 1722.

Young, on his examination, swore that he quitted the Exeter family, and refused an annuity of 100*l*. which had been offered him for his life if he would continue tutor to Lord Burleigh, upon the pressing solicitations of the Duke of Wharton, and his Grace's assurances of providing for him in a much more ample manner.   It also appeared that the Duke had given him a bond for 600*l*., dated the 15th of March, 1721, in consideration of his taking several journeys, and being at great expenses, in order to be chosen member of the House of Commons at the Duke's desire, and in consideration of his not taking two livings of 200*l*. and 400*l*. in the gift of All Souls College, on his Grace's promises of serving and advancing him in the world.

Of his adventures in the Exeter family I am unable to give
any account.   The attempt to get into Parliament was at
Cirencester, where Young stood a contested election.   His
Grace discovered in him talents for oratory as well as for
poetry.   Nor was this judgment wrong.   Young, after he took
orders, became a very popular preacher, and was much followed
for the grace and animation of his delivery.   By his oratorical
talents he was once in his life, according to the Biographia,
deserted.   As he was preaching in his turn at St. James's, he
plainly perceived it was out of his power to command the
attention of his audience.   This so affected the feelings of the
preacher, that he sat back in the pulpit and burst into tears.
But we must pursue his poetical life.

In 1719 he lamented the death of Addison, in a Letter addressed to their common friend Tickell.[17]   For the secret
history of the following lines, if they contain any, it is now vain
to seek :

> " *In joy once join'd*, in sorrow, now, for years—
> Partner in grief, and brother of my tears,
> Tickell, accept this verse, thy mournful due."

From your account of Tickell it appears that he and Young
used to " communicate to each other whatever verses they
wrote, even to the least things." [18]

In 1719 appeared a ' Paraphrase on Part of the Book of
Job.'   Parker, to whom it is dedicated, had not long, by
means of the seals, been qualified for a patron.   Of this work
the author's opinion may be known from his Letter to Curll :
" You seem, in the Collection you propose, to have omitted
what I think may claim the first place in it; I mean ' A
Translation from part of Job,' printed by Mr. Tonson."
The dedication, which was only suffered to appear in Mr. Tonson's edition, while it speaks with satisfaction of his present
retirement, seems to make an unusual struggle to escape from

---

[17] ' A Letter to Mr. Tickell, occasioned by the Death of the Right Honourable Joseph Addison, Esq.   By E. Young, LL.D., Fellow of All Souls College,
Oxon.'   Tonson, 1719, fol.

[18] This is confirmed by some rough drafts of Satires in Young's handwriting
still (1854) preserved among the Tickell Papers.

retirement. But every one who sings in the dark does not sing from joy. It is addressed, in no common strain of flattery, to a Chancellor of whom he clearly appears to have had no kind of knowledge.

Of his Satires it would not have been possible to fix the dates without the assistance of first editions, which, as you had occasion to observe in your account of Dryden, are with difficulty found. We must then have referred to the poems, to discover when they were written. For these internal notes of time we should not have referred in vain. The first Satire laments that " Guilt's chief foe in Addison is fled." The second, addressing himself, asks,

> " Is thy ambition sweating for a rhyme,
> Thou unambitious fool, at this late time ?
> A fool at *forty* is a fool indeed."

The Satires were originally published separately in folio, under the title of ' The Universal Passion.' These passages fix the appearance of the first to about 1725, the time at which it came out. As Young seldom suffered his pen to dry, after he had once dipped it in poetry, we may conclude that he began his Satires soon after he had written the ' Paraphrase on Job.' The last Satire was certainly finished in the beginning of the year 1726.[19] In December, 1725, the King, in his passage from Helvoetsluys, escaped with great difficulty from a storm by landing at Rye ; and the conclusion of the Satire turns the escape into a miracle, in such an encomiastic strain of compliment as poetry too often seeks to pay to royalty.

From the sixth of these poems we learn,

> " Midst empire's charms, how Carolina's heart
> Glow'd with the love of virtue and of art :"

since the grateful poet tells us, in the next couplet,

> " Her favour is diffus'd to that degree,
> Excess of goodness ! it has dawn'd on me."

---

[19] It was published in 1726, in folio.

Her Majesty had stood godmother and given her name to a daughter of the lady whom Young married in 1731, and had perhaps shown some attention to Lady Elizabeth's future husband.

The fifth Satire, ' On Women,' was not published till 1727, and the sixth [on the same subject] not till 1728.

To these poems, when, in 1728, he gathered them into one publication,[20] he prefixed a preface; in which he observes, that " no man can converse much in the world but, at what he meets with, he must either be insensible or grieve, or be angry or smile. Now to smile at it, and turn it into ridicule," he adds, " I think most eligible, as it hurts ourselves least, and gives vice and folly the greatest offence. . . . . Laughing at the misconduct of the world will, in a great measure, ease us of any more disagreeable passion about it. One passion is more effectually driven out by another than by reason, whatever some teach." So wrote, and so of course thought, the lively and witty satirist at the grave age of almost fifty, who, many years earlier in life, wrote the ' Last Day.' After all, Swift pronounced of these Satires, that they should either have been more angry or more merry.

Is it not somewhat singular that Young preserved, without any palliation, this preface, so bluntly decisive in favour of laughing at the world, in the same collection of his works which contains the mournful, angry, gloomy ' Night Thoughts ?'

At the conclusion of the preface he applies Plato's beautiful fable of the ' Birth of Love ' to modern poetry, with the addition, " that Poetry, like Love, is a little subject to blindness, which makes her mistake her way to preferments and honours; and that she retains a dutiful admiration of her father's family; but divides her favours, and generally lives with her mother's relations." Poetry, it is true, did not lead Young to preferments or to honours; but was there not something like blindness in the flattery which he sometimes forced her, and her

[20] ' Love of Fame, the Universal Passion, in Seven Characteristical Satires. The second edition, corrected and altered,' 1728. Tonson, 8vo. The fourth edition, also in 8vo., appeared in 1741.

sister Prose, to utter? She was always, indeed, taught by him to entertain a most dutiful admiration of riches; but surely Young, though nearly related to Poetry, had no connexion with her whom Plato makes the mother of Love. That he could not well complain of being related to Poverty appears clearly from the frequent bounties which his gratitude records, and from the wealth which he left behind him. By 'The Universal Passion' he acquired no vulgar fortune, more than three thousand pounds. A considerable sum had already been swallowed up in the South-Sea. For this loss he took the vengeance of an author. His muse makes poetical use more than once of a South-Sea Dream.

It is related by Mr. Spence, in his Manuscript Anecdotes, on the authority of Mr. Rawlinson, that Young, upon the publication of his 'Universal Passion,' received from the Duke of Wharton [21] two thousand pounds; and that, when one of his friends exclaimed, "Two thousand pounds for a poem!" he said it was the best bargain he ever made in his life, for the poem was worth four thousand.

This story may be true; but it seems to have been raised from the two answers of Lord Burghley and Sir Philip Sidney in Spenser's Life.

After inscribing his Satires, not perhaps without the hope of preferments and honours, to such names as the Duke of Dorset, Mr. Dodington, Mr. Spencer Compton, Lady Elizabeth Germaine, and Sir Robert Walpole, he returns to plain panegyric. In 1726 he addressed a poem to Sir Robert Walpole, of which the title sufficiently explains the intention. If Young must be acknowledged a ready celebrator, he did not endeavour, or did not choose, to be a lasting one. 'The Instalment' is among the pieces he did not admit into the number of his *excusable writings;* yet it contains a couplet which pretends to pant after the power of bestowing immortality!

> "Oh how I long, enkindled by the theme,
> In deep eternity to launch thy name!"

---

[21] In all the editions of these Lives that I have seen, it is "Grafton;" but "Wharton" is the Spence reading. The same error occurs in the story of the human skull with the candle in it, p. 332.

The bounty of the former reign seems to have been continued, possibly increased, in this.[22]   Whatever it might have been, the poet thought he deserved it ; for he was not ashamed to

[22] It was continued, but not increased. Young was a servile courtier, and in the following letter is seen in his most abject mood :—

To Mrs. Howard.

" Madam,   Monday Morning.

" I know his majesty's goodness to his servants, and his love of justice in general, so well, that I am confident, if His Majesty knew my case, I should not have any cause to despair of his gracious favour to me.

Abilities.
Good Manners.
Service.
Age.
Want.
Sufferings ⎫ for his
   and   ⎬
Zeal   ⎭ majesty.

These, madam, are the proper points of consideration in the person that humbly hopes his majesty's favour.

As to *Abilities*, all I can presume to say is, I have done the best I could to improve them.

As to *Good manners*, I desire no favour, if any just objection lies against them.

As for *Service*, I have been near seven years in his majesty's, and never omitted any duty in it, which few can say.

As for *Age*, I am turned of fifty.

As for *Want*, I have no manner of preferment.

As for *Sufferings*, I have lost £300 per ann. by being in his majesty's service; as I have shown in a *Representation* which his majesty has been so good as to read and consider.

As for *Zeal*, I have written nothing without showing my duty to their majesties, and some pieces are dedicated to them.

This, madam, is the short and true state of my case. They that make their court to the ministers, and not their majesties, succeed better. If my case deserves some consideration, and you can serve me in it, I humbly hope and believe you will: I shall, therefore, trouble you no farther; but beg leave to subscribe myself, with truest respect and gratitude,

Yours, &c.,
Edward Young.

P.S. I have some hope that my Lord Townshend is my friend; if therefore soon, and before he leaves the court, you had an opportunity of mentioning me, with that favour you have been so good to show, I think it would not fail of success; and, if not, I shall owe you more than any."—*Suffolk Letters,* vol. i. p. 285.

acknowledge what, without his acknowledgment, would now perhaps never have been known:

> " My breast, O Walpole, glows with grateful fire.
> The streams of royal bounty, turn'd by thee,
> Refresh the dry domains of poesy."

If the purity of modern patriotism will term Young a pensioner, it must at least be confessed he was a grateful one.

The reign of the new monarch [George II.] was ushered in by Young with ' Ocean, an Ode.' The hint of it was taken from the Royal speech, which recommended the increase and the encouragement of the seamen; that they might be " invited, rather than compelled by force and violence, to enter into the service of their country "—a plan which humanity must lament that policy has not even yet been able, or willing, to carry into execution. Prefixed to the original publication were an ' Ode to the King, Pater Patriæ,' and an ' Essay on Lyric Poetry.' It is but justice to confess that he preserved neither of them, and that the ode itself, which in the first edition and in the last consists of seventy-three stanzas, in the author's own edition is reduced to forty-nine. Among the omitted passages is a " Wish " that concluded the poem, which few would have suspected Young of forming, and of which few, after having formed it, would confess something like their shame by suppression.

It stood originally so high in the author's opinion that he intituled the poem ' Ocean, an Ode. Concluding with a Wish.' This wish consists of thirteen stanzas. The first runs thus:

> " O may I *steal*
> Along the *vale*
> Of humble life, secure from foes !
> My friend sincere,
> My judgment clear,
> And gentle business my repose ! "

The three last stanzas are not more remarkable for just rhymes; but altogether they will make rather a curious page in the life of Young:

> " Prophetic schemes,
> And golden dreams,

> May I, unsanguine, cast away!
>   Have what I *have*,
>   And live, not *leave*,
> Enamour'd of the present day!
>
>   My hours my own!
>   My faults unknown!
> My chief revenue in content!
>   Then leave one *beam*
>   Of honest *fame*!
> And scorn the labour'd monument!
>
>   Unhurt my urn
>   Till that great TURN
> When mighty Nature's self shall die,
>   Time cease to glide,
>   With human pride,
> Sunk in the ocean of eternity!"

It is whimsical that he, who was soon to bid adieu to rhyme, should fix upon a measure in which rhyme abounds even to satiety. Of this he said, in his ' Essay on Lyric Poetry,' prefixed to the poem, " For the more *harmony* likewise I chose the frequent return of rhyme, which laid me under great difficulties. But difficulties overcome give grace and pleasure. Nor can I account for the *pleasure of rhyme in general* (of which the moderns are too fond) but from this truth." Yet the moderns surely deserve not much censure for their fondness of what, by his own confession, affords pleasure, and abounds in harmony.

The next paragraph in his Essay did not occur to him when he talked of " that great turn " in the stanza just quoted. " But then the writer must take care that the difficulty is overcome. That is, he must make rhyme consistent with as perfect sense and expression as could be expected if he was perfectly free from that shackle."

Another part of this Essay will convict the following stanza of, what every reader will discover in it, " involuntary burlesque."

> " The northern blast,
>   The shatter'd mast,
> The syrt, the whirlpool, and the rock,
>   The breaking spout,
>   The *stars gone out*,
> The boiling strait, the monster's shock."

But would the English poets fill quite so many volumes if all their productions were to be tried, like this, by an elaborate essay on each particular species of poetry of which they exhibit specimens?

If Young be not a lyric poet, he is at least a critic in that sort of poetry; and if his lyric poetry can be proved bad, it was first proved so by his own criticism. This surely is candid.

Milbourne was styled by Pope "the fairest of critics," only because he exhibited his own version of Virgil to be compared with Dryden's which he condemned, and with which every reader had it otherwise in his power to compare it. Young was surely not the most unfair of poets for prefixing to a lyric composition an 'Essay on Lyric Poetry,' so just and impartial as to condemn himself.

We shall soon come to a work before which we find indeed no critical essay, but which disdains to shrink from the touchstone of the severest critic, and which certainly, as I remember to have heard you say, if it contain some of the worst, contains also some of the best things in the language.

Soon after the appearance of 'Ocean,' when he was almost fifty, Young entered into orders. In April 1728, not long after he put on the gown, he was appointed chaplain to George the Second.

The tragedy of 'The Brothers,' which was already in rehearsal, he immediately withdrew from the stage. The managers resigned it with some reluctance to the delicacy of the new clergyman. The Epilogue to 'The Brothers,' the only appendages to any of his three plays which he added himself, is, I believe, the only one of the kind. He calls it an historical Epilogue. Finding that "Guilt's dreadful close his narrow scene denied," he, in a manner, continues the tragedy in the Epilogue, and relates how Rome revenged the shade of Demetrius, and punished Perseus "for this night's deed."

Of Young's taking orders something is told by a former biographer of Pope,[23] which places the easiness and simplicity of the poet in a singular light. When he determined on the

---

[23] Ruffhead. See his 'Life of Pope,' p. 291.

Church, he did not address himself to Sherlock, to Atterbury, or to Hare for the best instructions in theology, but to Pope; who, in a youthful frolic, advised the diligent perusal of Thomas Aquinas. With this treasure Young retired from interruption to an obscure place in the suburbs. His poetical guide to godliness hearing nothing of him during half a year, and apprehending he might have carried the jest too far, sought after him, and found him just in time to prevent what Ruffhead calls "an irretrievable derangement."

That attachment to his favourite study which made him think a poet the surest guide in his new profession, left him little doubt whether poetry were the surest path to its honours and preferments. Not long indeed after he took orders, he published in prose, 1728, 'A true Estimate of Human Life,' dedicated, notwithstanding the Latin quotations with which it abounds, to the Queen; and a sermon preached before the House of Commons, 1729, on the martyrdom of King Charles, intituled, 'An Apology for Princes, or the Reverence due to Government.' But the 'Second Discourse,' the counterpart of his 'Estimate,' without which it cannot be called "a true estimate," though in 1728 it was announced as "soon to be published," never appeared; and his old friends the Muses were not forgotten. In 1730 he relapsed to poetry, and sent into the world 'Imperium Pelagi: a Naval Lyric, written in Imitation of Pindar's Spirit, occasioned by His Majesty's Return from Hanover, September, 1729, and the succeeding Peace.' It is inscribed to the Duke of Chandos. In the Preface we are told that the Ode is the most spirited kind of Poetry, and that the Pindaric is the most spirited kind of Ode. "This I speak," he adds, with sufficient candour, "at my own very great peril. But truth has an eternal title to our confession, though we are sure to suffer by it." Behold, again, the fairest of poets. Young's 'Imperium Pelagi' was ridiculed in Fielding's 'Tom Thumb;' but let us not forget that it was one of his pieces which the author of the 'Night Thoughts' deliberately refused to own.

Not long after this Pindaric attempt, he published two

Epistles to Pope, "concerning the Authors of the Age," 1730.
Of these poems one occasion seems to have been an apprehension
lest, from the liveliness of his satires, he should not be deemed
sufficiently serious for promotion in the Church.

In July 1730 he was presented by his College to the rectory
of Welwyn in Hertfordshire.   In May 1731 he married Lady
Elizabeth Lee, daughter of the Earl of Lichfield, and widow
of Colonel Lee.[24]   His connexion with this lady arose from his
father's acquaintance, already mentioned, with Lady Anne
Wharton, who was co-heiress of Sir Henry Lee, of Ditchley in
Oxfordshire.   Poetry had lately been taught by Addison to
aspire to the arms of nobility, though not with extraordinary
happiness.

We may naturally conclude that Young now gave himself up
in some measure to the comforts of his new connexion, and to
the expectations of that preferment which he thought due to his
poetical talents, or, at least, to the manner in which they had so
frequently been exerted.

The next production of his Muse was 'The Sea-piece,' in two
odes.

Young enjoys the credit of what is called an 'Extempore
Epigram on Voltaire;' who, when he was in England, ridiculed,
in the company of the jealous English poet, Milton's allegory of
'Sin and Death:'

> "You are so witty, profligate, and thin,
>   At once we think thee Milton, Death, and Sin."

From the following passage in the poetical Dedication of his
'Sea-piece' to Voltaire, it seems that this extemporaneous
reproof, if it must be extemporaneous (for what few will now
affirm Voltaire to have deserved any reproof?), was something
longer than a distich, and something more gentle than the distich just quoted:[25]

---

[24] They were married in the church of St. Mary-at-Hill, London, 27th May,
1731.

[25] It was on the occasion of Voltaire's criticism on the episode of 'Death
and Sin' that Dr. Young spoke that couplet to him:

Thou 'rt

> " No stranger, Sir, though born in foreign climes.
>   On *Dorset* downs, when Milton's page
>   With Sin and Death provok'd thy rage,
> Thy rage provok'd, who sooth'd with *gentle* rhymes ? "

By " Dorset downs " he probably meant Mr. Dodington's seat. In Pitt's Poems is ' An Epistle to Dr. Edward Young, at East-bury in Dorsetshire, on the Review at Sarum, 1722.'

> " While with your Dodington retir'd you sit,
>   Charm'd with his flowing Burgundy and wit," &c.

Thomson, in his ' Autumn,' addressing Mr. Dodington, calls his seat the seat of the Muses,

> " Where, in the secret bower and winding walk,
>   For virtuous Young and thee they twine the bay."

The praises Thomson bestows but a few lines before on Philips, the second

> " Who nobly durst, in rhyme-unfetter'd verse,
>   With British freedom sing the British song,"

added to Thomson's example and success, might perhaps induce Young, as we shall see presently, to write his great work without rhyme.

In 1734 he published ' The Foreign Address, or the best Argument for Peace, occasioned by the British Fleet and the Posture of Affairs. Written in the Character of a Sailor.' It is not to be found in the author's four volumes.

He now appears to have given up all hopes of overtaking Pindar, and perhaps at last resolved to turn his ambition to some original species of poetry. This poem concludes with a formal farewell to Ode, which few of Young's readers will regret :

> " My shell, which Clio gave, which *Kings applaud*,
>   Which Europe's bleeding Genius call'd abroad,
>   Adieu ! "

> Thou 'rt so ingenious, profligate, and thin,
> That thou thyself art Milton's Death and Sin.

Voltaire's objection to that fine episode was, that Death and Sin were non-existents.—*Spence by Singer*, p. 375.

In a species of poetry altogether his own, he next tried his skill, and succeeded.

Of his wife he was deprived in 1741. Lady Elizabeth had lost, after her marriage with Young, an amiable daughter, by her former husband, just after she was married to Mr. Temple, son of Lord Palmerston.[26]   Mr. Temple [27] did not long remain after his wife, though he was married a second time to a daughter of Sir John Barnard's, whose son is the present peer.[28]   Mr. and Mrs. Temple have generally been considered as Philander and Narcissa.   From the great friendship which constantly subsisted between Mr. Temple and Young, as well as from other circumstances, it is probable that the poet had both him and Mrs. Temple in view for these characters; though at the same time some passages respecting Philander do not appear to suit either Mr. Temple or any other person with whom Young was known to be connected or acquainted, while all the circumstances relating to Narcissa have been constantly found applicable to Young's daughter-in-law.[29]

At what short intervals the poet tells us he was wounded by the deaths of the three persons particularly lamented, none that has read the 'Night Thoughts' (and who has not read them?) needs to be informed.

> " Insatiate Archer! could not one suffice?
>   Thy shaft flew thrice; and thrice my peace was slain;
>   And thrice, ere thrice yon moon had fill'd her horn."

Yet how is it possible that Mr. and Mrs. Temple and Lady Elizabeth Young could be these three victims, over whom Young has hitherto been pitied for having to pour the 'Midnight Sorrows' of his religious poetry?   Mrs. Temple died in 1736; Mr. Temple four years afterwards, in 1740; and the poet's wife

---

[26] Anne Temple, wife of the Honourable Henry Temple, eldest son of the first Viscount Palmerston.   She died 8th Dec. 1735.

[27] Hon. Henry Temple died 18th August, 1740, having married, 12th Sept. 1738, a daughter of Sir John Barnard.

[28] Henry, second Viscount Palmerston (d. 1802), father of the present distinguished statesman.

[29] Sir Herbert should have written *step-daughter*.

seven months after Mr. Temple, in 1741. How could the insatiate Archer thrice slay his peace in these three persons, " ere thrice the moon had fill'd her horn?"

But in the short preface to 'The Complaint' he seriously tells us " that the occasion of this poem was real, not fictitious ; and that the facts mentioned did naturally pour these moral reflections on the thought of the writer." It is probable, therefore, that in these three contradictory lines the poet complains more than the father-in-law, the friend, or the widower.

Whatever names belong to these facts, or, if the names be those generally supposed, whatever heightening a poet's sorrow may have given the facts ; to the sorrow Young felt from them, religion and morality are indebted for the ' Night Thoughts.' There is a pleasure sure in sadness which mourners only know !

Of these poems the two or three first have been perused perhaps more eagerly and more frequently than the rest. When he got as far as the fourth or fifth, his original motive for taking up the pen was answered ; his grief was naturally either diminished or exhausted. We still find the same pious poet ; but we hear less of Philander and Narcissa, and less of the mourner whom he loved to pity.[30]

Mrs. Temple died of a consumption at Lyons, in her way to Nice, the year after her marriage ; that is, when poetry relates the fact, " in her bridal hour." It is more than poetically true, that Young accompanied her to the Continent.

> " I flew, I snatch'd her from the rigid North,
>   And bore her nearer to the sun."

But in vain. Her funeral was attended with the difficulties painted in such animated colours in Night the Third. After her death, the remainder of the party passed the ensuing winter at Nice.

The poet seems perhaps in these compositions to dwell with

---

[30] I have ordered Mr. Dodsley to wait on you with a thing called ' The Complaint,' and with the second as soon as printed, which will be soon. . . . Sir, I write this in confidence ; for I do not own myself the writer of it.—DR. YOUNG to Sir Thomas Hanmer, Nov. 20, 1742. (Hanmer Corresp. p. 229.)

more melancholy on the death of Philander and Narcissa than of his wife.   But it is only for this reason.   He who runs and reads may remember that in the 'Night Thoughts' Philander and Narcissa are often mentioned and often lamented.   To recollect lamentations over the author's wife, the memory must have been charged with distinct passages.   This lady brought him one child, Frederick, now [1780] living, to whom the Prince of Wales was godfather.

That domestic grief is, in the first instance, to be thanked for these ornaments to our language, it is impossible to deny.   Nor would it be common hardiness to contend, that worldly discontent had no hand in these joint productions of poetry and piety. Yet am I by no means sure that, at any rate, we should not have had something of the same colour from Young's pencil, notwithstanding the liveliness of his satires.   In so long a life, causes for discontent and occasions for grief must have occurred. It is not clear to me that his Muse was not sitting upon the watch for the first which happened.   'Night Thoughts' were not uncommon to her, even when first she visited the poet, and at a time when he himself was remarkable neither for gravity nor gloominess.   In his 'Last Day,' almost his earliest poem, he calls her " the melancholy maid,"

————— " whom dismal scenes delight,
Frequent at tombs and in the realms of Night."

In the prayer which concludes the second book of the same poem, he says—

" —Oh ! permit the gloom of solemn night
To sacred thought may forcibly invite.
Oh ! how divine to tread the milky way,
To the bright palace of Eternal Day ! "

When Young was writing a tragedy, Wharton is said by Spence [31] to have sent him a human skull, with a candle in it, as a lamp ; and the poet is reported to have used it.

What he calls " The *true* estimate of Human Life," which

[31] Spence, ed. Singer, p. 255.

has already been mentioned, exhibits only the wrong side of the tapestry ; and being asked why he did not show the right, he is said to have replied that he could not.   By others it has been told me that this was finished, but that, before there existed any copy, it was torn in pieces by a lady's monkey.

Still, is it altogether fair to dress up the poet for the man, and to bring the gloominess of the ' Night Thoughts ' to prove the gloominess of Young, and to show that his genius, like the genius of Swift, was in some measure the sullen inspiration of discontent ?

From them who answer in the affirmative it should not be concealed that, though " Invisibilia non decipiunt " appeared upon a deception in Young's grounds, and " Ambulantes in horto audiêrunt vocem Dei " on a building in his garden, his parish was indebted to the good humour of the author of the ' Night Thoughts ' for an assembly and a bowling-green.

Whether you think with me I know not ; but the famous " De mortuis nil nisi bonum " always appeared to me to savour more of female weakness than of manly reason.   He that has too much feeling to speak ill of the dead, who, if they cannot defend themselves, are at least ignorant of his abuse, will not hesitate by the most wanton calumny to destroy the quiet, the reputation, the fortune of the living.   Yet censure is not heard beneath the tomb any more than praise.   " De mortuis nil nisi verum—De vivis nil nisi bonum "—would approach much nearer to good sense.   After all, the few handfuls of remaining dust which once composed the body of the author of the ' Night Thoughts ' feel not much concern whether Young pass now for a man of sorrow, or for a " fellow of infinite jest."   To this favour must come the whole family of Yorick.   His immortal part, wherever that now dwell, is still less solicitous on this head.

But to a son of worth and sensibility it is of some little consequence whether contemporaries believe, and posterity be taught to believe, that his debauched and reprobate life cast a Stygian gloom over the evening of his father's days, saved him the trouble of feigning a character completely detestable, and

succeeded at last in bringing his "grey hairs with sorrow to
the grave."

The humanity of the world, little satisfied with inventing
perhaps a melancholy disposition for the father, proceeds next
to invent an argument in support of their invention, and chooses
that Lorenzo should be Young's own son. The 'Biographia'
and every account of Young pretty roundly assert this to be the
fact ; of the absolute impossibility of which the 'Biographia'
itself, in particular dates, contains undeniable evidence. Readers
I know there are of a strange turn of mind who will hereafter
peruse the 'Night Thoughts' with less satisfaction ; who will
wish they had still been deceived ; who will quarrel with me
for discovering that no such character as their Lorenzo ever yet
disgraced human nature, or broke a father's heart. Yet would
these admirers of the sublime and terrible be offended should
you set them down for cruel and for savage.

Of this report, inhuman to the surviving son, if it be true, in
proportion as the character of Lorenzo is diabolical, where are
we to find the proof ? Perhaps it is clear from the poems.

From the first line to the last of the 'Night Thoughts' no
one expression can be discovered which betrays anything like
the father. In the second 'Night' I find an expression which
betrays something else : that Lorenzo was his friend—one, it is
possible, of his former companions ; one of the Duke of Wharton's set. The poet styles him "gay friend"—an appellation
not very natural from a pious incensed father to such a being
as he paints Lorenzo, and that being his son.

But let us see how he has sketched this dreadful portrait,
from the sight of some of whose features the artist himself must
have turned away with horror—a subject more shocking, if his
only child really sat to him, than the Crucifixion of Michael
Angelo, upon the horrid story told of which Young composed a
short poem of fourteen lines in the early part of his life, which
he did not think deserved to be republished.

In the first 'Night' the address to the poet's supposed son is,

"Lorenzo, Fortune makes her court to thee."

In the fifth ' Night '—

> " And burns Lorenzo still for the sublime
> Of life? to hang his airy nest on high ? "

Is this a picture of the son of the rector of Welwyn ?
Eighth ' Night '—

> " In foreign realms (for thou hast travelled far) "—

which even now does not apply to his son.
In ' Night ' Five —

> " So wept Lorenzo fair Clarissa's fate,
> Who gave that angel-boy on whom he dotes,
> And died to give him, orphan'd in his birth ? "

At the beginning of the fifth ' Night ' we find—

> " Lorenzo, to recriminate is just,
> I grant the man is vain who writes for praise."

But, to cut short all inquiry, if any one of these passages, if
any passage in the poems be applicable, my friend shall pass for
Lorenzo.   The son of the author of the ' Night Thoughts ' was
not old enough, when they were written, to recriminate or to be
a father.   The ' Night Thoughts ' were begun immediately
after the mournful event of 1741.   The first ' Nights ' appear
in the books of the Company of Stationers as the property of
Robert Dodsley, in 1742.   The preface to ' Night ' Seven is
dated July the 7th, 1744.   The marriage, in consequence of
which the supposed Lorenzo was born, happened in May 1731.
Young's child was not born till June 1733.   In 1741 this Lorenzo,
this finished infidel, this father to whose education Vice had for
some years put the last hand, was only eight years old.

An anecdote of this cruel sort, so open to contradiction, so
impossible to be true, who could propagate ?   Thus easily are
blasted the reputation of the living and of the dead.

Who then was Lorenzo ? exclaim the readers I have mentioned.   If we cannot be sure that he was his son, which would
have been finely terrible, was he not his nephew, his cousin ?

These are questions which I do not pretend to answer.   For

the sake of human nature, I could wish Lorenzo to have been
only the creation of the poet's fancy : like the Quintus of Anti-
Lucretius, " quo nomine," says Polignac, "quemvis Atheum
intellige." That this was the case many expressions in the
' Night Thoughts' would seem to prove, did not a passage in
' Night' Eight appear to show that he had somebody in his
eye for the groundwork at least of the painting. Lovelace or
Lorenzo may be feigned characters ; but a writer does not feign
a name of which he only gives the initial letter.

> " Tell not Calista. She will laugh thee dead,
>   Or send thee to her hermitage with L——."

The 'Biographia,' [32] not satisfied with pointing out the son of
Young, in that son's lifetime, as his father's Lorenzo, travels
out of its way into the history of the son, and tells of his having
been forbidden his college at Oxford for misbehaviour. How
such anecdotes, were they true, tend to illustrate the life of
Young it is not easy to discover. Was the son of the author of
the ' Night Thoughts' indeed forbidden his college for a time,
at one of our Universities ? The author of ' Paradise Lost' is
by some supposed to have been disgracefully ejected from the
other. From juvenile follies who is free? But, whatever the
' Biographia' choose to relate, the son of Young experienced no
dismission from his college, either lasting or temporary.

Yet were nature to indulge him with a second youth, and to
leave him at the same time the experience of that which is past,
he would probably spend it differently—who would not ?—he
would certainly be the occasion of less uneasiness to his father.[33]

[32] The article on Young in the 'Biographia Britannica' appeared in 1766.
Some of the information it contains is said, in a note, to have been " communicated by Dr. Eyre, of Gray's-Inn, who was his schoolfellow at Winchester."

[33] The cause of quarrel between Young and his son, he [Johnson] told us,
was that his son insisted Young should turn away a clergyman's widow who
lived with him, and who, having acquired great influence over the father, was
saucy to the son. Dr. Johnson said she could not conceal her resentment at
him for saying to Young that " an old man should not resign himself to the
management of anybody." I asked him if there was any improper connection
between them? "No, Sir, no more than between two statues." He was past
fourscore, and she a very coarse woman. She read to him, and, I suppose,
made his coffee and frothed his chocolate, and did such things as an old man
wishes to have done for him.—*Boswell by Croker*, p. 357.

But, from the same experience, he would as certainly, in the same case, be treated differently by his father.

Young was a poet: poets, with reverence be it spoken, do not make the best parents. Fancy and imagination seldom deign to stoop from their heights—always stoop unwillingly to the low level of common duties. Aloof from vulgar life, they pursue their rapid flight beyond the ken of mortals, and descend not to earth but when compelled by necessity. The prose of ordinary occurrences is beneath the dignity of poets.

He who is connected with the author of the ' Night Thoughts,' only by veneration for the poet and the Christian, may be allowed to observe that Young is one of those concerning whom, as you remark in your account of Addison, it is proper rather to say " nothing that is false than all that is true."

But the son of Young would almost sooner, I know, pass for Lorenzo than see himself vindicated, at the expense of his father's memory, from follies which, if it may be thought blame-able in a boy to have committed them, it is surely praiseworthy in a man to lament, and certainly not only unnecessary but cruel in a biographer to record.

Of the ' Night Thoughts,' notwithstanding their author's professed retirement, all are inscribed to great or to growing names. He had not yet weaned himself from earls and dukes, from Speakers of the House of Commons, Lords Commissioners of the Treasury, and Chancellors of the Exchequer. In ' Night ' Eight the politician plainly betrays himself :

> " Think no post needful that demands a knave,
>   When late our civil helm was shifting hands,
>   So P—— thought : think better, if you can."

Yet it must be confessed that at the conclusion of ' Night ' Nine, weary perhaps of courting earthly patrons, he tells his soul,

> " Henceforth
>   Thy *patron* he, whose diadem has dropt
>   Yon gems of heaven ; Eternity thy prize ;
>   And leave the racers of the world their own."

The Fourth ' Night ' was addressed by " a much-indebted

Muse" to the Honourable Mr. Yorke, now Lord Hardwicke,
who meant to have laid the Muse under still greater obligation
by the living of Shenfield in Essex, if it had become vacant.

The First 'Night' concludes with this passage :

> " Dark, though not blind, like thee, Meonides ;
>   Or Milton, thee.   Ah ! could I reach your strain ;
>   Or his who made Meonides our own !
>   Man too he sung.   Immortal man I sing.
>   Oh had he prest his theme, pursued the track
>   Which opens out of darkness into day !
>   Oh had he mounted on his wing of fire,
>   Soar'd where I sink, and sung immortal man—
>   How had it blest mankind, and rescued me ! ' "

To the author of these lines was dedicated, in 1756, the first
volume of an 'Essay on the Writings and Genius of Pope,'
which attempted, whether justly or not, to pluck from Pope his
" Wing of Fire," and to reduce him to a rank at least one
degree lower than the first class of English poets.   If Young
accepted and approved the dedication, he countenanced this
attack upon the fame of him whom he invokes as his Muse.[34]

Part of " paper-sparing " Pope's Third Book of the ' Odyssey,' deposited in the Museum, is written upon the back of a
letter signed " E. Young," which is clearly the hand-writing
of our Young.   The letter, dated only May the 2nd, seems
obscure ; but there can be little doubt that the friendship he
requests was a literary one, and that he had the highest literary opinion of Pope.   The request was a prologue, I am told.

" May the 2nd.

" Dear Sir,—Having been often from home, I know not if you have
done me the favour of calling on me.   But, be that as it will, I much

---

[34] Young accepted the dedication by letter to Joseph Warton.

Nov. 9, 1755.

Dear Sir,—You do me an honour.   I shall not fail to keep your secret.   I
heartily wish you success in this and all things.   If this or any other occasion
calls you to town, I am but four hours from you; and you will be most welcome to,   Dear Sir,

Your obliged humble servant,

—Wooll's ' Warton,' p. 236.   Ed. Young.

want that instance of your friendship I mentioned in my last—a friendship I am very sensible I can receive from no one but yourself. I should not urge this thing so much but for very particular reasons; nor can you be at a loss to conceive how a ' trifle of this nature ' may be of serious moment to me; and, while I am in hopes of the great advantage of your advice about it, I shall not be so absurd as to make any further step without it. I know you are much engaged, and only hope to hear of you at your entire leisure.

> " I am, Sir, your most faithful and obedient servant,
>
> " E. YOUNG."

Nay, even after Pope's death, he says, in ' Night' Seven:

> " Pope, who could'st make immortals, art thou dead? "

Either the ' Essay,' then, was dedicated to a patron who disapproved its doctrine, which I have been told by the author [Joseph Warton] was not the case; or Young appears, in his old age, to have bartered for a dedication an opinion entertained of his friend through all that part of life when he must have been best able to form opinions.

From this account of Young, two or three short passages, which stand almost together in ' Night' Four, should not be excluded. They afford a picture, by his own hand, from the study of which my readers may choose to form their own opinion of the features of his mind and the complexion of his life.

> " Ah me! the dire effect
> Of loitering here, of death defrauded long;
> Of old so gracious (and let that suffice),
> *My very master knows me not.*
>
> .   .   .   .
>
> I 've been so long remember'd, I 'm forgot.
>
> .   .   .   .
>
> When in his courtier's ears I pour my plaint,
> They drink it as the Nectar of the Great;
> And squeeze my hand, and beg me come to-morrow.
>
> .   .   .   .
>
> Twice told the period spent on stubborn Troy,
> Court-favour, yet untaken, I *besiege.*
>
> .   .   .   .
>
> If this song lives, Posterity shall know
> One, though in Britain born, with courtiers bred,

> Who thought ev'n gold might come a day too late ;
> Nor on his subtle death-bed plann'd his scheme
> For future vacancies in church or state."

Deduct from the writer's age " twice told the period spent on stubborn Troy," and you will still leave him more than forty when he sat down to the miserable siege of court favour. He has before told us

> " A fool at forty is a fool indeed."

After all, the siege seems to have been raised only in consequence of what the General thought his " death-bed."

By these extraordinary poems, written after he was sixty, of which I have been led to say so much, I hope by the wish of doing justice to the living and the dead, it was the desire of Young to be principally known. He entitled the four volumes which he published himself, ' The Works of the Author of the Night Thoughts.' [35] While it is remembered that from these he excluded many of his writings, let it not be forgotten that the rejected pieces contained nothing prejudicial to the cause of virtue or of religion. Were everything that Young ever wrote to be published, he would only appear perhaps in a less respectable light as a poet, and more despicable as a dedicator : he would not pass for a worse Christian, or for a worse man. This enviable praise is due to Young. Can it be claimed by every writer ? His dedications, after all, he had perhaps no right to suppress. They all, I believe, speak, not a little to the credit of his gratitude, of favours received ; and I know not whether the author who has once solemnly printed an acknowledgment of a favour, should not always print it.

Is it to the credit or to the discredit of Young, as a poet, that of his ' Night Thoughts ' the French are particularly fond ?

Of the ' Epitaph on Lord Aubrey Beauclerk,' dated 1740, all I know is, that I find it in the late body of English poetry, and that I am sorry to find it there.

Notwithstanding the farewell which he seemed to have taken

[35] Croft alludes to the edition in four volumes published in 1762, and deservedly looked upon as the standard text of Young.

in the ' Night Thoughts ' of everything which bore the least
resemblance to ambition, he dipped again in politics.   In 1745
he wrote ' Reflections on the Public Situation of the Kingdom,
addressed to the Duke of Newcastle ;' indignant, as it appears,
to behold

> " — a pope-bred Princeling crawl ashore,
>   And whistle cut-throats, with those swords that scrap'd
>   Their barren rocks for wretched sustenance,
>   To cut his passage to the British throne."

This political poem might be called a ' Night Thought.'   Indeed it was originally printed as the conclusion of the ' Night
Thoughts,' though he did not gather it with his other works.

Prefixed to the second edition of Howe's ' Devout Meditations ' is a letter from Young, dated January 19, 1752, addressed to Archibald Macauly, Esq. ; thanking him for the
book, which, he says, " he shall never lay far out of his reach ;
for a greater demonstration of a sound head and a sincere
heart he never saw."

In 1753, when ' The Brothers ' had lain by him above thirty
years, it appeared upon the stage.[36]   If any part of his fortune

---

[36] At Drury Lane. It was acted eight nights, and brought 400*l.* to its author.
"Will it be hereafter believed that ' The Earl of Essex ' had a run, and
that a play of the author of the ' Night Thoughts ' was acted to thin houses
but just eight nights ?   The Doctor, you have heard, intended the benefit
accruing to an author to go to the Society for Propagating the Gospel. He,
finding it did not answer his expectations as to profits, took them to himself
(not 400*l.*), and gave a thousand guineas to that Society. I had some talk
with him on this great action. ' I always,' said he, ' intended to do something handsome to this Society.   Had I deferred it to my demise, I should
have given away my son's money: all the world are inclined to pleasure; I
myself love pleasure as much as any man; could I have given myself a greater
by disposing of the same sum to a different use, I should have done it.' "—
RICHARDSON (the novelist) to Lady Bradshaigh, Feb. 24, 1753.
Young seems to have obtained fair prices for his works from the booksellers.
Lintot gave him 42*l.* for a half share in his first tragedy. Dodsley gave him,
as appears by his own assignment, which I have seen, dated Nov. 24, 1743,
one hundred and sixty guineas for the first five parts of the ' Night Thoughts.'
Yet Warton says (Warton's ' Pope,' ix. 134) that he received from Dodsley
200 guineas for the first three Nights. The same publisher gave him, Jan.
26, 1744, sixty guineas for the sixth Night. From Millar he received, 7th April,
1749, 63*l.* for Nights seven, eight, and nine, and a ' Paraphrase of Job.'   On
the 19th Feb. 1755, he assigned to James Dodsley the copyright of ' The Centaur ' for 200*l.*

had been acquired by servility of adulation, he now determined
to deduct from it no inconsiderable sum, as a gift to the Society
for the Propagation of the Gospel. To this sum he hoped the
profits of ‘The Brothers’ would amount. In his calculation
he was deceived; but by the bad success of his play the Society
was not a loser. The author made up the sum he originally
intended, which was a thousand pounds, from his own pocket.

The next performance which he printed was a prose publication, entitled, ‘The Centaur not fabulous, in Six Letters to a
Friend on the Life in Vogue.’ The conclusion is dated November 29, 1754. In the third Letter is described the death-
bed of the “gay, young, noble, ingenious, accomplished, and
most wretched Altamont.” His last words were—“ My principles have poisoned my friend, my extravagance has beggared
my boy, my unkindness has murdered my wife!” Either Altamont and Lorenzo were the twin production of fancy, or Young
was unlucky enough to know two characters who bore no little
resemblance to each other in perfection of wickedness. Report
has been accustomed to call Altamont Lord Euston.

‘The Old Man’s Relapse,’ occasioned by an Epistle to
Walpole, if written by Young, which I much doubt, must have
been written very late in life. It has been seen, I am told, in
a Miscellany published thirty years before his death. In 1758
he exhibited ‘The Old Man’s Relapse’ in more than words,
by again becoming a dedicator, and publishing a sermon
addressed to the King.

The lively Letter in prose on ‘Original Composition,’ addressed to Richardson, the author of ‘Clarissa,’ appeared in
1759. Though he despair “ of breaking through the frozen
obstructions of age and care’s incumbent cloud, into that flow of
thought and brightness of expression which subjects so polite
require,” yet is it more like the production of untamed, un-
bridled youth, than of jaded fourscore. Some sevenfold volumes
put him in mind of Ovid’s sevenfold channels of the Nile at
the conflagration :

—————— “ ostia septem
Pulverulenta vocant, septem sine flumine valles.”

Such leaden labours are like Lycurgus's iron money, which was so much less in value than in bulk, that it required barns for strong boxes, and a yoke of oxen to draw five hundred pounds.

If there is a famine of invention in the land, we must travel, he says, like Joseph's brethren, far for food ; we must visit the remote and rich ancients. But an inventive genius may safely stay at home ; that, like the widow's cruse, is divinely replenished from within, and affords us a miraculous delight. He asks why it should seem altogether impossible that Heaven's latest editions of the human mind may be the most correct and fair? And Jonson, he tells us, was very learned, as Sampson was very strong, to his own hurt. Blind to the nature of tragedy, he pulled down all antiquity on his head, and buried himself under it.

Is this " care's incumbent cloud," or " the frozen obstructions of age?"

In this letter Pope is severely censured for his " fall from Homer's numbers, free as air, lofty and harmonious as the spheres, into childish shackles and tinkling sounds ; for putting Achilles in petticoats a second time :" but we are told that the dying swan talked over an Epic plan with Young a few weeks before his decease.

Young's chief inducement to write this letter was, as he confesses, that he might erect a monumental marble to the memory of an old friend. He who employed his pious pen for almost the last time in thus doing justice to the exemplary death-bed of Addison, might probably, at the close of his own life, afford no unuseful lesson for the deaths of others.

In the postscript he writes to Richardson, that he will see in his next how far Addison is an original. But no other letter appears.

The few lines which stand in the last edition, as " sent by Lord Melcombe to Dr. Young, not long before his Lordship's death," were indeed so sent, but were only an introduction to what was there meant by ' The Muse's latest Spark.' The poem is necessary, whatever may be its merit, since the preface

to it is already printed.   Lord Melcombe called his Tusculum
' La Trappe.'

> " Love thy country, wish it well,
>   Not with too intense a care ;
> 'T is enough that, when it fell,
>   Thou its ruin didst not share.
>
> Envy's censure, Flattery's praise,
>   With unmov'd indifference view ;
> Learn to tread Life's dangerous maze,
>   With unerring Virtue's clue.
>
> Void of strong desire and fear,
>   Life's wide ocean trust no more ;
> Strive thy little bark to steer
>   With the tide, but near the shore.
>
> Thus prepar'd, thy shorten'd sail
>   Shall, whene'er the winds increase,
> Seizing each propitious gale,
>   Waft thee to the Port of Peace.
>
> Keep thy conscience from offence
>   And tempestuous passions free,
> So, when thou art call'd from hence,
>   Easy shall thy passage be ;
>
> Easy shall thy passage be,
>   Cheerful thy allotted stay,
> Short the account 'twixt God and thee ;
>   Hope shall meet thee on the way :
>
> Truth shall lead thee to the gate,
>   Mercy's self shall let thee in,
> Where its never-changing state
>   Full perfection shall begin."

The poem was accompanied by a letter:

" La Trappe, the 27th of Oct., 1761.

" DEAR SIR,—You seemed to like the ode I sent you for your amusement ; I now send it you as a present.   If you please to accept of it, and
are willing that our friendship should be known when we are gone, you
will be pleased to leave this among those of your own papers that may
possibly see the light by a posthumous publication.   God send us health
while we stay, and an easy journey !

" My dear Dr. Young,

" Yours, most cordially,

" MELCOMBE."

In 1762, a short time before his death, Young published
' Resignation.' Notwithstanding the manner in which it was
really forced from him by the world, criticism has treated it
with no common severity.   If it shall be thought not to deserve
the highest praise, on the other side of fourscore, by whom except by Newton and by Waller has praise been merited?

To Mrs. Montagu, the famous champion of Shakespeare, I am
indebted for the history of ' Resignation.' Observing that
Mrs. Boscawen, in the midst of her grief for the loss of the
Admiral, derived consolation from the perusal of the ' Night
Thoughts,' Mrs. Montagu proposed a visit to the author.   From
conversing with Young, Mrs. Boscawen derived still further
consolation ; and to that visit she and the world were indebted
for this poem.   It compliments Mrs. Montagu in the following
lines :

> " Yet, write I must.   A Lady sues,
>   How shameful her request !
> My brain in labour with dull rhyme,
>   Her's teeming with the best ! "

And again :

> " A friend you have, and I the same,
>   Whose prudent, soft address
> Will bring to life those healing thoughts
>   Which died in your distress.
> That friend, the spirit of my theme
>   Extracting for your ease,
> Will leave to me the dreg, in thoughts
>   Too common ; such as these."

By the same lady I am enabled to say, in her own words,
that Young's unbounded genius appeared to greater advantage
in the companion, than even in the author ; that the Christian
was in him a character still more inspired, more enraptured,
more sublime than the poet ; and that, in his ordinary conversation,

> " —letting down the golden chain from high,
> He drew his audience upward to the sky."

Notwithstanding Young had said, in his ' Conjectures on

Original Composition,' that "blank verse is verse unfallen,
uncurst; verse reclaimed, re-inthroned in the true language of
the Gods:" notwithstanding he administered consolation to his
own grief in this immortal language, Mrs. Boscawen was comforted in rhyme.[37]

[37] The following letter was first printed by me, from the original long in
the possession of the late Thomas Hill, Esq.—the Hull of 'Gilbert Gurney,'
and the original of Paul Pry:—

To HERBERT CROFT, ESQ., SOUTHAMPTON ROW, LONDON.

Sandleford, Sept. 17, 1782.

MRS. MONTAGU presents her compliments to Mr. Croft, and would have
returned an answer to his letter sooner, but being in the country it was delayed on its way to her. In regard to 'Resignation,' the matter which gave
occasion to that poem was simply this: Mrs. Montagu having observed that
Mrs. Boscawen, in her great and just grief for the loss of the Admiral, seemed
to find some consolation in reading Dr. Young's 'Night Thoughts,' she wished
to give her an opportunity of conversing with him, having herself always
thought his unbounded genius appeared to greater advantage in the companion
than the author. The Christian was in him a character more inspired, more
enraptured, more sublime, than the Poet, and in his ordinary conversation,

— letting down the golden chain from high,
He drew his audience upward to the sky.

Mrs. M. therefore proposed to Mrs. Boscawen and Mrs. Carter to go with her
to Welwyn: it is unnecessary to add that the visit answered every expectation.

Mrs. Montagu is very sorry it is not in her power to furnish Mr. Croft with
any important circumstances in Dr. Young's life; but he was sunk into the
vale of years and quiet retreat before she had the honour and happiness of his
acquaintance, and his contemplation being then chiefly intent on things *above
the visible diurnal sphere,* he rarely talked of the earlier and more active part of
his life. From others she has heard many things greatly to his credit, particularly an act of uncommon liberality to his lady's daughter by her first
husband; but as they were delivered to her in the vague relations of common
discourse, she cannot speak of them with such certainty and precision as Mr.
Croft's purpose requires. This deficiency she greatly laments, not only on
account of the honour they would have done to the memory of her departed
friend, but likewise for the sake of the world, to whom they would have held
forth patterns of right and noble conduct. Though right and wrong are declared and made known to us by higher wisdom than human wisdom, yet such
is the perverseness of mankind, they are more apt to be influenced by the
example of persons celebrated for their parts than by pure precept; for the
same reason, in an unbelieving age, the interests of religion are connected with
the character of a man so distinguished for piety as Dr. Young. Though unable
to assist Mr. Croft, she must ever respect him for endeavouring to get information from Dr. Young's friends concerning him, instead of collecting from
the whispers of calumny idle tales by which to blast the memory of a good
man, and prevent the edification of a good example.

While the poet and the Christian were applying this comfort, Young had himself occasion for comfort, in consequence [1761] of the sudden death of Richardson, who was printing the former part of the poem.   Of Richardson's death he says:

> " When Heaven would kindly set us free,
>   And earth's enchantment end,
>   It takes the most effectual means,
>   And robs us of a friend."

To ' Resignation ' was prefixed an Apology for its appearance : to which more credit is due than to the generality of such apologies, from Young's unusual anxiety that no more productions of his old age should disgrace his former fame.   In his will, dated February, 1760, he desires of his executors, *in a particular manner*, that all his manuscript books and writings whatever might be burned, except his book of accounts.

In September, 1764, he added a kind of codicil, wherein he made it his dying entreaty to his housekeeper, to whom he left 1000*l.*, " that all his manuscripts might be destroyed as soon as he was dead, which would greatly oblige her deceased *friend*."

It may teach mankind the uncertainty of worldly friendships, to know that Young, either by surviving those he loved, or by outliving their affections, could only recollect the names of two *friends*, his housekeeper and a hatter, to mention in his will ;[38] and it may serve to repress that testamentary pride which too often seeks for sounding names and titles, to be informed that the author of the ' Night Thoughts ' did not blush to leave a legacy to his " friend Henry Stevens, a hatter at the Temple-gate."   Of these two remaining friends, one went before Young. But, at eighty-four, " where," as he asks in ' The Centaur,' " is that world into which we were born ?"[39]

The same humility which marked a hatter and a housekeeper

---

[38] This is not the case.   He left twenty shilling rings to Richardson, the novelist, and to Mr. Alderman Göstling.

[39] " Where is the world?" cries Young at eighty; " where
       The world in which a man was born?"   Alas!
      Where is the world of *eight* years past?   ' *Twas there*—
       I look for it—'tis gone, a globe of glass.
                                        BYRON: *Don Juan*, can. ii. 76.

for the friends of the author of the ' Night Thoughts,' had
before bestowed the same title on his footman, in an epitaph in
his ' Church-yard ' upon James Barker, dated 1749; which I
am glad to find in the late collection of his works.

Young and his housekeeper were ridiculed with more ill-
nature than wit in a kind of novel published by Kidgell in
1755, called ' The Card,' under the names of Dr. Elwes and
Mrs. Fusby.

In April, 1765, at an age to which few attain, a period was
put to the life of Young.

He had performed no duty for three or four years, but he
retained his intellects to the last.[40]

Much is told in the ' Biographia,' which I know not to have
been true, of the manner of his burial: of the master and
children of a charity-school, which he founded in his parish,
who neglected to attend their benefactor's corpse ; and of a bell
which was not caused to toll as often as upon those occasions
bells usually toll.   Had that humanity which is here lavished
upon things of little consequence either to the living or to the
dead, been shown in its proper place to the living, I should
have had less to say about Lorenzo.   They who lament that
these misfortunes happened to Young, forget the praise he
bestows upon Socrates, in the preface to ' Night ' Seven, for
resenting his friend's request about his funeral.

During some part of his life Young was abroad, but I have
not been able to learn any particulars.

In his seventh Satire he says,

> " When, after battle, I the field have SEEN
>   Spread o'er with ghastly shapes which once were *men*."

---

[40] "My friend," said Young to Dr. Cotton, about a fortnight before he was
seized with his last illness; " my friend, there are two considerations upon
which my faith in Christ is built as upon a rock : The fall of man, the redemp-
tion of man, and the resurrection of man, the three cardinal articles of our
religion, are such as human ingenuity could never have invented; therefore
they must be divine. The other argument is this : If the Prophecies have
been fulfilled (of which there is abundant demonstration), the Scripture must
be the word of God; and if the Scripture is the word of God, Christianity
must be true."—COWPER to Lady Hesketh. (Southey's ' Cowper,' vol. iii.
p. 250.)

It is known also that from this or from some other field he once wandered into the camp, with a classic in his hand, which he was reading intently ; and had some difficulty to prove that he was only an absent poet, and not a spy.

The curious reader of Young's life will naturally inquire to what it was owing, that, though he lived almost forty years after he took orders, which included one whole reign uncommonly long, and part of another, he was never thought worthy of the least preferment. The author of the ' Night Thoughts ' ended his days upon a living which came to him from his college without any favour, and to which he probably had an eye when he determined on the Church. To satisfy curiosity of this kind is, at this distance of time, far from easy. The parties themselves know not often, at the instant, why they are neglected, or why they are preferred. The neglect of Young is by some ascribed to his having attached himself to the Prince of Wales, and to his having preached an offensive sermon at St. James's. It has been told me that he had two hundred a year in the late reign,[41] by the patronage of Walpole : and that, whenever any one reminded the King of Young, the only answer was, " He has a pension." All the light thrown on this inquiry by the following letter from Secker only serves to show at what a late period of life the author of the ' Night Thoughts ' solicited preferment :

" Deanery of St. Paul's, July 8, 1758.

" GOOD DR. YOUNG,—I have long wondered that more suitable notice of your great merit hath not been taken by persons in power. But how to remedy the omission I see not. No encouragement hath ever been given me to mention things of this nature to his Majesty. And therefore, in all likelihood, the only consequence of doing it would be weakening the little influence which else I may possibly have on some other occasions. Your fortune and your reputation set you above the need of advancement ; and your sentiments above that concern for it, on your own account, which, on that of the public, is sincerely felt by

" Your loving Brother,

" THO. CANT."

----

[41] See about his pension, note at pp. 313, 314.

At last, at the age of fourscore, he was appointed, in 1761, Clerk of the Closet to the Princess Dowager.[42]

One obstacle must have stood not a little in the way of that preferment after which his whole life seems to have panted. Though he took orders, he never entirely shook off politics. He was always the Lion of his master Milton, " pawing to get free his hinder parts." By this conduct, if he gained some friends, he made many enemies.

Again, Young was a poet; and again, with reverence be it spoken, poets by profession do not always make the best clergymen. If the author of the ' Night Thoughts' composed many sermons, he did not oblige the public with many.

Besides, in the latter part of life, Young was fond of holding himself out for a man retired from the world. But he seemed to have forgotten that the same verse which contains " oblitus meorum," contains also " obliviscendus et illis." The brittle chain of worldly friendship and patronage is broken as effectually when one goes beyond the length of it as when the other does. To the vessel which is sailing from the shore, it only appears that the shore also recedes; in life it is truly thus. He who retires from the world will find himself, in reality, deserted as fast, if not faster, by the world. The public is not to be treated as the coxcomb treats his mistress; to be threatened with desertion, in order to increase fondness.

Young seems to have been taken at his word. Notwithstanding his frequent complaints of being neglected, no hand was reached out to pull him from that retirement of which he declared himself enamoured. Alexander assigned no palace for the residence of Diogenes, who boasted his surly satisfaction with his tub.

Of the domestic manners and petty habits of the author of the ' Night Thoughts,' I hoped to have given you an account from the best authority: but who shall dare to say, To-morrow I will be wise or virtuous, or to-morrow I will do a particular thing? Upon inquiring for his housekeeper, I learned that

[42] The mother of George III.

she was buried two days before I reached the town of her abode.[43]

In a letter from Tscharner, a noble foreigner, to Count Haller, Tscharner says he has lately spent four days with Young at Welwyn, where the author tastes all the ease and pleasure mankind can desire. " Every thing about him shows the man, each individual being placed by rule. All is neat without art. He is very pleasant in conversation, and extremely polite."

This, and more, may possibly be true ; but Tscharner's was a first visit, a visit of curiosity and admiration, and a visit which the author expected.

Of Edward Young an anecdote which wanders among readers is not true, that he was Fielding's Parson Adams. The original of that famous painting was William Young, who was a clergyman.[44] He supported an uncomfortable existence by translating for the booksellers from Greek ; and, if he did not seem to be his own friend, was at least no man's enemy. Yet the facility with which this report has gained belief in the world argues,

---

[43] Croft was misinformed. The death at Hertford of Mrs. Hallows, the housekeeper, is chronicled in the ' Gentleman's Magazine' of May, 1790, p. 476, as a death that had lately occurred.

" I have great joy in Dr. Young, whom I disturbed in a reverie. At first he started, then bowed, then fell back into a surprise; then began a speech, relapsed into his astonishment two or three times, forgot what he had been saying; began a new subject, and so went on. I told him your Grace desired he would write longer letters; to which he cried, "Ha!" most emphatically, and I leave you to interpret what it meant. He has made a friendship with one person here, whom I believe you would not imagine to have been made for his bosom friend. You would, perhaps, suppose it was a bishop or dean, a prebend, a pious preacher, a clergyman of exemplary life; or if a layman, of most virtuous conversation, one that had paraphrased St. Matthew, or wrote comments on St. Paul. . . . You would not guess that this associate of the Doctor's was—old Cibber! Certainly, in their religious, moral, and civil character there is no relation; but in their dramatic capacity there is some. . . . The waters have raised his spirits to a fine pitch, as your Grace will imagine when I tell you how sublime an answer he made to a very vulgar question. I asked him how long he stayed at the Wells: he said, As long as my rival stayed;—as long as the sun did.—Mrs. MONTAGU (from Tunbridge Wells, in 1745) to the Duchess of Portland."

[44] This is told by Murphy in his ' Life of Fielding.' William Young was buried Sept. 3, 1757. See Lysons's ' Environs,' under ' Chelsea.'

were it not sufficiently known, that the author of the ' Night Thoughts' bore some resemblance to Adams.[45]

The attention which Young bestowed upon the perusal of books is not unworthy imitation. When any passage pleased him, he appears to have folded down the leaf. On these passages he bestowed a second reading. But the labours of man are too frequently vain. Before he returned to much of what he had once approved, he died. Many of his books, which I have seen, are by those notes of approbation so swelled beyond their real bulk, that they will hardly shut.[46]

> " What though we wade in wealth, or soar in fame?
> Earth's highest station ends in *Here he lies!*
> And *dust to dust* concludes her noblest song."

The author of these lines is not without his *Hic jacet*.

By the good sense of his son, it contains none of that praise which no marble can make the bad or the foolish merit ; which, without the direction of a stone or a turf, will find its way, sooner or later, to the deserving.

> " M. S.
> Optimi parentis
> EDWARDI YOUNG, LL.D.
> Hujus Ecclesiæ rect.
> Et Elizabethæ
> fæm. prænob.
> Conjugis ejus amantissimæ
> Pio & gratissimo animo
> Hoc marmor posuit
> F. Y.
> Filius superstes."

---

[45] His forgetfulness — anything but an affectation — was well known to his friends. Warton had heard (Pope, vii. 163) that he is the author who forgot to dine, and who was so delighted with a bladebone of mutton that he asked its name, and how to cook it. See also 'Spence by Singer,' p. 355.

[46] I have seen volumes of Dr. Young's copy of 'The Rambler,' in which he has marked the passages which he thought particularly excellent, by folding down the corner of the page; and such as he rated in a supereminent degree are marked by double folds. Johnson was pleased when told of the minute attention with which Young had signified his approbation of his Essays.— BOSWELL: *ed. Croker,* p. 67.

Is it not strange that the author of the 'Night Thoughts' has inscribed no monument to the memory of his lamented wife? Yet what marble will endure as long as the poems? [47]

Such, my good friend, is the account which I have been able to collect of the great Young. That it may be long before anything like what I have just transcribed be necessary for you is the sincere wish of,

Dear Sir,

Your greatly obliged Friend,

Herbert Croft, Jun.

Lincoln's Inn, Sept. 1780.

P. S. This account of Young was seen by you in manuscript, you know, Sir; and, though I could not prevail on you to make any alterations, you insisted on striking out one passage, because it said, that if I did not wish you to live long for your sake, I did for the sake of myself and of the world. But this postscript you will not see before the printing of it; and I will say here, in spite of you, how I feel myself honoured and bettered by your friendship; and that if I do credit to the Church, after which I always longed, and for which I am now going to give in exchange the bar, though not at so late a period of life as Young took orders, it will be owing, in no small measure, to my having had the happiness of calling the author of 'The Rambler' my friend.

H. C.[48]

Oxford, Sept. 1782.

[47] The only portrait of Young is by Highmore, and was painted for Richardson, the novelist. See account of Highmore in 'Gent.'s Mag.' for 1780.

[48] This P.S. was not in the first edition of these Lives.
"We stopped at Welwyn, where I wished much to see, in company with Johnson, the residence of the author of 'Night Thoughts,' which was then possessed by his son, Mr. Young. Here some address was requisite, for I was not acquainted with Mr. Young; and had I proposed to Dr. Johnson to send to him, he would have checked my wish, and perhaps been offended; I therefore concerted with Mr. Dilly that I should steal away from Dr. Johnson and him, and try what reception I could procure from Mr. Young. If unfavourable, nothing was to be said; but if agreeable, I should return and notify it to them. I hastened to Mr. Young's; found he was at home; sent in word that a gentleman desired to wait upon him, and was shown into a parlour, where he

OF Young's poems it is difficult to give any general character ; for he has no uniformity of manner : one of his pieces
has no great resemblance to another.   He began to write early,
and continued long ; and at different times had different modes
of poetical excellence in view.   His numbers are sometimes
smooth, and sometimes rugged ; his style is sometimes conca-
tenated, and sometimes abrupt ; sometimes diffusive, and sometimes concise.   His plan seems to have started in his mind at
the present moment, and his thoughts appear the effect of
chance, sometimes adverse, and sometimes lucky, with very little
operation of judgment.

He was not one of the writers whom experience improves,

and a young lady, his daughter, were sitting.   He appeared to be a plain, civil
country gentleman ; and when I begged pardon for presuming to trouble him,
but that I wished much to see his place, if he would give me leave, he be-
haved very courteously, and answered, ' By all means, Sir ; we are just going
to drink tea ; will you sit down ?'   I thanked him, but said that Dr. Johnson
had come with me from London, and I must return to the inn to drink tea
with him ; that my name was Boswell ; I had travelled with him in the Hebri-
des.   ' Sir,' said he, ' I should think it a great honour to see Dr. Johnson
here.   Will you allow me to send for him ?'   Availing myself of this opening,
I said that ' I would go myself ; and bring him when he had drunk tea ; he
knew nothing of my calling here.'   Having been thus successful, I hastened
back to the inn, and informed Dr. Johnson that Mr. Young, son of Dr. Young,
the author of ' Night Thoughts,' whom I had just left, desired to have the
honour of seeing him at the house where his father lived.'   Dr. Johnson luckily
made no inquiry how this invitation had arisen, but agreed to go ; and when
we entered Mr. Young's parlour, he addressed him with a very polite bow :
' Sir, I had a curiosity to come and see this place.   I had the honour to know
that great man, your father.'   We went into the garden, where we found a
gravel-walk ; on each side of which was a row of trees, planted by Dr. Young,
which formed a handsome Gothic arch.   Dr. Johnson called it a fine grove.
I beheld it with reverence.

  " He sat some time in the summer-house, on the outside wall of which was
inscribed, *Ambulantes in horto audiebant vocem Dei*, and, in reference to a brook,
by which it is situated, *Vivendi rectè qui prorogat horam*, &c.   I said to Mr.
Young that I had been told his father was cheerful.   ' Sir,' said he, ' he was
too well bred a man not to be cheerful in company ; but he was gloomy when
alone.   He never was cheerful after my mother's death, and he had met with
many disappointments.'   Dr. Johnson observed to me afterwards ' that this
was no favourable account of Dr. Young ; for it was not becoming in a man to
have so little acquiescence in the ways of Providence as to be gloomy because he has not obtained as much preferment as he expected ; nor to continue gloomy for the loss of his wife.   Grief has its time.' "—BOSWELL: *ed.
Croker*, p. 693.

and who, observing their own faults, become gradually correct. His poem on ‘ The Last Day,’ his first great performance, has an equability and propriety which he afterwards either never endeavoured or never attained.   Many paragraphs are noble, and few are mean, yet the whole is languid ; the plan is too much extended, and a succession of images divides and weakens the general conception ; but the great reason why the reader is disappointed is, that the thought of the LAST DAY makes every man more than poetical, by spreading over his mind a general obscurity of sacred horror, that oppresses distinction, and disdains expression.

His story of ‘ Jane Grey’ was never popular.   It is written with elegance enough ; but Jane is too heroic to be pitied.

‘ The Universal Passion ’ is indeed a very great performance.   It is said to be a series of epigrams ; but if it be, it is what the author intended.   His endeavour was at the production of striking distichs and pointed sentences, and his distichs have the weight of solid sentiment, and his points the sharpness of resistless truth.

His characters are often selected with discernment, and drawn with nicety ; his illustrations are often happy, and his reflections often just.   His species of satire is between those of Horace and Juvenal ; and he has the gaiety of Horace without his laxity of numbers, and the morality of Juvenal with greater variation of images.   He plays, indeed, only on the surface of life ; he never penetrates the recesses of the mind, and therefore the whole power of his poetry is exhausted by a single perusal ; his conceits please only when they surprise.[49]

To translate he never condescended, unless his ‘ Paraphrase on Job ’ may be considered as a version, in which he has not, I think, been unsuccessful : he indeed favoured himself by choosing those parts which most easily admit the ornaments of English poetry.

---

[49] Young’s Satires were in higher reputation when published than they stand at present [1776].   He seems fonder of dazzling than pleasing; of raising our admiration for his wit, than our dislike of the follies he ridicules.—GOLDSMITH: *Works by Cunningham,* iii. 439.

He had least success in his lyric attempts, in which he seems to have been under some malignant influence : he is always labouring to be great, and at last is only turgid.

In his ' Night Thoughts' he has exhibited a very wide display of original poetry, variegated with deep reflections and striking allusions, a wilderness of thought, in which the fertility of fancy scatters flowers of every hue and of every odour. This is one of the few poems in which blank verse could not be changed for rhyme but with disadvantage. The wild diffusion of the sentiments, and the digressive sallies of imagination, would have been compressed and restrained by confinement to rhyme. The excellence of this work is not exactness, but copiousness ; particular lines are not to be regarded ; the power is in the whole, and in the whole there is a magnificence like that ascribed to Chinese plantation, the magnificence of vast extent and endless diversity.

His last poem was the ' Resignation ;' in which he made, as he was accustomed, an experiment of a new mode of writing, and succeeded better than in his ' Ocean' or his ' Merchant.' It was very falsely represented as a proof of decaying faculties. There is Young in every stanza, such as he often was in his highest vigour.

His tragedies not making part of the Collection, I had forgotten, till Mr. Steevens recalled them to my thoughts by remarking that he seemed to have one favourite catastrophe, as his three plays all concluded with lavish suicide ; a method by which, as Dryden remarked, a poet easily rids his scene of persons whom he wants not to keep alive. In ' Busiris' there are the greatest ebullitions of imagination ; but the pride of Busiris is such as no other man can have, and the whole is too remote from known life to raise either grief, terror, or indignation. The ' Revenge' approaches much nearer to human practices and manners, and therefore keeps possession of the stage : the first design seems suggested by ' Othello ;' but the reflections, the incidents, and the diction are original. The moral observations are so introduced, and so expressed, as to have all the novelty that can be required. Of ' The Brothers' I may be allowed to say nothing, since nothing was ever said of it by the public.

It must be allowed of Young's poetry, that it abounds in thought, but without much accuracy or selection. When he lays hold of an illustration, he pursues it beyond expectation, sometimes happily, as in his parallel of *Quicksilver* with *Pleasure*, which I have heard repeated with approbation by a lady,[50] of whose praise he would have been justly proud, and which is very ingenious, very subtle, and almost exact; but sometimes he is less lucky, as when, in his 'Night Thoughts,' having it dropped into his mind, that the orbs, floating in space, might be called the *cluster* of creation, he thinks on a cluster of grapes, and says that they all hang on the great vine, drinking the "nectareous juice of immortal life."

His conceits are sometimes yet less valuable. In the 'Last Day' he hopes to illustrate the re-assembly of the atoms that compose the human body at the 'Trump of Doom,' by the collection of bees into a swarm at the tinkling of a pan.

The Prophet says of Tyre, that " her Merchants are Princes." Young says of Tyre in his 'Merchant,'

> " Her merchants Princes, and each *deck a Throne*."

Let burlesque try to go beyond him.

He has the trick of joining the turgid and familiar: to buy the alliance of Britain, "Climes were paid down." Antithesis is his favourite: "They for kindness hate:" and "because she's right, she's ever in the wrong."

His versification is his own; neither his blank nor his rhyming lines have any resemblance to those of former writers; he picks up no hemistichs, he copies no favourite expressions; he seems to have laid up no stores of thought or diction, but to owe all to the fortuitous suggestions of the present moment. Yet I have reason to believe that, when once he had formed a new design, he then laboured it with very patient industry, and that he composed with great labour and frequent revisions.

[50] Mrs. Thrale.

His verses are formed by no certain model; he is no more
like himself in his different productions than he is like others.
He seems never to have studied prosody, nor to have had any
direction but from his own ear. But, with all his defects, he
was a man of genius and a poet.[51]

[51] Though the strain of the 'Night Thoughts' is stamped with the strongest
mannerism, and both the matter and the manner are of a kind to affect the
reader powerfully and deeply, Blair's 'Grave' is the only poem I can call to
mind which has been composed in imitation of it.—SOUTHEY: *Cowper's Works*,
ii. 143.

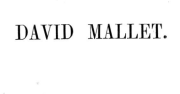

DAVID MALLET.

MALLET.

1698 ?–1765.

Born in the Highlands of Scotland — Educated at Edinburgh — Made
Tutor to the Sons of the Duke of Montrose — Visits London — Pub-
lishes ' William and Margaret,' a Ballad — Changes his name — Pub-
lishes ' The Excursion,' a Poem — Courts Pope by a Poem on ' Verbal
Criticism ' — Writes for the Stage — Made Under-Secretary to Frederick
Prince of Wales — Writes a ' Life of Bacon,' and undertakes a ' Life of
the Duke of Marlborough ' — Publishes ' Amyntor and Theodora,' a
Poem — Seeks to blacken the memory of Pope — Left Bolingbroke's
Literary Executor — His Pamphlet against Admiral Byng — Obtains
a Pension — Is twice married — Death and Burial — Works and
Character.

OF DAVID MALLET, having no written memorial, I am able
to give no other account than such as is supplied by the unauthorised loquacity of common fame, and a very slight personal
knowledge.

He was, by his original, one of the Macgregors, a clan that
became, about sixty years ago, under the conduct of Robin
Roy, so formidable and so infamous for violence and robbery
that the name was annulled by a legal abolition,[1] and when
they were all to denominate themselves anew, the father, I
suppose of this author, called himself Malloch.[2]

David Malloch was, by the penury of his parents, compelled
to be janitor of the High School at Edinburgh,[3] a mean office,

[1] Here is an error: the Clan Macgregor was outlawed long before Rob Roy's
day, by an Act of the Privy Council of James I. in 1603. See Scott's Introduction to ' Rob Roy.'

[2] The father, James Malloch, kept a small clachan, or publichouse, at Crieff,
on the borders of the Highlands, where his son David was born cir. 1698.
His mother's maiden name was Beatrix Clark.

[3] Johnson's statement is confirmed by subsequent researches (see Steven's
' History of the High School of Edinburgh,' p. 89). Mallet studied at
Aberdeen under Professor Ker; and Ker's kindness is spoken of in after-life
with thankfulness by the pupil, in a series of interesting letters, printed in
the ' European Magazine,' when under the direction of Isaac Reed. His first
situation, after leaving Aberdeen, was that of tutor to the four sons (the

of which he did not afterwards delight to hear.   But he sur-
mounted the disadvantages of his birth and fortune ; for when
[1723] the Duke of Montrose applied to the College of Edinburgh for a tutor to educate his sons, Malloch was recommended, and I never heard that he dishonoured his credentials.[4]

When his pupils were sent to see the world, they were
entrusted to his care ; and having conducted them round the
common circle of modish travels, he returned with them to
London, where, by the influence of the family in which he
resided, he naturally gained admission to many persons of the
highest rank and the highest character, to wits, nobles, and
statesmen.

Of his works, I know not whether I can trace the series.
His first production [5] was ' William and Margaret,' [6] of which,

eldest under fourteen) of a Mr. Home, near Edinburgh.   " He allows me
my learning, clothes, and diet," he writes to Ker in Oct. 1720, " but no fixed
salary."

[4] My encouragement is 30*l.*; and because the Duke's family is in England, I
am about the middle of August to depart for London, and from thence to Winchester.—MALLET to Ker, July, 1723.

[5] His first printed production was a Pastoral in the ' Miscellany ' of the
Edinburgh wits, where Thomson's poetic puerilities first appeared.   In 1721
he had completed a poem on the Transfiguration, " written," as he says to
Ker, " in imitation of Milton's style, copying his epithets, his periods, and the
elisions with which he abounds."

[6] Mallet's ' William and Margaret' was printed in Aaron Hill's ' Plain
Dealer,' No. 36, July 24, 1724.   In its original state it was very different from
what it is in the last edition of his works.—JOHNSON.

It first appeared in ' The Plain Dealer ' as the probable production of " an
Elizabethan writer; perhaps of Shakespeare himself."

This piece of serviceable flattery drew, of course, a contradiction from
Mallet.   " The gentleman is very young," writes Hill, " and received his education in the University of Edinburgh.   He possesses so sincere a modesty
that he declines being publicly named; but as he has obliged me with a letter
containing the short history of an unhappy accident which gave occasion to
his ballad, it will be an agreeable entertainment if I publish it as the author
sent it me."   As I have seen the letter nowhere save in its original publication,
I have copied it for insertion here:—

To the Plain Dealer.

SIR,—Your ' Plain Dealer' of July 24th was sent me by a friend. I must
own, after I had read it over, I was both surprised and pleased to find that a
simple tale of my writing had merited the notice and approbation of the author
of ' The Plain Dealer.'

After what you have said of ' William and Margaret,' I flatter myself that

though it contains nothing very striking or difficult, he has been envied the reputation, and plagiarism has been boldly charged, but never proved.

Not long afterwards he published 'The Excursion' (1728), a desultory and capricious view of such scenes of Nature as his

you will not be displeased with an account of the accident which gave birth to that ballad.

Your conjecture that it was founded on the real history of an unhappy woman is true. A vain young gentleman had for some time professed love to a lady then in the spring of her life and beauty. He dressed well, spoke loud, and talked nonsense with spirit. She had good understanding; but was too young to know the world. I have seen her very often. There was a lively innocence in her look. She had never been addressed to by a man of sense, and therefore knew not how despicable and unsincere a fool is. In time he persuaded her there was merit in his passion—she believed him, and was undone.

She was upon the point of bringing into the world the effect of her ill-placed love before her father knew the misfortune. Judge the sentiments of the good old man! Yet his affection outweighed his anger. He could not think of abandoning his child to want and infamy. He applied himself to her false lover with an offer of half his fortune; but the temper of the betrayer was savaged with cruel insolence. He rejected the father's offers, and reproached the innocence he had ruined with the bitterness of open scorn. The news was brought her when in a weak condition, and cast her into a fever; and in a few days after I saw her and her child laid in one grave together.

It was some time after this that I chanced to look into a comedy of Fletcher's, called 'The Knight of the Burning Pestle.' The place I fell upon was where old Merrythought repeats these verses:—

> When it was grown to dark midnight,
>   And all were fast asleep,
> In came Margaret's grimly ghost,
>   And stood at William's feet,

which I fancy was the beginning of some ballad commonly known at the time this author wrote. These lines, naked of ornament, and simple as they are, struck my fancy; I closed the book, and bethought myself that the unhappy adventure I have mentioned above, which then came fresh into my mind, might naturally raise a tale upon the appearance of this ghost. It was then midnight. All round me was still and quiet. These concurring circumstances worked my soul to a powerful melancholy. I could not sleep. And at that time I finished my little poem, such as you see it here. If it continues still to deserve your approbation, I have my aim, and am,

Sir,

Your most obliged and most humble servant,

[D. MALLOCH.]

— *Plain Dealer* of Aug. 28, 1724. The ballad enclosed was the correct copy, such, I believe, as it is to be found with his 'Excursion' and collected Works.

fancy led him, or his knowledge enabled him, to describe.[7] It is not devoid of poetical spirit. Many of the images are striking, and many of the paragraphs are elegant. The cast of diction seems to be copied from Thomson, whose 'Seasons' were then in their full blossom of reputation. He has Thomson's beauties and his faults.

His poem on 'Verbal Criticism' (April, 1733) was written to pay court to Pope,[8] on a subject which he either did not understand or willingly misrepresented; and is little more than an improvement, or rather expansion, of a fragment which

[7] His letters to Ker throw some light on the history of 'The Excursion.' "I have now finished," he says (May, 1727), "and am preparing for the press against winter, a poem in two books, which I began last year in the country. The first book has been perused by Mr. Molyneux, the Prince's Secretary; by Mr. Hill, Dr. Young, &c. It is now in the hands of Mr. Dennis; and as soon as that dread critic has condemned or approved of it, I shall wait on you by the way of Edinburgh. I will try the town with this before I venture out a tragedy that I have been long meditating."

By the July of the same year, it appears that Dennis had approved of it by letter, and that Mallet had sold it for twenty-five guineas. He was long in suspense to whom he should dedicate it. He had thought of the Duke of Dorset and the Earl of Scarborough, while it was yet in embryo; but since it had met with so much approbation in manuscript, he was preparing a dedication to the King, hoping by the influence of Molyneux and Montrose to gain an opportunity of introduction at Court.

[8] Pope procured him the situation of travelling tutor to the son of his friend and correspondent, Mrs. Newsham; an office of five years' continuance, spent in travelling abroad with profit and without expense.

"To prove to you how little essential to friendship I hold letter-writing, I have not yet written to Mr. Mallet, whom I love and esteem greatly; nay, whom I know to have as tender a heart, and that feels a friendly remembrance as long as any man. Pray send him the enclosed; 'tis all I can say, for (as I told you before) it makes me quite sick to be put upon the pikes, to be saying such things as can only be felt, not said."—Pope to Mrs. Newsham.

"May I never hope for the pleasure of hearing from you that you are well, and have not forgot me? By saying just that, and no more, you will give me the most agreeable piece of news I can receive or you yourself send. Believe me, I am in no treaty with Curll to furnish him any letters for his second volume. If he has no more influence with the clerks of the Post Office than with me, yours will come very safe, as it will be most welcome to,

"Dear Sir, your most affectionate, faithful servant,

"D. Mallet.

"P.S. Mr. N. is extremely your humble servant; and we beg leave to send by you a thousand good wishes to Mrs. Blount for the continuance of her good humour and good health."—Mallet to Pope. 'Gent.'s Mag.' for Oct. 1835.

Pope printed in a Miscellany long before he engrafted it into a regular poem.   There is in this piece more pertness than wit, and more confidence than knowledge.   The versification is tolerable, nor can criticism allow it a higher praise.

His first tragedy was 'Eurydice,' acted at Drury Lane in 1731, of which I know not the reception nor the merit, but have heard it mentioned as a mean performance.   He was not then too high to accept a prologue and epilogue from Aaron Hill, neither of which can be much commended.[9]

Having cleared his tongue from his native pronunciation so as to be no longer distinguished as a Scot,[10] he seems inclined to disencumber himself from all adherences of his original, and took upon him to change his name from Scotch *Malloch* to English *Mallet*, without any imaginable reason of preference which the eye or ear can discover.[11]   What other proofs he gave of disrespect to his native country, I know not ; but it was remarked of him, that he was the only Scot whom Scotchmen did not commend.[12]

[9] 'Eurydice' was published by Millar in the March of the same year, with a dedication to the Duke of Montrose.   Of the success of the performance or the publication, I am as ignorant as Johnson.   It occasioned, however, a sixpenny pamphlet of criticism, entitled 'Remarks on the Tragedy of Eurydice.'

I have seen a letter from Mallet to Andrew Millar, in which he says (22nd Aug. 1757), " If it ['Eurydice'] is not now the best play that has ever appeared in my time, the author and it ought to be buried together."

[10] Sir, when people watch me narrowly, and I do not watch myself, they will find me out to be of a particular county.   In the same manner Dunning may be found out to be a Devonshire man.   So most Scotchmen may be found out.   But, Sir, little aberrations are of no disadvantage.   I never catched Mallet in a Scotch accent; and yet Mallet, I suppose, was past five-and twenty before he came to London.—JOHNSON : *Boswell by Croker*, p. 232.

[11] In the octavo Abridgment of his Dictionary, published in 1756, Johnson has given, under the article *Alias*, ' Mallet alias Malloch.'   (See ' Boswell by Croker,' p. 730.)

The change occurred in 1726; for the verses to Thomson in this year are signed *Malloch*, while his name is found among the subscribers to Savage's Miscellany of the same year as *Mallet*.   He had thought of this renouncement of name as early as September, 1724.   " My cousin Paton," he says to Ker, " would have me write my name *Mallet*, for there is not one Englishman that can pronounce it."

Johnson was evidently ignorant of the proper pronunciation.   To a Scottish ear there is a considerable difference of name between *Mallock* and *Malloch*, and to an English ear, when pronounced by a Scot, a difference in sound.

[12] " This volume of Gascoigne's Works was bought for 1*l*. 13*s*. at Mr. Mallet's,

About this time Pope, whom he visited familiarly, published his 'Essay on Man,' but concealed the author; and when Mallet entered one day, Pope asked him slightly what there was new. Mallet told him that the newest piece was something called an 'Essay on Man,' which he had inspected idly, and seeing the utter inability of the author, who had neither skill in writing nor knowledge of his subject, had tossed it away. Pope, to punish his self-conceit, told him the secret.[13]

A new edition of the works of Bacon being prepared (1740) for the press, Mallet was employed to prefix a Life, which he has written with elegance, perhaps with some affectation; but with so much more knowledge of history than of science, that when he afterwards undertook the Life of Marlborough, Warburton remarked that he might perhaps forget that Marlborough was a general, as he had forgotten that Bacon was a philosopher.

When [1737] the Prince of Wales was driven from the palace, and setting himself at the head of the Opposition, kept a separate court, he endeavoured to increase his popularity by the patronage of literature, and made [June, 1742] Mallet his under-secretary, with a salary of two hundred pounds a year. Thomson likewise had a pension, and they were associated in the composition of the masque of 'Alfred,' which in its original state was played at Cliefden in 1740; it was afterwards almost wholly changed by Mallet, and brought upon the stage at Drury Lane in 1751, but with no great success.

Mallet, in a familiar conversation with Garrick, discoursing of the diligence which he was then exerting upon the 'Life of Marlborough,' let him know that in the series of great men, quickly to be exhibited, he should *find a niche* for the hero of the theatre. Garrick professed to wonder by what artifice he could be introduced, but Mallet let him know that, by a dexterous anticipation, he should fix him in a conspicuous place.

alias Mallock's, alias M'Gregor's sale, March 14, 1776. He was the only Scotchman who died in my memory unlamented by an individual of his own nation."—GEO. STEEVENS (Book sold at Heber's sale).

[13] This story is first told in Ayre's 'Life of Pope' (2 vols. 12mo. 1745), but without naming Mallet.

"Mr. Mallet," says Garrick, in his gratitude of exultation, " have you left off to write for the stage ?"   Mallet then confessed that he had a drama in his hands.   Garrick promised to act it, and ' Alfred ' was produced.

The long retardation of the Life of the Duke of Marlborough shows, with strong conviction, how little confidence can be placed in posthumous renown.   When he died, it was soon determined that his story should be delivered to posterity ; and the papers supposed to contain the necessary information were delivered to the Lord Molesworth, who had been his favourite in Flanders. When Molesworth died, the same papers were transferred with the same design to Sir Richard Steele, who, in some of his exigencies, put them in pawn.   They then remained with the old Duchess, who in her will assigned the task to Glover and Mallet, with a reward of a thousand pounds, and a prohibition to insert any verses.   Glover rejected, I suppose, with disdain the legacy,[14] and devolved the whole work upon Mallet, who had from the late Duke of Marlborough [died 1758] a pension to promote his industry, and who talked of the discoveries which he had made, but left not, when he died, any historical labours behind him.

While he was in the Prince's service he published [1739] ' Mustapha,' with a prologue by Thomson, not mean, but far inferior to that which he had received from Mallet for ' Agamemnon.'   The epilogue, said to be written by a friend, was composed in haste by Mallet, in the place of one promised, which was never given.   This tragedy was dedicated to the Prince his master.   It was acted at Drury Lane in 1739, and was well received, but was never revived.[15]

[14] Glover, in his ' Memoirs ' (p. 57), regrets that the " capricious restrictions of the will compelled him to reject the undertaking."   He alludes to the power vested in Lord Chesterfield of revising the whole.

[15] ' Mustapha ' was acted fourteen nights, and was attended by the whole of the Opposition.   Its success as a party piece was complete.

" The pit [the first night] was before five o'clock filled with gentlemen who made a very polite appearance, and were mostly of the Scots nation. . . . The whole play was acted without one hiss or mark of dislike. . . . The best description and the most moving distress passed in silence, while any casual expression which was capable of being interpreted into a meaning unintended,

In 1740 he produced, as has been already mentioned, the masque of ' Alfred,' in conjunction with Thomson.

For some time afterwards he lay at rest.   After a long interval, his next work was ' Amyntor and Theodora ' (1747), a long story in blank verse ; in which it cannot be denied that there is copiousness and elegance of language, vigour of sentiment, and imagery well adapted to take possession of the fancy. But it is blank verse.   This he sold to Vaillant for one hundred and twenty pounds.[16]   The first sale was not great, and it is now lost in forgetfulness.[17]

Mallet, by address or accident, perhaps by his dependence on the Prince, found his way to Bolingbroke ; a man whose pride and petulance made his kindness difficult to gain, or keep, and whom Mallet was content to court by an act which, I hope, was unwillingly performed.   When it was found [1744] that Pope had clandestinely printed an unauthorised pamphlet, called ' The Patriot King,' Bolingbroke, in a fit of useless fury, resolved to blast his memory, and employed Mallet (1749) as the executioner of his vengeance.   Mallet had not virtue, or had not spirit, to refuse the office ; and was rewarded, not long after [1751], with the legacy of Lord Bolingbroke's works.

Many of the political pieces had been written during the opposition to Walpole, and given to Francklin, as he supposed, in perpetuity.   These, among the rest, were claimed by the will. The question was referred to arbitrators ; but when they decided against Mallet, he refused to yield to the award, and by the

I believe, by the author met with the loudest applauses."—*Scots Magazine* for 1739, vol. i. p. 88.

[16] ' Amyntor and Theodora, or the Hermit.'   A Poem in Three Cantos. London: printed for Paul Vaillant in the Strand, 1747, 4to.

It appeared anonymously, with a dedication to the Earl of Chesterfield, who, before Mallet's ' Truth in Rhyme,' affixed the following:—

> It has no faults, or I no faults can spy;
> It has all beauty, or all blindness I.
>
> *Imprimatur :* Chesterfield.

[17] Vaillant advertised it as Entered at Stationers' Hall, and added in his advertisement that he would prosecute any one who pirated it.   For this poem Mallet received from Vaillant 120 guineas (Warton's ' Pope,' ix. 134).   It was published in May, 1747, price 3s. 6d.

help of Millar, the bookseller, published all that he could find, but with success very much below his expectation.[18]

In 1755, his masque of 'Britannia' was acted at Drury Lane, and his tragedy of 'Elvira' in 1763;[19] in which year he was appointed keeper of the Book of Entries for ships in the port of London.[20]

In the beginning of the last war,[21] when the nation was exasperated by ill success, he was employed to turn the public vengeance upon Byng, and wrote a letter of accusation under the character of a 'Plain Man.' The paper was with great industry circulated and dispersed; and he, for his seasonable intervention, had a considerable pension bestowed upon him, which he retained to his death.[22]

[18] The day of publication was the day of the death of Mr. Pelham, and occasioned an epigram by Garrick. Johnson's famous saying about the scoundrel and coward and the beggarly Scotchman is one of the best remembered, as it was certainly the first, in print of his many memorable sayings. (See 'Boswell by Croker,' p. 88, and 'Goldsmith's Works' by Cunningham, vol. iv. p. 179.)

[19] 'Elvira' was dedicated to the Earl of Bute, and was attacked by three Scotchmen in an octavo pamphlet, entitled 'Critical Strictures on the New Tragedy of "Elvira," written by Mr. David Malloch. London: printed for W. Flexney, near Gray's-Inn, Holborn, 1763,' with this prefatory "*Advertisement:*"—"We have followed the authority of Sir David Dalrymple and Mr. Samuel Johnson in the orthography of Mr. Malloch's name, as we imagine the Decision of these gentlemen will have more weight in the world of letters than even that of the said Mr. Malloch himself." This pamphlet (it has little wit) was written by the Honourable Andrew Erskine, George Dempster, and James Boswell. (See 'Boswell by Croker,' p. 139.)

[20] Worth 400*l.* a-year.

> Next Mallet came; Mallet who knows each art
> The ear to tickle and to soothe the heart;
> Who with a goose-quill, like a magic rod,
> Transforms a Scottish peer into a god.
> Oh! matchless Mallet, by one stroke to clear,
> One lucky stroke, four hundred pounds a-year.
> Long round a court poor Gay dependent hung
> (And yet most trimly has the poet sung),
> Twice six revolving years vain hoping pass'd,
> And unrewarded went away at last.
>
> SHAW: *The Race*, 1766.

The Scottish peer was the Earl of Bute.

[21] The war of 1756.

[22] TO LORD ANSON.

Wimpole, Oct. 10th, 1756.

MY DEAR LORD,—I have taken the opportunity of the Marquis of Rockingham's

Towards the end of his life he went with his wife to France ;[23] but after a while, finding his health declining, he returned alone to England, and died in April, 1765.[24]

He was twice married, and by his first wife had several children.[25] One daughter, who married an Italian of rank, named Cilesia, wrote a tragedy, called 'Almida,' which was acted at Drury Lane.[26] His second wife was the daughter of a noble-

doing me the honour of a visit, to return (by his servant) to Mr. Cleveland the *manuscript* of Mr. Mallet's pamphlet. I had read it quite through, and, upon the whole, cannot find much fault with it, though I must own I am not much enamoured with it. But this *entre nous*, for authors of this kind must not be discouraged by too much criticism. However, I have ventured to put down in the enclosed sheet of paper some remarks and queries, which I desire your Lordship will take the trouble to peruse, and to consider whether you think any of them improper, especially in what relates to maritime affairs and dispositions. Whatever you shall disapprove in this paper of mine, I desire you will strike out, and then deliver it to Mr. Cleveland, with my request to him to copy it over fair, and forthwith send such copy to Mr. Mallet, keeping my original. My reason (which I will tell your Lordship) for taking this method is, that I am not fond of giving a handle to be named as a joint author with this gentleman; but I have writ him a very civil letter, wherein I have informed him that he will very soon receive such a paper from Mr. Cleveland. I have also modestly suggested to him to add something further, by way of observation and argument, upon the points of conduct chiefly objected to, for in that part I suspect the performance to be chiefly deficient.

Ever yours,

—(Barrow's 'Anson,' 8vo., 1839.) HARDWICKE.

[23] His last dirty work was in the famous Hamilton and Douglas case:— "Know, then, that there is not a retailer of gingerbread nuts, a vender of brandy by the gill, or of mellow apples by the dozen, a dresser of bullock's liver for the Savoyards, or a washer of their linen shirts when shirts they have, from one end of the Faubourg St. Antoine to the other, with whom I am not particularly acquainted; for such, my Lord, are the marvellous engines with which the House of Hamilton is attempting to overturn that of Douglas."— MALLET to Lord Bathurst, Paris, Dec. 16, 1764 (MS.).

[24] By his will, dated 20th June, 1755, he leaves his wife Lucy Mallet his sole executrix. He was buried 27th April, 1765, I believe, at Putney, where he had long resided.

[25] 7th Oct., 1742, David Mallet, Esq., Under-Secretary to the Prince of Wales, to Miss Lucy Elstob.—*Gent.'s Mag.* for 1742, p. 546. This, I suspect, was his *second* wife.

[26] Mallet's widow, I hear, sets out on her return to France very soon; and, having despatched her daughter down to Scotland, there remains nothing in this country that can deprive the *beaux esprits* of Paris of the company of that unparalleled lady.—Bp. DOUGLAS to D. Hume, London, June 25, 1765: *Letters of Eminent Persons addressed to D. Hume,* 8vo. 1849, p. 20.

man's steward, who had a considerable fortune, which she took care to retain in her own hands.[27]

His stature was diminutive, but he was regularly formed; his appearance, till he grew corpulent, was agreeable, and he suffered it to want no recommendation that dress could give it. His conversation was elegant and easy.[28] The rest of his character may, without injury to his memory, sink into silence.[29]

As a writer, he cannot be placed in any high class. There is no species of composition in which he was eminent. His Dramas had their day, a short day, and are forgotten: his blank verse seems to my ear the echo of Thomson. His 'Life

[27] Mr. Mallet and his lady appeared to all the world to be the happiest couple in it, and I desire to have no doubt that they really were what they wished the world should think them. However, Mrs. Mallet to her excessive love joined the most consummate prudence. Every shilling of her fortune, which amounted to seven or eight thousand pounds, she settled upon herself; but then she took all imaginable care that Mr. Mallet should appear like a gentleman of distinction, and, from her great kindness, she always purchased everything that he wore: hat, stockings, coat, waistcoat, &c., were all of her own choice, as well as at her own cost ; and such was the warmth of her fondness, that she took care all the world should know the pains she bestowed on her husband's dress.—T. DAVIES: *Life of Garrick*, ii. 47.

[28] Mr. Mallet, a name among the English poets, is praised by an unforgiving enemy for the ease and elegance of his conversation, and his wife was not destitute of wit or learning.—GIBBON: *Autobiography.*

When Gibbon's father removed him from Oxford, he carried him to the house of his friend and neighbour at Putney—Mallet, "by whose philosophy," the future historian records, " I was rather scandalised than reclaimed." Gibbon attended the rehearsal and first night of Mallet's last play, and has left a long account of it in his journal.

" He [Johnson] said that Mallet was the prettiest dressed puppet about town, and always kept good company. That, from his way of talking, he saw, and always said, that he had not written any part of the Life of the Duke of Marlborough, though perhaps he intended to do it at some time, in which case he was not culpable in taking the pension."—JOHNSON: *Boswell by Croker*, p. 321.

" Mr. Mallet's favourite dress was a suit of black velvet."—T. DAVIES: *Life of Garrick*, ii. 47.

[29] " Mallet's boasts, however, should not, I imagine, have much effect with those who know him; for, from the knowledge I have of him, I feel an unaccountable propensity to believe the contrary of what he tells me. His conduct as commissioner has not at all belied the opinion you had of him. In one respect we have a little improved; we have made him less impertinent; but I can't boast that we have made him more candid."—ALEX. WEDDERBURN (Lord Loughborough) to D. Hume, Paris, 28th Oct., 1764.

of Bacon' is known as it is appended to Bacon's volumes, but is no longer mentioned. His works are such as a writer, bustling in the world, showing himself in public, and emerging occasionally from time to time into notice, might keep alive by his personal influence; but which, conveying little information and giving no great pleasure, must soon give way, as the succession of things produces new topics of conversation and other modes of amusement.[30]

---

[30] "Mallet had talents enough to keep his literary reputation alive as long as he himself lived; and that, let me tell you, is a good deal."—JOHNSON: *Boswell by Croker*, p. 257.

If Johnson had been fond of ballads, he could have said a word in favour of Mallet's 'Edwin and Emma,' 1760 (4to. Baskerville); but Johnson did not care for ballads. In his 'Life of Tickell' he is silent about 'Colin and Lucy.'

MARK AKENSIDE.

AKENSIDE.

1721–1770.

Born at Newcastle-on-Tyne — Educated at Edinburgh and Leyden — Determines to study Physic — Publishes ' The Pleasures of Imagination' — His Quarrel with Warburton — Writes a Poem against Pulteney — Publishes a volume of Odes — Mr. Dyson's friendship for him — His small practice as a physician — Death, and Burial in St. James's Church, Piccadilly, London.

MARK AKENSIDE was born on the 9th of November, 1721, at Newcastle-upon-Tyne. His father Mark was a butcher, of the Presbyterian sect ; his mother's name was Mary Lumsden.[1] He received the first part of his education at the grammar-school of Newcastle, and was afterwards instructed by Mr. Wilson, who kept a private academy.

At the age of eighteen he was sent to Edinburgh, that he might qualify himself for the office of a dissenting minister, and received some assistance from the fund which the Dissenters employ in educating young men of scanty fortune. But a wider view of the world opened other scenes and prompted other hopes : he determined to study physic, and repaid that contribution, which, being received for a different purpose, he justly thought it dishonourable to retain.

Whether, when he resolved not to be a dissenting minister, he ceased to be a Dissenter, I know not. He certainly retained an unnecessary and outrageous zeal for what he called and thought liberty ; a zeal which sometimes disguises from the world, and not rarely from the mind which it possesses, an envious desire of plundering wealth or degrading greatness, and of which the immediate tendency is innovation and anarchy, an

---

[1] "1710, August 10.—Mark Akenside and Mary Lumsden. Mar."—Register of St. Nicholas, Newcastle. ('Biographical Notice of Akenside,' by Robert White, p. 1.) His father wrote his name Akinside, and so did his son till he became distinguished.

impetuous eagerness to subvert and confound, with very little care what shall be established.[2]

Akenside was one of those poets who have felt very early the motions of genius, and one of those students who have very early stored their memories with sentiments and images. Many of his performances were produced in his youth;[3] and his greatest work, 'The Pleasures of Imagination,' appeared in 1744.[4] I have heard Dodsley, by whom it was published, relate, that when the copy was offered him, the price demanded for it, which was an hundred and twenty pounds, being such as he was not inclined to give precipitately, he carried the work to Pope, who, having looked into it, advised him not to make a niggardly offer, for "this was no every-day writer."[5]

---

[2] Akenside, when a student at Edinburgh, was a member of the Medical Society, then recently formed, and was eminently distinguished by the eloquence which he displayed in the course of the debates. Dr. Robertson (who was at that time a student of divinity in the same university) told me that he was frequently led to attend their meetings chiefly to hear the speeches of Akenside, the great object of whose ambition then was a seat in Parliament; a situation which he was sanguine enough to flatter himself he had some prospect of obtaining, and for which he conceived his talents to be much better adapted than for the profession he had chosen. In this opinion he was probably in the right, as he was generally considered by his fellow-students as far inferior in medical science to several of his companions.—DUGALD STEWART: *Elem. of the Phil. of the Human Mind*, iii. 501.

[3] He was very young when he became a poet in print, many of his boyish verses appearing in the pages of 'The Gentleman's Magazine.' One of his first attempts is in the number of that periodical for April, 1737, and is called 'The Virtuoso, in imitation of Spenser's Style and Stanza.' The letter with which it was sent, signed "Marcus," pleads excuse for its defects, as "the performance of one in his sixteenth year." This is not a common poem; but it is very unlike the style, though written in the stanza, of Spenser.

Akenside's next communication was in the August of 1738; 'A British Philippic, occasioned by the Insults of the Spaniards, and the present Preparations for War.' This noble-spirited poem, as it is called by Sylvanus Urban, is too near an echo of the 'Britannia' of Thomson; but it is no everyday cento; and so it was thought by Cave, who printed it at the same time in a sixpenny folio. "If the ingenious author," says Cave, "will inform us how we may direct a packet to his hands, we will send him our acknowledgments for so great a favour with a parcel of the folio edition."

[4] The poem appeared anonymously; and a scribbler of the name of Rolt went over to Dublin, published an edition of it as his own work, and lived for some months at the best tables on the fame which it brought him. (See Boswell by Croker, p. 121.) Akenside vindicated his right by publishing an edition with his name.

[5] What was thought of the new poet and his poem by some men of genius

In 1741 he went to Leyden in pursuit of medical knowledge, and three years afterwards (May 16, 1744) became doctor of physic, having, according to the custom of the Dutch Universities, published a thesis or dissertation. The subject which he chose was 'The Original and Growth of the Human Fœtus;' in which he is said to have departed, with great judgment, from the opinion then established, and to have delivered that which has been since confirmed and received.

Akenside was a young man, warm with every notion that by nature or accident had been connected with the sound of liberty,[6] and by an eccentricity which such dispositions do not easily avoid, a lover of contradiction, and no friend to anything established. He adopted Shaftesbury's foolish assertion of the efficacy of ridicule for the discovery of truth. For this he was attacked by Warburton, and defended by Dyson:[7] Warburton afterwards reprinted his remarks at the end of his dedication to the Freethinkers.

The result of all the arguments which have been produced in a long and eager discussion of this idle question may easily be collected. If ridicule be applied to any position as the test of truth, it will then become a question whether such ridicule be just; and this can only be decided by the application of truth as the test of ridicule. Two men fearing, one a real and the other a fancied danger, will be for a while equally exposed to the inevitable consequences of cowardice, contemptuous censure, and ludicrous representation; and the true state of both cases

of the time is painful to tell.   Three have left their opinions in writing. Gray thought it above mediocrity, now and then rising to the best, particularly in description, that it was often obscure, and at times unintelligible. "I have read 'The Pleasures of Imagination,'" writes Ambrose Philips; "there are in it frequent obscurities, and it glares too much." "There is a poem of this season," writes Shenstone, "called 'The Pleasures of Imagination,' worth your reading; but it is an expensive quarto: if it comes out in a less size, I will bring it home with me."

[6] Smollett ridiculed him (1751) in 'Peregrine Pickle' as the republican doctor; the purveyor of the inimitable dinner in the manner of the ancients. To complete the likeness, he has made him quote himself. (Compare 'Per. Pickle,' ii. 248, ed. 1751, and Akenside's note on his 'Ode to the Earl of Huntingdon.')

[7] Dyson's defence was an anonymous 'Epistle;' in which I think with Mr. Dyce, that there is more of Akenside than Dyson.

must be known before it can be decided whose terror is rational,
and whose is ridiculous—who is to be pitied, and who to be
despised. Both are for a while equally exposed to laughter,
but both are not therefore equally contemptible.

In the revisal of his poem, which he died before he had
finished, he omitted the lines which had given occasion to
Warburton's objections.

He published, soon after his return from Leyden (1745), his
first collection of odes; and was impelled by his rage of patriotism to write [1744] a very acrimonious epistle to Pulteney,
whom he stigmatizes, under the name of Curio, as the betrayer
of his country.[8]

Being now to live by his profession, he first commenced
[1744] physician at Northampton, where Dr. Stonehouse then
practised, with such reputation and success, that a stranger was
not likely to gain ground upon him. Akenside tried the con-

---

[8] Akenside's share in 'Dodsley's Museum,' and the remuneration he re-
ceived from Dodsley for his services in that work, have escaped his biographers.
All that Mr. Dyce says on the subject is as follows:—"He also contributed to
Dodsley's excellent periodical publication, 'The Museum, or Literary and
Historical Register,' several prose papers, which deserve to be reprinted."
The following document is in Akenside's handwriting, and is here printed
from the original in my possession:—

Jany. 20, 1745-6.

Dr. Akinside engages to Mr. Dodsley for six months, commencing the 25th
of March next,

To prepare and have ready for the press once a fortnight, one Essay, whenever necessary for carrying on a work to be called The Museum. And also

To prepare and have ready for the press once a fortnight an account of the
most considerable books in English, Latin, French, or Italian, which have been
lately published, and which Mr. Dodsley shall furnish: and the said Account
of Books shall be so much in quantity as along with the Essay above mentioned may fill a sheet and a half in small pica, whenever so much is necessary
for carrying on the said design.

Dr. Akinside also engages to supervise the whole, and to correct the press
of his own part—On condition

That Mr. Dodsley shall pay to Dr. Akinside fifty pounds on or before the
27th of September next.

'Tis also agreed that so long as Mr. Dodsley thinks proper to continue the
Paper, and so long as Dr. Akinside consents to manage it, the Terms above
mentioned shall remain in force, and not less than an hundred pounds per
annum be offered by Mr. Dodsley, nor more insisted on by Dr. Akinside,
as witness our hands.

MARK AKINSIDE.
ROBT. DODSLEY.

test awhile ; and having deafened the place with clamours for
liberty, removed [1747] to Hampstead, where he resided more
than two years, and then fixed himself in London,[9] the proper
place for a man of accomplishments like his.

At London he was known as a poet, but was still to make his
way as a physician ; and would perhaps have been reduced to
great exigencies, but that Mr. Dyson,[10] with an ardour of
friendship that has not many examples, allowed him three
hundred pounds a-year. Thus supported, he advanced gradually in medical reputation, but never attained any great
extent of practice, or eminence of popularity. A physician in
a great city seems to be the mere plaything of Fortune ; his
degree of reputation is, for the most part, totally casual : they
that employ him know not his excellence ; they that reject him
know not his deficience. By any acute observer, who had looked
on the transactions of the medical world for half a century, a
very curious book might be written on the ' Fortune of
Physicians.'

Akenside appears not to have been wanting to his own success : he placed himself in view by all the common methods ;[11]
he became [1753] a Fellow of the Royal Society ; he obtained
a degree at Cambridge, and was admitted [1754] into the
College of Physicians ; he wrote little poetry, but published,
from time to time, medical essays and observations ; he became
[1759] Physician to St. Thomas's Hospital ; he read [1755] the
Gulstonian Lectures in Anatomy ; but began to give, for the
Croonian Lecture, a history of the revival of Learning, from
which he soon desisted ; and, in conversation, he very eagerly
forced himself into notice by an ambitious ostentation of elegance
and literature.[12]

His Discourse on the Dysentery (1764) was considered as a

[9] In Bloomsbury Square.

[10] Jeremiah Dyson, Esq., of Stoke, near Guildford, in Surrey, many years
Secretary to the Treasury. Akenside obtained his acquaintance in Edinburgh,
where Dyson was studying law, and Akenside was studying physic. He died
Sept. 16, 1776.

[11] He was, it is said, somewhat harsh and unfeeling in his treatment of hospital patients, and made but little way either with the poor or the rich.

[12] Of all our poets, perhaps, Akenside was the best Greek scholar since
Milton.—Jos. WARTON: *Essay on Pope*, ii. 386, ed. 1782.

very conspicuous specimen of Latinity, which entitled him to
the same height of place among the scholars as he possessed
before among the wits ; and he might perhaps have risen to a
greater elevation of character, but that his studies were ended
with his life, by a putrid fever, June 23, 1770, in the forty-
ninth year of his age.[13]

AKENSIDE is to be considered as a didactic and lyric poet.
His great work is the 'Pleasures of Imagination ;' a performance
which, published as it was at the age of twenty-three, raised
expectations that were not very amply satisfied. It has undoubtedly a just claim to very particular notice, as an example
of great felicity of genius, and uncommon amplitude of acquisitions, of a young mind stored with images, and much exercised
in combining and comparing them.

With the philosophical or religious tenets of the author I have
nothing to do ; my business is with his poetry. The subject is
well chosen, as it includes all images that can strike or please,
and thus comprises every species of poetical delight. The only
difficulty is in the choice of examples and illustrations ; and it is
not easy in such exuberance of matter to find the middle point
between penury and satiety. The parts seem artificially disposed, with sufficient coherence, so as that they cannot change
their places without injury to the general design.

His images are displayed with such luxuriance of expression,
that they are hidden, like Butler's Moon, by a 'Veil of Light ;'
they are forms fantastically lost under superfluity of dress.
Pars minima est ipsa puella sui. The words are multiplied till
the sense is hardly perceived ; attention deserts the mind, and
settles in the ear. The reader wanders through the gay dif-

[13] By his will, dated 6th December, 1767, he left his "whole estate and
effects of whatever kind" to his friend Mr. Dyson. He died at his house in
Burlington Street, and was buried in the church of St. James', Piccadilly;
but his grave remains unmarked to this day.

"That 'Akenside when he walked in the streets looked for all the world like
one of his own Alexandrines set upright' was a saying of Henderson the actor,
for which I am indebted to a true poet of our own day, Mr. Rogers, who heard
it repeated many years ago."—DYCE: *Appendix to his Life of Akenside.*

The only portrait of Akenside is a characteristic profile by Arthur Pond,
drawn 1754, and engraved by E. Fisher 1772.

fusion, sometimes amazed, and sometimes delighted; but, after many turnings in the flowery labyrinth, comes out as he went in. He remarked little, and laid hold on nothing.

To his versification justice requires that praise should not be denied. In the general fabrication of his lines he is perhaps superior to any other writer of blank-verse; his flow is smooth, and his pauses are musical; but the concatenation of his verses is commonly too long continued, and the full close does not recur with sufficient frequency. The sense is carried on through a long intertexture of complicated clauses, and as nothing is distinguished, nothing is remembered.

The exemption which blank-verse affords from the necessity of closing the sense with the couplet betrays luxuriant and active minds into such self-indulgence, that they pile image upon image, ornament upon ornament, and are not easily persuaded to close the sense at all. Blank-verse will therefore, I fear, be too often found in description exuberant, in argument loquacious, and in narration tiresome.

His diction is certainly poetical as it is not prosaic, and elegant as it is not vulgar. He is to be commended as having fewer artifices of disgust than most of his brethren of the blank song. He rarely either recalls old phrases or twists his metre into harsh inversions. The sense however of his words is strained, when "he views the Ganges from Alpine heights;" that is, from mountains like the Alps. And the pedant surely intrudes (but when was blank-verse without pedantry?) when he tells how "Planets *absolve* the stated round of Time."

It is generally known to the readers of poetry that he intended to revise and augment this work, but died before he had completed his design. The reformed work as he left it, and the additions which he had made, are very properly retained in the late Collection. He seems to have somewhat contracted his diffusion; but I know not whether he has gained in closeness what he has lost in splendour. In the additional book, the 'Tale of Solon' is too long.

One great defect of his poem is very properly censured by Mr. Walker,[14] unless it may be said in his defence, that what

---

[14] 'Exercises for Improvement in Elocution,' p. 66.—JOHNSON.

he has omitted was not properly in his plan. "His picture of man is grand and beautiful, but unfinished. The immortality of the soul, which is the natural consequence of the appetites and powers she is invested with, is scarcely once hinted throughout the poem. This deficiency is amply supplied by the masterly pencil of Dr. Young; who, like a good philosopher, has invincibly proved the immortality of man, from the grandeur of his conceptions, and the meanness and misery of his state; for this reason, a few passages are selected from the 'Night Thoughts,' which, with those from Akenside, seem to form a complete view of the powers, situation, and end of man."

His other poems are now to be considered; but a short consideration will dispatch them. It is not easy to guess why he addicted himself so diligently to lyric poetry, having neither the ease and airiness of the lighter, nor the vehemence and elevation of the grander ode. When he lays his ill-fated hand upon his harp, his former powers seem to desert him; he has no longer his luxuriance of expression, nor variety of images. His thoughts are cold, and his words inelegant. Yet such was his love of lyrics, that, having written with great vigour and poignancy his 'Epistle to Curio,' he transformed it afterwards into an ode disgraceful only to its author.

Of his odes nothing favourable can be said: the sentiments commonly want force, nature, or novelty; the diction is sometimes harsh and uncouth, the stanzas ill-constructed and unpleasant, and the rhymes dissonant, or unskilfully disposed, too distant from each other, or arranged with too little regard to established use, and therefore perplexing to the ear, which in a short composition has not time to grow familiar with an innovation.

To examine such compositions singly, cannot be required; they have doubtless brighter and darker parts: but when they are once found to be generally dull, all further labour may be spared; for to what use can the work be criticised that will not be read? [15]

[15] The amplest and ablest memoir of Akenside is by Mr. Dyce in the Aldine edition of Akenside's Poems, 1837.

APPENDIX.

The following letters (three in number) are now published for the first time :—

AKENSIDE TO MR. DAVID FORDYCE.

To be left at the shop of Mr. Gavin Hamilton, Bookseller in Edinburgh.

Saturday night, ten o'clock.

DEAR SIR,—About ten minutes ago I received your letter. I hope I may congratulate you on the pleasures you are now enjoying at Edinburgh among those whose conversation I envy you, and to whom I envy your conversation.   Your reflections on the face of society in those countries you have been travelling through, are, I dare say, extremely just ; but I am afraid we have at present no prospect of any valuable change, any general introduction either of plenty or independence among the multitude, much less of that manly and rational spirit of thinking and acting which ought to be the very end of society, since it can never be obtained but by society, and is the best and noblest of those enjoyments which society produces.   I am very sensibly vexed when I hear people asserting that nine-tenths of the human species must, by the necessity of civil government, remain ignorant of this divine possession, brutal and without even a comprehension of the ends of life, which they spend in vain as to their own parts, going out of the world just as they came into it, without nourishment or growth to their minds, without advancing one step in the scale of nature.   What can I think of that scene of government which naturally leads men to a position so shocking and absurd ?

Your view of the Inquiry about the Sciences is perfectly congruous to mine.   As to your Initiation and Oath, I like it extremely—only do not you think those terms or appellations, the *Throne of Honour* and the *Chamber of heroic Virtue*, will look rather affected ?   If we conceive the thing as actually existing, and students at an academy calling chambers, &c., by such names, I am afraid we should think the fashion strained almost to pedantry.   The statues of Virtue and Liberty on each side the rostrum are, I think, very proper ; also the inscription and the other bustos, excepting only Machiavel.   He was, no doubt, a man of genius, and has wrote well as far as his materials allowed him to go ; but being conversant only with little Italian republics and principalities, where personal considerations are the principal or only springs of action, and consequently where government is often subservient to the worst passions, and carried on by the worst arts—from these causes having no comprehension of an extensive and virtuous plan of a Constitution, he has often wrote crudely, generally so monstrous wickedly, that I think you should not allow him a place among those heroes, but put Sir Thomas More in his stead.

I have enclosed the Oath as I would choose it : the alterations are marked with figures :—1. This passage redundant.   2. *Systems* too recluse and subtle a word.   3. *King* has naturally a bad or sordid idea.   4. *Honourable* more sober and moral than *glorious*.   5. *So,* &c., too vulgar and trivial a phrase.

As for the poem, I am just respiring from a pretty bold undertaking, not only in poetry, let me tell you, but even in philosophy—namely, to develope and describe the general species and laws of ridicule in the characters of men, and give an universal idea of it in every other subject.   I have been grievously put to it in the descriptive part.   The general idea of the poem is rather bashfully candid—excuse the phrase—and ill admits any appearance of satire, though this Inquiry was absolutely necessary to the plan as relating to the materials and ground of comedy.

> " Lo, thus far,
> With bold adventure to the Mantuan lyre,
> I sing of Nature's charms, and touch, well pleas'd,
> A stricter note.   Now haply must my song
> Unbend her serious measure, and declare,
> In sportive strains, how Folly's awkward arts
> Awake impetuous Laughter's gay rebuke,
> The lighter province of the comic scene." [16]

I am filing and re-touching every day, and confess I long to see the first book fairly and entirely transcribed ; and if I had it once off my hands, I imagine my thoughts would be freed from some constraint and anxiety. For to you I dare pretend to so much philosophy, as that I shall not be much disturbed about its success ; and I fancy my mind will be much more at leisure after putting an end to this task I have so long imposed on myself ; for, though this be but a small part of the design, yet I have no views of completing the remainder otherwise than in the most leisurely manner in the world ; for this, if it be worth aught, must answer all the ends I propose by it at present ; and you know that if it do answer them, I shall have other matters to mind than versifying.   I expect to finish the transcribing part in a fortnight or three weeks.   I must have a few notes too ; but I blush to have said so much.   I have been for these three weeks proposing every post to write to Mr. B., but shall certainly muster up courage to do it next post, for does it not require (if not courage) resolution, at least, and self-control ?   Remember me to all our friends, and believe me, dear Sir,

Yours most affectionately, M. A.

P.S.—Write to me soon, and in my next I will tell you what to do about those letters you are so good as to mention.

M. A.

---

[16] This was afterwards introduced into ' The Pleasures of Imagination,' book iii.

AKENSIDE TO MR. DAVID FORDYCE,

At Aberdeen, N. Britain.

Newcastle, 18th June, 1742.

DEAR SIR,—I should have answered your letter sooner, but that I was uncertain, till of late, whether to direct for you at Edinburgh or at Aberdeen. I durst not, however, reply in the language you wrote in; for, though I could perhaps have filled two or three pages with Italian words ranged in grammatical order, yet, without assuming the natural air and spirit of the language, you would no more think I had wrote Italian than you would call that a musical composition which was only a number of concords put together without any regard to the rhythm or style of the whole. This reason was stronger in writing to you, who have attained so perfectly the wild elegance, the *vagherra*, which the Italians are so fond of both in language and painting, and in which, I believe, they exceed all the moderns. What is good in the French authors is of a more sober, classical manner, and greater severity of design. The Spaniards, I imagine, approach much nearer to the Italian manner. Our English poetry has but little of it, and that chiefly among the older compositions of our countrymen—the juvenilia of Milton, and the fairy scenes of Spenser and Shakespeare. Our nervous and concise language does not willingly flow into this fanciful luxuriance ; besides that the genius of our poetry delights in a vehemence of passion and philosophical sublimity of sentiments much above its reach.

Since we parted, I have been chiefly employed in reading the Greek philosophers, especially the Stoics. Upton's edition of Arrian was published just as I got hither : it is in two small quarto volumes, neat enough ; the second consists principally of the editor's comments and the notes variorum. He has got a great many remarks of Lord Shaftesbury, but they are entirely critical, and contain very ingenious conjectures on the reading of several passages.

I have had great pleasure from the writers of this sect ; but, though I admire the strength and elevation of their moral, yet, in modern life especially, I am afraid it would lead to something splenetic and unconversable. Besides, it allows too little to domestic virtue and tenderness, it dwells too much on the awful and sublime of life ; yet even its sublimity resembles that of a vast open prospect in winter, when the sun scarce can shine through the atmosphere, and looks on the rigour of the season with a kind of sullen majesty ; to the generality of mankind, a much narrower landscape in the sunshine of a spring morning would be much more agreeable. I would therefore mix the Stoic with the Platonic philosophy ; they would equally temper and adorn each other ; for, if mere stoicism be in hazard of growing surly and unsocial, it is no less certain that Platonic enthusiasm has always run to extravagance, but where it was kept steady by a severe judgment ; besides that the constant pursuit of beauty and elegance is apt to fill the mind with high and florid desires, than which nothing is more dangerous to that internal freedom which is the basis of virtue. In short, the case seems much the same here as with the human sexes, either of which is liable to these very imperfections when apart, and therefore the perfection of human life is best found in their union. Were I a painter, and going to represent these two sects in an emblematic way, I would draw the genius of the Stoics like a man in his prime, or rather of a green and active old age, with a manly sternness and simplicity in his air and habit, seated on a rock overlooking the sea in a tempest of wind and lightning, and regarding the noise of the thunder and the rolling of the waves with a serene defiance. But the Platonic genius I would represent like another Muse—a virgin of a sweet and lively beauty, with wings to her head, and a loose robe of a bright azure colour. She should be seated in a garden, on the brink of a clear and smooth canal, while the sky were without a cloud, and the sun shining in the zenith. Our theological lady, conscious that her eyes could not endure the splendour of his immediate appearance, should be fixed in contemplating his milder image reflected from the water. But enough of this. I thank you for your account of the manner in which you dispose of your personages ; I am only afraid you will scarce find room for the full exercise of Philander's genius and virtue in the station you have assigned him, for the statutes of a college are too well known and too strictly observed to leave a probability of much improvement under any particular president or master. The rest, I think, are very well settled. You might find occasion, in the characters of Atticus and Sophron, to give a little good advice on the ancient and present state of our political constitution.

We have little news. I saw yesterday proposals by an Oxford man to publish an edition of Polybius. I am quite sick of politics—our present politics I mean. Within this last month or six weeks I have seen Richardson, Pickering, and Frank Hume, who all remembered you with affection ; the two former were for Paris, the last for Flanders with the regiment to which he is surgeon. I had a letter last post from Russell ; he has been ill of a quinsy, but is much better : all other friends are well. Roebuck is at Leyden, and takes his degree there this summer, as Allen has already done at St. Andrew's. Ogle died about a month after we left you.

I am, with great esteem and affectionate remembrance of the pleasures of our late conversations,

Dear Sir, your most faithful and obedient servant,

MARK AKINSIDE.

(Direct to be left at Mr. Akinside's,
    Surgeon in Newcastle-upon-Tyne.)

AKENSIDE TO MR. DAVID FORDYCE,

At Mr. Gavin Hamilton's, Bookseller in Edinburgh.

Newcastle, 30th July, 1743.

DEAR SIR,—With respect to Shaftesbury's Test of Truth, I apprehend the matter thus :—Ridicule is never conversant about bare abstract speculative truth—about the agreement or disagreement of ideas which merely inform the understanding without affecting the temper and imagination. It always supposes the perception of some quality or object either venerable, fair, praiseworthy, or mean, sordid, and ignoble. The essence of the το γελοιον consists in the unnatural combination of these in one appearance ; and hence you will observe the origin of that difference which is made between true ridicule and false ; for I, by a wrong imagination, may apprehend that to be sordid and ignoble which really is not ; I may also apprehend it inconsistent with the other appearances of reverence or beauty, when they are in fact perfectly coincident. Take an instance of each. I remember to have heard you condemn the late comic romance of Joseph Andrews, for representing Joseph's temperance against the offers of his lady in a ridiculous light ; your sentence was perfectly just, for it is custom, corrupted custom, and not nature, which teaches us to annex ideas of contempt to such an abstinence ; for by vicious conversations and writings the world is deceived, to think it *incongruous, inconsistent* with the character and situation of a man, and therefore ridiculous. An instance of the second kind may be this : suppose a gentleman nobly drest, a person of a public character, perhaps in the robes of his office, walking in a foul street, without any conceited airs or self-applause from his splendid appearance ; suppose, by an accident or fall, his garment quite stained and defaced,—the opposition between the splendour of one part of his dress, and the foul appearance of the other, might perhaps excite the sense of ridicule in a light, superficial mind ; but, to a man of taste and penetration, the ridicule would immediately vanish, because, as our gentleman's *mind* was not fondly prepossessed with any conceit of worth or *considerable* splendour in his habit, so neither will the change produced in it give him any sensation of real disgrace or shame ; consequently, in his *mind* there is no incongruity produced by this external circumstance, therefore nothing ridiculous in the *man,* in *sentiment,* in *life :* now take away all ideas of this intellectual and *feeling* species, and then try whether ridicule can have any place in an object ; you will find, I believe, none at all. But alter the example a little, and suppose the person so begrimed to have been a fop, whose whole appearance and gesture showed how much he valued himself on his finery, there the ridicule will [be] irresistible and just, because the incongruity is real. Now, as to the test of our divine Master. This sense of ridicule was certainly given us for good ends—in a word, for the same sort of end as the sense of beauty and veracity and gratitude ; to supply the slow deductions of our reason, and lead us to avoid and depress at first sight some certain circumstances of the mind which are really prejudicial to life, but would otherwise have required a longer investigation to discover them to be so than we are usually at leisure for. If, therefore, by any unfairness in an argument, certain circumstances relating to a point in question be concealed, to apply the ridicule is to drag out those circumstances, and set them (if they be opposite) in the fullest light of opposition to those others which are owned and pleaded for, and thus render the claim *incongruous* and ridiculous. Is there any great mystery or danger in this? and is not Mr. Warburton—are not all the priests in Christendom—at full liberty to inquire whether these circumstances which I represent as opposite and incongruous, be really so; and whether they are any way connected with the claim? If they be not, my procedure is certainly itself ridiculous, as connecting in my own mind the idea of the το γελοιον with what is no way related to it, and very inconsistent with it.

I have not yet fixed either the day of my departure or my route, being detained by some accidents longer than I expected, only I am pretty sure I shall set forward in the second week of August. If you could be at leisure to send me two or three letters enclosed in one to myself, the carrier who sets out every Thursday from Bristow Port would bring them safe enough, especially if you tell him I will give him sixpence or a shilling for his trouble. You or Russell might send them to his lodging by a cadie: you see my impudence, but you taught me it by your too great complaisance. There is another carrier, who sets out from the head of the Cow-gate; so that if one should not be in the way, you will find the other. I was half angry in mirth, that you should so misapprehend me about my difficulty in writing to Philostratus; I thought the word *self-control* would have given you a different idea of the matter than a diffidence and terror of appearing under so formidable an eye. I assure you, Sir, I wrote a very simple letter, without correction, without brilliancy, without literature. I wrote to Cleghorn last night, to make him laugh, to puzzle and astonish him in this combination of woes. As I make no doubt but he would think me distracted, you may be so good as tell him that you have received a letter, wrote the next morning, in which, after passing an easy night, with nine hours' sleep, there appears some pretty favourable symptoms of a return to my senses. I want letters from him and   , and Russell and Blair, immediately; for I have waited too long for them. Farewell: I shall write from London. Commend me to all ours.

I am, dear Fordyce, your affectionate friend and obedient servant,

M. A.

LORD LYTTELTON.

LYTTELTON.

1709–1773.

Son of Sir Thomas Lyttelton, of Hagley, in Worcestershire — Educated at Eton and Oxford — Visits France and Italy — Obtains a seat in Parliament — Made Secretary to Frederick Prince of Wales — His Friendship with Pope and Thomson — Is twice married — Publishes his ' Observations on the Conversion of St. Paul ' — Inherits his Father's Baronetcy — Is created a Peer — Writes ' The History of the Reign of Henry II.' — Death, and Burial at Hagley.

GEORGE LYTTELTON, the son of Sir Thomas Lyttelton, of Hagley in Worcestershire,[1] was born in 1709. He was educated at Eton, where he was so much distinguished, that his exercises were recommended as models to his school-fellows.

From Eton he went to Christ-Church, where he retained the same reputation of superiority, and displayed [1728] his abilities to the public in a poem on ' Blenheim.'

He was a very early writer, both in verse and prose. His ' Progress of Love ' [1732], and his ' Persian Letters,' were both written when he was very young ; and indeed the character of a young man is very visible in both.[2] The verses cant of shepherds and flocks, and crooks dressed with flowers ; and the letters have something of that indistinct and headstrong ardour for liberty which a man of genius always catches when he enters the world, and always suffers to cool as he passes forward.[3]

He stayed not long at Oxford ; for in 1728 he began his

---

[1] By Christian, the younger of two sisters of Sir Richard Temple of Stowe, created successively Baron and Viscount Cobham.

[2] His ' Blenheim,' fol., 1728, is his earliest production in print.

[3] In the ' Persian Letters,' as in all his other works, Lyttelton is but an imitator :—the idea, the name, and some of the details are borrowed from the ' Lettres Persannes ' of the President Montesquieu, then in high repute.— CROKER: *Quar. Rev.*, No. 155, p. 229.

travels, and saw France and Italy.[4] When he returned, he
obtained [April, 1735] a seat in Parliament,[5] and soon distinguished himself among the most eager opponents of Sir Robert
Walpole, though his father, who was Commissioner of the
Admiralty, always voted with the Court.

For many years the name of George Lyttelton was seen in
every account of every debate in the House of Commons. He
opposed the standing army ; he opposed the Excise ;[6] he supported the motion for petitioning the King to remove Walpole.
His zeal was considered by the courtiers not only as violent, but
as acrimonious and malignant ; and when Walpole was at last
hunted from his places, every effort was made by his friends,
and many friends he had, to exclude Lyttelton from the secret
committee.

The Prince of Wales, being (1737) driven from St. James's,
kept a separate court, and opened his arms to the opponents of
the ministry. Mr. Lyttelton became [Oct. 1737] his secretary,
and was supposed to have great influence in the direction of his
conduct. He persuaded his master, whose business it was now
to be popular, that he would advance his character by patronage. Mallet was made under-secretary, with 200l., and Thomson had a pension of 100l. a year. For Thomson Lyttelton
always retained his kindness, and was able at last to place him
at ease.

Moore[7] courted his favour by an apologetical poem, called
' The Trial of Selim,' for which he was paid with kind words,
which, as is common, raised great hopes, that were at last disappointed.

Lyttelton now stood in the first rank of opposition ; and Pope,
who was incited, it is not easy to say how, to increase the
clamour against the ministry, commended him among the other

[4] He entered as a Gentleman Commoner of Christ-Church, 4th December,
1725. Some of his verses are dated from Oxford in 1725, which must be the
old style for the spring of 1726; and he seems not to have left it till the spring
of 1728.—CROKER : Quar. Rev., No. 155, p. 227.

[5] He sat for Okehampton.

[6] He could not have opposed the Excise, as that scheme was brought forward
in 1733, when Lyttelton was not a member.

[7] Edward Moore, author of ' The Gamester,' and editor of ' The World,'
died 1757.

patriots.[8]   This drew upon him the reproaches of Fox, who, in
the House, imputed to him as a crime his intimacy with a lampooner so unjust and licentious.   Lyttelton supported his friend,
and replied, that he thought it an honour to be received into
the familiarity of so great a poet.[9]

While he was thus conspicuous, he married (1741) Miss
Lucy Fortescue, of Devonshire,[10] by whom he had a son, the
late Lord Lyttelton, and two daughters, and with whom he
appears to have lived in the highest degree of connubial
felicity : but human pleasures are short ; she died in childbed
about five years afterwards,[11] and he solaced his grief by writing
a long poem to her memory.[12]

He did not, however, condemn himself to perpetual solitude
and sorrow ; for, after a while, he was content to seek happiness

---

[8]   Sometimes a patriot, active in debate,
       Mix with the world, and battle for the state;
       Free as young Lyttelton her cause pursue,
       Still true to virtue, and as warm as true.

                                    Imitations, Book i., Ep. i.

Pope has mentioned him in two more places:—

       If any ask you, " Who's the man so near
       His prince, that writes in verse, and has his ear ?"
       Why, answer Lyttelton, and I 'll engage
       The worthy youth shall ne'er be in a rage.

                                    Epilogue to Satires, Dialogue I.

       Cobham 's a coward, Polwarth is a slave,
       And Lyttelton a dark designing knave.

                                    Epilogue to Satires, Dialogue II.

This is said ironically.   He has also remembered him in his will.   " Item,
I desire Mr. Lyttelton to accept of the busts of Spenser, Shakespeare, Milton,
and Dryden, in marble, which his royal master the Prince was pleased to give
me."   These interesting busts are still at Hagley.   They are smaller than life,
and on black marble pedestals.

[9]   Compare Johnson in his ' Life of Pope,' p. 82.

[10]   Daughter of Hugh Fortescue, of Filleigh, Devon.

[11]   19th January, 1746-7, aged 29.

[12]   ' To the Memory of a Lady lately deceased, a Monody.'   Millar [Novem-
ber], 1747, fol., pp. 15; and one of the last poems, if not the very last, that
appeared in folio, a fashion that prevailed between 1680 and 1750.   A parody
appeared at the time also, in folio, entitled ' A sorrowful Ditty, or the Lady's
Lamentation for the Death of her favourite Cat.   A Parody.   London: printed
for J. Tomlinson, near St. Paul's, 1748.'   The Burlesque Ode on the Monody
by Smollett in ' Peregrine Pickle,' under the notion of a Pastoral on the death
of his Grandmother, is different from this.

again by a second marriage [10 Aug., 1749] with the daughter
of Sir Robert Rich ; but the experiment was unsuccessful.[13]

At length, after a long struggle, Walpole gave way, and
honour and profit were distributed among his conquerors.
Lyttelton was made (December, 1744) one of the Lords of the
Treasury, and from that time was engaged in supporting the
schemes of the ministry.

Politics did not, however, so much engage him as to withhold
his thoughts from things of more importance. He had, in the
pride of juvenile confidence, with the help of corrupt conversation, entertained doubts of the truth of Christianity ; but he
thought the time now come when it was no longer fit to doubt
or believe by chance, and applied himself seriously to the great
question. His studies being honest, ended in conviction.[14] He
found that religion was true, and what he had learned he endeavoured to teach (1747), by 'Observations on the Conversion
of St. Paul ;' a treatise to which infidelity has never been able
to fabricate a specious answer.[15] This book his father had the

[13] Gilbert West speaks of Miss Rich as "an intimate and dear friend of his
former wife, which," he adds, "is some kind of proof of her merit."—*Letter
to Doddridge, dated Wickham*, 17th June, 1749.

"Mr. Lyttelton has not married a woman without fortune or a reasonable
share of beauty : she has five thousand pounds at present, and will have as
much more at her father's death. She has a good complexion, fine hair, and
good teeth; has very good sense; lived a more reasonable retired life than
young ladies now do; was an intimate friend of his first wife's; and from that
friendship sprung his affection. He is a man who gives into neither the vices
nor pleasures of the gay world; likes his own home; and those domestic sort
of men always marry, and love their *wife*, be she who she will."—LADY HERVEY.
Aug. 23, 1749 (' Letters,' p. 161).

[14] There is at Wickham a walk made by Pitt; and what is of far more importance, at Wickham Lyttelton received that conviction which produced his
' Observations on St. Paul.'—JOHNSON : *Life of West.*

[15] The Observations on St. Paul were written to satisfy the scruples of the
author of 'The Seasons':—

"My refuge and consolation is in philosophy—Christian philosophy—which
I heartily wish you may be a disciple of as well as myself. Indeed, my dear
friend, it is far above the Platonick. I have sent you a pamphlet on a subject
relative to it, which we have formerly talked of. I writ it in Kew Lane last year;
and I writ it with a particular view to your satisfaction. You have therefore
a double right to it; and I wish to God it may appear to you as convincing as
it does to me, and bring you to add the faith to the heart of a Christian.—
LYTTELTON to Thomson, May 21, 1747. (Phillimore's 'Lyttelton,' i. 307.)

happiness of seeing, and expressed his pleasure in a letter which deserves to be inserted :—

" I have read your religious treatise with infinite pleasure and satisfaction. The style is fine and clear, the arguments close, cogent, and irresistible. May the King of kings, whose glorious cause you have so well defended, reward your pious labours, and grant that I may be found worthy, through the merits of Jesus Christ, to be an eye-witness of that happiness which I don't doubt he will bountifully bestow upon you. In the mean time I shall never cease glorifying God for having endowed you with such useful talents, and giving me so good a son.

" Your affectionate father,

" THOMAS LYTTELTON."

A few years afterwards (1751), by the death of his father,[16] he inherited a baronet's title with a large estate, which, though perhaps he did not augment, he was careful to adorn by a house of great elegance and expense, and by much attention to the decoration of his park.[17]

As he continued his activity in parliament, he was gradually advancing his claim to profit and preferment, and accordingly was made in time (1754) cofferer and privy counsellor : this place he exchanged next year for the great office of Chancellor of the Exchequer,—an office, however, that required some qualifications which he soon perceived himself to want.

The year after his curiosity led him into Wales, of which he has given an account, perhaps rather with too much affectation of delight, to Archibald Bower,[18] a man of whom he had conceived an opinion more favourable than he seems to have deserved, and whom, having once espoused his interest and

---

[16] 14th Sept. 1751.

[17] 16th Sept. 1774.—We [Johnson and Mr. and Mrs. Thrale] went to Hagley, where we were disappointed of the respect and kindness that we expected— [from Lord Westcote. The poet, Lord Lyttelton, died the year before].

17th Sept.—We saw the house and park, which equalled my expectation. The house is one square mass. The offices are below ; the rooms of elegance on the first floor, with two stories of bedchambers, very well disposed above it. The bedchambers have low windows, which abates the dignity of the house. The park has one artificial ruin, and wants water; there is, however, one temporary cascade. From the farthest hill there is a very wide prospect. —JOHNSON: *Journal of Tour in Wales*. (' Boswell by Croker,' ed. 1847, p. 424.)

[18] Author of the ' History of the Popes.' London, 1748-66. 4to. 7 vols.

fame, he never was persuaded to disown. Bower, whatever was his moral character, did not want abilities ; attacked as he was by an universal outcry, and that outcry, as it seems, the echo of truth, he kept his ground ; at last, when his defences began to fail him, he sallied out upon his adversaries, and his adversaries retreated.

About this time Lyttelton published his 'Dialogues of the Dead,'[19] which were very eagerly read, though the production rather, as it seems, of leisure than of study, rather effusions than compositions. The names of his persons too often enable the reader to anticipate their conversation; and when they have met, they too often part without any conclusion. He has copied Fenelon more than Fontenelle.

When they were first published, they were kindly commended by the 'Critical Reviewers ;' and poor Lyttelton, with humble gratitude, returned, in a note which I have read, acknowledgments which can never be proper, since they must be paid either for flattery or for justice.

When, in the latter part of the last reign, the inauspicious commencement of the war made the dissolution of the ministry unavoidable, Sir George Lyttelton, losing with the rest his employment, was [19th Nov. 1757] recompensed with a peerage, and rested from political turbulence in the House of Lords.[20]

His last literary production was his 'History of Henry the Second,' elaborated by the searches and deliberations of twenty years, and published with such anxiety as only vanity can dictate.

The story of this publication is remarkable. The whole work was printed twice over, a great part of it three times, and many

---

[19] First published April, 1760. The 26th, 27th, and 28th Dialogues were written by Mrs. Montagu.

[20] Sir George Lyttelton and Legge were as opposite in their manners; the latter concise and pointed, the former diffuse and majestic. Legge's speeches seemed the heads of chapters to Sir George Lyttelton's dissertations.—WALPOLE'S *George II.*

Sir George Lyttelton was an enthusiast both in religion and politics; absent in business, not ready in a debate, and totally ignorant of the world: on the other hand, his studied orations were excellent; he was a man of parts, a scholar, no indifferent writer, and by far the honestest man of the whole society.—LORD WALDEGRAVE'S *Memoirs,* p. 25.

sheets four or five times. The booksellers paid for the first impression; but the charges and repeated operations of the press were at the expense of the author, whose ambitious accuracy is known to have cost him at least a thousand pounds. He began to print in 1755. Three volumes appeared in 1764, a second edition of them in 1767, a third edition in 1768, and the conclusion in 1771.

Andrew Reid, a man not without considerable abilities, and not unacquainted with letters or with life, undertook to persuade Lyttelton, as he had persuaded himself, that he was master of the secret of punctuation; and, as fear begets credulity, he was employed, I know not at what price, to point the pages of 'Henry the Second.' The book was at last pointed and printed, and sent into the world. Lyttelton took money for his copy, of which, when he had paid the printer, he probably gave the rest away, for he was very liberal to the indigent.

When time brought the History to a third edition, Reid was either dead or discarded; and the superintendence of typography and punctuation was committed to a man originally a comb-maker, but then known by the style of Doctor.[21] Something uncommon was probably expected, and something uncommon was at last done; for to the Doctor's edition is appended, what the world had hardly seen before, a list of errors in nineteen pages.[22]

But to politics and literature there must be an end. Lord Lyttelton had never the appearance of a strong or of a healthy man; he had a slender, uncompacted frame, and a meagre face;

[21] Dr. Saunders. See Nichols's 'Life of Bowyer,' 4to. 1782, p. 427.

[22] Our Journal for the year 1767, under the title of 'Mémoires Littéraires de la Grande Bretagne,' was soon finished and sent to the press. For the first article, 'Lord Lyttelton's History of Henry II.,' I must own myself responsible; but the public has ratified my judgment of that voluminous work, in which sense and learning are not illuminated by a ray of genius.—GIBBON : *Autobiography.* Ed. Milman, p. 218.

There is a good letter from Lyttelton to Joseph Warton about his History in Wooll's 'Warton,' p. 321, 4to.

He [Johnson] talked of Lord Lyttelton's extreme anxiety as an author, observing that "he was thirty years in preparing his History, and that he employed a man to point it for him; as if (laughing) another man could point his sense better than himself." Mr. Murphy said he understood his History was kept back several years for fear of Smollett.—*Boswell by Croker,* ed. 1847, p. 504.

he lasted, however, sixty years, and was then seized with his last illness. Of his death a very affecting and instructive account has been given by his physician,[23] which will spare me the task of his moral character.

"On Sunday evening the symptoms of his Lordship's disorder, which for a week past had alarmed us, put on a fatal appearance, and his Lordship believed himself to be a dying man. From this time he suffered by restlessness rather than pain ; though his nerves were apparently much fluttered, his mental faculties never seemed stronger when he was thoroughly awake.

"His Lordship's bilious and hepatic complaints seemed alone not equal to the expected mournful event ; his long want of sleep, whether the consequence of the irritation in the bowels, or, which is more probable, of causes of a different kind, accounts for his loss of strength and for his death very sufficiently.

"Though his Lordship wished his approaching dissolution not to be lingering, he waited for it with resignation. He said, ' It is a folly, a keeping me in misery, now to attempt to prolong life ;' yet he was easily persuaded, for the satisfaction of others, to do or take anything thought proper for him. On Saturday he had been remarkably better, and we were not without some hopes of his recovery.

"On Sunday, about eleven in the forenoon, his Lordship sent for me, and said he felt a great hurry, and wished to have a little conversation with me, in order to divert it. He then proceeded to open the fountain of that heart from whence goodness had so long flowed, as from a copious spring. ' Doctor,' said he, ' you shall be my confessor : when I first set out in the world, I had friends who endeavoured to shake my belief in the Christian religion. I saw difficulties which staggered me, but I kept my mind open to conviction. The evidences and doctrines of Christianity, studied with attention, made me a most firm and persuaded believer of the Christian religion. I have made it the rule of my life, and it is the

---

[23] Dr. Johnstone, "a skilful physician of Kidderminster." See the account, dated Aug. 28, 1773, in the 'Gentleman's Magazine' for Nov. 1773, p. 604.

ground of my future hopes. I have erred and sinned, but have repented, and never indulged any vicious habit. In politics and public life, I have made public good the rule of my conduct. I never gave counsels which I did not at the time think the best. I have seen that I was sometimes in the wrong, but I did not err designedly. I have endeavoured, in private life, to do all the good in my power, and never for a moment could indulge malicious or unjust designs upon any person whatsoever.'

"At another time he said, 'I must leave my soul in the same state it was in before this illness ; I find this a very inconvenient time for solicitude about any thing.'

"On the evening, when the symptoms of death came on, he said, 'I shall die, but it will not be your fault.' When Lord and Lady Valentia came to see his Lordship, he gave them his solemn benediction, and said, ' Be good, be virtuous, my Lord ; you must come to this.' Thus he continued giving his dying benedictions to all around him. On Monday morning a lucid interval gave some small hopes, but these vanished in the evening, and he continued dying, but with very little uneasiness, till Tuesday morning, August 22, when, between seven and eight o'clock, he expired, almost without a groan."

His Lordship was buried at Hagley, and the following inscription is cut on the side of his Lady's monument :

> " This unadorned stone was placed here
> By the particular desire and express
> Directions of the Right Honourable
> GEORGE Lord LYTTELTON,
> Who died August 22, 1773, aged 64." [24]

---

[24] For further particulars of the Life of Lord Lyttelton see 'Memoirs and Correspondence of George, Lord Lyttelton,' by Robert Phillimore, 2 vols. 8vo., 1845, and Mr. Croker's article on the work, in ' Quarterly Rev.,' No. 155. . . The *good* Lyttelton, as he is called, was succeeded by his only son, commonly called the *bad* Lord Lyttelton. He had great but misapplied talents, and died childless 27th Nov. 1779, when his father's barony became extinct. The present barony of Lyttelton was revived in 1794 by the creation of the brother of the *good* Lord Lyttelton to that title. For a full account of the *bad* Lord Lyttelton see ' Quar. Rev.' for Dec. 1851, in which it is sought to prove that the *bad* Lord L. was Junius.

Fielding immortalized the personal virtues of Lord Lyttelton in the Dedicatory Letter to ' Tom Jones;' and Smollett in the first edition of ' Peregrine Pickle ' held his tall gaunt figure up to ridicule as Gosling Scrag, Esq.

Lord Lyttelton's Poems are the works of a man of literature and judgment devoting part of his time to versification. They have nothing to be despised, and little to be admired. Of his ‘ Progress of Love,’ it is sufficient blame to say that it is pastoral. His blank verse in ‘ Blenheim ’ has neither much force nor much elegance. His little performances, whether Songs [25] or Epigrams, are sometimes sprightly, and sometimes insipid. His epistolary pieces have a smooth equability, which cannot much tire, because they are short, but which seldom elevates or surprises. But from this censure ought to be excepted his ‘ Advice to Belinda,’ which, though for the most part written when he was very young, contains much truth and much prudence, very elegantly and vigorously expressed, and shows a mind attentive to life, and a power of poetry which cultivation might have raised to excellence. [26]

[25] Lord Lyttelton's Delia was a Mrs. Boughton.   See Walpole to Mann, Sept. 10, 1761.

[26] Bolingbroke's idea of a Patriot King was originally written in the form of a letter to Lyttelton.   The letter was meant for Frederick Prince of Wales, in whose service Lyttelton then was.   The only good portrait of Lyttelton is at Hagley; a Kitcat by Sir Joshua Reynolds.

“ Have you seen Lyttelton's Monody on his wife's death?   There are parts of it too stiff and poetical; but others truly tender and elegiac, as one would wish.” —GRAY to Wharton, Nov. 30, 1747.

“ I am not totally of your mind as to Mr. Lyttelton's Elegy, though I love kids and fawns as little as you do.   If it were all like the fourth stanza, I should be excessively pleased.”—GRAY to Walpole (n. d.).

> In vain I look around
> O'er all the well-known ground,
> My Lucy's wonted footsteps to descry!
> Where oft we used to walk,
> Where oft in tender talk
> We saw the summer sun go down the sky;
> Nor by yon fountain's side,
> Nor where its waters glide
> Along the valley, can she now be found:
> In all the wide-stretch'd prospect's ample bound
> No more my mournful eye
> Can aught of her espy,
> But the sad sacred earth where her dear relics lie.
>
> LYTTELTON: *Monody*, st. 4.

Johnson should have said a word in praise of Lyttelton's Prologue to Thomson's last play: one of the best Prologues in the English language.

THOMAS GRAY.

G R A Y.

1716–1771.

Born in Cornhill, London — Educated at Eton and Cambridge — Accompanies Horace Walpole into Italy — His Quarrel with Pope — Publishes his ' Elegy written in a Country Churchyard ' — Its immediate popularity — Publishes his Odes — Refuses the Laurel — Made Professor of Modern History at Cambridge — Death, and Burial at Stoke Pogeis in Buckinghamshire — Works and Character.

THOMAS GRAY, the son of Mr. Philip Gray, a scrivener of London, was born in Cornhill, November 26, 1716. His grammatical education he received at Eton under the care of Mr. Antrobus, his mother's brother,[1] then assistant to Dr. George ; and when he left school, in 1734, entered a pensioner at Peterhouse in Cambridge.

The transition from the school to the college is, to most young scholars, the time from which they date their years of manhood, liberty, and happiness ; but Gray seems to have been very little delighted with academical gratifications ; he liked at Cambridge neither the mode of life nor the fashion of study, and lived sullenly on to the time when his attendance on lectures was no longer required. As he intended to profess the Common Law, he took no degree.

When he had been at Cambridge about five years, Mr. Horace Walpole, whose friendship he had gained at Eton, invited him to travel with him as his companion. They wandered through France into Italy ; and Gray's letters contain a very pleasing account of many parts of their journey. But unequal friendships are easily dissolved : at Florence they quarrelled,[2] and parted ; and Mr. Walpole is now content to have it

---

[1] Mr. William Antrobus died at Everden, Northamptonshire, 22nd May, 1742, and was buried in the chancel of that church.

[2] They quarrelled at Reggio.

told that it was by his fault.[3] If we look, however, without prejudice on the world, we shall find that men whose consciousness of their own merit sets them above the compliances of servility, are apt enough in their association with superiors to watch their own dignity with troublesome and punctilious jealousy, and in the fervour of independence to exact that attention which they refuse to pay. Part they did, whatever was the quarrel, and the rest of their travels was doubtless more unpleasant to them both. Gray continued his journey in a

---

[3] " I am conscious that in the beginning of the differences between Gray and me the fault was mine. I was too young, too fond of my own diversions; nay, I do not doubt, too much intoxicated by indulgence, vanity, and the insolence of my situation as a Prime Minister's son, not to have been inattentive and insensible to the feelings of one I thought below me; of one, I blush to say it, that I knew was obliged to me; of one whom presumption and folly, perhaps, made me deem not my superior *then* in parts, though I have since felt my infinite inferiority to him. I treated him insolently: he loved me, and I did not think he did. I reproached him with the difference between us, when he acted from conviction of knowing he was my superior; I often disregarded his wishes of seeing places which I would not quit other amusements to visit, though I offered to send him to them without me. Forgive me if I say that his temper was not conciliating. At the same time that I will confess to you that he acted a more friendly part, had I had the sense to take advantage of it; he freely told me of my faults. I declared I did not desire to hear them, nor would correct them. You will not wonder that with the dignity of his spirit, and the obstinate carelessness of mine, the breach must have grown wider, till we became incompatible. After this confession, I fear you will think I fall far short of the justice I promised him in the words which I should wish to have substituted to some of yours. If you think them inadequate to the state of the case, as I own they are, preserve this letter, and let some future Sir John Dalrymple produce it to load my memory."—WALPOLE to Mason, March 2, 1773.

" The quarrel between Gray and me arose from his being too serious a companion. I had just broke loose from the restraint of the university, with as much money as I could spend, and I was willing to indulge myself. Gray was for antiquities, &c., whilst I was for perpetual balls and plays: the fault was mine."—WALPOLE: *Walpoliana*, vol. i. p. 95, art. cx.

Mr. Roberts, of the Pell Office, who was likely to be well informed, told me at Mr. Deacon's, 19th April, 1799, that the quarrel between Gray and Walpole was occasioned by a suspicion Mr. Walpole entertained that Mr. Gray had spoken ill of him to some friends in England. To ascertain this he clandestinely opened a letter and re-sealed it, which Mr. Gray with great propriety resented: there seems to have been but little cordiality afterwards between them.—ISAAC REED : *MS. Note in Wakefield's Life of Gray; Mitford's Gray,* ii. 175.

Compare Norton Nicholls's Reminiscences in Mitford's ' Gray,' v. 48.

manner suitable to his own little fortune, with only an occasional servant.

He returned to England in September, 1741, and in about two months afterwards buried his father; who had, by an injudicious waste of money upon a new house, so much lessened his fortune, that Gray thought himself too poor to study the law.[4] He therefore retired to Cambridge, where he soon after became Bachelor of Civil Law; and where, without liking the place or its inhabitants, or professing to like them, he passed, except a short residence in London, the rest of his life.

About this time [1742] he was deprived of Mr. West, the son of a chancellor of Ireland, a friend on whom he appears to have set a high value,[5] and who deserved his esteem by the powers which he shows in his letters and in the ' Ode to May ' which Mr. Mason has preserved, as well as by the sincerity with which, when Gray sent him part of 'Agrippina,' a tragedy that he had just begun, he gave an opinion which probably intercepted the progress of the work, and which the judgment of every reader will confirm. It was certainly no loss to the English stage that ' Agrippina ' was never finished.

In this year (1742) Gray seems first to have applied himself seriously to poetry; for in this year were produced the ' Ode to Spring,' his ' Prospect of Eton,'[6] and his ' Ode to

---

[4] Philip Gray (the father) was born 27th July, 1676; died 6th November, 1741; and was buried in the church of St. Michael's, Cornhill, London. He was the son of Thomas and Alice Gray, and was baptized in the church of St. Olave, Hart Street, London. Dorothy Antrobus (the mother) made her will 23rd January, 1753. It commences touchingly: "In the name of God, Amen. This is the last will and desire of Dorothy Gray to her son Thomas Gray." She speaks of her "lining close," and desires to be buried in "lining" in a coffin of polished oak, with black nails, in the same vault with her sister, Mary Antrobus. The hearse was to be accompanied by one mourning coach. Gray's own request in his will is that he should be buried by the side of his mother, "in a coffin of seasoned oak, neither lined nor covered." She died 11th March, 1753. The story of the wedded life of the father and mother of Gray is told in a Case submitted to counsel in 1735, when the poet was entering his twentieth year. See Appendix.

[5] Richard West died in his 26th year. Mr. Mitford, I am glad to think, is collecting his works for publication.

[6] The Ode on Eton College was published in May, 1747, and was Gray's first *English* poem that was published.

When

Adversity.' He began likewise a Latin poem, ' De principiis cogitandi. ' [7]

It may be collected from the narrative of Mr. Mason, that his first ambition was to have excelled in Latin poetry : perhaps it were reasonable to wish that he had prosecuted his design ; for though there is at present some embarrassment in his phrase, and some harshness in his lyric numbers, his copiousness of language is such as very few possess ; and his lines, even when imperfect, discover a writer whom practice would quickly have made skilful.

He now lived on at Peterhouse, very little solicitous what others did or thought, and cultivated his mind and enlarged his views without any other purpose than of improving and amusing himself; when Mr. Mason being elected Fellow of Pembroke Hall, brought him a companion who was afterwards to be his editor, and whose fondness and fidelity has kindled in him a zeal of admiration which cannot be reasonably expected from the neutrality of a stranger, and the coldness of a critic.

In this retirement he wrote (1747) an ode on the ' Death of Mr. Walpole's Cat ;' and the year afterwards attempted a poem of more importance, on ' Government and Education,' of which the fragments which remain have many excellent lines.

His next production (1751) was his far-famed ' Elegy in the Church-yard,' which, finding its way into a Magazine, first, I believe, made him known to the public.[8]

An invitation from Lady Cobham about this time gave occasion to an odd composition called ' A Long Story,' which adds little to Gray's character.[9]

When Gray published his exquisite Ode on Eton College—his first publication—little notice was taken of it.—Jos. WARTON: *Essay on Pope*, ii. 230, ed. 1782.

[7] No; he *began* it at Florence in 1740.

[8] Afterwards (1751) published in 4to. 'An Elegy wrote in a Country Church Yard. London: printed for R. Dodsley, in Pall-Mall; And sold by M. Cooper in Pater-noster-Row, 1751. Price Sixpence.' A fourth edition appeared the same year.

[9] To Thomas Gray, Esq.

Sunday morning.

Sir,—I am as much at a loss to bestow the commendations due to your Performance as any of our modern Poets wou'd be to imitate it. Ev'ry body that

Several of his pieces were published (1753), with designs by Mr. Bentley, and, that they might in some form or other make a book, only one side of each leaf was printed. I believe the poems and the plates recommended each other so well, that the whole impression was soon bought. This year he lost his mother.

Some time afterwards (1756) some young men of the college, whose chambers were near his, diverted themselves with disturbing him by frequent and troublesome noises, and, as is said, by pranks yet more offensive and contemptuous. This insolence, having endured it a while, he represented to the governors of the society, among whom perhaps he had no friends; and, finding his complaint little regarded, removed himself to Pembroke Hall.

In 1757 he published 'The Progress of Poetry' and 'The Bard,' two compositions at which the readers of poetry were at first content to gaze in mute amazement.[10] Some that tried them confessed their inability to understand them, though Warburton said that they were understood as well as the works of Milton and Shakespeare, which it is the fashion to admire. Garrick wrote a few lines in their praise. Some hardy champions undertook to rescue them from neglect, and in a short time many were content to be shown beauties which they could not see.[11]

has seen it is charm'd, and Lady Cobham was the first (tho' not the last) that regretted the loss of the 500 stanzas. All that I can say is, your obliging intention in sending it has fully answer'd, as it not only gave us amusement the rest of the Evening, but always will upon reading it over. Lady Cobham and the rest of the Company hope to have yours tomorrow at din'er.

I am, Sir, Your most obliged and obedient

HENRIETTA JANE SPEED.

—*Mason and Penn MSS.*

[10] Odes by Mr. Gray. ΦΩΝΑΝΤΑ ΣΥΝΕΤΟΙΣΙ.—Pindar, Olymp. ii. Printed at Strawberry Hill, for R. and J. Dodsley, in Pall-Mall, 1757, 4to. "The words of Pindar prefixed to them (Vocal to the Intelligent alone) were prophetic of their fate: very few understood them; the multitude of all ranks called them unintelligible."—GRAY: MS. Note on his own copy, now (1854) in the possession of Mr. George Daniel of Canonbury.

[11] "Even my friends tell me that they [the Odes] do not succeed, and write me moving topics of consolation on that head. In short, I have heard of no-

Gray's reputation was now so high, that, after the death of
Cibber [1757], he had the honour of refusing the laurel, which
was then bestowed on Mr. Whitehead.

His curiosity, not long after, drew him away [1759] from
Cambridge to a lodging near the Museum, where he resided
near three years, reading and transcribing; and, so far as can
be discovered, very little affected by two odes on 'Oblivion'
and 'Obscurity,' in which his lyric performances were ridiculed
with much contempt and much ingenuity.[12]

When [1762] the Professor of Modern History at Cambridge died, he was, as he says, "cockered and spirited up"
till he asked it of Lord Bute, who sent him a civil refusal; and
the place was given to Mr. Brocket, the tutor of Sir James
Lowther.

His constitution was weak, and believing that his health was
promoted by exercise and change of place, he undertook (1765)
a journey into Scotland, of which his account, so far as it
extends, is very curious and elegant : for, as his comprehension
was ample, his curiosity extended to all the works of art, all the
appearances of nature, and all the monuments of past events.
He naturally contracted a friendship with Dr. Beattie, whom he

body but a player [Garrick] and a doctor of divinity [Warburton] that profess
their esteem for them."—GRAY to Dr. Hurd, Aug. 25, 1757.

"I yet reflect with pain upon the cool reception which those noble odes,
'The Progress of Poetry' and 'The Bard,' met with at their first publication;
it appeared that there were not twenty people in England who liked them."—
WHARTON to Mason, May 29, 1781. (MS.)

"These two Odes, it must be confessed, breathe much of the spirit of Pindar;
but then they have caught the seeming obscurity, the sudden transition, and
hazardous epithet of his mighty master; all which, though evidently intended
for beauties, will probably be regarded as blemishes by the generality of his
readers. In short, they are in some measure a representation of what Pindar
now appears to be, though perhaps not what he appeared to the states of
Greece, when they rivalled each other in his applause, and when Pan himself
was seen dancing to his melody."—GOLDSMITH: *Monthly Review* for Sept. 1757;
Works by Cunningham, iv. 316.

[12] By Colman and Lloyd. The 'Ode to Obscurity' was directed chiefly
against Gray; that to 'Oblivion' against Mason.

"It was some time after publication before the 'Odes' of Gray were relished
and admired. They were even burlesqued by two men of wit and genius,
who, however, once owned to me that they repented of the attempt."—JOS.
WARTON: *Pope's Works*, i. 236.

found a poet, a philosopher, and a good man. The Mareschal College at Aberdeen offered him the degree of Doctor of Laws, which, having omitted to take it at Cambridge, he thought it decent to refuse.

What he had formerly solicited in vain was at last given him without solicitation. The Professorship of History became again vacant, and he received (1768) an offer of it from the Duke of Grafton. He accepted, and retained it to his death ; always designing lectures, but never reading them ; uneasy at his neglect of duty, and appeasing his uneasiness with designs of reformation, and with a resolution which he believed himself to have made of resigning the office, if he found himself unable to discharge it.

Ill health made another journey necessary, and he visited (1769) Westmoreland and Cumberland. He that reads his epistolary narration wishes that to travel, and to tell his travels, had been more of his employment ; but it is by studying at home that we must obtain the ability of travelling with intelligence and improvement.

His travels and his studies were now near their end. The gout, of which he had sustained many weak attacks, fell upon his stomach, and, yielding to no medicines, produced strong convulsions, which (July 30, 1771) terminated in death.[13]

His character I am willing to adopt, as Mr. Mason has done, from a letter written to my friend Mr. Boswell by the Rev. Mr. Temple, rector of St. Gluvias in Cornwall ; and am as willing as his warmest well-wisher to believe it true.[14]

[13] He died at Pembroke Hall, Cambridge, and was buried by his own desire in the churchyard of Stoke-Pogeis, in Buckinghamshire.

[14] This character of Gray originally appeared in the ' London Magazine ' for March, 1772. Mr. Temple died 1796.

" Mr. James Boswell, the friend of Paoli and Dr. Johnson, has writ me a very Scotch letter about Gray's character, to tell me it was written by a friend of his, Mr. Temple, and that he put it into the ' London Magazine ' without his leave. I writ him a very plain English answer, which I hope will quit me of this correspondent."—MASON to Walpole, June 17, 1775.

" I never saw Mr. Gray ; but my old and most intimate friend, the Rev. Mr. Temple, Rector of Mainhead, in Devonshire, knew him well. He knew his foibles, but admired his genius, and esteemed his virtues. I know not if you were acquainted with Mr. Gray. He was so abstracted and singular a man that

" Perhaps he was the most learned man in Europe.   He was equally acquainted with the elegant and profound parts of science, and that not superficially, but thoroughly.   He knew every branch of history, both natural and civil ; had read all the original historians of England, France, and Italy ; and was a great antiquarian.   Criticism, metaphysics, morals, politics, made a principal part of his study ; voyages and travels of all sorts were his favourite amusements ; and he had a fine taste in painting, prints, architecture, and gardening.   With such a fund of knowledge, his conversation must have been equally instructing and entertaining ; but he was also a good man, a man of virtue and humanity.   There is no character without some speck, some imperfection ; and I think the greatest defect in his was an affectation in delicacy, or rather effeminacy, and a visible fastidiousness, or contempt and disdain of his inferiors in science. He also had, in some degree, that weakness which disgusted Voltaire so much in Mr. Congreve : though he seemed to value others chiefly according to the progress they had made in knowledge, yet he could not bear to be considered himself merely as a man of letters ; and though without birth, or fortune, or station, his desire was to be looked upon as a private independent gentleman, who read for his amusement.   Perhaps it may be said, What signifies so much knowledge, when it produced so little ?   Is it worth taking so much pains to leave no memorial but a few poems ?   But let it be considered that Mr. Gray was to others at least innocently employed ; to himself, certainly beneficially.   His time passed agreeably ; he was every day making some new acquisition in science ; his mind was enlarged, his heart softened, his virtue strengthened ; the world and mankind were shown to him without a mask ; and he was taught to consider every thing as trifling, and unworthy of the attention of a wise man, except the pursuit of knowledge and practice of virtue in that state wherein God hath placed us." [15]

I can suppose you and him never having met."—BOSWELL to GARRICK, 18th Sept. 1771.

[15] "I agree with you most absolutely in your opinion about Gray.   He is the worst company in the world.   From a melancholy turn, from living reclusely,

To this character Mr. Mason has added a more particular account of Gray's skill in zoology. He has remarked, that Gray's effeminacy was affected most " before those whom he did not wish to please ; " and that he is unjustly charged with making knowledge his sole reason of preference, as he paid his esteem to none whom he did not likewise believe to be good.

What has occurred to me from the slight inspection of his letters in which my undertaking has engaged me, is, that his mind had a large grasp ; that his curiosity was unlimited, and his judgment cultivated ; that he was a man likely to love much where he loved at all, but that he was fastidious and hard to please. His contempt, however, is often employed, where I hope it will be approved, upon scepticism and infidelity. His short account of Shaftesbury I will insert.

" You say you cannot conceive how Lord Shaftesbury came to be a philosopher in vogue ; I will tell you : first, he was a lord ; secondly, he was as vain as any of his readers ; thirdly, men are very prone to believe what they do not understand ; fourthly, they will believe any thing at all, provided they are under no obligation to believe it ; fifthly, they love to take a new road, even when that road leads nowhere ; sixthly, he was reckoned a fine writer, and seems always to mean more than he said. Would you have any more reasons ? An interval of above forty years has pretty well destroyed the charm. A dead lord ranks with commoners ; vanity is no longer interested in the matter, for a new road is become an old one."

Mr. Mason has added, from his own knowledge, that though Gray was poor, he was not eager of money ; and that out of the little that he had he was very willing to help the necessitous.[16]

and from a little too much dignity, he never converses easily : all his words are measured and chosen, and formed into sentences ; his writings are admirable ; he himself is not agreeable."—HOR. WALPOLE to Montagu, Sept. 3, 1748.

" Mr. Gray's chamber windows were ever ornamented with mignonette, or other sweet-scented herbs and flowers, elegantly planted in china vases, as were other parts of his room, in which the utmost neatness and delicacy prevailed, as well as in his person."—COLE, the Antiquary. (MS. note in Mason's ' Gray.')

[16] Gray's features have been preserved to us, though there is no good portrait of him. Mason made an etching of his head, alluded to by Gray in a

As a writer he had this peculiarity, that he did not write his pieces first rudely and then correct them, but laboured every line as it arose in the train of composition ; and he had a notion not very peculiar, that he could not write but at certain times, or at happy moments ; a fantastic foppery, to which my kindness for a man of learning and of virtue wishes him to have been superior.[17]

Gray's Poetry is now to be considered ; and I hope not to be looked on as an enemy to his name, if I confess that I contemplate it with less pleasure than his life.

His ode on 'Spring' has something poetical, both in the language and the thought ; but the language is too luxuriant, and the thoughts have nothing new.   There has of late arisen a practice of giving to adjectives derived from substantives, the termination of participles ; such as the *cultured* plain, the *daisied* bank ; but I was sorry to see, in the lines of a scholar like Gray, the *honied* Spring.[18]   The morality is natural, but too stale ; the conclusion is pretty.

The poem 'On the Cat' was doubtless by its author considered as a trifle, but it is not a happy trifle.   In the first stanza "the azure flowers *that* blow," show resolutely a rhyme is sometimes made when it cannot easily be found.   Selima, the Cat, is called a nymph, with some violence both to language and

letter to the Rev. James Brown, of Oct. 23, 1760; and from this and other sources (equally slight) the profile medallion was compiled by Bacon for the monument which Mason erected to his memory in Westminster Abbey.

[17] Compare Johnson, in vol. i. p. 118, on Milton's mental submission to the seasons.

[18] Gray has Shakespeare and Milton on his side, and what deserves to be mentioned, Johnson has admitted into his Dictionary the word he now objects to:—

> His sweet and *honied* sentences.
>
> > SHAKESPEARE: *King Henry V.*
>
> While the bee with *honied* thigh.
>
> > MILTON : *Il Penseroso.*
>
> That on the green turf suck the *honied* showers.
>
> > MILTON: *Lycidas.*
>
> The bait of *honied* words.
>
> > MILTON: *Samson Agonistes.*

sense ; but there is good use made of it when it is done ; for of the two lines,

> " What female heart can gold despise ?
> What cat 's averse to fish ? "

the first relates merely to the nymph, and the second only to the cat. The sixth stanza contains a melancholy truth, that " a favourite has no friend ;" but the last ends in a pointed sentence of no relation to the purpose : if *what glistered* had been *gold*, the cat would not have gone into the water ; and if she had, would not less have been drowned.

The ' Prospect of Eton College ' suggests nothing to Gray which every beholder does not equally think and feel. His supplication to Father Thames, to tell him who drives the hoop or tosses the ball, is useless and puerile. Father Thames has no better means of knowing than himself.[19] His epithet " buxom health " is not elegant ; he seems not to understand the word. Gray thought his language more poetical as it was more remote from common use : finding in Dryden " honey redolent of Spring," an expression that reaches the utmost limits of our language, Gray drove it a little more beyond common apprehension by making " gales " to be " redolent of joy and youth."

Of the ' Hymn to Adversity,' the hint was at first taken from " O Diva, gratum quæ regis Antium ; " but Gray has excelled his original by the variety of his sentiments, and by their moral application. Of this piece, at once poetical and rational, I will not by slight objections violate the dignity.

My process has now brought me to the *wonderful* " Wonder of Wonders," the two Sister Odes ; by which, though either vulgar ignorance or common sense at first universally rejected

---

[19] " Are we by this rule of criticism to judge the following passage in the twentieth chapter of ' Rasselas '? " As they were sitting together, the Princess cast her eyes upon the river that flowed before her : ' *Answer*,' said she, ' *great Father of Waters*, thou that rollest thy floods through eighty nations, to the invocation of the daughter of thy native king : *Tell me if thou waterest* through all thy course a single habitation from which thou dost not hear the murmurs of complaint ? ' "—Rev. John Mitford.

them, many have been since persuaded to think themselves
delighted. I am one of those that are willing to be pleased,
and therefore would gladly find the meaning of the first stanza
of the 'Progress of Poetry.'

Gray seems in his rapture to confound the images of "spreading sound and running water." A "stream of music" may be
allowed; but where does "music," however "smooth and
strong," after having visited the "verdant vales, roll down the
steep amain," so as that "rocks and nodding groves rebellow to
the roar?" If this be said of music, it is nonsense; if it be said
of water, it is nothing to the purpose.

The second stanza, exhibiting Mars's car and Jove's eagle,
is unworthy of further notice. Criticism disdains to chase a
school-boy to his common-places.

To the third it may likewise be objected that it is drawn from
mythology, though such as may be more easily assimilated to
real life. Idalia's "velvet-green" has something of cant.[20] An
epithet or metaphor drawn from nature ennobles art: an epithet
or metaphor drawn from art degrades nature. Gray is too
fond of words arbitrarily compounded. "Many-twinkling"[21]
was formerly censured as not analogical; we may say "many-
spotted," but scarcely "many-spotting." This stanza, however,
has something pleasing.

Of the second ternary of stanzas, the first endeavours to tell
something, and would have told it had it not been crossed by
Hyperion: the second describes well enough the universal prevalence of poetry; but I am afraid that the conclusion will not
rise from the premises. The caverns of the North and the
plains of Chili are not the residences of "glory and generous

[20] Pope was laughed at in his lifetime for his "velvet plain," a copy, says the
critic, "after Brughell," who still passes by the name of Velvet Breughell.
('Gulliveriana and Alexanderiana,' 8vo., 1728, p. 288.)

[21] Or rustling turn the many-twinkling leaves
Of aspen tall.—THOMSON: *Spring.*

Mrs. Garrick admired the expression, and observed with peculiar reference
to it, "that Mr. Gray is the only poet who ever understood dancing." (Walpole to Lyttelton, Aug. 25, 1757.)

shame." But that poetry and virtue go always together is an opinion so pleasing, that I can forgive him who resolves to think it true.

The third stanza sounds big with "Delphi," and "Egean," and "Ilissus," and "Meander," and "hallowed fountains," and "solemn sound;" but in all Gray's odes there is a kind of cumbrous splendour which we wish away. His position is at last false: in the time of Dante and Petrarch, from whom we derive our first school of poetry, Italy was over-run by "tyrant power" and "coward vice;" nor was our state much better when we first borrowed the Italian arts.

Of the third ternary, the first gives a mythological birth of Shakespeare. What is said of that mighty genius is true; but it is not said happily: the real effects of this poetical power are put out of sight by the pomp of machinery. Where truth is sufficient to fill the mind, fiction is worse than useless; the counterfeit debases the genuine.

His account of Milton's blindness, if we suppose it caused by study in the formation of his poem—a supposition surely allowable—is poetically true, and happily imagined. But the *car* of Dryden, with his *two coursers*, has nothing in it peculiar; it is a car in which any other rider may be placed.

'The Bard' appears at the first view to be, as Algarotti and others have remarked, an imitation of the prophecy of Nereus. Algarotti thinks it superior to its original, and if preference depends only on the imagery and animation of the two poems, his judgment is right. There is in 'The Bard' more force, more thought, and more variety. But to copy is less than to invent, and the copy has been unhappily produced at a wrong time. The fiction of Horace was to the Romans credible; but its revival disgusts us with apparent and unconquerable falsehood. *Incredulus odi.*

To select a singular event, and swell it to a giant's bulk by fabulous appendages of spectres and predictions, has little difficulty; for he that forsakes the probable may always find the marvellous. And it has little use: we are affected only as we believe; we are improved only as we find something to be imitated or declined. I do not see that 'The Bard' promotes any truth, moral or political.

His stanzas are too long, especially his epodes; the ode is finished before the ear has learned its measures, and consequently before it can receive pleasure from their consonance and recurrence.

Of the first stanza the abrupt beginning has been celebrated; but technical beauties can give praise only to the inventor. It is in the power of any man to rush abruptly upon his subject that has read the ballad of 'Johnny Armstrong:'

"*Is there ever a man in all Scotland.*"

The initial resemblances, or alliterations, "ruin, ruthless, helm or hauberk," are below the grandeur of a poem that endeavours at sublimity.

In the second stanza the Bard is well described; but in the third we have the puerilities of obsolete mythology. When we are told that "Cadwallo hush'd the stormy main," and that "Modred made huge Plinlimmon bow his cloud-topp'd head," attention recoils from the repetition of a tale that, even when it was first heard, was heard with scorn.

The *weaving* of the *winding sheet* he borrowed, as he owns, from the Northern bards; but their texture, however, was very properly the work of female powers, as the act of spinning the thread of life in another mythology. Theft is always dangerous; Gray has made weavers of slaughtered bards, by a fiction outrageous and incongruous. They are then called upon to "weave the warp, and weave the woof," [22] perhaps with no great propriety; for it is by crossing the *woof* with the *warp* that men *weave* the *web* or piece; and the first line was dearly bought by the admission of its wretched correspondent, "Give ample room and verge enough." [23] He has, however, no other line as bad.

---

[22] This objection had been previously made in the 'Critical Review,' vol. iv. p. 167.

[23] I have a soul, that like an *ample* shield
Can take in all; and *verge enough* for more.
                    DRYDEN : *Don Sebastian*, Act i. sc. 1.

The third stanza of the second ternary is commended, I think, beyond its merit. The personification is indistinct. *Thirst* and *hunger* are not alike ; and their features, to make the imagery perfect, should have been discriminated. We are told in the same stanza how " towers are fed." But I will no longer look for particular faults ; yet let it be observed that the ode might have been concluded with an action of better example ; but suicide is always to be had without expense of thought.

These odes are marked by glittering accumulations of ungraceful ornaments ; they strike, rather than please ; the images are magnified by affectation ; the language is laboured into harshness. The mind of the writer seems to work with unnatural violence. " Double, double, toil and trouble." He has a kind of strutting dignity, and is tall by walking on tiptoe. His art and his struggle are too visible, and there is too little appearance of ease and nature.

To say that he has no beauties, would be unjust : a man like him, of great learning and great industry, could not but produce something valuable. When he pleases least, it can only be said that a good design was ill directed.

His translations of Northern and Welsh poetry deserve praise ; the imagery is preserved, perhaps often improved ; but the language is unlike the language of other poets.

In the character of his Elegy [24] I rejoice to concur with the common reader ; for by the common sense of readers uncorrupted with literary prejudices, after all the refinements of subtilty and the dogmatism of learning, must be finally decided all claim to poetical honours. The ' Church-yard ' abounds with images which find a mirror in every mind, and with sentiments to which every bosom returns an echo. The four stanzas beginning " Yet even these bones " are to me original : I have

---

[24] The only existing copy of the ' Elegy in a Country Churchyard ' in the handwriting of its author was sold 4th August, 1854, for One Hundred and Thirty-one Pounds. It is written in his small neat hand (he wrote with a crow-quill) on one half of a sheet of yellow foolscap, folded into two.

never seen the notions in any other place ; yet he that reads
them here, persuades himself that he has always felt them.   Had
Gray written often thus, it had been vain to blame, and useless
to praise him.[25]

[25] "I am too proud to make this apology to any person but my bookseller,
who will be the only real loser by the defect.   Those readers who believe that
I do not write immediately under his pay, and who may have gathered, from
what they have already read, that I am not so passionately enamoured of Dr.
Johnson's biographical manner as to take that for my model, have only to
throw these pages aside, and wait till they are new-written by some one of
his numerous disciples who may follow his master's example; and should
more anecdote than I furnish him with be wanting (as was the Doctor's case
in his Life of Mr. Gray), may make amends for it by those acid eructations of
vituperative criticism which are generated by unconcocted taste and intellectual indigestion."—MASON : *Life of Whitehead*, 8vo. 1788, p. 129.

The amplest account of Gray's Life may be seen in an article in the 'Quarterly Review' for December, 1853.   We are still in want of an edition of his
works which will embody all his recently-printed letters.   This, I am told,
we are likely to receive, and soon, from his accomplished editor, the Rev.
John Mitford.

APPENDIX.

CASE

From Mitford's ' Gray,' i. xcvi. ed. 1836.

" Philip Gray, before his marriage with his wife (then Dorothy Antrobus, and who was then partner with her sister Mary Antrobus [26]),
entered into articles of agreement with the said Dorothy and Mary, and
their brother Robert Antrobus, that the said Dorothy's stock in trade
(which was then 240*l.*) should be employed by the said Mary in the said
trade, and that the same, and all profits arising thereby, should be for the
sole benefit of the said Dorothy, notwithstanding her intended coverture,
and her sole receipts alone a sufficient discharge to the said Mary and her
brother Robert Antrobus, who was made trustee.   But in case either the
said Philip or Dorothy dies, then the same to be assigned to the survivor.

" That, in pursuance of the said articles, the said Mary, with the assistance of the said Dorothy her sister, hath carried on the said trade for near
thirty years, with tolerable success for the said Dorothy ; that she hath
been no charge to the said Philip, and during all the said time hath not
only found herself in all manner of apparel, but also for all her children,
to the number of twelve, and most of the furniture of his house, and
paying 40*l.* a-year for his shop, *almost providing everything for her son
whilst at Eton School, and now he is at Peter-house at Cambridge.*

" Notwithstanding which, almost ever since he hath been married he
hath used her in the most inhuman manner, by beating, kicking, punching,
and with the most vile and abusive language, that she hath been in the
utmost fear and danger of her life, and hath been obliged this last year to
quit her bed and lie with her sister.   *This she was resolved, if possible, to
bear ; not to leave her shop of trade, for the sake of her son, to be able to
assist in the maintenance of him at the University, since his father wo'nt.*

" There is no cause for this usage, unless it be an unhappy jealousy of
all mankind in general (her own brother not excepted) ; but no woman
deserves or hath maintained a more virtuous character ; or it is presumed
if he can make her sister leave off trade, he thinks he can then come into
his wife's money, but the articles are too secure for his vile purposes.

" He daily threatens he will pursue her with all the vengeance possible,
and will *ruin himself to undo her and his only son*, in order to which he
hath given warning to her sister to quit his shop, where they have carried
on their trade so successfully, which will be almost their ruin ; but he
insists she shall at Midsummer next ; and the said Dorothy, his wife,

---

[26] Mary Antrobus, of St. Michael's, Cornhill, made her will in 1742, leaving
her sister, Dorothy Gray, her executrix :—200*l.* to each of her three sisters,
Rogers, Oliffe, and Gray, and 100*l.* to her nephew, Thomas Gray.

in necessity must be forced to go along with her, to some other house and shop, to be assisting to her said sister, in the same trade, for *her own and son's support.*

" But if she can be quiet, she neither expects or desires any help from him ; but he is really so very vile in his nature, she hath all the reason to expect most troublesome usage from him that can be thought of.

" *Question.*—What he can or possibly may do to molest his wife in living with her sister and assisting in her trade for the purposes in the said articles ; and which will be the best way for her to conduct herself in this unhappy circumstance, if he should any ways be troublesome, or endeavour to force her to live with him ? And whether the said Dorothy, in the lifetime of the said Philip, may not, by will or otherwise, dispose of the interest or produce which hath or may arise or become due for the said stock as she shall think fit, it being apprehended as part of her separate estate ?

" *Answer.*—If Mrs. Gray should leave her husband's house, and go to live with her sister in any other, to assist her in her trade, her husband may and probably will call her, by process in the Ecclesiastical Court, to return home and cohabit with him, which the court will compel her to do, unless she can show cause to the contrary. She has no other defence, in that case, than to make proof before the court of such cruelties as may induce the judge to think she cannot live in safety with her husband, then the court will decree for a separation.

" This is a most unhappy case, and such a one as I think, if possible, should be referred to and made up by some common friend—sentences of separation, by reason of cruelty only, being very rarely obtained.

" What the cruelties are which he has used towards her, and what proof she is able to make of them, I am yet a stranger to. She will, as she has hitherto done, bear what she reasonably can, without giving him any provocation to use her ill. If, nevertheless, he forces her out of doors, the most reputable place she can be in is with her sister. If he will pro-ceed to extremities, and go to law, she will be justified, if she stands upon her defence, rather perhaps than if she was plaintiff in the cause.

" As no power of making a will is reserved to Mrs. Gray by her mar-riage settlement, and not only the original stock, but likewise the produce and interest which shall accrue and be added to it are settled upon the husband if he survives his wife, it is my opinion she has no power to dis-pose of it by will or otherwise.

" JOH. AUDLEY.

" Doctors' Commons, Feb. 9th, 1735."

ADDITIONAL NOTES.

ADDITIONAL NOTES.

Vol. i. p. 6, note 8.

It appears from Cowley's Will (at p. 63) that he was subsequently a successful candidate for admission to Trinity College, Cambridge.

Vol. i. p. 100.

I should have appended a note to the statement in the text, that Milton was suspected of having interpolated into the book called 'Icon Basilike' a prayer from Sidney's 'Arcadia.' The statement is now generally disbelieved. (*See* Mitford's 'Milton,' vol. i. p. lxviii., ed. 1851; and Todd's 'Milton,' vol. i. p. 73, ed. 1852.)

Vol. i. p. 104, note 44.

Milton's second marriage is also registered in the parish of St. Margaret, Westminster :—

" John Milton, of this parish, Esqr., and Mrs. Katherin Woodcocke, of the parish of Aldermanbury, spinster. Published October 22, 27, Nov. 3, 1656."

To this I will add (from the same register) what I believe has escaped the biographers of the poet, the baptism of Milton's only child by his second wife :—

" 19 Oct. 1657. Katherin Milton, d. to John, Esq., by Katherin."

Vol. i. p. 219, note 3.

Waller was not so nearly related to Cromwell as is stated in the note. The exact relationship has not been satisfactorily made out.

Vol. i. p. 237, l. 6.

Waller's " last ingenious biographer " was the writer of the Life prefixed to an edition of Waller published in 1773, by Percival Stockdale.

Vol. ii. p. 83, note 7, add—

Johnson follows the writer of Halifax's Life before his Poetical Works. 1716. 8vo.

Vol. ii. p. 116, add—

" The Life of Rowe is a very remarkable instance of the uncommon strength of Dr. Johnson's memory. When I received from him the MS. he complacently observed, 'that the criticism was tolerably well done, considering that he had not read one of Rowe's plays for thirty years.' "— JOHN NICHOLS (*Note in Johnson's Lives*).

Vol. ii. p. 121, add—

" This fact was communicated to Johnson in my hearing by a person of unquestionable veracity, but whose name I am not at liberty to mention. He had it, as he told us, from Lady Primrose, to whom Steele related it with tears in his eyes. The late Dr. Stinton confirmed it to me by saying that he had heard it from Mr. Hooke, author of the Roman History ; and he from Mr. Pope."—SIR JOHN HAWKINS.

Johnson should have added that the story is to be found, with some additional particulars, in Ben Victor's *Letters*, 1776, i. 328.

Vol. ii. p. 227.

For the four letters (now first published) from Prior to his patron and friend, the witty Earl of Dorset, I am indebted to the kindness of the Rev. J. E. Mayer, of St. John's College, Cambridge. Mr. Mayer transcribed them from the originals in St. John's College (Prior's own College), where they are preserved with this memorandum :—

" May 17, 1751.

" These original Lres of Mr. Prior were given me by the Rev^d. Mr. Upton, Prebend of Rochester, to be deposited in St. John's College Library.

" JOHN TAYLOR."

The notes attached have been supplied by Mr. Mayer.

PRIOR TO THE EARL OF DORSET.

[Now first published.]

Hague, y^e $\frac{14}{4}$ May. 94.

MY LORD,—By an Expres from Dresden We have an acc^t that the Elector of Sax [1] dyed there the $\frac{27 \text{ Ap.}}{7 \text{ May}}$ of the same distemper and almost in the same manner as his Countesse : [2] this may give some change to our affaires on that side, since his Brother and successour [3] is in good English a resty

---

[1] John George IV.

[2] The Elector's mistress, Magdalena Sibylle of Neitzschütz, created Countess of Rochlitz in 1693, died on the 4th of April, 1694.

[3] (Frederick) Augustus II., *the Strong.*

Brute, of too much stubborness to be convinced by any Man, and too much ferocity to be softened by any Woman, a true Dane, and gouverned by one of that Nation who is a little too partial to the French Interest.

The French begin to move in Flanders, our letters from France are all filled with the Misery and Desolation of that Kingdom, which is really very pressing.[4]

This letter may end like my last, with my Prayers for yor Lordships health and Happiness.

> Spare Dorsett's sacred life, decerning fate,
> And Death shall march thrô Courts & Camps in state,
> Emptying his Quiver on the vulgar Great;
>
> Round Dorsett's board lett Peace and Plenty dance
> Far off lett Famine Her sad reign advance
> And War walk deep in Blood thrô conquer'd France.
>
> Apollo thus began the Mystic Strain,
> The Muses Sons all bow'd and sayd Amen.

> I am with eternall Duty and respect
> My Lord
> Yo^r Lordsp's most ob^t
> and most humble Ser^t
>
> M. PRIOR.

PRIOR TO THE EARL OF DORSET.

[Now first published.]

Hag. $\frac{28}{18}$ June 97.

MY LORD,—I have hoped that our Treaty[5] might long before this have afforded something material enough for me to have troubled yor Lord^{ps} with, but by what has been written to yor Excell^{ces} in general on that subject, you see, my Lord, that we are advanced but little beyond our Preliminaries, and that in 15 meetings we have hardly agreed to the first Article either of the Imperialists or Spaniards thô they contain little more than *Pax sit*. I think that the Mystery of this slowness on the French side is that they have a mind to see the Event of what they hope as well from the West-Indies as from Barcelona.

We are thinking of that part of the treaty wch regards Us, and then England and Holland will certainly have quicker answers towards making a good peace, or break off those conferences wch as yet advance so little

---

[4] Compare Prior to Secretary Blathwayt (Hague, $\frac{22}{12}$ Sepr. 94), in *Ellis's Letters of Eminent Literary Men* (Camd. Soc.) p. 213.

[5] Of Ryswick.

towards it. Yo[r] Lord[sp] will see by the inclosed Protestation in what a posture K. James' affairs stand : this is the last Entry he is likely to make ; the Mediat[r] when He showed it to the Congress declared He received and looked upon it as neither valid or of consequence, but read it only as a Curiosity.

I am never to write to yor Lord[sp] without repeating my acknowledgements for all yor favours : I wish yor Lord[sp] all that pleasure and satisfaction to yor self wch you deserve, and which yor place of Chamberlain kept you frõ enjoying so entirely as you desired : but I hope, my Lord, you will never leave the Court so absolutely as not to be near it in every case wherein the welfare of the Nation may ask yor assistance.

The King has been pleased to name Me his Secretary in Ireland, I wish the business I have here may give me leave to go to my new charge soon, and behave my self in it as One ought to do who owes his education to my Lord Dorsett's peculiar kindness to him.

                         I am ever
                    With all imaginable respect
                         My Lord
                    Yo[r] Lordsp's most ob[t]
                              and most humble Ser[t]

L[d] Dorsett.   M. PRIOR.

PRIOR TO THE EARL OF DORSET.

[Now first published.]

                                   Paris the ²⁷⁄₁₇ Dec[r]
                                        1698.

MY LORD,—Your Lord[sp] as one of our Regents has seen what commonly occurred here from your secretary Mr. Yard, and indeed to have sent it to you more particularly would have been only to have desired you to read the Postboys a day or two before they appeared in print : so little is there really in all that Mystery which amuses the World that I can hardly in 6 Months find enough to furnish a letter to my Lord of Dorsett, tho' I could have written with ease twice a week to S[r] James Forbiss :

It is beyond contradiction that the King of Spain has made his Will, and by it constituted the Electoral Prince of Bavaria his heir, and the Queen to be Regent in case his Maj[ty] dyes during the Minority of the Prince : thus the Lineal right is kept to the younger Sisters Grandson and heir, the renonciation that France made when the King married the eldest Sister is confirmed to be valid, and the Dauphin (or as France was projecting) one of his younger Sons, excluded ; as well as the Archduke of Austria : the Queen had a great sway in this business, and the reasons that most probably inclined Her to this choice were that She might exalt the Palatine family of which your Lord[sp] knows the house of Bavaria and That of Neubourg from whence She is are equally branches : and that by this contrivance She might hold the Gouvernment longer which is not the least of a Woman's aim in such cases, the Electoral Prince not being above 8 year old, and as well the Archduke as the Duke of Berry 5 or 6 years nearer manhood. The French in general seem to be nettled at this affair, but, I think, those of them that have best sence are not so really : for all their natural heat and Impatience, and the pride they take in the greatness of their Monarchy, they begin to see that these notions has impoverish'd and enslaved Them ; and the treaty of Ryswick has a good deal instructed them, and their own affairs at home convinced them, that they have grasped at more then they could secure, and that neither their King nor they are the better for the expence of fortifying and keeping garisons 8 years together in 30 towns which they have been obliged to give back in the ninth : the Monarch himself is old, and, I think, has a good mind to be quiett, to say the truth o'nt, he is quite cowed by King William, and since the taking of Namur he has as fairly wheeled and run as ever any Cock did in a pitt; with this, the people are farr enough from being in an estate of beginning a new Warr, for they still feel the weight of That which is past very sensibly lying upon them, wch is so evident, that as yet they are not in a condition of redressing their Mony to it's intrinsique value, and by consequence can not open a Commerce upon a good foott wth their neighbours : so that I hope We may have Peace in our time.

The Succession of Spain is mostly our King's contrivance and effecting : some faults he has, or else he would not be a Man : as to his Character of a Prince he has carryed his reputation to a prodigious height, and this affair must be allowed to be a proff (sic) of it beyond denial :

The Emperour is a good deal angry at us, but he can do us no harm, god knows ; the Dutch Ambassad^r assures me that the Truce between his Imperial Maj^{ty} and the Turk was concluded the 28th of Novr for 25 years ; this will reconcile the Emperour to us again and is a new Epoche in the King's honour, and a great advantage to our reputation at Constantinople.

Poor King James [6] is hardly thought on or mentioned, an Italian and a Scotch Priest govern him and his whole concerns, he is so directly the same Man he ever was, persecuting the few Protestants about Him, tho' they are ruined and banished for their adhering to him, and rewarding and encouraging any sorry Creature that He can make a Convert of, the Child they Call the Prince of Wales they breed up with all the abhorrence imaginable to Heresy.

I should wrong your Lordsp's goodness to Me if I did nott tell you the State of my own private affairs ; I have played the Minister here in my Lord Jersey's absence, and now he is returned we are preparing for his Entry, so I am to appear with him as I did with my Lord Portland,[7] in

---

[6] Compare a letter of Prior's to Halifax (Paris, $\frac{30}{20}$ Aug. 1698) in *Ellis's Letters of Eminent Literary Men* (Camd. Soc.), p. 265. "I faced old James and all his Court the other day at St. Cloud: *vive Guillaume.* You never saw such a strange figure as the old bully is, lean, worn, and riv'led."

[7] "On the 27th of February [1698], he [the E. of Portland] made his

a new gaudy coat and with an expensive equipage: I must own to
your Lord^{sp} I am weary of this dancing on the high-rope in spangled
breeches; and if my Lord Jersey be Secretary of State (as it is thought he
may be some time) I'l endeavour to gett home, and seat my self in a
desk in his office; for I had rather be Mat Prior near my dear Lord
Dorsett, (yor Lord^{sp} must pardon Me the familiarity of the Expression)
then Monsieur L'envoyé in any court in Christendome, and I know not
how it is, life runs away before one is aware of it, and I shall hardly have
time enough in that part of it which is to come, to testify the Obligations
I have to yor Lord^{sp} for so many years past.

I am ever with entire respect

and duty

My Lord

Yo^r Lordsp's most ob^t

and most humble Ser^t

E. of Dorsett.   M. PRIOR.

PRIOR TO THE EARL OF DORSET.

[Now first published.]

Tuesday, 7 in the   [Feb. 13. $\frac{1699}{1700}$]. [8]
Evening.

MY LORD,—I have been at Westminster, the Question that was aimed
at my Lord Chancell^r and wch was to this sence, *that the procuring or
enjoying any Grant whilst the Nation was in war and oppressed with heavy*

---

public entry with such extraordinary splendor, as had never been seen at the
court of France since the Duke of Buckingham's embassy. . . . The Earl of
Portland left Paris the 8th of June, after a stay of above four months. This
embassy cost the King fourscore thousand pounds to little purpose."—
Tindal, xiv. 446, 447. Compare Burnet, ii. 224, folio. Kennett (p. 753) mentions Prior as having accompanied the Earl.

[8] " Towards the middle of *February* ($\frac{1699}{1700}$), the Commons in a Grand Committee
consider'd the State of the Nation, and a Motion being made, and the Question
put, *That the Procuring or Obtaining of grants of Estates belonging to the Crown,
by any publick Minister concerned in the Directing or Passing such Grants, to or for
their own Use or Benefit, whilst the Nation lay under the heavy taxes of the late War,
was highly injurious to his Majesty, and prejudicial to the State, and a violation of
the Trust reposed in them;* the Court party carried it in the Negative; but at
the same Time, they gave their Consent to an order for bringing in a Bill *To
resume the Grants of all Lands and Revenues of the Crown, and all Pensions granted
by the Crown, since the 6th of February,* 1684, *and for applying the same to the use
of the Publick.*"—KENNETT: *Compl. Hist.* iii. pp. 772-3. Cf. Tindal, xiv. 500.

The Commons' Journals (Tuesd. Feb. 13, $\frac{1699}{1700}$) give the numbers who voted,

taxes was injurious to the King and Nation &c this was carried in the Negative by 50 voices, S*ʳ* Richard Onslow put an other question, *if the grants made by the King ought not to be resumed ?* this question was afterwards inlarged and put, *if the grants made since the 7ᵗʰ of Feb*ʳʸ *8⅘, w*ᶜʰ *includes all King James' Grants ought not likewise to be reassumed,* and this was carried by a plurality that a bill be brought in to that effect : this is the Substance of this days sitting, angry speeches have passed, one particularly between Jack How and Maj*ʳ* Stringer, Harcourt and Seymour were ag*ᵗ* recalling the Grants, fearing it should clogg the Irish bill, and Jack How was pushed in his own defence to say that he thought grants might be taken provided it was in a time when the Nation was not so greatly taxed, my Lord Chancell*ʳ* has on all sides had a great commendation of his personal merit, Jack How said he did not aim at persons but at things, and intimated that some within those Walls were guilty, by which he meant Montagu : lett who so will be accused or brought off, I remain eternally

My Lord
Yo*ʳˢ*
PRIOR.

Vol. ii. p. 326.

The kindness of Edward Tickell, Esq., Q.C., the great-grandson of the poet, and who is in possession of the poet's papers, has enabled me to add some particulars to the Life of Tickell.

Here, in the first place, is Lord Carteret's letter of introduction and recommendation of Addison's friend to the Lords Justices :—

TO THE RIGHT HONBLE. THE LORDS JUSTICES, &c.

[Now first published.]

Arlington Street, May 17th, 1724.

MY LORDS,—Mr. Tickell, who will have the honour to present to your Lordships this Letter, having been appointed by Mr. Clutterbuck to succeed Mᵣ. Maddockes, has desir'd me to give him a recommendation to your Lordships. He served under me as Under Secretary all the time that I

---

182 for, 232 against ; but they differ both from Prior and Kennett in fixing the 5th Feb. 168⅘ as the limit after which grants should be resumed.

On the Monday night, Feb. 12, Prior wrote (Cole's ' Memoirs,' p. 103, and thence in Prior's ' Misc. Works,' i. 164) to Lord Manchester : " Tomorrow is the great Day when we expect that my Lord Chancellor will be fallen upon." And on the 30 Nov. / Dec. 10 previous : " My Lord Chancellor is the Man aimed at, and some Grants he has are the visible Pretext." (Cole, p. 84 ; Prior, p. 140.)

was Secretary of State, and in the same station was he under Mr. Craggs and Mr. Addison during the time that they were Secretaries of State, in which office he justly got the reputation both of ability and integrity ; so that I am persuaded that your Lordships will have reason to be satisfied with his conduct in whatever you shall think fit to employ him. I am, my Lords, with great respect,

Your Lordships
most faithfull humble Servant,

CARTERET.

Tickell had a small villa near the village of Glasneven, in the neighbourhood of Dublin, and was buried in Glasneven churchyard. A tablet to his memory in Glasneven church has this inscription :—

Sacred
to
The Memory of
THOMAS TICKELL, Esq.,
who was born in 1686,
At Bridekirk in Cumberland ;
He married, in 1726, Clotilda Eustace,
Died in April, 1740, at Bath,
And was buried in this Churchyard.
He was for some time Under Secretary in England,
And afterwards, for many years,
Secretary to the Lords Justices of Ireland ;
But his highest Honor was that of having been
The Friend of Addison.

The said Clotilda Eustace
Was the Daughter and one of the Coheiresses
of
Sir Maurice Eustace, Kt.
of Harristown, in the County of Kildare.
She died in July, 1792,
In the 92d Year of her Age,
And was also buried in this Churchyard.

By his will he left his wife his executrix and the guardian of his children. " She was," writes her great-grandson, " a very clever and most excellent woman."

He left two sons, John and Thomas, and two daughters. Thomas died unmarried. Richard Tickell, the poet, was the grandson of Addison's friend, and the uncle of Edward Tickell, Esq., Q.C.

Mr. Tickell has " a very good portrait " of his great-grandfather by Vanderbank. The portrait at Queen's College, Oxford, was presented by the father of Mr. Edward Tickell, Q.C. The poet's library was sold in 1792, at the death of his widow.

Vol. ii. p. 289, note 20, add—

" To my knowledge, she [the Countess of Suffolk] sincerely tried to serve some; but without effect: she could not even procure a place of 200*l.* a year for John Gay, a very poor and honest man, and no bad poet, only because he was a poet, which the King considered as a mechanic."—LORD CHESTERFIELD (character of Lady Suffolk, first published in Lord Mahon's ' Chesterfield,' ii. 441).

Vol. ii. p. 331, add—

" The death of poor Hammond was the only event that disturbed the tranquillity of my mind : he died in the beginning of a career which, if he had lived, I think he would have finished with reputation and distinction. But such is the folly, knavery, and futility of the world, and such was his truth, fidelity, and attachment to me, that in my opinion I have lost more by his death than he has."—CHESTERFIELD to Lyttelton, Bath, June 19, 1742 (Phillimore's ' Lyttelton,' i. 215).

Vol. ii. p. 370, note 45.

" R." (the former annotator) was Isaac Reed.

Vol. ii. p. 440.

Savage sat to John Ellis, a painter of several theatrical portraits. Mrs. Vannost, or Van Ost, the wife of the sculptor, had the picture. Ben Victor, who tells us this (*Letters*, 8vo., 1776, i. 264), calls her Savage's sister.

Vol. iii. p. 21, add—

" Mr. Pope's ' Eloisa to Abelard ' is such a *chef-d'œuvre*, that nothing of the kind can be relished after it. Yet it is not the story itself, nor the sympathy it excites in us, as Dr. Johnson would have us think, that constitutes the principal merit in that incomparable poem. It is the happy use he has made of the monastic gloom of the Paraclete, and of what I will call Papistical machinery, which gives it its capital charm ; so that I am almost inclined to wonder (if I could wonder at any of that writer's criticisms) that he did not take notice of this beauty, as his own superstitious turn certainly must have given him more than a sufficient relish for it."—MASON : *Life of Whitehead*, 8vo., 1788, p. 35.

ERRATA.

Mr. Cunningham will feel obliged to any one who will correct an error either in the text or notes of this edition of Johnson, so that he may secure in the end a perfect text of this British Classic.

   Vol. i., Preface, p. xxiv. line 6, for *hexameters* read *heroics*.
    „   „   „   line 30, for *blank verse over rhyme* read *rhyme over blank verse*.
    „ p. 74, note 18, for *Lewisdon* read *Lewesdon.*
    „ p. 86, l. 24, dele *not.*
    „ p. 88, note 18, for *Aug.* read *April.*
    „ p. 89, l. 6, for *preservation* read *preservative.*
    „ p. 94, note 27, for *Spinstow* read *Spurstow.*
    „ p. 95, l. 4, for *content that* read *content them that.*
    „ p. 103, l. 30, for *agis* read *agas.*
    „ p. 109, l. 4, for *like with* read *like of.*
    „ p. 110, l. last, for *necessarily* read *necessary.*
    „ p. 115, l. 28, for *low* read *law.*
    „ p. 141, l. 21, for *inventions* read *invention.*
    „ p. 191, l. 14, for *consequences* read *conferences.*
    „ p. 215, l. 6, for *tarriers* read *terriers.*
   Vol. ii. p. 37, note 11, for 1852 read 1854.
    „ p. 125, note 20, for *youth* read *lad.*
   Vol. iii. p. 127, note 269, for *had* read *has.*

INDEX.

Note.—The Roman numerals i., ii., iii., refer to the Volumes, the Arabic numerals to the pages.

A.

ADDISON, JOSEPH; on burlesque poetry, i. 185 note. His retort upon Edmund Smith, ii. 51, 52. His complaint of the neglect of Smith's tragedy, 53. His opinion of Rowe, 114, 115. His birth, parentage, and tutors, 119. Takes the lead in a " barring-out ", 119, 120, and notes. His early friendship with Steele, 120. His treatment of Steele in a matter of debt, 121, and note [4], and vol. iii. 424. His success at college, ii. 121. His fondness for his Latin compositions, 122. His interviews with Malbranche and Boileau, ib. note [7]. Admiration of Boileau for his Latin poems, 122, 123, and note [8]. Begins to write English poetry, 123. Dryden's eulogium on his 'Georgics', ib. Influence of his introduction to Montague (Halifax) on his prospects, 124. Obtains a pension and proceeds on his travels, 125. His ' Dialogue on Medals '; controversy as to where ' Cato ' was written, ib. and notes [20] [21]. His ' Epistle ' to Halifax, 126, and note [23]. Consequences of the non-remittance of his pension, ib. Publishes his 'Travels,' 126, 127, and notes [25-27]. His projected tutorship to the son of the " proud Duke ", 127, and note [28]. Writes his 'Campaign'; his attic study, ib. and note [29]. His rewards, 128. Fate of his opera of ' Rosamond '; its dedication, ib. and notes [32] [33]. Its merit, 160, 161. His Irish secretaryship; contrast between him and his chief, 128, 129. Swift's comments upon the conjunction of the two, 129, and notes [35] [36]. Mr. Macaulay on Addison's Irish parliamentary career, ib. note [37]. His reasons for taking fees from his friends, 130, and note [38]. His participation in ' The

Tatler ', ib. and notes [38] [39]. Commencement of ' The Spectator '; its objects, 131. Addison's view of the effects of his periodicals, 133, and note [44]. His share in 'Theophrastus', ib. and note [45]. His jealous care of Sir Roger de Coverley, 134, 135. Interference of the stamp with the sale of ' The Spectator', 135, and note. Completion of ' Cato ' for the stage, 135, 136. The author's coquettings relative thereto, 136, 137. Its performance and success, 137, 138. Why published without a dedication, 138. Dennis's assaults upon it, and Pope's equivocal defence, 138, 139, and notes [55] [57]. Its various translations and performances abroad, 139, and note [63]. Addison's share in ' The Guardian'; his equal love of fame and profit, 140, 141, and notes [64-66]. His silence on the authorship of ' The Drummer', 141, and notes [67] [68]. Short life of his ' Whig Examiner '; its merits, 142, and notes [69-72]. Revival of ' The Spectator '; his papers in it, 142, 143. His difficulty in a State crisis, 143. His ' Freeholder '; Steele's remark upon it, 144. His infelicitous marriage; character of his wife, 144, 145, and note [76]. Becomes Secretary of State; cause of his resignation, 145, and notes [77] [78]. His further literary projects; Tonson's sneer at his piety, 146. His quarrel with Steele, 147. Their pamphleteering skirmishes, 148. His approaching end and unexplained interview with Gay, 149. His deathbed monition to Lord Warwick, 150, and note [83]. His death, burial-place, and portraits, ib. and note [85]. His personal character; his alleged bashfulness, 151. His literary egotism and jealousy, 152. His fluency of composition and anxiety for correctness of style, 153. His daily life; devo-

2 F

His only allusion to his religion, 75. His introduction of Lord Bathurst's name, and remark of the latter, 76, and note [165]. His poem on the ' Characters of Men', and theory expounded in it, 76, 77. His 'Characters of Women' and treatment of the Duchess of Marlborough therein, 77, 78, and note [170]. His imitations of Horace and fondness for that kind of composition, 78, 79. His Epistle to Arbuthnot, and oft corrected lines on Addison therein, 79, 80, and note [173]. His quarrel with Lord Hervey, and indecent attack on Lady Mary, 80, 81, and notes [174-179]. His Satirical Dialogues (1738), and junction with the Prince of Wales, 81, and note. Fox's denunciation of him to Lord Lyttelton, and spirited reply of the latter, 81, 82, and note [181]. Lines which occasioned Fox's reproach, 393, note [8]. Warning given to him by Paul Whitehead's citation before the Lords, 82, and note [182]. Object of the ' Memoirs of Scriblerus', and writers joined in the work, 82, 83, and notes [184 185]. Publication of his fourth book of the Dunciad, 84, and note [187]. His attack on Cibber, and reprisals of the latter, 85-87, and notes. His reason for satirizing Osborne, 87, and notes [192 193]. Effect of Cibber's second Pamphlet upon him, 87, 88, and notes [194-196]. His acquaintance with Martha Blount, and mistakes of his biographers regarding her, 89, 90, and note [128]. His last days, and Walpole's anecdote of him, ib., and note [200]. His death, burialplace, and literary executors, 91, and notes [207-210]. His ' posthumous offence ' to Bolingbroke, and controversy which ensued, 91-93, and notes [213-217]. Presumed cause of his contemptuous mention of Allen in his will, 93, 94, and notes [219-221]. His personal appearance and portraits, deformity, and infirmities, 95-97, and notes. His habits and indulgences, 97-99, and notes [222-229]. His witticism on a dictionary maker, and alleged bickerings with Lady Mary Wortley, 100, and notes [200 201]. Did he ever laugh? ib., and note [202]. His " paper sparing" habit, and Swift's fling at it, 101, and note [233]. Wine story told of him, ib. His delight in talking of his possessions, and sneers at his antagonists' poverty, 101, 102.

Why did he dedicate his ' Homer' to Congreve? 102, and note [238]. His love for men of rank, 102, 103, and notes [236 237]. Johnson's remarks on his friendship for lords, 103, note [239]. His social qualities, as exhibited in his letters, 103, 104, and note [240]. His pretended contempt for his own poetry and for his critics, 105. His dislike to courts, ib., and notes. His affected fear of the post-office, 106, and note [242]. Comparison between his letters and Swift's, 107. His wantonness of attack and meanness in retreat, 108. His liberality and constancy to his friends, ib. Defamatory life of Swift ascribed to him, 109, and note [248]. His religion, ib., and note [249]. Extent of his learning: his desire to travel, 110, and note [250]. His intellectual characteristics, and mode of composition, 110-112, and notes [251 253]. Voluntariness of his effusions. His deliberateness in publishing, 112, 113. His punctilious revision of his works, 114, and note [254]. His style compared with that of Dryden, 114-116, and note [256]. Examination of his works: his Pastorals, 116, 117, and note [257]. His ' Windsor Forest'; its elegance and variety, 117. Its weak points, 118, and note [258]. Why his ' Temple of Fame' obtained but small notice, 118. Moral objections to his ' Verses on an Unfortunate Lady ', 118, 119. His ' Ode for St. Cecilia's Day,' compared with Dryden's Ode, 119, 120, and notes [259 260]. Excellence of his ' Essay on Criticism ', 120. Beauty of his simile of the Alps, 121, and note. His skill in the use of representative metre, 122, 123, and notes. Novelty of the machinery introduced into his ' Rape of the Lock', 124, 125, and note [266]. Purpose of the poem: critical objections considered, 125, 126, and note [267]. His skilful adaptation of the story of Eloisa and Abelard, 126, and note [268]. Mason's note thereon, 431. His translation of the Iliad a " poetic wonder", 127. His departures from the text of the original defended, 128, 129. His own letter on the same subject, 138, 139. His comments, and the objections to which they are open, 129, 130. First design of his ' Dunciad', 130, and note [271]. Necessity for printing all the variations of ' The

W.

THE END.

LONDON : PRINTED BY W. CLOWES AND SONS, STAMFORD STREET,
AND CHARING CROSS.